Okanagan College

D1554816

FC 2923.1 .T37 V53 1986
Vigod, Bernard L., 1946-
    Quebec before Duplessis

DATE DUE        82639

| | | | |
|---|---|---|---|
| NOV 2 0 1991 | | | |
| JAN 0 4 2001 | | | |
| | | | |
| | | | |
| | | | |
| | | | |
| | | | |
| | | | |
| | | | |
| | | | |

**OKANAGAN COLLEGE
LEARNING RESOURCE CENTRE
BRITISH COLUMBIA
V1Y 4X8**

*Quebec before Duplessis:*
*The Political Career of*
*Louis-Alexandre Taschereau*

Born into French Canada's traditional elite, a legal and landholding aristocracy, Louis-Alexandre Taschereau emerged as the leading champion of industrial development in early twentieth-century Quebec. As premier from 1920 to 1936, and previously as chief lieutenant in the Liberal government of Sir Lomer Gouin, Taschereau vigorously advocated the development of Quebec's immense hydraulic, forest, and mineral resources as the key to a prosperous future. His policy of encouraging private, usually non-French-Canadian entrepreneurs earned him the undying enmity of nationalist and conservative forces, yet he defended his position openly and won four general elections despite an unfavourable economic climate during much of his premiership.

Bernard L. Vigod provides the first balanced assessment of Taschereau's long career, countering the popular image of him – largely the creation of his political opponents – as the leader of a corrupt, reactionary regime tied to "foreign" financiers. Vigod shows that Taschereau possessed a coherent vision of French-Canadian society, a liberal one which welcomed material and intellectual progress and rejected the isolationism and resistance to change favoured by traditional nationalist and ultramontane thinkers. He gives Taschereau credit for his courageous attempt to guide Quebec through the depression, without ignoring his fatal inability to deal with the issues of social security and the "electricity trust." This study reveals in its subject an intense if partisan commitment to Wilfrid Laurier's ideal of tolerance and compromise in Canadian political life. It also testifies to a genuine sense of public duty in a politician who was far more than a "Duplessis with manners."

Bernard L. Vigod is professor of history and coordinator of French language policy at the University of New Brunswick.

OKANAGAN COLLEGE LIBRARY
BRITISH COLUMBIA

# *Quebec before Duplessis*

# The Political Career of Louis-Alexandre Taschereau

BERNARD L. VIGOD

82639

McGill-Queen's University Press
Kingston and Montreal

© McGill-Queen's University Press 1986
ISBN 0-7735-0588-1

Legal deposit 1st quarter 1986
Bibliothèque nationale du Québec

Printed in Canada

This book has been published with the help of a grant from the
Canadian Federation for the Humanities, using funds provided by
the Social Sciences and Humanities Research Council of Canada.

**Canadian Cataloguing in Publication Data**

Vigod, Bernard L., 1946–
    Quebec before Duplessis
    Bibliography: p.
    Includes index.
    ISBN 0-7735-0588-1
    1. Taschereau, Louis-Alexandre, 1867-1952. 2. Prime
    ministers — Quebec (Province) - Biography.
    3. Politicians - Quebec (Province) - Biography.
    4. Quebec Liberal Party. 5. Quebec (Province) -
    Politics and government - 1897-1936. I. Title.
    FC2923.1.T37V53 1986        971.4'03'0924        C85-099378-4
    F1053.T37V53 1986

PICTURE CREDITS
All pictures are from the Public Archives of Can-
ada: Union libérale members PA143060; Sir Lomer
Gouin C21910; Taschereau before World War I
PA53709; Ferguson, King, and Taschereau
PA125133; Taschereau with his wife Adine C19515;
Taschereau in 1935 PA74622

COVER Louis-Alexandre Taschereau during his last
campaign in 1935 PA74624

# Contents

# Preface

The cool breezes of the lower St Lawrence River offered welcome relief from the stiflingly hot Quebec summer of 1936. But for the solitary figure who daily strode the steep paths between his summer home at Pointe Rivière du Loup and the river's south shore, there was little comfort. Unaccustomed to idleness in any circumstances, Louis-Alexandre Taschereau felt especially restless with a provincial election campaign going on. For half a century he had fought in every federal and provincial election battle waged by the Quebec Liberal party. Now he was forced to remain silent while long-time Conservative and clerical nationalist opponents avenged years of defeat by maligning the family name he bore so proudly. Worse still, they did so virtually unchallenged by the Liberals, whom he had served in the legislature since 1900, the cabinet since 1907, and the premier's office since 1920. Even from supposed friends, there could be no public recognition of a long, successful, and distinguished political career; suddenly a liability to party fortunes, Taschereau was now a man to be ignored. Most later showed greater personal consideration, appreciating his need for some kind of symbolic vindication. But active politicians seemed anxious above all to let the Taschereau regime fade from public memory.

Since then, historians have likewise paid scant attention to Alexandre Taschereau's political career. This is much more surprising than what Taschereau himself called the "ingratitude of political life," the unseemly rush of allies and clients to dissociate themselves from his fallen regime.[1] For whatever their judgment of this figure, historians can hardly escape the fact that Taschereau occupied a central place in Quebec during critical phases of that province's economic and social development, not to mention its political evolution. Nor can Taschereau be dismissed as a mere bystander, a chance political survivor amidst changes wrought by external forces. For while such an image may suit some ideological preferences, the most cursory examination is enough to establish that Taschereau maintained a consistent and comprehensive view of Quebec's needs and priorities and of the role of government throughout his adult life.[2] And whatever its deficiencies and despite its conservative-nationalist bias, Robert Rumilly's chronicle of political life during the Taschereau era has made a wealth of basic information on the subject available since the 1950s.[3]

Yet Taschereau has been largely ignored in scholarly treatments of urbanization and industrialization in Quebec, even those focused on matters in which provincial policy was a crucial factor.[4] When he has appeared, Taschereau has usually been a nationalist's caricature, the foil for ideological and political opponents who were the objects of investigation.[5] Two recent studies tried to break out of this tradition, acknowledging Taschereau as the protagonist in substantive debates over the nature and future of Quebec society.[6] Even they suffered, unfortunately, from an inability to "humanize" Taschereau, to understand his position as a product of personal and historical experience. One result of the historians' failure to take Taschereau seriously is that despite a proliferation of excellent monographs, Quebec historiography still lacks a good narrative synthesis of his era. The most commendable textbook is being written, not surprisingly, by scholars committed to a structuralist approach which eschews narration and minimizes the significance of political leadership.[7]

There are a number of reasons for this odd failure. Academic historians in French Canada have never been very interested in political biography. This tradition long predates the Marxist determinism which became prevalent around 1970. For years historical interest and research were focused almost exclusively on French Canada's "golden age" prior to the British Conquest, while debate on the impact of the Conquest expanded the field of inquiry no further than the early nineteenth century. Alienated from politics for most of the twentieth century, moreover, French-Canadian intellectuals have dismissed their society's political leaders as weak, ineffectual, or downright corrupt; provincial politics especially have been regarded as unimportant and sordid. This attitude has endured even while a sister discipline, political science, has developed some interest and expertise in the field, and English-Canadian historians have studied at least some aspects of important political careers.[8] Few major studies of post-Confederation Quebec politics have been published by French-Canadian academic historians. Apart from compilations of election data, those dealing with the present century have focused on one important but limited theme, the frustrations of Quebec Conservatives in federal politics.[9]

One factor which has sustained this aversion may be described as the "Duplessis archetype syndrome." It consists of an assumption that the characteristics of Maurice Duplessis and his postwar regime were essentially the same as those of his Liberal predecessors. Thus, for example, the theory of the "Negro King" and the explanations for the longevity of the Union Nationale government developed by its contemporary critics are given general application to earlier leaders and governments without actual investigation or regard for different circumstances.[10] This ahistorical tendency came naturally to supporters of Quebec's Quiet Revolution, who divided history into the "uniform bleakness of ... 'la grande noirceur' and the long-delayed liberation" which followed the election of the Lesage government in 1960. In such an undifferentiated prerevolutionary past, Taschereau is but "a Duplessis with better manners; corrupt, self-serving, allied to the forces of reaction in matters economic, cultural and spiritual."[11] The Quiet Revolution itself has since been attacked from a radical perspective, but all seem content with its historical mythology.[12]

Finally, there are a number of obstacles to the writing of a biography of Taschereau in particular. Even by normal Quebec standards, let alone by the measure of Duplessis, he was not a flamboyant or charismatic political leader. In fact, his oratorical talents were distinctly substandard, he distrusted "demagogues," and the image of business-like efficiency he cultivated did little to excite the popular imagination. Nor did he exhibit the kind of eccentric personal behaviour which would capture the interest of a modern psycho-historian – although some might well attribute his preoccupation with family honour and responsibility more to personal experience than to prevailing values.

More serious has been the problem of inadequate sources. There is no single collection to "anchor" a Taschereau biography, even for the period of his premiership. The Taschereau Papers deposited in the Archives Nationales du Québec contain several excellent dossiers, but the gaps are enormous. Clearly, Taschereau or an executor eliminated some material, since many letters appearing in the papers of his correspondents are missing here. However, most of the correspondence a biographer would desire probably never existed. Taschereau was rarely separated from his family and closest friends and associates long enough to bother with revealing personal letters, and while he was premier there appears to have been a preference for verbal consultation among ministers and face-to-face negotiation leading to formal agreements with private interests. Although Taschereau made no secret of this procedure,[13] it obviously makes historians vulnerable to what David Hackett Fischer calls

the furtive fallacy ... the erroneous idea that facts of special significance are dark and dirty things and that history itself is a story of causes mostly insidious and results mostly invidious. It begins with the premise that reality is a sordid, secret thing; and that history happens on the back stairs a little after midnight, or else in a smoke-filled room ... It is something more, and something other than merely a conspiracy theory, though that form of causal reduction is a common component. The furtive fallacy is a more profound error, which combines a naive epistemological assumption that things are never what they seem to be, with a firm attachment to the doctrine of original sin.[14]

Thus, for example, historians would be just as wrong to assume that kickbacks were the key to Taschereau's approval of resource development projects as they would be to ignore the realities of party financing and the blatant conflicts of interest he permitted. This particular question of motivation is both highly emotional and critically important, and the would-be biographer is reduced (at best) to highly impressionistic conclusions.

For the years of his premiership there is fortunately some compensation for the inadequacies of the Taschereau Papers. Quebec departmental records were not very carefully preserved, but the government did spend generously on the publication of Sessional Papers which contained considerable internal administrative information. There is much relevant correspondence in the papers of Taschereau's political contemporaries, especially federal and Ontario provincial leaders. As premier he naturally attracted a good deal of press coverage whose very partisanship can be useful: critics pulled few punches, while a fawning Liberal press printed the full text of speeches and dutifully reported social and family as well as political occasions. In the absence of an official record of legislative debates, government and opposition newspapers between them provided a fairly complete account.[15] The author was able to interview several well-informed survivors of the period, and a few other contemporaries have published their memoirs.[16]

A different form of compensation exists for the period of Taschereau's maturation, the years preceding his entry into the legislature. Such fragmentary evidence as does exist suggests that many of the habits and beliefs which gave purpose to and sustained his political career, and also some of those which spurred criticism and ultimately contributed to his rather sad and sordid political demise, were well established by 1900. Admittedly, this is an observation born of hindsight, and since it pertains as much to his early adulthood as to his childhood, it would be fatuous to posit some sort of "life script." But one can certainly point out the remarkable consistency between certain early experiences and later behaviour, and recall Taschereau's own references, albeit superficial and often self-serving, to the days of his youth.

The lack of a narrative synthesis of Quebec history during the Taschereau years represents a serious gap in Canadian as well as Quebec historiography. It is not only a case of contributing to French-English understanding by shedding light on a critical phase of Quebec's evolution, important as this may be. It is also a matter of recognizing that the recent study of governments, parties, and leaders in other provinces has considerably enhanced our understanding of the Canadian political system as a whole, and that this work must include Quebec. The historian should not be discouraged, therefore, by the remaining source problems or the likelihood that continuing ideological commitments in a wide segment of the Quebec academic community will prejudice the reception of such a book. One is required only to be honest, avoiding dogmatic assertions where the evidence warrants a reasonable inference and acknowledging personal biases. This book assumes that political biography is especially valuable as a check on monistic and deterministic historical interpretations. In particular, it takes a "liberal" approach to the "national" question: it does not attribute the problems of the age or Taschereau's reaction to them exclusively to the unique character and minority position of French-Canadian society. This is hardly an original position,[17] but it needs restating in the light of a general reluctance to view Quebec developments and Taschereau's performance in a wider and comparative context.

For enabling me to survive the frustration occasioned by fragmentary sources and other difficulties, I owe much to the patience and encouragement of colleagues at the University of New Brunswick, to the constructive suggestions of readers who undoubtedly would have approached the subject differently, to the sympathetic attitude of the editors of McGill-Queen's University Press, and above all to the loving forbearance of my wife and daughters. In addition to gratitude I must express a profound regret: that several individuals with personal knowledge of the Taschereau era, who took a genuine interest in the project and provided me with invaluable insights and information, have not lived to receive the published work.

Ginger group: Members of the Union libérale club, c. 1890; L.-A. Taschereau and Adélard Turgeon are standing (second and third from right), Edouard Taschereau is seated (second from left)

Friend and ally: Sir Lomer Gouin, premier of Quebec, 1905–20

The heir apparent: Taschereau before World War I, when he was minister of public works and labour in the Gouin government

First ministers: G. Howard Ferguson, premier of Ontario, Prime Minister Mackenzie King, and Taschereau at the Dominion-Provincial Conference in 1927

"My Opposition Leader": Adine Taschereau travelling with her husband in the 1930s

The last campaign: Taschereau addressing an election rally in November 1935

*Quebec before Duplessis*

## CHAPTER ONE

# "The Glorious Name of Taschereau"

"Which is the outstanding name belonging to the French race in Canada?" asked Wilfrid Laurier in 1892.

Is it Papineau? Lafontaine? Papineau and Lafontaine were like meteors in the night, but we also have a permanent star which I believe shines far brighter. I speak of that noble family in which talent, character, honour, force and work are hereditary; which in every generation for a hundred years has furnished patriots and men of action who influenced the people and events of their time; which early in this century produced a martyr to liberty in Governor Craig's prison; which has given five judges to the magistracy, an archbishop to the Canadian Church and a Cardinal to the Universal Church! Let us toast the glorious name of Taschereau! Let us do so with respect, for this name is the symbol of those manly virtues which alone create great peoples and great nations.[1]

Louis-Alexandre Taschereau was twenty-five years old when he listened to this tribute, the climax of a banquet honouring his uncle, Cardinal-Archbishop Elzéar-Alexandre Taschereau of Quebec. By then he was already highly conscious of his family's stature, proud of it but also impressed by the obligations it placed upon him. His father, the Hon. Jean-Thomas Taschereau, had taught him the national history of French Canada as a record of the exploits of his ancestors. He was able to envision these events by exploring the historic sites of Quebec City, where he was born on 5 March 1867, as well as the family's original seigneurial estate, where he spent several summers. The first Taschereau in Canada was Thomas-Jacques, who had relatives in the nobility of the French province of Touraine, but had crossed the Atlantic in 1720 as a mere secretary to the Intendant Dupuy. Within ten years he was an important official in his own right, a successful businessman, and connected by marriage to a prominent Canadian family. Before his death in 1749 he was recognized as a full-fledged member of the colonial elite: King Louis xv appointed him to the Superior Council and granted him the substantial seigneury called Sainte Marie, south of Quebec.

After the British Conquest, the Taschereau name and property were continued by Gabriel-Elzéar, the youngest surviving son and the only one to remain in the colony. As Roman Catholics, French Canadians were at first not permitted to hold official positions under British rule. But Gabriel-Elzéar succeeded in business and also developed the potential wealth of Sainte Marie. Then, as a reward for active loyalty to Britain during the American Revolution, he became the first French-Canadian judge appointed by the British. When an elected legislature was established in 1792, Taschereau was chosen to represent the county of Dorchester. Although defeated in 1796, he held a number of government positions in the remaining thirteen years of his life.

Gabriel-Elzéar's most illustrious offspring was Jean-Thomas (Senior). Elected to the legislature at the age of twenty-two, he helped found French Canada's first newspaper, *Le Canadien*, and its first political party, the Parti canadien. He was the Taschereau jailed by Governor James Craig, basically for his militancy in defending the right of French Canadians to preserve their language and culture. He nevertheless remained loyal to Britain and fought against American invaders at the Battle of Châteauguay during the War of 1812. In later years, when radical young lawyers took over the Parti canadien, Taschereau was considered too loyal and lost his seat in the Assembly. He then became a distinguished judge and also built up a new seigneury on land purchased for him by his father.

The two sons of Jean-Thomas Taschereau were the uncle and father of Louis-Alexandre. Elzéar-Alexandre entered the church and began teaching at the Quebec Seminary in 1842. In 1860 he became supérieur-général (principal) of the seminary as well as rector of Laval University. He was appointed Archbishop of Quebec in 1871, and in 1887 became the first Canadian cardinal. Jean-Thomas, Jr entered the legal profession, studying in Paris as well as Quebec during the tumultuous 1830s. An outstanding trial lawyer in both criminal and civil cases for many years, he became a judge just prior to Confederation. With the creation of a Canadian Supreme Court in 1875, his appointment was a foregone conclusion. Unfortunately, ill health forced him to retire after only three years, but he lived to see all five of his sons enter the legal profession as attorneys or notaries.[2]

Young Alexandre understood that he belonged not only to an historically prominent family but also to the contemporary elite of French Canada. When he was nine there were, in addition to his father and uncle, three close relatives prominent in public life. His maternal grandfather, René-Edouard Caron, had been mayor of Quebec during the 1840s and a major figure in LaFontaine's campaign for responsible government, and was now serving as lieutenant-governor of Quebec. He also had a step-brother representing the nearby county of Montmagny in Parliament and a cousin presiding as superior court judge.

Alexandre and his three brothers and three sisters were products of the second marriage of Jean-Thomas, to Joséphine Caron. The boys received the education usual for sons of the French-Canadian elite. They learned the rudiments from their mother at home, and then proceeded to the Petit Séminaire de Québec, the leading classical college. Alexandre quickly distinguished himself upon entering the Petit Séminaire in 1878, finishing in the top half of his class despite a two-month illness. Promoted directly to the third level (and not missing a single day of class), he rose to second in a class of more than thirty by the end of the year. In his remaining four years he was never lower than third and captured numerous subject prizes, especially in Latin and English.[3] If later reminiscences are reliable, Alexandre cared little for the rigid and humiliating discipline of the school. His father told him, in fact, to refuse to kiss the floor – a form of penitence frequently demanded by one teacher for trivial offences. Beatings had been officially abolished at the school, but "cuffing" was frequent and suspension or expulsion awaited those guilty of more serious misconduct. As a day student, Alexandre was fortunately able to escape much of the dreary morning and evening routine, not to mention the inevitably monotonous and bland diet. And while he participated in the usual assortment of student pranks and "secret" societies, he was never considered a ringleader or a disciplinary problem by school authorities.[4]

The curriculum of the Petit Séminaire contained all the elements of a classical education. Taschereau studied Greek, Latin, English, and French languages and literature, ancient, medieval, and modern (to 1815) history, rhetoric, arithmetic, geography, and, naturally, Catholicism. With due regard for political sensitivities, the Séminaire added a course in Canadian history based on the liberal interpretation of F.-X. Garneau (*Histoire du Canada*) and the clerical version of J.-B.-A. Ferland (*Cours d'histoire du Canada*) as well as L.-P. Turcotte's chronicle *Le Canada sous l'Union*. There was no science, but art and musical instruction were organized by interested faculty members on a voluntary basis. Taschereau does not seem to have taken advantage of these, preferring instead the competitive rhetorical and debating activities. There was no organized athletic competition, although the Séminaire acquired some gymnastic equipment in 1879. The favourite outdoor activities appear to have been skating, marbles, and snowball fights.[5]

The better students generally appreciated capable and inspiring teachers, and learned to tolerate the eccentric and the mediocre with reasonable grace. And although the priests encouraged a highly competitive atmosphere, Taschereau formed his closest and most enduring friendships with the other top students. Two of these, Joseph Gignac and François Pelletier, later entered the church and gave Taschereau important moral support during conflicts with ultramontane clergy.[6] Alfred Morriset became a doctor by profession but also shared in Taschereau's early political adventures, sat in the legislature for several years, and later served as clerk of the Assembly. Two of Alexandre's brothers attended the Petit Séminaire at about the same time and both did well. Antoine was three years older but only one year ahead, and Edmond was a year younger but two years behind him. Judging by later events, however, it appears that Alexandre became more closely attached to his oldest brother Edouard, who was four years ahead and thus moved on to Laval University soon after Alexandre entered the Petit Séminaire.

The classical program of the Petit Séminaire led almost invariably to the Arts course at Laval. Alexandre Taschereau followed this normal route and received his BA in 1886, but without spectacular achievement. This he saved for his law degree, sweeping every prize and medal except the one for criminal law when he graduated in 1889.[7] Alexandre may well have been ready to sprint ahead of his class at this point simply on the basis of his own intelligence and strong motivation. But he undoubtedly derived some benefit from the encouragement and example of Edouard, and from his contact with a number of Edouard's friends who were also recent graduates in law. Edouard had been an outstanding student, and was already considered the heir-apparent to the family's great judicial tradition. He was thus an ideal mentor, who made it possible for Alexandre to be articled in his office, that of a prestigious firm headed by François Langelier.

Edouard also influenced his favourite brother's political and courting activities. In 1888 he and his contemporaries welcomed Alexandre into the Union libérale, a political club they had founded. Alexandre wrote for the club's weekly newspaper of the same name, became an officer of the organization, and eventually stood as its candidate in a hopeless provincial election adventure. While at university, Alexandre began courting Adine Dionne, the younger sister of Edouard's wife Amélie. There was actually a much older relationship between the two families. The girls' father, a legislative councillor and former provincial cabinet minister, Elisée Dionne, was the brother of Jean-Thomas Taschereau's first wife, and the two men had briefly practised law together. Alexandre and Adine had almost certainly known each other since childhood, for she had attended a convent school in Quebec City. But after his cabinet stint (1882-4) Dionne had moved his family back to the seigneurial estate at Ste Anne de la Pocatière.[8] One can therefore reasonably suppose that Alexandre's courtship was helped along, at least initially, by the social opportunities arising from Edouard's marriage. Adine was an attractive and quick-witted woman, which no doubt explains Alexandre's interest. Moreover, her family background had prepared her to meet the social demands of elite society – entertaining, doing charitable work, patronizing the arts – and to understand and accept the infectious disease called politics to which Alexandre progressively succumbed. Many years later, in a graceful tribute to her Conservative parentage as well as her ability to deflate excessive pretensions, he conferred upon his wife the title of "my Opposition Leader." The deeply religious orientation of her family, which led two of her brothers into the priesthood, became an additional source of reassurance when other priests presumed to denounce Alexandre and his political colleagues in the name of Catholicism.[9]

Their predictably happy marriage, consecrated by Cardinal Taschereau on 26 May 1891, nevertheless began amidst a succession of tragedies whose effect on Taschereau's personality and later career naturally cannot be measured, but must have been profound. Within two months, the false optimism with which family and friends had witnessed Edouard's painful fight with cancer was shattered by his death in a New York hospital. Amélie was carrying his second child at the time. In October, one of Alexandre's two step-sisters died and sixteen months later the other was widowed. In August 1892 Elisée Dionne died suddenly at only sixty-four, and exactly a year later Alexandre and Adine's first child died in infancy. Jean-Thomas Taschereau died three months after that. At the same time Elzéar-Alexandre Taschereau began to evince signs of physical as well as mental infirmity as he approached his mid-seventies. In addition to being emotionally disruptive in themselves, these events left Alexandre, still in his mid-twenties and trying to launch his own career, the effective leader of the Taschereau family. Formally, he was the executor of his father's estate. Morally, he felt responsible for the happiness as well as the material comfort of middle-aged and young widows and of fatherless children. And from Edouard's death arose the deepest summons, the task of continuing that record of distinguished achievement to which Laurier had paid such eloquent homage. In later interviews Taschereau never mentioned Edouard in the context of his own ambition to be a justice of the Supreme Court. But he did acknowledge the family tradition, and it is clear that this accomplishment had been widely expected of Edouard. At least one journalist did sense the connection quite strongly.[10]

The political and philosophical attachments formed during Taschereau's youth were moderate in substance but deeply felt and enduring. Jean-Thomas was a Liberal in politics, but there were Taschereaus and other relations – Caron and Elisée Dionne, for example – in the Conservative camp. In fact, Alexandre long recalled witnessing the funeral procession of George-Etienne Cartier,[11] whose heroic stature no one around him questioned. "Rouge" or "Bleu," the Taschereaus were basically Whigs: believers in the British constitutional system, in leadership by an educated elite, in progress through gradual change, in religion as a matter of personal conscience but also as a beneficial stabilizing influence in society. It was the religious dimension which assumed prominence during Taschereau's formative years, almost certainly determined his ultimate devotion to the Liberal party, and echoed loudly throughout his political career.

Jean-Thomas and (obviously) Elzéar-Alexandre Taschereau did not belong to the radical, anticlerical wing of the Liberal party – the original Rouges. However, they did not escape involvement in the war which ultramontane Catholics had been waging since the early 1850s against real and imagined enemies of their faith, both in politics and within the church itself. In its worldwide context, nineteenth-century ultramontanism was an arch-conservative, authoritarian reaction to liberal influences and revolutionary events. French-Canadian ultramontanism drew unusual strength, however, from one peculiar characteristic: its compatibility with nationalism. Whereas most European nationalists were revolutionaries and considered the church an integral part of the old order, French-Canadian nationalism became increasingly an ideology of conservation following the unsuccessful rebellions of 1837–8. "La survivance," national survival, required vigilant defence of the traditional faith and religious institutions.

Ultramontane influence in French Canada reached a peak in 1858, when Bishop Bourget of Montreal persuaded the Papacy to condemn the spiritual centre of French-Canadian liberalism, the Institut canadien of Montreal. By the 1870s ultramontanes were in a much more defensive posture, fighting to preserve the concept that religious authority took precedence over secular power. Archbishop Taschereau opposed those clergy and laymen who attempted, through a manifesto known as the "Catholic Programme" and other tactics directed against liberals, to put this doctrine into practice politically. Jean-Thomas wrote the Supreme Court decision which brought clerical pressure within the definition of "undue influencing" of voters. Both before and after the Papacy finally instructed all clergy to respect Canadian laws, ultramontane frustration caused the Taschereaus to be bitterly denounced – even their religious faith was questioned.[12]

As a child Alexandre probably did not understand this conflict fully, but his later statements and highly personal reaction to echoes of *castorisme* suggest that he did sense the anger and injustice felt by members of his family.[13] Whatever memories he retained were certainly reinforced by his experience with the Union libérale, which also gave him the opportunity to articulate his beliefs on a wide range of issues. The Union was founded by young Liberals in Quebec City who, while admiring Honoré Mercier, were deeply suspicious of the disaffected Conservatives who helped Mercier become premier of Quebec following the 1886 provincial election. Most of these so-called National Conservatives were *castors* whose ideas, Union libérale members thought, had no place in the Liberal party and whose loyalty to Mercier's "national" government could not be trusted anyway. Taschereau's special assignment with the club newspaper was to criticize the Conservative press, and his favourite targets initially were ultramontane journalists like Senator F.-X. Trudel ("F.-X. Anselme") and Jules-Paul Tardivel, publisher of *La Verité*. Writing as "Turpin," he took particular delight in ridiculing the pretensions of Tardivel, the self-appointed prophet and conscience of French Canada, and was overjoyed when Tardivel made the mistake of responding. "M. Tardivel (Notre Pasteur Québécois), fortified by a powerful antidote and armed with that telescope which detects freemasons invisible to the naked eye, has focused his wonderful instrument upon the Union libérale. The interest of science does not permit him to reveal everything he has seen. He has, however, discovered some very suspicious germs whose initial symptoms take the form of a slightly too advanced liberalism."[14]

While careful not to criticize Mercier directly, "Turpin" never hid his discomfort at the alliance with the *castors*. He applauded Laurier for repudiating any such alliance in federal politics. "The Liberal party can only gain by ridding itself of these parasites." Let the religious fanatics tear apart the Conservative party, he wrote prophetically in 1890. Sane and moderate French-Canadian Conservatives would eventually come over to the Liberals, especially with Ontario Tories falling prey to Protestant and imperialist fanaticism. So purified, the Liberal party would represent religious and commercial freedom, national independence, racial harmony – in short, all "generous ideas and noble sentiments." When the National Conservatives held a meeting to consolidate their provincial organization, "Turpin" took it as a sign of bad faith and of treachery to come. He celebrated when Mercier was overwhelmingly reelected in June 1890 while most National Conservatives were defeated. The *Union libérale* newspaper suspended publication for almost two years, from March 1891, and therefore did not cover the demise of Mercier. In a retrospective analysis, however, "Turpin" suggested that one cause was Mercier's failure to heed the warnings of true Liberals. Thereafter, he attacked the *castor* de Boucherville and Taillon ministries unceasingly, delighting in evidence of their lack of moral purity and even daring to question the propriety of certain grants to religious orders. The most severe criticism was reserved for Louis-Philippe Pelletier, the provincial secretary.[15]

The enmity toward Pelletier is not difficult to explain. He was the leading National Conservative who turned against Mercier when the Bay of Chaleurs scandal broke out; in fact, he helped make possible Mercier's dismissal from office by the lieutenant-governor. Convinced that Pelletier's motives were entirely personal, the Union libérale group decided to oppose his reelection for Dorchester in the 1892 election. With Mercier now discredited and many Liberals shunning association with him, it was not difficult to secure any "parti national" nomination. The Union libérale chose Taschereau, several of whose ancestors had represented the county. His chances of victory were negligible, but Taschereau's candidacy livened up the midwinter campaign with charges and counter-charges hurled at large, boisterous *assemblées contradictoires*, Quebec's legendary oratorical duels in which candidates and seconds vied for popular acclaim.

It was evidently more than sport, for Pelletier was not a gracious winner. After capturing every poll on election day, 8 March, he refused Taschereau and his followers the usual courtesy of a ride back to Quebec City on his private train. Taschereau and two friends had to hire a carriage to Lévis and then walk through bitter cold across the frozen St Lawrence and up to his residence, arriving well past midnight. The feud simmered for years and boiled over as late as 1911 when Pelletier figured in the Conservative-nationalist alliance against Laurier and then joined the federal government of Robert Borden.[16]

Much of Taschereau's writing for *L'Union libérale* was superficial or self-indulgent. Yet the very persistence of his crusade against ultramontanism in politics and religion makes this aspect of his liberalism seem sincere enough; even distant and obscure cases of religious intolerance brought his condemnation.[17] Despite his declarations of support for the nationalism of Mercier, moreover, Taschereau's real affinity was clearly with Wilfrid Laurier: fear that *castorisme*, far from protecting French-Canadian Catholicism, served to provoke and confirm English-Canadian prejudices and risked isolating Quebec politically; confidence, however, that the numbers and credibility of Conservative partisans among the clergy were in decline and that the Liberal party was the vehicle to unite the tolerant majority of English and French Canadians.[18] The events surrounding Mercier's rise and fall also tempered the idealistic conception of politics with which the young often begin their involvement. Taschereau saw that politics was a rough business governed by opportunity and self-interest more often than loyalty and duty, and that "the best governments" and "the most honest administrators" were prone to abuse if not properly scrutinized.[19] "A bit cynical about men, motives and ambition" was the apt description applied by C.G. Power, a close observer of Taschereau's later political career.[20]

Taschereau's attitude to politics was not, of course, shaped solely by his association with the Union libérale. For practical purposes, the launching of his own professional career was probably much more important. Born to French Canada's "aristocracy" and setting his sights on high judicial honours, Taschereau was not motivated by the desire for wealth *per se*. However, achieving excellence and recognition meant reaching for the top of his profession. Courtroom skill, based on meticulous preparation as well as keen intelligence, was certainly crucial to a lawyer's reputation. At least equally important, though, was the clientele attracted to a practice. Here Taschereau was strongly influenced by Charles Fitzpatrick, an uncle by marriage, with whom be began the practice of law in 1889, and later by Simon-Napoléon Parent. Fifteen years older than his nephew, Fitzpatrick had been an equally brilliant law student with a special flair for criminal cases. He had helped prepare the defence for Louis Riel in 1885 and now lectured on criminal procedure at Laval. By the time Taschereau joined him, however, Fitzpatrick had decided that corporate law provided greater challenges and opportunities, opening up the world of finance, commerce, and industry as well as judicial careers. Political connection seemed important, so in 1890 Fitzpatrick secured a seat in the legislature as a Mercier supporter.[21] Between 1892 and 1896, however, the Conservatives were in power both federally and provincially. To a Liberal firm this meant little chance for legal work from the government itself or from private interests hoping to secure political good will through their choice of attorneys. Yet Taschereau apparently used the period to establish an outstanding legal reputation, for major clients came quickly to the firm once the Liberals regained power. At the same time, his occasional contributions to *L'Union libérale* began to reflect a conviction that survival of the traditional French-Canadian elite would require acceptance of and participation in large-scale enterprise.[22] Fitzpatrick's name may have helped after 1896, but it was Taschereau whose legal skills were actually being hired, since the senior partner had gone to Ottawa as solicitor general in Laurier's administration. Moreover, many corporate clients were dealing with the provincial rather than the federal government; as outsiders they naturally sought the most prestigious local firm.

Not only for his own career but for the subsequent political and economic history of Quebec, Taschereau's most important new association was with Parent. Appointed provincial minister of lands, mines and forests in 1897, while still mayor of Quebec City, Parent could not also manage his own extensive business and legal affairs. He was therefore anxious to delegate this work to a full-time lawyer, and in December of 1898 he concluded a five-year partnership agreement with Taschereau and Fitzpatrick.[23] Without quite realizing it himself, Parent was a new breed of Quebec politician. He had risen from modest origins to graduate first in law at Laval in 1881, and won acceptance in the Quebec City business community. Elected to city council in 1890 and chosen mayor by his fellow aldermen in 1894, Parent emphasized "progressive" administration. Primarily, this meant modernizing Quebec with new public buildings and transportation facilities, planning city growth in a rational manner, and operating on the basis of efficiency rather than partisan or other kinds of favouritism. This did not preclude reserving a piece of the action for public officials – Parent himself formed a company to build a bridge spanning the St Lawrence and was a director of the Quebec Railway, Light and Power Company – nor did it prevent the development of fierce interest group rivalries. What it did provide were criteria for contracts and franchises awarded to private corporations: they must contribute to the economic development of the city at reasonable cost to the taxpayer. The emphasis on efficient, modern development and the downplaying of partisanship were even less familiar in provincial politics when Parent brought them to bear in 1897. A backbench Liberal since 1890, but not implicated in either the scandals or the "betrayal" of Mercier, Parent accepted office in F.-G. Marchand's new administration. Immediately he set about promoting the rapid and efficient exploitation of Quebec's natural resources by changing regulations, reassigning leases and grants, and other devices. The clear, stated purpose was to attract the capital and expertise, regardless of party or nationality, necessary to transform the province's forest, mineral, and hydro-electric potential into real wealth.[24]

In accepting Parent's vision of an industrial future for Quebec, Taschereau was of course adapting his own ambitions to a changed environment. This adaptation did not, however, demand any real departure from his earlier philosophical orientation. The moderate liberal's faith in human progress and the "perfectibility of man," for example, could be expressed in material as well as intellectual and moral terms. Thus the progress of French-Canadian society now meant achieving economic as well as intellectual modernity, and Taschereau quite naturally regarded the critics of industrialization who soon appeared as a new generation of *castors* seeking to obstruct that progress. Unfortunately, Taschereau also accepted without much question Parent's assumption that private gain by public officials and their associates was compatible with good government, while at the same time forgetting his own warnings about the temptations of power. This is clear from the terms of the partnership agreement with Parent and Fitzpatrick. It was explicitly stated that only Fitzpatrick and Parent could engage in "politics, finance and business." Taschereau was to be the full-time lawyer. He and Ferdinand Roy (a salaried employee whose brilliance in law school meant more to Taschereau than his Conservative affiliation) would handle the important and lucrative legal work which the others steered to the firm, along with work they themselves had attracted; the profits would be shared three ways. As long as Parent did not actually require companies he dealt with in his public role to retain Taschereau, none of this was illegal. And indeed, political opponents at first did not seem to recognize the full implications of such a system; the earliest backlash occurred among Liberals who resented the virtual monopoly of favour secured by one group.[25] When the inevitable challenge came to this standard of public morality, Taschereau developed the habit of defending it by attacking the motives of the critics – with more self-righteousness than common sense once public opinion would no longer tolerate it.

All that lay in a future political career which no one would have predicted for Taschereau in 1900. He was as well connected politically as anyone could possibly be, he willingly performed organizational services for the Liberal party, and he had strong views on many public issues. But at thirty-three his original career plans remained fully in force. He was well on his way to the top of the legal profession as measured both by skill in court (where he never ceased accepting criminal and charity cases) and by the importance of his corporate clients.[26] Even his physical appearance and mannerisms seemed to match his calling: a slimness and straight posture which made him look taller than his five feet nine inches, sharp features, wiry brown hair, an elongated stride when in motion and a nervous impatience when still. He listened carefully, and responded precisely and logically. (Thirty-five years later the hair was grey and he would spin the telephone dial instead of drumming his fingers on his desk. Little else changed.)[27] Neither his own ambition to succeed nor the desire to extend the Taschereau tradition of public service at the highest level required his entry into active politics. However strongly early experiences influenced his eventual political career, Taschereau was actually drawn towards the premiership of Quebec by a series of unplanned, unforeseeable developments.

## CHAPTER TWO

# "The Party of Progress"

Most Canadians witnessed the dawn of the twentieth century with great optimism, and justifiably so. For after a generation of agonizingly slow and forced expansion, the vision of the political and economic elites who established Confederation seemed finally on the verge of fulfilment. Worldwide prosperity provided the capital and markets so long denied, while the filling of the American West redirected the transatlantic tide of immigration northward to farm Canadian land, man Canadian factories, and consume Canadian production. As a modern state sharing the great moral and technological progress of the age, Canada would occupy an increasingly important place in the affairs of the British Empire and of the world.

Quebec had every reason to share this enthusiasm. Lacking the coal and iron resources essential to industrial expansion in the late nineteenth century, and helplessly watching the centre of North American economic gravity shift westward to the Great Lakes region, the province had fallen into severe stagnation. The CPR upheld Montreal as Canada's commercial and transportation capital, tariffs fostered and protected textile, leather, and other "sweating" industries, and specialization in dairying raised some farmers above subsistence agriculture. But these activities could not begin to absorb the exceedingly high natural increase in population, or even reward those employed in manufacturing and transportation with reasonable security or a decent wage. Every year, thousands of French Canadians emigrated from their homeland, mostly to work in New England mills which themselves paid meagre wages. In desperation, some French Canadians promoted the "colonization" of marginal farmland on the edge of the Laurential Shield. Although this crusade drew considerable praise, not to speak of provincial railway subsidies to open up the area, its effectiveness in slowing emigration was negligible.[1]

Fortunately the new era offered Quebec an escape from its stagnation. National prosperity of course meant a revitalization of the St Lawrence as a commercial highway, and if a second transcontinental railway were to follow the north shore of the river, then Quebec City in particular could escape the isolation to which the CPR's route had condemned it. But the carrying trade was cyclical and not a mass employer. The real opportunity lay in exploiting the immense natural resources of Quebec's interior, above all the force of rivers descending from the Shield into the St Lawrence Valley. With the advent of hydroelectric technology and the availability of American capital, Quebec suddenly had a bright industrial future. No longer need heavy industry shun the province because of its costly dependence upon imported coal. On the contrary, once a sufficient proportion of its hydroelectric potential had been harnessed, Quebec would enjoy a competitive advantage. Cheap power would provide jobs for hundreds of thousands of French Canadians, permanently stemming the tide of emigration. Power was not the only resource. Already Quebec's spruce and pine forests were being eyed covetously by American newsprint manufacturers whose domestic pulpwood reserves were rapidly diminishing. Even if Quebec pulpwood were initially exported for manufacture in existing American mills, this would compensate for the chronic decline in lumbering activity. And within a few years, electrical power would encourage the establishment of paper mills within the province. Finally, the inestimable mineral wealth hidden in the Shield would be gradually uncovered, contributing still further to overall employment and general prosperity.[2]

Nevertheless, some French Canadians viewed the propsect of material advance with mixed emotions. It was true that industry could be the salvation of dying towns and villages, and provide a dramatically expanded market for agricultural producers. But on the whole, the industrialization of Quebec must inevitably destroy the predominantly rural and agrarian character of French-Canadian society. No longer would the mass of the population live a poor but independent existence, isolated from the Protestant materialism which prevailed elsewhere in North America. A few leaders concluded that such developments were incompatible with the survival of French Canadians as a distinct people, and rejected industrialization as an acceptable course.[3] That extreme view was so divorced from reality that only a tiny minority openly espoused it. But there were many more who shared the underlying sentiment. For unlike most English-

Canadian leaders, who embraced the idea of progress and had been awaiting their country's material advance with great concern and impatience, important sections of the French-Canadian elite felt threatened by the prospect of rapid, large-scale industrialization. The doctrine and institutional power of the church and the social influence of the clergy were sure to be challenged as they had been by similar changes elsewhere. French-Canadian lawyers, businessmen, and financiers had to maintain their status amidst a process initiated and controlled by cultural aliens who were operating in a continental economic system. Nor did the empire and world in which English-Canadian nationalists looked forward to playing a role seem necessarily hospitable to French Canadians. Those leaders who welcomed the new age unreservedly and sought a place in the new industrial order had no doubt that theirs was the right course. But critics, whatever their motives, had a receptive audience for accusations of treason against the progressives.

This fundamental and emotional issue provided the fulcrum for provincial politics during the first decade of the twentieth century. The exaggerated theatrics and questionable morality of individuals which usually captured the spotlight were symptoms but not the cause of tension within and between the political parties. The Liberals reaffirmed their commitment to industrialization, but lost the support of young nationalists originally attracted to the party by Laurier and also suffered from factionalism among followers competing for favour. Taking no clear position as a party, Conservatives became identified with growing clerical-nationalist resistance to industrialization. This weakened the impact of legitimate criticism of Liberal practices and cost them traditional support among businessmen, especially English-speaking ones, even men who maintained their Conservative allegiance in federal politics. It was in this turbulent atmosphere that Alexandre Taschereau's political career began – and very nearly ended.

In the first months of 1900 it became more unlikely than ever that Taschereau would depart from the partnership agreement and seek elected office. Fitzpatrick and Parent were advancing their careers relentlessly; the former's performance in Ottawa would soon earn him promotion to full cabinet rank as minister of justice while the latter's fellow aldermen continued to trust his ability to ride two horses and elected him to a fourth term as mayor of Quebec. In his provincial role Parent was now treating actively with American investors for large-scale development of hydroelectric resources on the St Maurice and Saguenay rivers. As senior practising member of the most powerful and prestigious law firm in Quebec City,

Taschereau was supervising Roy and another bright new graduate, Arthur Cannon. The firm would obviously collapse if Taschereau sought and won a seat in the federal election scheduled for 1900. A seat in the local legislature might be considered some day, just for recreation. But no provincial election was expected for more than a year, there were no Liberals in the Quebec City area willing to retire, and the district was so well served and represented in cabinet that no one felt the need for a "strong new voice."

However, the outlook changed dramatically in September with the sudden death of Premier Marchand. The natural successor, enjoying general caucus support, was Attorney General J.-E. Robidoux, a veteran Rouge who had served under Mercier. While in no way hostile to the man, Prime Minister Laurier had reservations about such a choice: it could herald a return to the extravagance of earlier administrations, threaten the truce between the Liberal party and the Catholic hierarchy, and alienate the moderate Conservatives whom Laurier had recruited to the Liberal cause. Laurier's preference was for Parent, whose past was untainted, administrative competence proven, and views moderate. He also shared Laurier's constituency, and was associated with Fitzpatrick; hence he could be relied upon to cooperate in keeping the party faithful harmonious and contented. Robidoux and the caucus bowed to Laurier's desires, and Simon-Napoléon Parent became premier of Quebec.[4]

Not all Liberals were pleased. It meant another setback to long-time party supporters who resented sharing the fruits of office with former rivals, and Montrealers had understandable qualms about the treatment they might receive from the mayor of Quebec. Parent recognized the importance of broadening his support, especially within the caucus. Naturally this meant winning the confidence of present members, but, come the next election, it would also help to bring more of his own partisans into the legislature. Although two years still remained in the life of the existing legislature, Parent decided that his best chance on both counts lay in an immediate election. Part of the reason was Laurier, who at the time of Parent's accession was about to enter his first federal reelection campaign. Despite some misgivings about Canadian participation in the Boer War, most Quebec Liberals rallied behind Laurier and on 7 November they swept all but seven seats in the province. Wishing to exploit Laurier's popularity and the organizational readiness of the party, Parent waited only a week before seeking dissolution. Provincial elections were set for 7 December, with Parent's need for a personal mandate the only excuse offered.

Unquestionably, Parent's legal associate would be a valuable asset to him in the legislature. Taschereau had some doubts about whether Roy and Cannon, both young bachelors still engaged in "charming the ladies" as well as in the practice of law, were ready to assume greater responsibilities. And his own family was still so young – the fourth child, Charles, arrived three days before the federal election. But ultimately that "craving for politics without which the nation would lack saviours" proved irresistible, and Adine, who recognized the growing ambition, consented gracefully.[5] Despite the generally demoralized state of the Conservative opposition, however, there would be nothing automatic about Taschereau's election.[6]

Trying to displace an incumbent Liberal in Quebec City was out of the question – it would only create a grievance against Parent. Although Taschereau happened to live and work in Quebec West, the one constituency in the capital which had voted Conservative in 1897, this seat was traditionally reserved for an anglophone. Taschereau therefore set his sights on the Conservative riding of Montmorency, which comprised the Ile d'Orléans and the Beaupré coast just below Quebec. This choice had several advantages: if elected, he would not be far from his constituents; he was already known in the riding, having campaigned there for others; perhaps most importantly, winning it would be a genuine accomplishment. The federal member was Tom Chase Casgrain, his former professor of criminal law. He was highly regarded and had survived the Laurier sweep largely because of his personal prestige and strong local organization. The provincial deputy, Edouard Bouffard, was also popular and shared the same organization. If Parent's associate could defeat Bouffard, it might persuade doubtful Liberals that their new leader did in fact have some political clout.

The nomination meeting took place on a cold Friday night, 23 November, at Quebec City's Delmonico Hotel. Taschereau was not the only contestant, and he was in fact somewhat troubled by the affair. Philéas Corriveau, a friend and colleague in Union libérale days, had come close to upsetting Casgrain in the federal vote and felt the provincial seat was within his grasp. Quebec City organizers thought, however, that Corriveau had not demonstrated much electoral flair against Casgrain, and they wanted a stronger candidate. Delegates from the constituency itself were naturally receptive to being represented by a close associate of the premier, and so Taschereau won the nomination handily. Corriveau actually finished third in the voting, and was visibly antagonized. It took several days for Taschereau and the others to soothe his feelings, but finally Corriveau joined in the campaign.[7]

With Bouffard already renominated, the battle could begin immediately. The first *contradictoires* were held on the following Sunday at Ste Famille and St Jean on the island. In 1900 residents of the Ile d'Orléans enjoyed a fairly prosperous existence based upon farming and fishing, though none of the modern amenities. On election night, voting results would be signalled to the mainland by a series of bonfires. Casgrain was present to second Bouffard, but Taschereau was also ably assisted by Dr Henri Béland, already acclaimed in his own constituency. Cheered on by a sympathetic audience, Taschereau promised virtually everything he could think of. It was a friendly affair – Bouffard and Casgrain were both spirited yet gentlemanly debaters – and Taschereau felt it had gone fairly well.

In subsequent days campaigning shifted to the mainland, with its striking natural beauty and enchanting historic sites: Montmorency Falls, the ancient church at Château-Richer towering over a frequent colonial battlefield, the shrine at Ste Anne de Beaupré, the inland settlements recently cleared by Quebec's modern colonists. Here the outcome was similar. While Taschereau took the advice of his organizers and toned down the promises, both sides realized that the prospect of material rewards from the party in power was swaying many voters. And since a Liberal majority was assured on nomination day, Bouffard could not even pretend for rhetorical purposes that his party was going to win. The only surprise on election day was the margin of Taschereau's victory, more than 600 in a poll of 2,000 voters.[8]

Although Taschereau attacked his new responsibilities with customary enthusiasm and thoroughness, most of his time was still devoted to the practice of law. In fact, a spectacular legal case in 1902 brought him more public attention than any political activity during his first term in the legislature. This was the Gaynor and Green extradition proceeding, which began as a fairly harmless comedy but ended by exposing Canadian judicial integrity to international question.[9] Col. John F. Gaynor and Capt. Benjamin Green of the United States Army were charged with defrauding the American government in a Savannah, Georgia, public works project. Apprehended in Syracuse, N.Y., they jumped bail and headed for Quebec, reportedly with close to a million dollars in stolen funds still in their possession. As soon as American agents located them and applied for extradition, Gaynor and Green sought legal counsel. Hospitable as ever towards American tourists, and not wishing to see their guests depart before they had spent the greater portion of their money, the good citizens of Quebec naturally recommended the best firm in town: Fitzpatrick, Parent, Taschereau, Roy, and Cannon.

Realizing the "popularity" of Gaynor and Green in Quebec City, the American authorities were anxious to have their extradition case heard in Montreal. So on 15 May they swore out warrants in Montreal, and in a night-time operation led by Montreal Chief of Detectives Carpenter, they kidnapped Gaynor and Green from their Quebec City hotel and hustled them on board a tugboat. A witness woke Cannon, who quickly obtained a writ of habeas corpus. Ignoring the shouts from Quebec police who chased him down the St Lawrence in a second vessel, and also avoiding the attempt of Three Rivers authorities to intercept him, the captain of the tug made it to Montreal by morning. The fugitives were remanded in court, and at this point Taschereau took over the case.

Within four days, and after being forcibly prevented by a dozen goons from seeing his clients at the Windsor Hotel, Taschereau had exposed enough irregularities for Gaynor and Green to be ordered returned to Quebec. On his advice they went to jail to await trial, rather than risk another abduction. This was no ordinary incarceration, however: given special treatment, Gaynor and Green held a reception which made the social page of local newspapers. Taschereau's defence of the pair rested basically on the fact that the original charge against them, receiving stolen money, was not an extraditable offence. But he also unleashed a flurry of counter-attacks (seeking a contempt citation against Carpenter, for example), jurisdictional challenges, and other means of delay. By the end of June, he had reduced the Montreal prosecutors who were acting for the United States to a state of frustrated rage, and it was in this condition that one of them laid a charge of political and judicial impropriety. The federal minister of justice was Taschereau's law partner, the provincial attorney-general (Horace Archambault) belonged to a Montreal firm working with Taschereau on the case, and somehow this explained Taschereau's successes in court. American newspapers went further, mentioning that Cannon's father was deputy attorney general and that a minor Taschereau aide was the son of an extradition commissioner. Called upon by superiors at home to explain his original unorthodox procedure (instigating the abduction), U.S. Attorney Marion Erwin claimed that Taschereau had been retained precisely and only because of his professional and family connections. The only "evidence" of improper influence was the spectacle of two judges reversing their own and each other's decisions, and Parent laughingly dismissed the charges as absurd. But it was becoming a question of justice seeming to be done, and rumours circulated that an international incident was brewing. The U.S. government, previously acting only for the State of Georgia, was reported ready to press the case on its own behalf and to launch a diplomatic protest in London.

In July, the "trial" at Quebec served as the major tourist attraction. In August came a bombshell. Although Taschereau had petitioned merely to have the case heard in Quebec City, Judge Caron threw the entire American case out of court, declaring the accused to be free men. A great celebration ensued on the Dufferin Terrace, but outside Quebec City editorialists were scandalized. Even the *Quebec Chronicle* declared the decision without precedent and in contravention of fact.[10] In September Erwin was quoted as saying that no appeals would be launched in Quebec City, but that "other action" would be taken. Other action turned out to be an appeal to the Judicial Committee of the Privy Council. Taschereau was initially confident, having been advised by senior British officials that the Privy Council was hearing the case only out of international courtesy.[11] But after a long delay, the council ruled in favour of the American authorities, describing Caron's decision as extraordinary. In the end, Gaynor and Green were ordered extradited by a Montreal judge, and in 1906 were convicted in a Savannah court.

Even before his British court appearance, however, Taschereau had become preoccupied with a far more momentous series of developments, the political demise of Simon-Napoléon Parent. Naturally Taschereau worked to forestall his colleague's fall from power and grace. For a while this seemed to ensure that he would share Parent's fate, but fortuitous circumstance and widespread appreciation of his talent eventually enabled Taschereau to achieve much greater political prominence than he ever would have with Parent still in control.

Parent was to some extent a victim of his own inadequacies. From the outset of his premiership he enjoyed many advantages, including weak parliamentary opposition, the trust and close cooperation of Laurier, a previous reputation for sound, progressive administration, and at least the outward loyalty of colleagues who had favoured Robidoux for the leadership of the party. But these did not prove sufficient. Lacking oratorical flair and any real enthusiasm for partisan debate, he was a totally uninspiring leader in the legislature. He did not even exercise strong leadership in cabinet, preferring to let ministers design and defend their departmental policies individually. On the other hand, he carried multiple responsibilities himself, retaining not only the Quebec mayoralty but also the provincial Crown Lands portfolio. Finally, he suffered from chronic bronchitis, which compounded all the other problems. In mid-1903

vague misgivings in caucus gave way to a state of alarm in the face
of accusations from young Liberal militants concerning the administration of Crown Lands and even Parent's personal integrity. The
major complaint of these militants, increasingly identified as *nationalistes*, was that the provincial government did not adequately
support colonization in the Quebec interior. Rather, they charged,
Parent discriminated against French-Canadian settlers and in favour
of forestry companies in the allocation of land, with the result that
many potential colonists were emigrating to the United States.[12]

When Parent failed to respond vigorously, fear spread to Ottawa
as well. Laurier was already concerned about the *nationalistes* because
they were admirers of Henri Bourassa, the Liberal MP who had rebelled
against Canadian participation in the Boer War of 1899-1902. They
had founded their Ligue nationaliste less to criticize Parent's economic policies than to mobilize Quebec opinion against further
Canadian involvement in British military affairs and to popularize
the idea of a bicultural Canada. The danger now was that if they
were alienated from Liberal governments at both Ottawa and Quebec,
the young militants might be completely and irretrievably lost to
the party. Moreover, if scandals and weak leadership drove the
Liberals from office provincially, Laurier's own political fortunes
would be severely threatened. Amidst all kinds of rumours, including
one which had Bourassa entering the provincial cabinet, Laurier
accepted the necessity of Parent's eventual retirement and counselled
patience and loyalty on the part of the various factions.[13]

Parent might well have retired honourably during this period to
the chairmanship of Laurier's imminent Transcontinental Railway
Commission. His integrity would be vindicated by the Colonization
Commission he had appointed to placate *nationaliste* sentiment,
while the new position would accommodate his talents, interests,
and even his physical disability. Although there was no single obvious
successor in the cabinet, there were at least three credible candidates,
any one of whom could probably have taken over without serious
internal conflict. But Parent was not allowed such an honourable
and peaceful withdrawal, largely because of one man's fanatical
determination to destroy him. Philippe-Auguste Choquette was a
curious political figure. Neither a *nationaliste* nor a genuine radical
of the old Rouge tradition, he was an effective political organizer
whom Laurier had rewarded with a judicial appointment in 1898.
But for reasons which have never been entirely clear, he hated
Fitzpatrick and Parent passionately. Although quite young, he
identified himself with that group of long-time faithful Liberals
whom Laurier had largely ignored in order to make room in his

cabinet for new business-oriented Quebec recruits like Fitzpatrick. The choice of Parent over Robidoux as premier had disappointed much the same group. Choquette fancied that he personally had been denied cabinet rank in Ottawa because of Fitzpatrick's influence, and that Fitzpatrick and Taschereau had somehow forced Parent's entry into the Marchand government and then into the premiership.[4] The lack of political preferment undoubtedly carried material consequences, for Choquette had his own set of business connections which needed government favour to flourish.[15] But Choquette's grievance seemed to run even deeper than this, for despite a distinguished performance at Laval University he never felt accepted by the closely knit elite of Quebec City. Tracing his other frustrations to the favouritism and exclusivism practised by this group, he took aim at its most successful representatives, the Fitzpatrick-Parent-Taschereau "cabal." Choquette was not the only man ever to express such resentment, and he would later find a receptive audience in the city.[16]

Choquette's gift for organization extended beyond electioneering; the ironical counterpart of his persecution complex was a compulsion to scheme. When Conservatives captured two supposedly safe Liberal seats in provincial by-elections early in 1904, Choquette abandoned his judgeship and sprang into action. Although he suspected Choquette's plan, which was to acquire the Liberal newspaper *Le Soleil* and use it against Parent, Laurier appointed him to the Senate and gave him the responsibility of organizing the Quebec district in time for the coming federal election. Harmony reigned among Quebec Liberals during the October campaign, Choquette even sharing a platform with Taschereau and Parent's son Georges, who was in the process of defeating Casgrain in Montmorency. But in order to retire voluntarily and on his own terms, Parent then launched a preemptive strike. He dissolved the legislature the day after Laurier's 3 November reelection, and called a provincial election for the 25th. Conservatives naturally protested that this snap election was "undemocratic," but no one believed they could win an election any time during the coming year. It was in fact a Conservative newspaper which accurately commented that Parent "has some dear friends in the legislature [i.e., potential Choquette allies] who he thinks would adorn private life, with more credit to themselves and more comfort to him."[17] More importantly, he wanted to give Choquette the least possible time to contest the renomination or election of loyal Liberals and to promote a rival for the premiership.

Parent's strategy failed. With most Conservatives boycotting the "unfair" election, Liberal dissidents could challenge Parent candidates without fear of their party losing control of the legislature. The result was one of the bitterest and most closely fought one-party elections in parliamentary history. Even a private meeting between Choquette and Parent ended in an exchange of personal insults. Choquette's Senate colleague J.-H. Legris, chairman of the Colonization Commission which had found much to criticize but no evidence of corruption on Parent's part, suddenly reversed himself. Parent had, Legris charged, behaved "like a fool or a criminal ... and Mr Parent is not a fool." On election day one of Choquette's candidates defeated a cabinet minister, and although only six Conservatives won seats, it was not at all clear whether Parent could control the new legislature. Choquette schemed feverishly to rally the undecided behind Lomer Gouin, the talented and energetic minister of public works.[18]

Gouin was ambitious and particularly popular among Montreal Liberals, two assets which probably explain why he rather than Agriculture Minister Adélard Turgeon became the alternative to Parent. But he had no particular interest in a palace coup, bloody or otherwise, and seemed content with an understanding reached in cabinet on 30 November. Parent would launch a libel suit against Legris and Choquette; his name cleared, the question of his leadership could then be considered fairly and rationally. Laurier also tried to arrange an honourable retirement for Parent by organizing a "peace conference" in Montreal on 28 December.[19] Then, in January, Parent tried to conciliate both the *nationaliste* and "Gouiniste" dissidents by adding the highly regarded Dominique Monet to his cabinet. But these developments would not satisfy the bloodlust of Choquette, who ignored Laurier's direct order to desist and virtually blackmailed Gouin and two other ministers into resigning. (He threatened to reveal the participation of Gouin, Turgeon, and William Weir in a conspiratorial meeting on 20 November.)[20] Once the three ex-ministers had denounced Parent – for failing to lead and consult adequately, not for dishonesty – the premier quickly lost control of the situation. Only twenty-seven members attended an official caucus he summoned on 8 February, whereas fifty-two had attended a rebel caucus earlier the same evening. Of these forty-four (a legislative majority) signed a round robin criticizing Parent and supporting the late ministers. On 22 February Parent agreed to resign as soon as a legislative committee had cleared his name, and to recommend Gouin as his successor. Laurier would appoint Parent to the chairmanship of the Railway Commission, and Gouin would begin the process of constructing a cabinet which Parent loyalists could support.[21]

This agreement by no means concluded the war between Parent and Choquette, which was merely transferred to other arenas. Here, in the courts and in municipal politics, Taschereau's role became more visible and central. Spared all opposition in Montmorency, Taschereau had spent the election campaign trying unsuccessfully to save the Parentiste candidate in Quebec East. Thereafter he seconded Parent at Laurier's December peace conference, represented the premier in other negotiations, and finally took charge of his libel suit against Choquette. Taschereau would undoubtedly have played a prominent role in the hearings of the legislative committee, but Choquette and Legris would not repeat their accusations in so formal a setting. With no evidence to consider beyond the findings of the previous Colonization Commission, the committee could do little other than write a brief report exonerating Parent.[22]

Legris was found guilty of defamation in a separate proceeding. Choquette tried for over a year to escape with ambiguous retractions, but each time Taschereau called him to account by threatening to reactivate the suit. In the most highly publicized episode, Choquette and Taschereau negotiated a settlement by which Choquette would disclaim first-hand knowledge of Parent's wrongdoing, throwing the burden of proof upon Legris. Before the agreement could be formalized in court, however, Choquette published almost identical accusations in *Le Soleil*. Taschereau argued successfully that these attacks violated the preliminary agreement and that Parent was no longer bound by his commitment to withdraw the suit.[23] By the time he did force Choquette into an unequivocal retraction, Taschereau found himself in an even fiercer battle in the arena of Quebec City politics. Shortly after resigning as premier, Parent surrendered the mayoralty of Quebec as well. Were it merely a question of combining the administrative responsibilities with his job as chairman of the Railway Commission, he might have remained – as his followers on City Council urged. But he would not have the time or the energy to withstand a serious political challenge, and in this respect a familiar scenario was unfolding. Reform forces genuinely disturbed by some of the practices of his regime were being organized and harnessed by Choquette, who unleashed a steady barrage of personal attacks. This time, Parent preferred to retire early, and allow a sympathetic successor to thwart Choquette's designs. Acceding to Parent's wishes, the council elected Alderman Georges Tanguay to serve out the unexpired weeks of his term.

If he proposed to continue as mayor, however, Tanguay would have to survive a head-on clash with Choquette in the municipal elections scheduled for 19 February 1906. Choquette announced that he himself was a candidate for mayor, an unusual step since Quebec's mayor was elected not directly but by council following the aldermanic elections. Technically, therefore, Choquette (and Tanguay) were only candidates for council, and were not running in the same ward. Choquette was in effect declaring himself leader of a party faction, and solicited commitments from other candidates to support him later for mayor. His major asset was neither personal magnetism nor popularity, but editorial control of *Le Soleil*, by far the largest and most widely read newspaper in the capital. Under the managing editorship of Ernest Pacaud, *Le Soleil* had tried to represent all Liberals as fairly as was consistent with its status as official spokesman for provincial and federal party leaders. But Pacaud's retirement and death, coinciding almost exactly with the growth of internal opposition to Parent, provoked a scramble for control from which Choquette emerged victorious early in 1905. As he had warned Laurier, and in spite of the prime minister's subsequent pleas, Choquette used this control to launch all manner of accusations against Parent and Taschereau.[24]

By early January 1906, it seemed inevitable that Choquette would ride to the mayoralty as self-appointed leader of the reform forces. With even greater certainty it could be predicted that his administration would spend more time punishing friends of the former regime and seeking evidence of corruption than in implementing positive reforms. Tanguay, although competent and well respected as long-time chairman of Quebec's finance committee, could not prevent this by himself. He lacked the vigour, the political talents, and the financial resources to preserve anything more than his own aldermanic seat. What is more, he was so closely identified with the Parent regime that his candidacy for mayor would merely lend credibility to Choquette's charges. He would be portrayed as a puppet of Parent, directed to protect special interests and hide corruption. In these circumstances Taschereau entered the fray, not with any personal ambition to be mayor – Edmond was the family's municipal politician – but simply determined to stop Choquette. He succeeded in this purpose, first by luring Choquette into making demonstrably false accusations and then by appealing to the civic tradition against factional or party politics in City Hall. Both Choquette's present approach and his proposal to have future mayors elected directly would, Taschereau argued, discourage "responsible businessmen" who lacked the time or money to build a city-wide electoral organization; the post would go by default to professional politicians.[25] Towards the end of the campaign, Taschereau accordingly renounced his own quest for the mayoralty, promised instead to support a suitable businessman, and invited Choquette to do the same. His own credibility damaged by the libel suit and by his more recent false charges, Choquette had to accept a face-saving device offered by Laurier; he would withdraw in the interests of Liberal party unity. Laurier's price was the surrender of Le Soleil to himself and Gouin.[26]

Just narrowly elected to council, Taschereau joined in the unanimous selection of Georges Garneau as mayor. Garneau was a suitable "responsible businessman," associated with neither of the warring factions. Some strains inevitably arose, since dispossessed Parent favourites looked to Taschereau for protection and since Garneau did authorize an investigation of Choquette's charges against the previous regime. But there was no real purge or discrimination against interests simply because they had dealt with Parent, and the investigation turned out to be a fair one and exonerated Parent. With no great interest or future in municipal politics Taschereau soon turned his attention back to the provincial scene, where the Gouin administration was already in difficulty.

Gouin became premier on 19 March 1905. After some weeks of minor shuffling of both men and departmental combinations, he emerged with a cabinet including Turgeon, Weir, Jules Allard, and Jean Prévost, all close allies during the "coup." Graceful exits were arranged for Parent loyalists Archambault and Robitaille, while two ministers sworn in during Parent's final weeks, Monet and Némèse Garneau, were dumped unceremoniously. From the late government Gouin retained only Provincial Treasurer J.C. McCorkill, who retired to the bench in 1906, to be replaced as Irish Catholic representative by John C. Kaine, an anti-Parent Liberal independent elected in 1904. To shore up Quebec district representation Gouin went beyond the capital, appointing Auguste Tessier of Rimouski and Rodolphe Roy of Kamouraska.

Beyond this internal reorganization, Gouin was anxious to stabilize the political situation by reassuring various outside interests that the change in government posed them no threat. Prominent among these were the Roman Catholic hierarchy, wary of changes in educational policy, and the business and financial community, concerned about a return to the reckless government spending under Mercier and the Conservative regime of 1892-7. With regard to education, Gouin dissociated himself from the radicalism of his friend Godfroy Langlois, the new member for Montreal St Louis, and even persuaded him to restrain his public utterances. No stranger to the business community, on account of his legal career and role in Montreal municipal politics, Gouin needed only to demonstrate that as premier he would maintain his faith in economic progress, based on a proper mixture of fiscal responsibility and encouragement of private enterprise. He would not revive memories of his late father-in-law, Honoré Mercier.

Perhaps the most difficult group to reconcile were the Parentistes of the Quebec City area. It was awkward at first to control local patronage quarrels, especially the inclination of erstwhile "out" groups to exclude friends of the former regime from a reasonable share.[27] As a major figure in Parent's ouster, Turgeon could not effectively arbitrate such disputes; yet he was the lone French-Canadian cabinet minister from the Quebec City district. It was impossible, moreover, to heal wounds at the provincial level as long as Senator Choquette was using Le Soleil in his campaign to drive Parent and his associates from City Hall. This was why Gouin and Laurier together purchased Choquette's controlling interest in the newspaper and why a Gouin appointee, Henri d'Hellencourt, replaced Choquette as political editor. Genuine reconciliation was a slow process, however, and it required an external threat to the Liberal party to hasten it. The form taken by this reconciliation was a steady rapprochement between the Gouin administration and Alexandre Taschereau, culminating in Taschereau's entry into the cabinet on 17 October 1907.

The external threat was posed by Henri Bourassa and his na-tionaliste followers. Naturally this group did not abandon its concern about the problems of colonization simply because Parent had been removed from office. They continued to suspect that French-Canadian agricultural expansion was being impeded by industrial corporations, mostly foreign, which dictated the province's forest exploitation policies. In fact by the end of 1906 the focus of nationalist agitation was shifting perceptibly from federal to provincial politics. This partially reflected the situation in Ottawa, where Bourassa and Armand Lavergne were bitterly frustrated over Laurier's handling of the Northwest Automony question, and positively contemptuous of Quebec Liberal MPs whose venality they held responsible for Laurier's "surrender." But the growing concern about resource administration and other early problems of industrialization in Quebec was undoubtedly genuine, and on such issues it was even possible to imagine the official opposition party as an ally. This was a far cry from the federal situation, in which French-Canadian nationalists were isolated and therefore ineffectual. When the scent of scandal raised prospects for a serious assault on Gouin, Bourassa and his followers could not resist.[28]

The scandal consisted of accusations made against two cabinet

OKANAGAN COLLEGE LIBRARY
BRITISH COLUMBIA

ministers by an improbable Belgian calling himself Baron de l'Epine.
No one ever discovered whether the title was genuine, or whether
he had invented it to gain sympathy and trust. In either case he
did win the sympathy of Adélard Turgeon soon after arriving in
Canada in 1902. To help this cultured but impecunious aristocrat
begin restoring his fortunes, Turgeon arranged a few small, quite
proper favours through the provincial government. Ambition grew,
however, and de l'Epine soon organized a Belgian syndicate to acquire
land along an anticipated Grand Trunk Pacific Railway route
through the Abitibi region of northern Quebec. Although mineral
exploitation was mentioned, the major pretext offered for this
speculative venture was colonization of the territory by French-
speaking Belgian settlers. When this scheme fell through in 1906
and he was refused a permanent government job by the minister
of colonization, mines and fisheries, Jean Prévost, de l'Epine turned
on his erstwhile benefactors. He accused Prévost of extravagance
during official travel abroad and incompetent departmental administration at home, the combination of which "had forever ruined
Belgian emigration to the province." When Turgeon defended his
colleague by attacking the credibility of the accusor, de l'Epine
returned to Quebec to charge Turgeon himself with outright corruption. The minister of lands and forests, he alleged, had demanded
a contribution of thirty cents an acre of Abitibi land to the Liberals'
election fund, with seventy cents an acre going to the provincial
treasury. The deal had fallen through, de l'Epine continued, because
the syndicate would not purchase enough land to finance the
acquisition of certain newspapers by the Liberals. A committee of
the legislature briefly investigated these charges, but concluded little
more than that de l'Epine had tried to blackmail Prévost.[29] The substance of the accusations was tested not in the political arena but
in the courts, where Prévost launched a defamation suit against the
young *nationaliste* militant, Olivar Asselin. Asselin's weekly *Le
Nationaliste* had first reported de l'Epine's charges, and the editor
had directed additional insults at Prévost, whom he referred to as
"Jean Sans-Tête."[30]

When Taschereau agreed to represent Prévost in court, it marked
the first public indication of a Gouin-Taschereau rapprochement.
(Gouin had already made the first conciliatory gesture by having
Taschereau elected chairman of the legislature's private bills committee.)[31] When the civil action was dropped in favour of a prosecution
for criminal libel, Taschereau became the crown prosecutor. The
exact priority of Taschereau's motives can only be surmised, but
there were a number of considerations which must have encouraged

him to undertake this responsibility. He bore no particular love for
Asselin, a former Liberal and an employee of the Colonization
Department who had been an original source of charges against
Parent. In his affection for Laurier, Taschereau was strongly opposed
to Asselin's spiritual and political leaders, Bourassa and Lavergne,
and no doubt saw the trial as an opportunity to strike at the credibility
of the nationalist movement generally. As he had demonstrated in
his dealings with Choquette, and as he was to reveal on several future
occasions, Taschereau refused to accept the notion that political
figures must suffer irresponsible and malicious accusations which
no other citizen would tolerate.[32] On the wider question of coming
to Gouin's aid, there was probably some ambivalence. So similar
were the charges against Prévost and Turgeon to those made previously against Parent, that the downfall of the Gouin regime on
their account would constitute a form of poetic justice. Conservative
newspapers openly suggested that Parentistes might merely sit back
to enjoy such a spectacle, and on this basis discounted the possibility
of Taschereau's entry into the cabinet until it was an accomplished
fact.[33] Even if he seriously considered this course of passive revenge,
however, Taschereau recognized a more constructive opportunity in
Gouin's predicament. He could demonstrate his value to the government and win the premier's gratitude. To thus evade the cul-de-
sac towards which his own career seemed to be rapidly heading was
hardly to betray Parent. He had been unswervingly loyal to his former
colleague, even permitting himself to become the target for Parent's
enemies.[34] Finding himself criticized in *Le Soleil* as late as February
1907, Taschereau even volunteered to quit politics if Laurier considered him an obstacle to party unity. While chiding him for
oversensitivity, Laurier responded with the desired reassurance.[35]
Political advancement aside, and merely to maintain the prestige
and clientele of his firm, Taschereau could hardly be expected to
dissociate himself from the provincial government indefinitely. Perhaps it was reasonable to continue hoping for revenge against
Choquette, but what was the point of regarding Gouin as an eternal
enemy? Gouin was not Choquette and had tried since before taking
office to dissolve his *mariage de convenance*. Though his means
were limited, the premier had endeavoured to rise above factional
warfare in Quebec City.

There was, moreover, a major issue of public policy at stake.
Superficially the Gouin administration was under fire for alleged
maladministration and corruption, but beneath the specific charges
and the muckraking style of the *nationalistes* Taschereau recognized
a fundamental challenge to the government's entire policy of eco-

nomic development. Like his two Liberal predecessors, Gouin favoured the rapid and immediate exploitation of Quebec's natural resources. Perhaps even more than Marchand and Parent, he recognized and accepted the implications of such a policy: that French Canada's future was predominantly industrial rather than agricultural; that at least in the short run, ownership of resource-based industries would rest primarily in the hands of non-French Canadian entrepreneurs who enjoyed access to capital and to technological expertise; that long-range hope for indigenous control lay not in defiance of the North American system of private enterprise (i.e., through government regulations favouring small French-Canadian interests), but in a more vocationally oriented concept of education and a generally more materialistic and progressive attitude within French-Canadian society. Although careful never to disparage traditional values, Gouin was really advocating the antithesis of the *nationaliste* program. Colonization was a fine ideal, but only the rapid growth of industrial employment could possibly slow the flood of French-Canadian emigration to New England. Catholicism could and should continue to be the touchstone of French-Canadian nationality, but not by rejecting progress in favour of an antimaterialist dream-world in which the vast majority of French Canadians would refuse to live. Sincere though they might be, nationalist sentiments were not a wise prescription for the future health of the community.[36]

Alexandre Taschereau shared this basic outlook. Because of differences in background he was probably more conservative than Gouin, more uneasy, for example, about the social conflict inherent in the process of industrialization. Yet his early experiences also led Taschereau to react more violently than Gouin against certain nationalist criticisms. When the nationalists invoked religious authority for their "industry versus agriculture" argument, for example, Taschereau recognized a familiar and odious ultramontane theme: that human progress was incompatible with Catholicism, and by implication with French-Canadian survival. That the theme was now being expressed in economic rather than intellectual terms did not change its essence. A liberal observer could hardly avoid perceiving the Ligue nationaliste in the context of other new organizations of the time, ominously labelled "Catholic Action." Both the Association catholique de la jeunesse canadienne-française and Action sociale (a publishing company whose first effort would be a newspaper of the same name) seemed clearly inspired by hostility to modern developments. And it was almost certain that cynical and desperate Conservative politicians would exploit the crusade with a reversion to *castor* tactics. Even before the first issue of *L'Action sociale* (later *L'Action catholique*) appeared, both Laurier and Gouin predicted the political and religious controversy it would create.[37] Taschereau knew from personal experience what to expect from *L'Action sociale*'s first editor, Dr Jules Dorion. Dorion had attacked him personally in his Quebec City weekly, *La Libre Parole*, during the 1906 municipal elections, and thereafter exchanged constant fire with *La Vigie*, a new weekly founded by friends of Taschereau.[38]

Historians would recognize that there was more to the *nationaliste* movement than clerical reaction. It shared a great deal with American progressivism in criticizing the excesses of modern industrial capitalism, and contained genuine radicals like Asselin and Jules Fournier operating in the shadow of the more conservative Bourassa.[39] But Taschereau could never believe that attacks on political leaders like Gouin and Turgeon, and upon lawyers like himself, successfully finding a place in the new industrial order, were merely a protest against "corrupt" government. They were designed to discredit the entire philosophy of those French Canadians who favoured the modernization of Quebec, and to brand the industrial age itself as corrupt. If this fundamental issue was to become the fulcrum of provincial politics, then Gouin must be supported.[40]

The Asselin-Prévost trial, which began on 13 May 1907, did not long remain an examination of Prévost's conduct. Rather, it became an inquiry into accusations against Turgeon, and since those charges involved the Liberals' alleged *caisse électorale*, the whole Gouin government was really on trial. It was de l'Epine's word against Turgeon's, and Taschereau did a masterful job of destroying the Belgian's credibility during cross-examination.[41] The jury could not reach a decision regarding Asselin and Prévost, but presiding Judge Bossé remarked that the evidence heard had clearly exonerated Turgeon. His Honour also urged the combatants to transfer their political warfare to a more suitable arena, which they did with unbridled enthusiasm.[42]

In July Bourassa declared his complete disillusionment with federal politics and hinted that provincial affairs might be more susceptible to purification. Taking their cue, his Quebec City supporters scheduled a major rally for 6 August at the Jacques Cartier market, St Roch, in the heart of Laurier's own constituency. Liberal chiefs in the capital decided that this gesture was a direct appeal for the allegiance of their own supporters, as well as an insult to Laurier himself. Whether they ordered the shower of vegetables and stones which drove Bourassa from the platform is a moot point, but Taschereau, conspicuous among the hecklers along with d'Hellencourt and Georges Parent, took most of the blame from Bourassa and the Conservative press. (Taschereau sued *La Patrie* for quoting Bourassa's charges that he had spent public funds on liquor for the demonstrators. He won a retraction, but that proved nothing about his responsibility for the violence itself.)[43]

Far from discouraging Bourassa, the St Roch affair afforded him the prestige of a martyr. Admirers elsewhere in the province organized further rallies at which he denounced the provincial government in increasingly strong terms, while *Le Nationaliste* kept up its own steady stream of accusations. By mid-August, Gouin and his ministers felt obliged to launch a counter-offensive in which they not only denied allegations of corruption but also justified their policy of industrial development. On the 21st, Turgeon sued *Le Nationaliste* for stating that he had committed perjury in the Prévost trial. Although the original case was about to be retried before a new jury, Taschereau undertook Turgeon's complaint as well. Nominally preoccupied with "legal" work, therefore, Taschereau had assumed complete resonsibility for one theatre of Gouin's war against the *nationalistes*.

On the last day of September Prévost resigned his portfolio, citing the desire to concentrate fully on clearing his name. Conservative newspapers reported that Gouin had fired him, and had tried but failed to dismiss Turgeon as well. When Auguste Tessier retired innocently to the bench, the same sources claimed that the government was in an advanced state of disintegration. That was probably wishful thinking, but Gouin and his colleagues were beginning to fear the combined impact of Bourassa, a possible electoral alliance between Conservatives and *nationalistes*, and the behaviour of disaffected Parentistes. And with an election only a year away, the appearance of a cabinet crisis could be as harmful as the reality. Clearly, the situation called for dramatic initiatives. Turgeon, a former Union libérale colleague whose friendship with Taschereau had only briefly been strained by the events of 1905, was authorized to determine the terms on which the leader of the Parentiste faction would enter the cabinet. Taschereau was not too demanding, and it remained only for Gouin and Laurier to persuade the last of the anti-Parent fanatics that this reconciliation was necessary.[44]

Taschereau was sworn in as minister of public works and labour on Thursday morning, 17 October. The only other portfolio considered was that of attorney general, which would have suited his legal talents and interests but otherwise posed too many problems. He could no longer practise law, and in fact would be under pressure to abandon his firm of which he was now titular head. (Parent and

Fitzpatrick, now chief justice of the Supreme Court, had withdrawn upon accepting their federal appointments.) There would also be some question of Taschereau's impartiality in cases already before the courts. Asselin, for example, was still under indictment for criminal libel and a warrant had been issued for his arrest. Public Works and Labour, on the other hand, possessed some positive advantages. Public Works assured Parentistes of fair access to the pork barrel, and labour legislation was a subject which had attracted Taschereau's interest as a backbencher.[45] The appointment was well received in most quarters, even by opponents of the government who hoped that the signs of Liberal unity were false. Neither Taschereau nor his colleagues were likely to feel comfortable, predicted the *Chronicle*, for "the memory of Mr Parent will assist, like the ghost of the murdered Banquo, at every ministerial feast." Nevertheless, "it is a decided advantage to Mr Gouin to have secured the only brain, it is said with bated breath, in the Liberal ranks in the Legislature."[46] Two Parent loyalists of 1905, Monet and Archambault, paid tribute to Taschereau's earlier "abnegation" and celebrated his triumph over the influence of Choquette. And from Tom Casgrain, who despite party differences always maintained a fond regard for his former student, some good-natured teasing: "tu es digne d'un meilleur entourage."[47]

Taschereau and his new colleagues thought they had a second cause to celebrate that day, for Judge Cimon found *Le Nationaliste* guilty of libelling Turgeon. Unfortunately, he appended such a harsh personal denunciation of Asselin (and even of his attorney) that a backlash developed. Had the custom of fighting political battles in court finally reached its inevitable conclusion, compromising the dignity of the judicial process? This disturbingly pertinent question was repeated a week later, when Asselin was unnecessarily jailed overnight for failure to appear at a resumption of the Prévost case.[48] There was yet another major development on 17 October: upon receiving his favourable judicial decision, Turgeon resigned from the legislature, challenged Bourassa to a by-election duel in his constituency of Bellechasse, and asked Gouin for a Royal Commission to clear him of de l'Epine's allegations once and for all. When Bourassa accepted the challenge, the other pending by-elections took on unexpected importance. Taschereau, required by law to seek reelection, Bernard Devlin, another new cabinet minister switching from the federal scene, and a new member for Tessier's riding would not receive the customary acclamations or token fights. The government was going to be challenged in at least three constituencies by a growing alliance of Conservatives and *nationalistes* hoping to "give the signal for [Gouin's] downfall.''[49]

Naturally Bellechasse became the focus of attention, ministers and *nationaliste* spokesmen descending upon it almost daily. But Montmorency, separated from Turgeon's constituency only by the width of the St Lawrence and still having a strong Conservative tradition, was easily the second most popular battleground. Besides, the *nationalistes* had already developed much of the personal hostility toward Taschereau which would characterize the next thirty years of Quebec politics. For his part, Taschereau made no attempt to deny that the integrity of the government was an issue, and strongly defended his colleagues.[50] Taschereau and J.-B. Bernier, the Conservative candidate, agreed to a series of *assemblées contradictoires*, the first of which on 27 and 28 October were well attended despite heavy rain. It soon became evident, however, that despite determination in the opposition camp, the electors of Montmorency would not seriously consider rejecting a cabinet minister. Local mayors and councillors nearly fell over each other competing for Taschereau's attention (and future gratitude). When Bernier charged at a meeting in Château Richer that the Liberals were buying votes, Taschereau had to plead with the audience to let his opponent finish speaking. With similar generosity, Georges Parent declined to speak after Casgrain was prevented from doing so. For the last week of the campaign both sides went through the motions. Like everyone else they were more interested in developments across the river.[51]

On polling day, 4 November, all three ministers were returned by healthy majorities. Rimouski went to an independent Liberal, but that simply involved a local organizational squabble, and the victor immediately pledged support for the government. Taschereau brought his troops home for a victory celebration late the same night. The following evening, at a public rally honouring himself, Turgeon, and Devlin, Taschereau modestly dwelt on the significance of the Bellechasse result. Implicitly, however, his words offered an explanation of his own motives for joining the cabinet.

The Bellechasse victory reestablishes the authentic position of the Liberal party, which has just purged itself completely of the nationalist faction. The latter party, if it still is one, has helped reunite the ranks among real Liberals, and the Liberal party is again the party of Mercier and of Laurier. We are the party of progress, and our work is productive. The last decade proves this abundantly ... It is to be hoped that we will continue the work so happily begun, for there are still great things to be done.[52]

Taschereau's assessment was certainly accurate so far as it went;

the *nationaliste* movement no longer had a place in the Liberal party. But that hardly meant the end of the threat. On the contrary, both Gouin and Bourassa treated the by-election as a preliminary skirmish, with the decisive battle still to come. And although neither Bourassa nor the Conservative leader, Pierre-Evariste Leblanc, favoured a fusion of Bleus and *nationalistes*, supporters of each began to negotiate local agreements whereby a single candidate would oppose the government in the next provincial election. Gouin used a preelection session of the legislature primarily to forestall expected criticism of his resource policies. The outright sale of public lands and waterfalls was replaced by a system of conditional leases, while mining, hunting, and fishing rights were reserved to the public domain. Devlin assumed a high profile as minister of colonization, promising more effective assistance and protection to colonists. The government was not entirely defensive, however, for Gouin pushed ahead with his controversial pet project, the Ecole des hautes études commerciales in Montreal. Against the background of radical pronouncements by Godfroy Langlois (who was finding silence a difficult burden), religious authorities read highly sinister intentions into the independent status conferred upon the new institution.[53]

With a tiny and mediocre parliamentary delegation, the opposition had to launch its campaign outside the legislature. In fact, Bourassa's chief ally inside the House was Jean Prévost, who embarrassed the government with his insider's critique of the Colonization Department. (Prévost's eventual defection to the *nationalistes* gave credence to earlier rumours of his dismissal by Gouin, but the former minister never did confirm it.) Bourassa and Lavergne stumped the province preaching primarily moral reform, a cause which could unite a wide variety of viewpoints and disguise some fundamental differences. Though decrying party spirit, Bourassa was effectively displacing Leblanc as leader of the opposition. More and more Conservatives concluded that their best hopes for electoral success lay in identifying themselves with the *nationaliste* leader and cause.

Wary of their opponents, Gouin and his colleagues were nevertheless sufficiently confident to eschew the electoral tactics to which Parent had twice resorted. They would not wait for a federal election, hoping to exploit Laurier's popularity, and they would leave more than a month between dissolution and polling day, 8 June 1908. Even before making a formal announcement, Gouin revealed his desire to clear the political air before Quebec City's tercentenary celebrations, scheduled for July. As a senior cabinet minister, Taschereau bore new responsibilities and enjoyed new prominence in this campaign. He was on the platform at major rallies throughout the province, experiencing for the first time the tumultuous atmosphere of politics in Montreal. Taking charge of the Quebec district, he emphasized his department's past and future work in preparing Quebec City for the arrival of the new transcontinental railway. In terms of organization, he set his sights on two ridings in particular. Charlevoix had been won in 1904 by Conservative Pierre d'Auteuil with considerable assistance from Senator Choquette. This time the Liberals would be united, but they would still have to contend with Rodolphe Forget, the county's powerful member of Parliament. Certain of reelection in Montmorency, Taschereau decided to contest this neighbouring constituency personally. The other special target was Dr Albert Jobin, who had won Quebec East as an anti-Parent Liberal in 1904 but then caused Gouin difficulty as well. Denying him the government nomination, Taschereau arranged for the nomination of Louis Letourneau, his own campaign manager on the Ile d'Orléans in 1900 and 1907.[54]

Although most opposition candidates throughout the province were nominally Conservative, it was Bourassa who as expected led the challenge to Gouin. Leblanc virtually disappeared from view, with no program worthy of the name and a weak campaign even in his own constituency.[55] Bourassa waged a bitter campaign against the premier in Montreal St Jacques, and both men were sufficiently uncertain of the outcome that they secured second nominations in safer ridings. He drew great crowds, and supplied Conservative candidates with an enthusiasm and confidence they could not obtain from their own leader. Yet at least in retrospect, there was something incongruous about Bourassa's campaign. It was never really clear, for instance, where he disagreed with Gouin on the question of natural resources. Considering the reforms already introduced or promised, and the vagueness of Bourassa's charges about systematic corruption, it seemed as if he was opposed to any rapid, large-scale development. But he never said so directly. Similarly, he emphasized provincial autonomy without pointing to an instance where Gouin was less than vigilant. He was in favour of educational reform, but identified himself with clerical opposition to Gouin's innovations. He preached purity and patriotism in provincial politics, in order to strengthen the hand of Laurier, whom he had recently denounced. It was naturally difficult for Gouin to engage Bourassa in substantive debate, so after defending Turgeon's integrity, the premier could only expound upon his own formulae for progress.[56]

The result of the election was also somewhat incongruous. Bourassa won both St. Jacques and St Hyacinthe, Lavergne won his seat, and Conservative candidates won twelve more. The opposition

considered these modest gains a great moral victory, Bourassa re-
joicing at the imminent dawn of a new age and the Conservatives
feeling that they had laid the groundwork for a return to power.
In reality, however, the Liberals were stronger than they had been
for years, united under strong leadership and with a healthy majority
honestly won. And Taschereau had particular reason to be satisfied.
Only one Liberal seat was lost in his district (Montmagny, to
Lavergne), he himself nearly overcame d'Auteuil's strong majority
in Charlevoix, and Letourneau ousted Jobin in Quebec East. A
surprising and immensely satisfying result occurred in Dorchester,
where Alfred Morisset finally avenged the insult of 1892 by defeating
L.-P. Pelletier. Both the Gouin regime and Taschereau's political
stature were now firmly established.

## CHAPTER THREE

# Bête noire *of the* *Nationalists*

During the summer of 1908, most residents of Quebec City were happy to forget the feverish politics of the past year and celebrate their tercentenary. The local, provincial, and federal governments spared no effort or expense, for they were commemorating not only the founding of a city but also the birth of the French-Canadian nation. And they succeeded in eliciting participation and expressions of good will from every corner of Canada as well as from the governments of Britain, the other Dominions, France, and the United States. During the official festivities in late July, eight brilliant pageants recalled the religious and military glories of New France (that portraying the decisive battle of 1759 discreetly ignoring the outcome). The Association catholique de la jeunesse canadienne-française staged an impressive tribute to Samuel de Champlain, the founder and real "guest of honour." Costumes and decorations in the streets of Quebec similarly recreated life under the French regime. Huge crowds attended the various events, and more than a few Quebeckers were financially saddened when the tourists finally departed. As a permanent memento of the tercentenary, the governor general, Lord Grey, initiated plans to establish a national park and museum on the Plains of Abraham.[1]

Only a few young *nationaliste* journalists and politicians seemed reluctant to share the spirit of the occasion. They first exaggerated and then carped at the "imperial" content of the festivities: the lavish welcome accorded to the prince of Wales, Lord Grey's park and museum (whose location supposedly implied the celebration of a French-Canadian defeat), and standard rhetoric about French-Canadian liberty under British rule. When the prince of Wales conferred imperial decorations on Prime Minister Laurier, Premier Gouin, and Mayor Garneau, *Le Nationaliste* boldly informed him that "The French Canadians with whom you have spoken, and those whom you have decorated reflect in no possible manner the sentiment and character of their fellow-citizens ... Thank God, we are better than they. If in fact all the French Canadians were like them you would have been right to suppose that we possessed so little dignity as to be satisfied with Lord Grey's Imperial masquerade. If we were really like those people, we would indeed be ripe for the grave and this demonstration would be nothing more nor less than our funeral."[2] Henri Bourassa celebrated the birth of his nation by taking a European holiday. One is tempted to regard the *nationalistes'* behaviour as petty, in the sense that it was motivated more by their dislike for the men in office than by the actual content of the festivities. But it did serve notice that they were emboldened by the spring election result and ready to engage Gouin's government in a battle which knew no bounds, including at times those of civility.

Alexandre Taschereau's contempt for the *nationalistes*, born of their personal attacks on Laurier, Parent, and Turgeon as well as their philosophy, was without doubt unsurpassed among cabinet members. Following the law suits and the St Roch debacle, Bourassa and his friends were no better disposed toward the new minister. Yet, in the early weeks of the eagerly anticipated 1909 session, Taschereau did not loom as a central figure in the Liberal-*nationaliste* confrontation. Surprisingly, it was William Weir who responded with bitter sarcasm to the outstanding maiden speech delivered by Bourassa.[3] And once the drama of Bourassa's mere presence had subsided, the government's most violent critic continued to be Prévost, who was infuriated by Gouin's refusal to reappoint him to the cabinet but had no particular bone to pick with Taschereau. Prior to the session, Taschereau applied his characteristic diligence to the preparation of important new labour legislation, particularly North America's first Workman's Compensation Act. When the new legislature met, Taschereau gently chided his opponents but expressed confidence in their capacity for reasoned debate and constructive criticism. He even played the diplomat, settling a bitter row between Prévost and Liberal backbencher John Hall Kelly. Bourassa and Lavergne responded in kind: the former delivered intelligent critiques of bills introduced by Taschereau, and the latter dropped his accusation of bribery concerning Taschereau's promises to the voters of Montmorency.[4]

Marxist analysis often assumes that, in capitalist societies, apparently progressive labour or social legislation is enacted only to benefit the dominant class. Thus a recent study of Quebec legislation declares that workman's compensation arose not from union requests or from the inability of most workers to win compensation through civil actions (the reasons given by Taschereau),[5] but from the fear of employers that awards to employees who did sue successfully could become astronomically high under a certain interpretation of the Quebec Civil Code.[6] Apart from the fact that it is not supported by any reference to actual cases and ignores other reasons given by manufacturers, this interpretation neglects factors other than employer interest which influenced labour legislation during the Gouin era. One such factor was personal: the zeal and expertise of Louis Guyon, Quebec's chief factory inspector and an observer at two European conferences on labour reform.[7] Another was the belief of Gouin and Taschereau, in company with many other Canadian political and business leaders of the day, that "enlightened" labour legislation was essential to industrial progress. The philosophy was clearly paternalistic: it did not, for example, imply strengthening the legal right of organized labour to negotiate economic benefits for workers, and so disrupt the "free market." Rather, it presumed that the state, legislating for the general welfare, could best define, protect, and advance the interests of the working class. From that perspective, the definition of "labour legislation" was extremely broad, encompassing factory laws, job placement, the resolution of industrial disputes, public health and safety regulations, and even technical and commercial education. In fact, only during Taschereau's tenure of the portfolio did "Public Works and Labour" begin to connote two distinct spheres of government activity: construction and industrial relations. The creation of a Conciliation Bureau in 1910 would be the first major sign of this development, while Taschereau would finish his term in 1919 by creating a separate Department of Labour with Guyon as its deputy minister.

In defending the compensation bill, Taschereau demonstrated both a genuine commitment to the reform and a crucial limitation in his (and the government's) conception of labour legislation. Justifiably, he claimed to have anticipated loopholes through which employers might escape liability; hence, provisions which made awards inalienable and exempt from seizure, nullified prior "agreements" wherein employees waived their right to compensation, and prevented employers from deducting any portion of accident insurance premiums from wages. When an employers' delegation urged amendments obviously designed to weaken the worker's position, Taschereau was totally unresponsive. Only with evidence that an injury was intentionally self-inflicted or due to the "inexcusable fault" of the worker or a third party could the employer contest his liability. Bourassa welcomed the legislation in principle, but declared the levels of compensation to be grossly inadequate: normally between $1,000 and $2,000 (four times the annual wage) for death or permanent, total disability, and between $3.50 and $6.50 a week (half of wages lost) for temporary or partial disability. Taschereau refused categorically to consider raising these figures, arguing that they were in line with benefits in a similar British plan. What emerged as Bourassa and others pursued the matter was that Taschereau did not consider it relevant whether such compensation provided an adequate standard of living for the victim and his family. The government could not impose liabilities which compromised the viability of enterprise – that would be contrary to employee interests as well.[8] Taschereau would convey this same attitude even more clearly during the 1910 and 1911 sessions, on the subject of hours of work in wool and textile factories: while legislating slight reductions, he warned of the grave danger that Canadian manufacturers would become uncompetitive in international markets.[9]

The second measure which drew Taschereau and Bourassa into a substantive debate concerned the right of hydroelectric companies to expropriate land adjacent to their power sites. This issue illustrated almost perfectly the conflict between Liberals and *nationalistes* over industrial development. Bourassa complained that such legislation facilitated the growth of foreign trusts and monopolies at the expense of small French-Canadian enterprise. Taschereau freely admitted the desire to encourage large-scale development of Quebec's hydroelectric potential, for he considered it crucial to overall industrial expansion. While avoiding explicit reference to the inadequacies of French-Canadian entrepreneurship, he insisted that the law would free serious investors not from legitimate local competition but from artificial and capricious obstruction.[10] This debate could have been one of the most significant in Quebec's parliamentary annals. What probably kept it from such heights was the mutual suspicion of insincerity. Bourassa would not credit Taschereau with an objective analysis of Quebec's economic needs: he was merely "l'avocat des gros intérêts." Taschereau still believed that Bourassa's criticisms and national criteria were really intended to discredit industrialization *per se*.[11] A further limitation was Bourassa's refusal to advocate public ownership and development of the resource, for this was the only plausible alternative to foreign control. Gouin himself had recently declared himself ideologically neutral on the subject, at least one loyal Liberal (Maurice Perrault) was an advocate of nationalization, and Ontario Hydro provided nearby model. But Bourassa did not force Taschereau to defend the principle of private development.[12]

By the time Taschereau's compensation and expropriation bills had been debated, however, tempers in the House were extremely short. This was almost entirely due to the efforts of Jean Prévost, who day after day attacked the alleged maladministration of colonization. Speeches exceeding five hours kept members in their seats (or at the bar, reopened at Lavergne's suggestion) through half the night, and after two months there was scarely a dent in the government's legislative agenda. For a while it greatly amused the opposition to hear an ex-minister damn his former colleagues with "inside" information. But as the government lost its patience and began to blame Conservatives and *nationalistes* for encouraging Prévost, threats and accusations flew in every direction. On 18 May, following yet another tiresome debate on the Abitibi affair, Taschereau suddenly found himself in the middle of the battle.

A few weeks earlier, someone had sent Baron de l'Epine's former Belgian associates a cablegram over Lomer Gouin's name, obviously in the hope of eliciting incriminating evidence. The reply to this forgery bore the Montreal address where Olivar Asselin boarded, and in condemning the prank Taschereau not surprisingly implied that Asselin was involved. Several minutes later, as Taschereau made his way to the Speaker's chambers with a stack of books under each arm, Asselin came down from the press gallery to confront him. Why, shouted the young journalist, had Taschereau accused him of receiving the return cable, when he knew perfectly well that Asselin had not been present when it arrived? Taschereau denied making such a statement, and in fact he had not uttered that specific accusation. But Asselin was in no mood for technicalities, and punched the defenceless minister hard enough to open a cut on his lip. Taschereau thought briefly of retaliating, then summoned police to arrest his much smaller assailant. Asselin spent the night in custody and the following morning Taschereau pressed a charge of common assault.[13]

When the legislature reconvened a few hours later, Taschereau channelled his anger into a "brief [but] effectively virulent" tirade. Asselin's resort to physical violence was no surprise, he charged. Rather, it was the ultimate argument for a disciple of Bourassa nationalism, the logical culmination of a campaign to destroy the reputation of anyone and everyone respectable – judges and governors as well as political opponents. Asselin was in jail but Bourassa, who never did anything positive either in Ottawa or at Quebec, was morally responsible for the offence. Then Taschereau sat down, thinking the matter closed. Bourassa might disclaim responsibility, but surely no one was going to defend Asselin.[14]

He was wrong. The *nationalistes* and even some Conservatives felt obliged to declare Asselin a martyr. First they cited irregularities in Asselin's arrest and overnight confinement. Then they claimed that his violence had been a just retaliation for Taschereau's complicity in the St Roch riot in 1907. Taschereau would probably have let those comments pass, for in spite of them the whole incident appeared to have sobered the legislators. Realizing that the episode was being widely attributed to their own performance, and that newspapers all over Canada were questioning the maturity of French Canadians, the members finally controlled their personal animosities and began disposing of legislative business. Outside the legislature, however, the Asselin incident brought Taschereau into open conflict with *L'Action sociale*. Prominent Liberals had, as already noted, expected trouble with this unofficial spokesman for the Quebec City hierarchy ever since its founding in 1907, and Taschereau was not surprised to find himself the first real target of his old enemies from *La Libre Parole*.

While careful to repudiate the resort to physical violence editorially, *L'Action sociale* gave prominence to *nationaliste* excuses for Asselin. Then, Jules Dorion explained that his first editorial had not intended to deny the possibility that Taschereau deserved to be struck.[15] Taschereau denounced the *nationaliste* mentality in stronger terms than ever, then questioned whether a newspaper which condoned violence ought to be distributed in the *collèges classiques*, much less enjoy the endorsement of the archbishop of Quebec. The defence of Asselin revealed "the spirit of this accursed school ... which under the cover of religion hides the bitterest fanaticism ... [and] has drawn through the mire members of my family who have occupied high ecclesiastical positions." An alliance between Bourassa nationalism and a revived Castorism had been consummated with the obvious blessing of Archbishop Bégin. "The religious peace" (political neutrality of the clergy) was again at the mercy of "pious editors ... who when attacked hide behind their altars and cry that their religion is attacked." Now Taschereau found himself accused of anticlericalism, and obliged to specify that the term "accursed school" referred to the journalists, not Bégin.[16] The truth was, nevertheless, that Taschereau had no faith in Bégin's neutrality or good will. This feeling dated at least from an unreported incident of the 1908 federal election. On the day before voting, Father J.-A. Trudel, superior of the Redemptorists of Ste Anne de Beaupré, denounced Georges Parent, Taschereau, and the local mayor from his pulpit. "You must vote against these young lawyers," he declared, "who charm their way in, who don't practise, aspire to honours and spend their time with other men's wives."[17]

As Parent observed, this was not mere political meddling; it was slander. Taschereau collected numerous affidavits to establish the contents of Trudel's sermon, and further testimony that Trudel had pressured persons absent from church to contradict the reports of Taschereau's witnesses. Upon receiving this documentation, Bégin conducted an "investigation" closed to the complainants, showed the affidavits to Trudel, and finally dismissed the matter on the basis of undisclosed counter-evidence. Meanwhile Trudel continued denouncing the Liberals and threatened witnesses with excommunication. Further angered by Bégin's refusal to receive him, yet still reluctant to drag the church into court, Taschereau appealed to Mgr Sbaretti, the apostolic delegate in Ottawa. There is little record of what transpired thereafter, but whatever mild satisfaction Taschereau and Parent received can only have created resentment in archdiocesan circles.

By the end of the session it was widely observed that Taschereau had emerged as Gouin's right hand, especially when it came to battling nationalism and clericalism.[18] However, Taschereau had yet to commit his ultimate, unforgivable sin in *nationaliste* eyes. That came at the very end of 1909, and it had little to do with either Gouin or provincial politics. The issue was imperialism, source of the original antagonism between Bourassa and Sir Wilfrid Laurier and now the spark which rekindled *nationaliste* interest in federal politics. The new controversy would mark "the birth of a double prejudice which would influence the history of the province of Quebec: that of Alexandre Taschereau towards *L'Action sociale* and that of the nationalists toward Alexandre Taschereau."[19] Taschereau had become the *nationalistes'* permanent *bête noire*.

At the beginning of 1909, Britain had informed the Dominion governments that Germany was in a position to challenge British naval supremacy. An official request for support, together with enthusiastic expressions of English-Canadian concern, forced Laurier to articulate a policy. In place of a resolution submitted by Conservative MP George Foster, Laurier proposed that "the organization of a Canadian naval service in cooperation with and in close relation to the British navy ... and in full sympathy with the view that the naval supremacy of Great Britain is essential to the security of commerce, the safety of the Empire and the peace of the world." Unlike the Foster resolution, whose emphasis on Canadian financial responsibility raised the spectre of an integrated imperial navy under British control, Laurier's version affirmed the principle of Canadian autonomy. At the same time, it proclaimed that Canadian loyalty to the empire in face of the German threat was based on self-interest, not subservience.[20]

When his resolution was passed unanimously in the House of Commons, Laurier felt that he was in a strong bargaining position vis-à-vis the British Admiralty and legislation establishing a navy primarily for Canadian coastal defence would enjoy wide support. Only British officials and the more extreme English-Canadian imperialists would be disappointed. That turned out to be a gross miscalculation. In November Frederick Monk, the federal Conservative leader in Quebec, stated his opposition to any naval expenditures on the grounds that they would be useless and apt to draw Canada into imperial wars. He had earlier acquiesced in the Laurier resolution, he claimed, only as a gesture of loyalty at a time of crisis for Britain. More likely, his opinion had been altered by communication with *nationalistes* who were already agitating against the anticipated naval bill.[21]

This was the atmosphere when Gouin and Taschereau led an official Quebec delegation to Toronto for discussions with Ontario leaders. At a formal luncheon on 14 December, where all speakers emphasized the importance of cooperation between the two governments and of mutual understanding between citizens of the "sister" provinces, Taschereau raised the subject of imperial defence. Citing the past loyalty of French Canadians, including the heroism of his grandfather at Châteauguay in 1813, he assured his listeners that "Quebec is willing and able to do her share. The call from the mother country should be answered. We leave the form in which assistance should be given to the men at the wheel and whatever they decide will be cheerfully assented to. If we build a fleet our boys will prove that the descendants of the great sailors of the dawning days of the colony, of Jacques Cartier and Champlain, have lost nothing of the courage, energy and seamanship of their forefathers, and I hope some day we will hear of the great deeds of Admiral Jean Baptiste ... When the call is heard, as true Canadians, we will say 'Here we are'."[22]

This was hardly a militaristic outburst, but neither was it likely to be a popular sentiment among French Canadians. And since the speech does not seem to have been an unmeasured or spontaneous contribution to the spirit of the occasion, one is tempted to speculate about Taschereau's possible motives. He probably feared, as did Laurier, that the naval issue could become more and more racially divisive. If the *nationalistes* appeared to speak for French Canada, then English Canadians might interpret Laurier's stance not as a positive assertion of Canadian autonomy but as a concession to anti-

British sentiment. French-Canadian Liberals had so far been very reluctant to admit that the proposed navy might actually participate in a war, lest they nourish the fear of conscription which the *nationalistes* had already planted. But at some point they had to face the issue, or else concede the *nationaliste* premise that Canada had no military obligations. In order to ensure moderate attitudes in both English and French Canada, it was therefore necessary to counteract *nationaliste* agitation. And with Laurier slated to introduce his naval legislation early in the new year, there could be no delay.[23]

Still, as a provincial cabinet minister, Taschereau might not have risked his political standing on such an issue without some sort of genuine personal commitment. The reference to his grandfather is a reminder of his awareness that ancestors had served and prospered under British authority and institutions; he may have been sensitive to the implication that the British Empire and civilization did not deserve the loyalty of patriotic French Canadians. Taschereau's attachment to Laurier far surpassed that of other provincial ministers, and he would naturally spring to Laurier's defence in any critical confrontation. Laurier had been the ally of Taschereau's father and uncle in the bitter religious controversies of the 1870s; frequent republication indicates that Laurier's 1892 tribute to the Taschereau family was never forgotten; more recently, Laurier had echoed Taschereau's complaint that the *nationalistes* were the heirs of those who had slandered the cardinal;[24] and even before the St Roch affair, Taschereau had become Laurier's chief political ally in the Quebec City district. Taschereau had also developed a fair degree of respect for the moderate imperialist sentiments of those English Canadians he knew best, the business elite of Quebec City. These were people whose "imperialism" seemed as positive and progressive as their economic outlook and never degenerated into denigrations of French-Canadian culture.[25] (During bitter wartime debates, he would contrast their tolerance with the bigotry of Ontario fanatics.)[26] Moreover, Taschereau no doubt viewed *nationaliste* agitation on the naval question in a manner consistent with his general interpretation of their philosophy. Whatever pretexts they might formulate, their anti-imperialism sprang ultimately from a desire to discourage French Canadians from broadening their horizons, on the ground that the world beyond the St Lawrence was irrelevant or hostile to their individual and collective aspirations. Taschereau expressed no surprise when the religious zealots at *L'Action sociale*, those guardians of French-Canadian purity, joined Bourassa's crusade against Laurier's naval policy.[27] It was another engagement in the familiar war between progress and stagnation.

Whatever his motives, "le plus impérialiste des ministres" quickly felt the consequences of his Toronto speech. Bourassa himself was busy founding a daily newspaper, *Le Devoir*, with financial help from anonymous Montreal Conservatives. But Lavergne, Prévost, and the younger Conservative MLA's like Arthur Sauvé wasted no time labelling Taschereau a jingo and a traitor to his race. Prévost was the most imaginative, claiming that Taschereau had offered his countrymen as cannon fodder for the imperialist adventures launched by the heirs of Joseph Chamberlain and Cecil Rhodes. Prevented by government corruption and mismanagement from colonizing Quebec's hinterland, he added, French Canadians would be forced either to enlist or to emigrate.[28] Far from apologizing, Taschereau went to the defence of Laurier's naval bill when it was introduced into Parliament. *Le Devoir*'s campaign against a Canadian navy, he told the Legislature, served mainly to inspire "a spirit of hatred and calumny without precedent in the history of Canadian journalism."[29] Nevertheless, the attacks on Taschereau evidently affected a few rural Liberal deputies: fearful of being associated with the naval bill itself, they absented themselves from the vote on Prévost's motion censuring Taschereau.[30]

A late summer federal by-election in the presumed Liberal stronghold of Drummond-Arthabaska soon proved that their fears were legitimate. Conservative and *nationaliste* forces combined to sponsor an "independent Liberal" candidate opposed to Laurier's Naval Service Act, which had now become law. Taschereau wisely kept a low profile in this campaign, but he was far from indifferent to the outcome. Laurier's prestige in French Canada was at stake, the constituency lay within Taschereau's Quebec district, and the official Liberal candidate was Edouard Perrault, a good friend and distant relation who had served the mass at his wedding and subsequently articled with his firm. So he played a "back room" organizational role, and witnessed first hand the stunning and acutely embarrassing victory of Bourassa's anti-imperialist candidate.

While no Quebec Liberal was happy about this blow to Laurier, the Gouin administration did gain indirectly from the result in Drummond-Arthabaska. Even prior to the campaign, opposition members of the provincial legislature had seemed impatient to get out and campaign against the Naval Service Act, and therefore made possible a much quicker and quieter session than that of 1909. Now they were convinced that a Conservative-*nationaliste* alliance had greater possibilities in the federal than in the provincial arena, and redirected their interest and energies accordingly. Bourassa ceased attending the legislature regularly, entrusting the opposition leadership to an uninspiring new Conservative chief, Mathias Tellier. Lavergne stayed on, but submerged himself in the Conservative ranks and seemed content to develop a reputation as Taschereau's personal nemesis. In fact the *nationaliste* challenge to Gouin was over almost as quickly as it had begun, and it would be many years before the provincial Liberals were seriously threatened again. Only Jean Prévost sustained his attack, but his obsession was becoming tiresome even to sympathizers.

In these circumstances, Gouin and Taschereau dared to hope that they would also be less harassed by *L'Action sociale*, with a resulting improvement in their strained relationship with the Quebec City hierarchy. Gouin began the quest for reconciliation at the 1910 Montreal Eucharistic Congress by endorsing the "faith and language" doctrine of French-Canadian nationality. Ministers attended every religious ceremony they possibly could, and Taschereau made certain that clergy were invited to christen virtually every public work.[31] It is reasonable to believe that Taschereau had the avoidance of a religious controversy in mind when he resisted pressure for a compulsory school attendance law. Proponents of this measure saw it as a means to control child labour, and Taschereau virtually admitted that the existing mechanism (a literacy test administered by factory inspectors) was inadequate.[32] But he could also predict both the official objection, that the state should not arrogate to itself a parental responsibility, and the imputation of anticlerical motives which would follow in *L'Action sociale*. In truth, there was some reason to fear that compulsory education might presage further challenges to clerical control over education. In 1897 the Liberals had tried to reestablish a Department of Education under ministerial authority; more recently, Gouin had insisted upon the independence of his Ecole des hautes études commerciales from Laval University, and spoken of technical schools and other projects in terms which suggested a whole network of vocational institutions outside the confessional system. Now, two leading proponents of compulsory education, Godfroy Langlois, MLA, and labour leader Gustave Francq, had just been exposed as members of the Emancipation Lodge of Freemasons, a militantly anticlerical secret society.[33]

However, no amount of deference and caution could satisfy Jules Dorion and Omer Héroux, who continued to flail away at everything Liberal in the pages of *L'Action sociale*. When *Le Soleil* and *La Vigie* counterattacked, Archbishop Bégin intervened with surprising force. In a pastoral letter read throughout the Diocese of Quebec, he condemned the two Liberal papers for questioning his vigilance over *L'Action sociale*. The cabinet and caucus were as much dumbfounded as enraged, but finally decided that Bégin had given them an excellent excuse to appeal for papal intervention. Taschereau drafted the memorandum and assembled the dossier.[34] First he drew attention to the contradiction between the principles enunciated by ecclesiastical authorities in launching *L'Action sociale*, and the paper's subsequent editorial policy. Founded to promote Catholic social and moral ideals, it was to observe strict political neutrality. In reality it had hired two sworn enemies of the Liberal party as its editors and, on issues having nothing to do with religion, slanted both its reporting and its commentaries against the Liberals. The dossiers documented five of the most obvious cases of political bias: unrelenting criticism of the Naval Service Act, automatic endorsement of every Bourassa accusation against the provincial government, slurs of its own against individual Liberals, constant exaggeration of Bourassa's prestige and influence (in the manner of a party newspaper idolizing its leader), misstatements of fact meant to excuse criminal acts by Asselin and his fellow journalist Fournier, and finally scurrilous attacks on Liberal newspapers and journalists.

The purpose of this appeal, Taschereau claimed, was not to silence *L'Action sociale*. All that Liberals sought was the right of their own newspapers to reply, just as they would to any other political opponent. But Archbishop Bégin was apparently claiming the exclusive right to judge the admissibility of all criticism; any public challenge to that judgment constituted a defiance of religious authority. This was the clear implication of his warning to *Le Soleil* and *La Vigie*, but surely it did not reflect papal teaching.

Despite our great respect for diocesan authority, we cannot accept that His Eminence should approve from his high office all the attacks and criticisms which *L'Action sociale* has directed toward our party and our leaders. Nor can we allow him to confer upon this newspaper a form of immunity which would make it a privileged and untouchable publication in our political arena. We insist respectfully but energetically, as much for ourselves as for our publicists, the right to reply to the editors of *L'Action sociale* when they attack us or accuse us unjustly, when they criticize our opinions or political acts. Denied this right, we would find ourselves in a weak and embarrassing position vis-à-vis our fellow citizens of other faiths; the smooth operation of our political system would be in jeopardy; and the clergy would inevitably lose its healthy influence over the Catholic population of our province.

We repeat to Your Holiness that we wish the greatest harmony between Church and State. We desire religious peace, without which our faith and institutions can only decline. But we firmly believe that this peace cannot long endure among us if Catholics must abdicate the sacred right they have always enjoyed in purely political matters, that of defending their acts and opinions, replying to accusers and opponents.[35]

Transmitting their memorandum in strict confidence through Mgr Stagni, the apostolic delegate, the Liberals anticipated that "Your Holiness will render justice and find means to end the truly alarming situation which we have brought to His attention." Some serious attention may well have been given to this petition, since the reply took more than a year to be communicated and *L'Action sociale* began exercising some restraint. Other circumstances could equally explain such moderation, however. *Nationalistes* were acutely embarrassed by the naval policy of the Conservative government which they had helped to elect federally in 1911, several of their formerly emotional provincial issues (especially Prévost's colonization exposés) were becoming tiresome, and Héroux had taken his vitriolic pen over to *Le Devoir*. In any case Rome finally supported its senior Canadian ecclesiastic, thus renewing the courage of Mgr P.-E. Roy and other Dorion sympathizers within the Bégin entourage. The open hostility between Liberals and Quebec City Catholic militants had only temporarily subsided, to be rekindled following World War I.

The 1911 and 1912 sessions at Quebec passed even more peacefully than that of 1910. Taschereau and Lavergne never ceased trading taunts and accusations, but merely in the process of dispatching a fairly heavy legislative program. In fact, Taschereau stood back from two episodes which had important implications for his own later career. One was the controversy surrounding Charles Lanctôt, Gouin's extremely able deputy attorney general. His annual salary of $4,500, even when augmented by special fees for work on the Revised Statutes of Quebec, was far less than he could earn in private practice. Having eleven children, he also found it inadequate to support his cherished membership in the elite society of Quebec City. Gouin therefore allowed him to moonlight, but this created a worse problem. Lanctôt's clientele consisted mainly of organizations on whose behalf he drafted petitions ("private bills") for presentation to the legislature. Since his official duties required him to make sure such bills did not contradict provincial statutes and to provide other legal advice to the Assembly's Private Bills Committee, there was a blatant conflict of interest. Critics were initially content to object in principle, and Tellier suggested a pay raise so that Lanctôt could serve the state at less financial sacrifice. In truth, however, Lanctôt was bitterly resented on both sides of the House for his insufferable arrogance and was widely considered a "legislative tollgate" by school and municipal commissions as well as private companies who felt obliged to retain his services. Thus while Gouin could dampen the immediate controversy by raising Lanctôt's salary and curtailing his most objectionable activities, he could not diminish his aide's unpopularity.[36] No rumours about him were too damning to strain credibility in subsequent years: he was said to harass personal enemies through provincial police investigations and blackmail persons on the basis of information acquired through his office. It is understandable that Taschereau came to admire this man's legal brilliance and capacity for work, which matched his own. But they had little else in common, and witnesses to their relationship could never explain Taschereau's blind loyalty to such a detestable individual.[37] Long before political opponents exposed his embezzlement of public funds in 1936, Lanctôt's unpopularity would be one of the greatest liabilities borne by Taschereau's own government.

The second ominous development involved the control of public utilities in Quebec City. Both public transportation and the supply and distribution of electrical power were in the hands of the Quebec Railway, Light and Power Company, commonly known as "the Merger." This firm was controlled by two powerful Montreal Conservative financiers, Rodolphe Forget and Herbert Holt. To exploit growing resentment against the Merger, several Liberals formed a rival company called Dorchester Electric and retained Taschereau's firm as solicitors. Arthur Cannon was in fact a director, and from his seat on City Council their chief political advocate. He helped secure Dorchester's first major victory, the street lighting concession. If it could fulfil its promise to halve rates previously charged, public favour might well carry the company to complete dominance in the capital. Forget counterattacked politically, personally ousting Georges Parent in the 1911 federal election and threatening unlimited financial support for opponents of Taschereau and Cannon in coming provincial and municipal elections. On the economic front, the Merger did its best to obstruct the launching of Dorchester's operations.[38]

Forget did not actually campaign against Taschereau in 1912, largely because the Conservative nominee was Armand Lavergne, whose sudden influence in the party he keenly resented. Nor was Dorchester Electric immediately successful in its challenge to the Merger. The real significance of this affair lay in the direct participation of Taschereau's close associates and relations in a quest for control of municipal services, and more generally in the advent of formal links between the hydroelectric industry and the Liberal party leadership. Montreal entrepreneur E.-A. Robert, for example, entered politics as a Liberal in 1912 in order to protect his growing interests. His solicitors were Robert Taschereau, son of Alexandre's step-brother, and J.-L. Perron. By the early 1920's E.-A. Robert controlled the Merger and Perron was in the provincial cabinet. Meanwhile Dorchester Electric had become a Shawinigan Water and Power subsidiary called the Public Service Corporation. Cannon was still its leading advocate, and now related to Taschereau by marriage as well as legal partnership. Lomer Gouin had joined Shawinigan's Board of Directors after leaving the premiership. Taschereau managed to remain neutral in the ensuing struggle between Liberal interests, won by the PSC. But the new monopoly, renamed the Quebec Power Company, still retained the law firm, which now included Taschereau's oldest son Paul as well as Cannon. Soon brother Edmond became a director of the QPC, while Lanctôt was rumoured to enjoy a retainer from the parent company. Thus the trap which ultimately destroyed public confidence in Taschereau began to form more than twenty years before it was sprung.

All that was of course unforeseeable in 1912. As Gouin sought a second renewal of his mandate, both the government's and Taschereau's stature seemed unassailable and still rising. Liberal election propaganda that year stressed two themes with which Taschereau was personally identified. One was material progress itself, which already seemed to have vindicated the policy of industrialization launched by Parent fifteen years earlier. Hydroelectric power had allowed Quebec to capitalize on the western wheat boom, expanding its traditional light manufacturing and its iron and steel capacity for railway construction. French-Canadian emigration from Quebec was slowing dramatically, and the province's growing reputation among foreign investors promised still greater economic opportunities at home. As much as Gouin's embargo on the export of pulpwood from crown lands, for example, it was cheap power which inspired plans to build large, integrated pulp and paper mills. The Liberals' second theme, their actual legislative record, cited numerous measures drafted or sponsored by Taschereau. Workman's Compensation was a natural showpiece, as were the provincial employment bureaus created to save workers from exploitation by unscrupulous private agencies. As minister of public works Taschereau had announced two important initiatives in transportation: the gradual abolition of toll roads and the construction of a rail link between Montreal and the Canadian Northern line now running through northern Ontario and Quebec. And although the policy was rightly identified with Gouin, Taschereau's department bore the actual responsibility for building new technical schools. As if to emphasize their confidence that these measures had won the gratitude of the working class, the Liberals had also moved to widen the franchise substantially and had eliminated multiple voting by men who owned property in more than one constituency.[39]

Although well organized and buoyed by their party's control of federal patronage, the Conservatives did not really pose as serious a threat as they had in 1908. They still had not articulated a coherent alternative philosophy, they offered few substantive criticisms of government policy, and the enthusiasm of Bourassa and other nationalist allies had subsided. Lavergne agreed to become chief election organizer for the Quebec district and personally challenged Taschereau in Montmorency. This created some real excitement at the constituency level, highlighted by a riotous *contradictoire* in Ste Anne de Beaupré,[40] but it was insufficient to topple any Liberal incumbents. The province-wide result was similar: modest Conservative gains in the popular vote in rural constituencies, but absolutely no gain in seats. The Liberals captured two urban Conservative ridings, and five of seven newly created constitutencies.

In retrospect, the 1912 election can be seen as a watershed in Quebec politics, not because of the party standings, but because of an apparent consensus on provincial issues. Industrialization was an established fact and generally a welcome one. The future promised greater material progress: resource based industries would create more highly skilled and better paid jobs, for which technical schools would train the local population. Shawinigan's success in harnessing the St Maurice River and attracting large industries to purchase its power inspired plans for major hydroelectric projects on other rivers, especially the Saguenay. The Ungava territory just ceded to Quebec by Ottawa was known to hold immense mineral and forest wealth. Even the long-suffering agricultural sector was gaining from the expansion of urban markets. Of course not everyone approved. But those idealists who still opposed industrialization as a threat to French-Canadian nationality spoke for an isolated and shrinking constituency. This was so even though their worst fears were being realized in the increasingly cosmopolitan nature of Montreal, the circulation of secular ideas, and the growth of secular institutions. New problems were arising, to which sincere critics could point without constant reference to French Canada's pastoral and religious vocation. The status of the French language in Quebec was threatened by "foreign" economic control and a vogue for English even among certain French-Canadian entrepreneurs. The living conditions of the working class properly outraged some, though too few, observers. Aspects of corporate behaviour, especially concerning public utilities, still gave rise to legitimate complaint.[41] But, at least for the moment, critics tended not to blame provincial authorities or conclude that the whole policy of industrialization was wrong.

Thus the thirteenth Quebec legislature was devoid of sharp conflict on provincial issues. There was only one major controversy, the rather nasty Mousseau affair. An English-language Montreal newspaper conspired to trap an unsuspecting and highly regarded Liberal MLA in a clear case of influence-peddling. To justify his elaborate conspiracy (which included the use of an American detective and electronic surveillance), the editor claimed that he was exposing a practice in which practically all deputies regularly engaged. Taschereau was named chairman of an inquiry into both Mousseau's activities and the blanket accusation. The committee's work was thorough and reasonably nonpartisan, for the reputation of the entire legislature and of the province itself was at stake. Mousseau's promising career ended in disgrace, and one legislative councillor was also implicated. The charge of systematic corruption was carefully refuted, and the motives of the newspaper questioned. Although this scandal had implications for the whole question of relationships between government and private interests, it was not perceived at the time as a challenge to the Liberal government and its policies.[42] Upon dissolution of the leglislature in 1916, Lavergne declared that the Liberals had enacted every major social and economic reform envisaged in the original *nationaliste* program. Of course this was an exageration, born of Lavergne's contempt for Philémon Cousineau, the latest Conservative leader. Still, his virtual endorsement of Gouin presaged a provincial election in which the Liberals were not seriously challenged on any issue.

External pressure also contributed to an internal consensus. At the same time that movements were under way to protect and advance the status of French in commerce and industry within Quebec, the language rights of French Canadians in other provinces suffered a new series of defeats. First, the Borden government extended Manitoba's boundaries without protecting separate school rights in the new territory, known as Keewatin. Later in 1912, Ontario effectively abolished French as a language of instruction. The latter decision, announced in a Department of Education directive known as Regulation XVII, was the response to a highly complex and emotional situation. It sprang not only from the traditional religious prejudices of the Protestant majority, but also from the insecurity felt by Irish Catholic citizens and clergy, a new aggressiveness on the part of the rapidly growing Franco-Ontarian population, and general alarm about the performance of the educational system. The Whitney government had to decide whether instruction in the French language, long accepted in practice, was to be considered a right of Ontario citizens. Or, in Whitney's terminology, would a third school system for the French race join the public and separate systems provided under the British North America Act? Clearly a negative response to that question was expected by the overwhelming majority of English-speaking Ontarians. Where the Catholic hierarchy and the Orange Order agreed, no politician could safely dissent.[43]

But in Quebec Regulation xvii was perceived simply as an attack on the French-Canadian population and it stirred a resentment far more profound and pervasive than any previous schools issue. Ontario was not distant, it was the neighbouring province. The size of its French-Canadian population far exceeded that of any western province, or even that of New Brunswick. Many Franco-Ontarians were recent immigrants from Quebec, settled near the Quebec border, and presumably retaining family ties to their former homes. Through the defiance of Regulation xvii by local separate school trustees, Ottawa quickly became the focal point of the controversy. This fact ensured extensive newspaper coverage, and made it all the more difficult for French-Canadian federal politicians to avoid involvement.

Perhaps the most important reason why French Canadians of Quebec took such offence at the measure was that it repudiated the very compelling and attractive vision of Canada being promoted by Henri Bourassa. In the pages of *Le Devoir* and from public platforms, Bourassa was arguing that French Catholic communities must be allowed to flourish in every part of Canada. Belief in cultural duality was the complement, if not the ultimate source, of Bourassa's insistence upon Canadian automony and his hostility to imperialism. Empires in general were homogenizing forces, intolerant of minorities; as long as English Canadians defined their nationality in terms of the British Empire, they would not likely accept the legitimacy of a bicultural state.[44] On many questions of the day Bourassa spoke for a minority, but who in French Canada could reject the ideals of mutual respect and equal collective rights between two communities? And who could fail to interpret Regulation xvii as a rejection of these ideals, and ultimately of the worth of French-Canadian nationality?

The outbreak of World War I also helped forge a consensus, or more accurately a common front, among French-Canadian leaders. Understandably, English Canadians responded more spontaneously and enthusiastically to Britain's call for assistance. But for all the hypothetical arguments and fine constitutional distinctions developed during the naval debate, no French-Canadian spokesmen now questioned the Borden government's immediate commitment of human and material resources to a united imperial front against Germany. Even Bourassa initially acknowledged Canada's moral obligation to help defend British and French civilization. A small number of French Canadians, primarily an intellectual elite which had personal contact with France, were genuinely attached to the cause of their rediscovered mother-country. In 1915, an "Aid to Belgium" fund-raising campaign would strike a similarly responsive chord in such circles. A far greater number, including Laurier, acted from a sincere admiration of and loyalty to British institutions and civilization. This was a period in which the whig interpretation of Canadian history, according to which the British Conquest of New France had been an ultimate blessing for French Canadians, enjoyed its widest acceptance in Quebec. There was also the stark recognition that Canada had substantial economic interests in a British victory.

Yet such convictions only partly account for the unreserved support promised and maintained by French-Canadian leaders, not only the politicians of both major parties but also religious authorities and businessmen. A sense of responsibility and one of foreboding were also important. Any loyal opposition would lean over backwards to avoid weakening public confidence in the government at such a critical time. French-Canadian leaders were acutely aware how tenuous support for the war effort might actually be in Quebec, especially in rural areas where the *nationalistes* had most successfuly cultivated and exploited the fear of military involvement. Criticism of the government therefore carried the risk of encouraging and justifying opposition to full-scale Canadian participation in the war. This in turn would inflame English-Canadian opinion, immoderate segments of which were always ready to characterize French Canada as disloyal to the empire. In their determination to prevent such a crisis in French-English relations, French-Canadian elites set aside internal differences and with one voice urged their compatriots to enlist, to make other sacrifices, and subsequently to ignore major grievances and provocations in their support of the war effort. Although Bourassa soon raised his pen and voice in dissent, it is significant that *L'Action sociale* (now called *L'Action catholique*) did not follow.[45]

Although a secondary figure in this campaign to ensure French-Canadian support for the war effort, Taschereau was unquestionably one of those Liberals who set partisanship aside and staked his political reputation on the good faith of English Canadians in general and the Borden government in particular. Genuinely tolerant of English-Canadian attitudes to the war and fearful of extremists on both sides, he never ceased preaching and hoping for moderation. His statements about Regulation xvii illustrate his patience, all the more so because his brother-in-law, Senator Philippe Landry, became a major spokesman for the Franco-Ontarian cause and no doubt informed him of the bigotry he encountered. For three years after the directive was issued, Taschereau made no public comment at all. Then in 1915 he concluded the legislative debate on the resolution by W.S. Bullock, which called upon Ontario to accord its French-Canadian minority the same privileges enjoyed by English-speaking Quebeckers. Taschereau echoed the insistence of earlier speakers that respect for the educational rights of Franco-Ontarians involved both elemental justice and the spirit of the Canadian Confederation. Therefore, he insisted, Quebec legislators were neither challenging the authority of the Ontario legislature nor interfering in the "domestic" politics of the neighbouring province by expressing their wish. But Taschereau developed a more original theme as well. Citing the Entente Cordiale and military cooperation between Britain and France, the efforts of Canadian soldiers of all races to save France, and his personal knowledge of Ontario leaders and Anglo-Quebeckers, he argued that conflict between the two cultures in Canada was unnecessary and aberrant. Soon, he predicted, English-Canadian soldiers, favourably impressed by France and its people, would return to promote the ideal of harmony even more strongly. But that might be too late if "gunslingers" (*franc-tireurs*) on both sides were allowed to begin firing. "Ontario leaders give me the impression that this is a question they would like to settle, but that they fear certain corners of their province where the modern British spirit, so broad, generous and tolerant, has not yet penetrated. Perhaps they fear certain groups too much." Let them summon their courage, he added, if only to prevent Quebec extremists from using the issue "for other purposes" – that is to say, for discouraging the war effort.[46]

A year later, Taschereau was still insisting that the Ontario schools issue must be kept separate from the war effort. He chastised Lavergne for claiming that Ontario "Prussianism" absolved French Canadians of the responsibility of fighting tyranny abroad. Such an argument merely served the interests of English-Canadian fanatics who were always ready to accuse French Canada of disloyalty. If French Canadians actually did make their participation conditional upon the repeal of Regulation xvii, they would become "pariahs" with no hope of restoring their rights outside Quebec. Similarly, Taschereau rejected the idea of using the Quebec Patriotic Fund (for the relief of soliders' dependents) to support defiant school boards in Ontario. But Taschereau also began to question the good faith of Ontario politicians. With an uncharacteristic mixture of anger and melancholy, he told members that their message was evidently being ignored. The depth of sentiment and Taschereau's sense of betrayal were well understood as he went on to express Quebec's "profound annoyance and impatience." Sustained applause followed from both sides of the legislature, and even Lavergne knew better than to respond "I told you so." Senator Landry, conspicuous in the gallery, watched approvingly.[47] And in yet another intervention, Taschereau insisted upon his right to speak French in every court in the country, and to be understood. For this to happen French must be taught throughout Canada, and only the federal government could ensure it. Taschereau had been sufficiently provoked to raise the more fundamental issue which lay beneath the Ontario schools question, equality of language rights throughout Canada. It was a virtual endorsement of Bourassa's vision.[48]

Regarding the war effort itself, Taschereau made few striking declarations. No doubt he was as sincere as any French Canadian in proclaiming his support for the imperial cause, though he spoke soberly of duty and honour, not glory or conquest.[49] Like other Liberals he tried to resist partisan sniping at the Borden regime, and as a provincial minister accepted the extension of federal authority which war demanded. He appeared on the platform at major recruiting and patriotic rallies near Quebec City, although there were usually so many senior political, ecclesiastical, and military officials present that he was seldom required to speak. He did perform regularly at lesser gatherings, however, and helped organize the Patriotic Fund and Aid to Belgium appeals. He also participated in the ill-fated Quebec City Home Guard, which was supposed to be a civil defence organization for men too old for active military service but instead became a justly ridiculed exhibition of upper-class conceit.[50]

Following the example Gouin and Laurier, Taschereau refused to let a growing list of French-Canadian grievances diminish his support for the war effort. Most irritating was Borden's toleration of Sir Sam Hughes, who as minister of militia had begun gratuitously insulting French Canada even before war was declared and maintained the habit after he took charge of Canadian mobilization. One such insult was the removal of Senator Landry's son, Col. J.-P. Landry, from command of a brigade on the eve of its departure for France in 1915. There were predictable rumours that Hughes's action was calculated to reward the replacement, a personal friend, and to punish Landry's father for his advocacy of Franco-Ontarian educational rights. It was bad enough that French Canadians loathed Hughes personally. More tragic was the belief that his attitude reflected a widespread English-Canadian mentality. Making no allowance for years of failure to recruit and promote French-Canadian officers, and refusing to acknowledge the insecurity and isolation suffered by unilingual French-Canadian volunteers in English-speaking units, Canadian military authorities considered it an unjustifiable inconvenience to meet the special needs of French Canadians. It took enormous political pressure just to compel the formation of a single French-Canadian regiment. Thus French Canadians were entreated to defend France, the source of their culture, and the British Empire, protector of their collective rights, within an institution which failed to recognize their collective existence or respect their language – and this in the shadow of Regulation XVII. Understandably, more and more French Canadians agreed with Bourassa that the Canadian war effort was really an exercise in Anglo-Saxon racial assertiveness.

The Hughes syndrome involved more than language. Since Hughes was a proud and vocal Orangeman, it became difficult for French-Canadian leaders to dismiss the provocative editorials of ultra-Protestant newspapers as the rantings of a fanatical and powerless minority. It was here that French Canadians were accused of disloyalty at the first sign of lagging enlistment, and that compulsory military service was first proposed as a means to punish them. If the war effort really was not an English Protestant crusade, then Borden should have repudiated Hughes long before he dismissed him for other reasons – insubordination, administrative laxness, and the suspicion of outright corruption. But Hughes remained until the end of 1916, probably never even suspecting the misery he created for French-Canadian leaders who answered his call for new recruitment campaigns.[51]

Despite Hughes and despite Regulation XVII, Taschereau's faith in the good intentions of most English-Canadian leaders persisted. In the face of Bourassa's escalating attacks on both the justice of the war and Canada's disproportionately heavy contribution, he pointedly insisted that Laurier was still the true spokesman for French Canada.[52] As the call intensified to "make French Canadians do their part," he publicly accepted Borden's assurance that there would be no conscription.[53] Despite grave nation-wide suspicions that R.B. Bennett's National Service Registration campaign in late 1916 was a prelude to compulsory military service, again he took the federal government at its word.[54]

But by now the credibility as well as the patience of "loyal" French-Canadian leaders was near exhaustion. It could no longer be pretended that the mass of French Canadians supported the war effort. The exact number of French Canadians to have volunteered was in dispute, but not the fact that it was proportionally very low – especially when the remarkable Acadian figure was subtracted. A highly publicized midsummer campaign had yielded precisely ninety-two Quebec recruits and occasioned several hostile demonstrations.[55] Although most French Canadians ultimately returned their National Service forms in January 1917, Bennett and his representatives met similar hostility when they tried to explain their scheme publicly. This reality, together with the knowledge of a looming manpower crisis in the army, forced a basic choice on French-Canadian political and religious authorities. At the risk of appearing to support nationalist opponents of the war effort, some began to argue that Canada's military obligation was real but not unlimited. Many leading churchmen, criticized for going overboard in their initial support for the war and fearing complete estrangement from the lower clergy, moved in this direction. So did politicians closely attached to rural communities and farmers' organizations; J.-E. Caron, Gouin's minister of agriculture, was among them. The harder choice was to try to alter French-Canadian opinion. Conservatives were almost forced to do this, but many of them along with some Liberals took the risk out of conviction: for all the callousness and stupidity of the regime, the war really had to be won.[56]

Taschereau tried to find a middle road, largely by lashing out at Ontario Conservatives for placing him in this predicament. "From the outset of the war," he told Montreal Liberals in late April 1917,

our province has been the target of attacks more spiteful and malicious than ever before. It is frightening to imagine what the future hides, and whether Europe's postwar disorders will not have their echoes here ... [While I commend the Bonne Entente movement] why can't we have mutual understanding with the majority in our sister province, when we French Canadians get along so well with our English-Canadian compatriots of Quebec? I am sincerely afraid that the shameful campaign carried on against us by part of the Ontario press, and which must necessarily reflect the opinion of part of the Ontario population, will have disastrous effects.

... The attack has been too systematic, too persistent, too unjust not to be the result of a methodically conducted campaign. They are using the war to hurl the accusation that our province doesn't do its share.

After defending Quebec's war record, especially its contributions on the home front, Taschereau explored the historical background to the problem of recruiting.

Only a few years ago ... the Conservative party in alliance with the Nationalist party undertook that memorable campaign against militarism, a campaign led by the Quebec Conservative party and financed by the Tory party of Ontario.

I would like to believe that these same men of 1911 now recognize their error and are trying to repair it ... Probably they are, but the seeds they planted are not so easy to destroy.

Moreover, our neighbours should realize that since the Conquest ... the authorities have not encouraged military enthusiasm among our French-Canadian population. [Prior to the war] we were systematically ignored in the Department of Militia. If they wanted us to come forth in time of trouble, should we not have had our fair share of favours during the serenity of peacetime?[57]

Taschereau would return to this theme, "l'oeuvre néfaste de 1911," a year later, after the Borden government had completely betrayed his faith. There were three distinct phases to that betrayal, beginning with the announcement of compulsory military service at the end of May 1917. Taschereau and other Liberals understandably had difficulty viewing this as a courageous decision by Borden, setting vital national interests above his own previous undertakings. They suspected that he had finally caved in to growing anti-French Canadian sentiment, particularly in Ontario. "Conscription is a measure specially aimed against the Province of Quebec," Taschereau said simply.[58] But beyond their assessment of Borden's motives lay the real grievance: he had made fools of them in the eyes of their constituents. Taschereau's charge that "it was a crime thus to deceive the people who trusted him" can be understood in both a broad and a narrow sense.[59] Bourassa, Lavergne, and other *nationalistes*, whom Liberal leaders held in such contempt, had effectively been proven correct about the nature of the Canadian war effort. One might almost wish that the government *had* surrendered to extreme opinions it feared but did not share, for the evidence suggested that "moderate" English Canadians had now turned against them as well. Ontario leaders of the Bonne Entente organization, who had enlisted the patronage of Gouin and Mayor Garneau among other prominent Quebeckers, were now in the forefront of the conscriptionist "Win-the-War Movement." And in Parliament Arthur Meighen, the minister responsible for steering through the Military Service Act, unashamedly declared that "the most backward elements" of Canadian society were opposed to conscription.[60] This was precisely the attitude of so-called fanatics earlier in the war.

Most French-Canadian Liberals regarded the subsequent formation of a Union government as a continuation of the betrayal. It was not a genuine national coalition, argued Taschereau, simply because a few Liberals had accepted portfolios. Its intent was obviously not to unify Canadians, but rather to keep in office a government which had bungled voluntary recruitment and could not by itself survive a general election.[61] The legislation which then disenfranchised naturalized east European immigrants, gave the vote to soldiers' female relatives, and allowed soldiers' votes to be concentrated in close constituencies was a virtual admission of the government's weakness. While followers of Laurier did not publicly question the motives of Unionist Liberals, they must certainly have done so privately. French-Canadian Liberals could be used to raise soldiers and funds for the war, but the patriotism of a new Laurier government could not be trusted. Laurier could be admitted to the coalition only by agreeing to support conscription – in other words, if he agreed to be used further.

Once it became public, this questioning of Laurier's patriotism constituted the third, and by far the most insulting and inexcusable phase of the betrayal. Despite all that French-Canadian Liberals had done prior to conscription, despite their continued support of the allied war effort thereafter, and despite their calls for public order in the face of near-riots against conscription, Unionists freely labelled them as traitors during the election campaign of November and early December 1917. Any wartime government is naturally tempted to claim a monopoly on patriotism for electoral purposes. But no French Canadian could accept Unionist propaganda as mere partisan excess, let alone genuine patriotism. Once a leading minister had declared that "every Hun sympathizer from Berlin to the trenches, from Berlin to the Cameroons, wishes success to Laurier with his anti-conscriptionist campaign," there was no stopping the English-Canadian press.[62] Laurier's followers were "the cockroaches of the kitchens of Canada" and their votes were "for Germany, the Kaiser, Hindenburg, von Tirpitz and the sinker of the Lusitania." Quebec was "the plague spot of the whole Dominion," and could not be permitted to "rule Canada." Acknowledging no distinction between

Laurier and Bourassa (who declared his intention to vote Liberal but openly opposed the war effort), a recognized Unionist publicity committee asserted that Quebec favoured "deserting our men, breaking our pledge ... and trailing Canada's honour in the mud of world opinion." And Laurier was "a demagogue, a charlatan and a mountebank"![63]

Campaigning for Liberal candidates in the Quebec district, Taschereau adopted an air of condescension toward their French-Canadian Unionist opponents. He pleaded with hostile crowds to let them be heard, afforded physical protection to one, and referred to them as "fantômes" whose names were on the ballot just to prevent the entire province from going Liberal by acclamation. "You have the same opinion of conscription as we do," he told one Unionist who later virtually admitted that his defence of the Borden government was less than sincere. "I offered my name and my efforts," the candidate explained, "because I believed that in the circumstances honour required partisans of the government to defend its program before the electors of Quebec." While toying with a helpless opponent, Taschereau was also driving at an important truth, that party differences among French Canadians were no longer meaningful in the face of a concerted external attack. At this "grave hour of our history, all men of good will must put forth the best of their hearts and minds to save our race from the danger which threatens us ... [and] rally behind Sir Wilfrid, who is devoting the last years of his life to saving his own people."[64]

French-Canadian solidarity became even more evident once the election was over. The victorious Union government had not a single French Canadian on its side of the new House of Commons, while Laurier had the support of a mere sixteen English Canadians from outside Quebec. It could no longer be pretended, as Taschereau and other Liberals had during the campaign, that there was enough sympathy for Laurier and opposition to conscription elsewhere in the country to defeat the government. The voting legislation and a last-minute promise to exempt farmers' sons from the draft had made the political isolation of French Canada a certainty. Now came additional grievances. The exemption promised to students in Quebec seminaries, a condition of the hierarchy's acquiescence in conscription, was forgotten. As Taschereau had predicted, moreover, the belief grew quickly that the military and judicial authorities were enforcing conscription more thoroughly and unsympathetically in Quebec than elsewhere. Liberal deputy J.-N. Francoeur accurately portrayed the mood of the French-Canadian elite, a mixture of bitterness and powerlessness, when he proposed his famous resolution to the Quebec legislature: "that this House is of the opinion that the province of Quebec would be disposed to accept the breaking of the federal pact of 1867 if in the other provinces, she is considered an obstacle to the unity, to the progress and to the development of Canada."[65]

It would be misleading to dismiss the debate on Francoeur's motion as an occasion "orchestrated" by Sir Lomer Gouin to let French Canada vent its spleen in a safe, orderly manner.[66] It is true that no vote was taken, the sponsors withdrawing their resolution after Gouin's climactic speech on 22 January. But none of the speakers sounded like participants in a charade. All recognized the serious implications of merely having such a motion before them, and several Liberals were evidently troubled by having to admit that they had been betrayed. Gouin's own conclusion was far from a ringing endorsement of Confederation: "We complain of injuries and of appeals to prejudice, but our fathers have always suffered from these. For sixty years the parties have resorted to them. That has not prevented our fathers from accomplishing their mission. We will do the same in the framework of the Canadian Confederation. Even with its imperfections, it's still the best form of government we could adopt."[67]

Taschereau had prepared the most thoughtful and forceful speech of his political career to that time, but for unexplained reasons never delivered it. He was scheduled to speak just before Gouin, and may simply have been called away from the legislature on the final day of debate.[68] He certainly would not have suppressed it on the ground of redundancy, for while his catalogue of French-Canadian grievances resembled those of others, some of the contents were unique. For one of the few times in his life he borrowed arguments from Henri Bourassa, notably the complaint that French Canadians had been labelled disloyal for adopting precisely the same attitude toward conscription as the majority of Australians and New Zealanders. He acknowledged that for historical reasons French Canadians were more "closely tied to the soil" and "parochial" in their outlook on world affairs. But as in his 1917 Montreal speech, he condemned Ontario imperialists for reinforcing these attitudes prior to the war. They had financed *nationaliste* propaganda efforts, made the Canadian militia a totally English institution, and even discouraged French-Canadian educators from introducing military exercises and ceremonies into their schools.

Taschereau was ready to insist that no matter how the legislature voted, the appeal of separatism was growing in Quebec. Men of good will could see that racial conflict was chronic and growing worse, not better; that French-Canadian opinion counted for nothing on great national questions, even when the same opinions were respectable elsewhere in the empire; that Quebec's economic interests were now threatened by the growth of western political influence. It was easy to conclude that separation was the logical answer, allowing each side to proceed with important tasks. Personally he rejected this conclusion: it was neither feasible to dismantle national economic structures, nor likely that French and English Canada could resist absorption by the United States separately. Even if they could, a separate French Canada risked stagnating on its own. More positively, both history and personal sentiment attached him to the whole of Canada, imperial connection and all. The majority of Canadians were not really fanatics; the problem was to control the minority on both sides who were. And with that injunction Taschereau's text returned to where it started, the needless but malicious provocation which sapped the will and undermined the work of French-Canadian moderates.[69]

While the Francoeur debate allowed French Canada to protest "officially" the injustices it had suffered, there were still more insults and provocations to come. Generally, French Canadians resisted the conscription law by legal or at least passive means. A total of 113,291 out of 115,602 men called up from Quebec claimed exemption, and about 105,000 were granted them by local tribunals.[70] Numerous other conscripts, along with some deserters, hid from the military authorities. There were several public disturbances, which some English newspapers predictably described as an attempt to duplicate the Irish uprising of 1916, but almost all political and religious leaders urged compliance with the law. In reality, most violence was a reaction against reportedly unfair administration of the Military Service Act, rather than a planned resistance to the law itself. French Canadians who believed that conscription had been legislated primarily to punish them naturally assumed that it was being enforced more harshly and rigorously in Quebec than elsewhere. This suspicion was reinforced because military and RCMP authorities, refused the cooperation they enjoyed from local police forces elsewhere in Canada, resorted to the use of spies, informers, and an intimidating physical presence.

Taschereau witnessed the last and most serious outbreak of violence, which started at Quebec City on Thursday, 29 March, 1918, and escalated during the Easter weekend with the help of typical bungling by the government and military. The RCMP entered a pool hall and arrested one Joseph Mercier, who claimed (truthfully) that he had been exempted from military service but had left his certificate at home. An angry and growing crowd followed Mercier and his captors, storming the police station when it appeared their friend would be locked up. There was substantial damage to the building, several officers were injured, and rumour spread that there would be a further demonstration the next day at the army's administrative centre. This rumour was self-fulfilling, at least to the extent of attracting a throng of spectators including Taschereau, who lived nearby. With nothing much actually happening, children began lobbing snowballs at municipal policemen. Soon older people were throwing harder substances, someone proposed "burning the [draft] records," and a group of invaders succeeded in setting fire to the building before military reinforcements could arrive. When troops did arrive to expel them, some of the rioters ransacked the offices of two proconscriptionist newspapers. Mayor Lavigueur and other local officials apparently believed that accumulated popular anger had now spent itself. However, military and federal authorities came to the opposite conclusion: that a revolutionary situation existed, created by provocateurs able to manipulate the crowds and civilian authorities lacking the ability or determination to stop them.

A smaller and more peaceful crowd gathered on Saturday night in front of the drill hall, also near Taschereau's home on the Grande Allée. Despite the number of women and children present, mounted soliders charged through several times to break it up. Later that night large military reinforcements, entirely English-speaking, arrived by train. Word spread quickly through the city, which now became uniformly angry. Early Sunday mobs began assembling in the Lower Town and breaking into commercial establishments where weapons might be found. By noon troops patrolled the streets, scattered shots could be heard, and one company fired into a crowd from which ice and snow had been hurled. With a full-scale, bloody riot looming despite the pleas of clergy and civic leaders for people to stay home, the military district commander was reduced to calling upon Armand Lavergne to use his influence. Lavergne's popularity had recently soared in the Lower Town, on account of his tireless, often unpaid efforts to secure exemptions from military service. Lavergne did persuade the crowds to disperse for that evening, but there is considerable dispute whether the rhetoric he used to do it calmed or further roused the anger of Quebeckers. In any case, Monday night, 1 April, witnessed the tragic climax. Although martial law had been declared, large crowds kept assembling, and finally soldiers were assailed by bricks and bottles and (according to some accounts) bullets. Soldiers began firing, killing at least four innocent civilians, and charged into crowds with drawn swords. Before the rioting ended around midnight, several soldiers and dozens of civilians were wounded.

That ended the violence, for the army demonstrated its control of the situation. A coroner's inquest into the four deaths allowed Mercier, Lavigueur, his police chief, Lavergne, and other Quebec residents to register their version of events, but that brought little comfort. All the actions of the military were retroactively authorized and legalized by the government. The charge of French-Canadian disloyalty was raised again in Parliament and in the English-Canadian press. This time the clergy were singled out for counselling evasion of the law, and Borden himself accused local tribunals in Quebec of granting military exemptions too freely. Then the government cancelled most remaining grounds for exemption from military service. Although this decision was taken entirely for military reasons, and although it cost the government most of its support in rural English Canada, French Canadians naturally interpreted it in the context of the Quebec riots. It was another form of punishment.[71]

Having counselled the population against further violence, and having no influence with the federal government, French-Canadian leaders could do little but wait for the wartime nightmare to end. Provincial ministers went about their normal political and administrative duties, and even when the armistice finally came in November, neither their mood nor their routine suddenly changed. Peace abroad was not an instant cure for injuries suffered at home, and the initiative for a gradual reconciliation between French and English Canada seemed to lie anywhere but in Quebec. Yet in the legislative session which began in January 1919, Taschereau and his colleagues began responding to other problems which had developed during the war. Most of these problems could be traced to the rapid acceleration of social and economic change. Wartime demand, both for traditional Quebec products like clothing and processed food and for munitions and small hardware, had drawn tens of thousands more people into the industrial labour force. Industrial expansion was not only quantitative, moreover. The establishment of electro-chemical and aluminum industries, the conversion of many existing manufacturing enterprises to the use of electrical energy, and the sudden burgeoning of pulp and paper production all signified a substantial fulfilment of Quebec's long-recognized hydroelectric potential. The spectacular success of the Shawinigan Water and Power Company in profiting from wartime opportunities ensured that private capital would be available to develop large new power sites in the near future. With industrialization came its inevitable social concomitant, greater urbanization. The 1921 census would show Quebec with an urban majority for the first time, some of it distributed among new or revitalized centres around the province but most of it concentrated on the Island of Montreal.[72]

Taschereau freely acknowledged that "the labour question" was one of the most important economic problems arising out of the war. Although Quebec's long-term economic prospects were bright, it was apparent that unemployment would be severe as the country demobilized and war production ceased. Traditional industries, meanwhile, were relying more than ever on female and child labour. As long as living costs remained high, parents would encourage the exploitation of their children, even to the extent of falsifying their age and school attendance certificates. Yet returned soldiers and others who had made sacrifices during the war rightfully expected the opportunity to earn a decent living. Governments must therefore listen carefully to the views of unions, whose membership was growing rapidly, even if it was not possible to accept every demand.[73]

These comments were accompanied by a virtual torrent of labour legislation, beginning with provision for the appointment of a deputy minister of labour under whose direction government services to the working class could expand. While continuing to be combined with Public Works as a ministerial portfolio, Labour now had the status of a separate department. In order to facilitate and augment federal programs, Taschereau's bills expanded provincial employment services, placed new controls on private employment bureaus with a view to eliminating them entirely, enabled Quebec municipalities to begin construction of working class housing, and made farmland available free to returning servicemen. Another law authorized the appointment of a commission to set minimum wages for women in industrial establishments, although Taschereau was undoubtedly horrified to see this celebrated as a precedent for further departures from the principles of economic liberalism. (Significantly, the commission was not actually appointed until 1925.) There was also a minor amendment to the Workman's Compensation Act, extending benefits to sons whose wages were the prime source of family income.[74]

Taschereau's best-known initiative was a major amendment to the Industrial Establishments Act concerning the employment of children. Provisions of the act would now apply to virtually all kinds of employment rather than just factories, and to children up to sixteen years old instead of fourteen. The power and responsibility of inspectors to enforce the "literacy" requirement were considerably enhanced. Parents and employers must not only document the age of working children but also the fact that they had completed six years of education. If suspicious, the inspector could still administer a literacy test. One loophole still remained: a working child could be enrolled in night courses to meet educational requirements, and it would be difficult to make sure he actually attended. But the terms of the amendment, the tone of debate, and the expressed intention to raise the quality and quantity of labour inspection generally all seemed to promise a serious government attack on the problem.[75]

This law was not merely a response to the rapid wartime increase in child labour. It was also the government's reaction to a strong current of opinion favouring compulsory school attendance legislation. Until recently such a measure had been viewed primarily as a means of keeping children out of the factories, but, because of its alleged philosophical implications, only those willing to be labelled anticlerical advocated it openly. Quebec Protestants had even been persuaded to forgo compulsory attendance for their children, lest they be accused of setting a precedent for use by "enemies" of the Roman Catholic Church. Rapidly, however, education itself was becoming the focus of concern. A broad consensus had formed among "respectable" French-Canadian leaders (not just anticlericals) that there had to be a much higher standard of mass education in an increasingly urban and industrial society. In a highly publicized petition addressed to Archbishop Bruchési of Montreal in January 1919, one hundred prominent citizens expressed the opinion that a compulsory attendance law was a necessary condition for such improvements. Meanwhile T.-D. Bouchard, who had succeeded Godfroy Langlois as the most renowned anticlerical in the provincial Liberal caucus, accused Catholic education officials of systematically falsifying school attendance statistics in their defence of the voluntary system.[76]

No one, however, seriously denied the need for educational reform *per se*. The Catholic Committee of the Council of Public Instruction established a commission to revise the entire eight-year curriculum offered by its schools, while French-Canadian educators in Montreal argued for a high school system parallel to those of Protestants and English Catholics in the city. The legislature held a curious, rather ethereal debate on the need for an "intellectual elite" to inspire and guide the renaissance of French-Canadian society as a whole.[77] Speaking to an organized labour delegation, Taschereau acknowledged that French Canadians must be well educated not only to cope as individuals with industrial society, but also to survive collectively as their contacts with the surrounding alien majority increased.[78] Yet the government had good reason to be cautious. In ecclesiastical circles compulsory attendance remained a hated symbol of secularism, the dreaded precedent for unlimited state intervention in education. No matter how intricate and learned the theological defence of "parental responsibility" became, it was of course not the parents' but the church's loss of control over education that the religious authorities feared. A compulsory attendance law would almost certainly shatter the truce which circumstances had forged between the hierarchy and the Gouin government, and free the anti-Liberal zealots at *L'Action catholique* and elsewhere from wartime constraints. (For Taschereau this truce had a personal dimension: he had been trying to serve as an intermediary in the vexatious question of independence for the Montreal campus of Laval University, to which his friend Mgr Pelletier, the rector, was opposed.)[79] The general popularity of compulsory attendance was also doubtful. Opponents could easily characterize it as English and Protestant in inspiration, a damaging accusation in the context of French Canada's wartime alienation and the continuing appearance of books and articles by Protestants critical of French-Canadian society and culture.[80] Beyond that, the enforcement of compulsory attendance risked a serious backlash. It could deprive urban families of irreplaceable, indispensable income, and in fact saddle them with new expenses for tuition and books. Farm children could still contribute to their families with unpaid labour, but formal education was less highly valued in rural areas and any increase in school taxes would be strongly resisted. No one even conceived of the provincial government mitigating these economic consequences with direct expenditures or general minimum wage laws for adult males.

Speaking for the government, Taschereau therefore argued that the controversy over compulsory attendance was a "distraction" from the real task at hand. The new restrictions on child labour would, he said, eliminate any incentive for parents to withdraw their children from school prematurely. Anticipated curricular reforms and further advances in vocational education would ensure that Quebec children were equipped for modern life. So where was the need for compulsion, and for the inevitably bitter dispute the issue caused? In light of conscription and the treatment of French-Canadian minorities outside Quebec, compulsion should be as repugnant to liberal as to religious sensitivities.[81] Considering the passions which had been raised on both sides, this position was a highly successful compromise. The hierarchy heaved a collective sigh of relief. The *Montreal Star*, a long-time proponent of compulsory education, declared that the child labour bill "practically" achieved this purpose.[82] Senator Raoul Dandurand, Gouin's close friend and chief organizer of the Montreal petition, also accepted the bill, his confidence enhanced by the promotion of Louis Guyon to the new post of deputy minister. Dandurand also believed that the campaign had been a propaganda victory, effectively challenging the complacency of educational authorities.[83] Controversy continued over the state's proper role in education, and new battles were soon fought over the curriculum. But the government had avoided a showdown with the hierarchy and directed the energies of educational reformers into more substantial projects.

Taschereau's prominence during the 1919 session took on considerable political significance as evidence mounted that Lomer Gouin would soon retire from the premiership. There was speculation about the state of his health, but no report of any sudden illness or deterioration. More likely, the problem was a combination of boredom and fatigue after fourteen years in office. A revealing tale, if true, is that he was excessively irritated by the minor political meddling of the new lieutenant-governor, Charles Fitzpatrick.[84] Clearly he wanted a change of scenery, and he listened politely as Robert Borden proposed that he join the Union government. It was unlikely that he would enter federal politics to save the authors of conscription, but he did foresee the possibility of a permanent political realignment based on tariff policy. In such circumstances, many of his protectionist allies would be Borden's present followers. When Gouin called a provincial election for 23 June, two full years before his mandate would expire, the question became not "whether" but "when" he would announce his resignation. With the Conservatives totally unprepared to put up a fight, this was surely a case of providing his successor with the majority and the time to meet a variety of looming challenges: farm and labour militancy, reaction against the administrative commission he had imposed on Montreal in the hope of restoring municipal finances, and the liquor question. After the election, Gouin gave up the attorney general's portfolio to Taschereau, found judicial positions for two long-time cabinet colleagues, and placed three relatively young men in major cabinet posts. Observers were understandably surprised when this "state of imminence" lasted through a session of the new legislature early in 1920.[85]

Taschereau knew he was considered the heir apparent to Gouin, and that he could become premier without any resistance within Liberal party ranks. The candidacy of his only possible rival, J.-E. Caron, was largely a figment of anglophone journalistic imagination. In a sense the speculation was understandable. Agrarian political protest was spreading like wildfire throughout Canada; Caron was a recognized champion of Quebec farmers; Liberals would draft him to head off a movement which could threaten their hold on power. Caron's harmony with popular sentiment seemed demonstrated, moreover, at the Liberals' federal leadership convention in mid-August 1919. Long an outspoken anti-imperialist, Caron actively supported W.L. Mackenzie King, a Laurier loyalist in 1917, against W. S. Fielding, a conscriptionist Liberal. Gouin and Taschereau forgave Fielding, who had not personally denounced Laurier, because they considered the former minister of finance a more reliable defender of the tariffs which protected Quebec's manufacturing industries. For the vast majority of Quebec delegates, the memory of Laurier, just six months dead, was far too sacred for such a hard-headed choice.[86]

Where the journalists erred was in assuming any personal antagonism or serious policy differences between Taschereau and Caron in the provincial context. Although he was a spokesman for the farmers, Caron did not oppose industrialization or regard Taschereau as hostile to agrarian interests. And while aware that Taschereau lacked certain political talents such as oratorical flourish and the ability to set people at ease on first acquaintance, Caron also understood his own more serious limitations. If anything he was too sensitive about his modest rural origins, feeling insecure among the urbane professionals who surrounded him in the cabinet.[87] If Taschereau did not exercise his right of succession, then Caron might well be a candidate against Léonide Perron, the Montreal lawyer. But that was a different question, and there is no evidence that Caron sought to discourage Taschereau from making a positive choice.

## CHAPTER FOUR

# Prosperity Delayed

Alexandre Taschereau's elevation to the premiership of Quebec began formally on 21 June 1920, when Lomer Gouin delivered a farewell speech to the Young Liberals in Montreal. Gouin's preference for Taschereau as his successor was no secret: respect for his colleague's ability and judgment had grown constantly since 1907, and he was also a more reassuring choice politically. As heir apparent for several years, his authority had begun to transcend regional and other divisions among Liberals. The leading alternatives, Caron and Perron, lacked anything like Taschereau's broad acceptability. In fact some Liberals feared that these two would symbolize the rural-urban or agrarian-industrial division which was threatening political stability throughout Canada, and that a leadership contest between them would severely embarrass the party. While his own federal ambitions were a factor, Gouin had been delaying his announcement primarily because of Taschereau's hesitation.[1] With no intention of forming a brief, caretaker government, Taschereau was well aware what he would be sacrificing: the opportunity to spend more time with his family, to practise law with sons Paul and Robert, to achieve still greater financial security, and finally to begin his judicial career while still relatively young and healthy. Friends and colleagues appealed strongly to his sense of public duty and of party loyalty before Taschereau finally agreed to serve.[2]

The decision made, Taschereau and Gouin left on 25 June for the Moisie River, the north shore salmon-fishing paradise where they had first retreated in 1907 to discuss Taschereau's entry into the cabinet. Between fishing expeditions, they spent a week discussing the transfer of power and the immediate plans of both men. They returned to Quebec on 2 July, consulted the cabinet, and paid an official call upon Fitzpatrick. On 8 July, one day after Arthur Meighen succeeded the ailing Robert Borden as prime minister of Canada, Gouin resigned. On the morning of 9 July, Louis-Alexandre Taschereau became the fourteenth premier of Quebec.[3]

Sworn in with Taschereau was a "furnished house," a virtually complete cabinet as reorganized by Gouin a year earlier. Taschereau remained attorney general, thus restoring Gouin's practice of combining the two posts and avoiding an otherwise inevitable collision between Charles Lanctôt and a "lesser" minister. The veteran Caron would naturally continue in Agriculture, as would J.-A. Tessier, who was also the mayor of Three Rivers, in Roads. Honoré Mercier, son of the illustrious premier and brother-in-law of Sir Lomer, had the sensitive Lands and Forests portfolio. Walter Mitchell had been provincial treasurer since 1914, and in 1918 he had become Quebec's first minister of municipal affairs in order to increase his authority in dealing with the desperate financial plight of Montreal and its suburbs. He was also the acknowledged spokesman for Protestant education interests, having served on the Protestant Committee of the Council of Public Instruction since entering the legislature and cabinet. Fluently bilingual and still only forty-three years old, he was expected to be an enduring strength of the Taschereau government, not the St James Street watchdog of nationalist caricature.[4] The three ministers first appointed in 1919 were Antonin Galipeault in Public Works and Labour, Edouard Perrault in Colonization, Mines and Fisheries and Athanase David as provincial secretary. Galipeault had practised law with several prominent figures and was involved in a number of business interests, but he also had a record of sympathy for labour dating from his years as a Quebec City alderman. Perrault, loser in the famous Drummond-Arthabaska federal by-election before entering provincial politics, enjoyed a certain tolerance among moderate nationalist elements. While expected by the latter to devote great energy to the sacred mission of colonization, Perrault was already more interested in the mining possibilities of northwestern Quebec. At thirty-eight, David was the youngest cabinet minister and a deeply committed educational and social reformer. Fortunately, he did not fully share the anticlerical reputation of his father, the renowned journalist, politician, and man of letters, Laurent-Olivier David.

Four ministers were sworn in without portfolio. Joseph Kaine and Napoléon Séguin were token Irish and labour representatives. Narcisse Pérodeau, alert and active in business, law, and politics at nearly seventy years of age, would remain government leader in the Legislative Council. Léonide Perron was the only new member of the government, but his talents and energy were well known through his legal and business activities in Montreal. It was evident that he would receive a portfolio at the first opportunity. The average age of ministers with portfolio was less than forty-eight, so that despite marked continuity with the previous regime, Taschereau's first administration contained some promise of a modern, energetic approach to postwar problems.

This dual theme of continuity and departure also characterized Taschereau's inaugural address as premier on 27 July. The occasion was a banquet organized in his honour at the Chateau Frontenac, attended by over 250 guests including most deputies and legislative councillors, a delegation of federal MP's led by Ernest Lapointe, civic leaders, long-time supporters from Montmorency, and Taschereau's closest friends. After Adélard Turgeon had presided with his customary eloquence and humour over a succession of testimonials, Taschereau delivered an optimistic yet sincere assessment of Quebec's future. Outwardly the emphasis was on continuity, for Taschereau, like others during the preceding two weeks, wanted to acknowledge fully the accomplishments of Sir Lomer Gouin. Thus, "the first principle of my program is to continue vigorously the beneficial policy of my predecessor, to develop it as fully as can be, to enlarge and complete it according to new requirements in each sphere of activity." The central priority would remain economic progress, especially the fullest possible exploitation of hydroelectric and other natural resources. His government's duty was "to open our doors wide to capitalists, to discuss their projects like businessmen, to say no immediately when we must say no, and when the projects are beneficial, to accept them without delay or indecision." Progress in education must also continue if French Canadians hoped "to occupy the front rank in our factories and gradually succeed the outsiders who direct them." This would require not only advanced technical training, but also secondary institutions to bridge the gap between primary schools and technical academies. Other sectors would also receive their customary just consideration: the farmer and colonist "because we realize that agriculture is the strongest root of our national security"; the working man; the city of Montreal, which, despite his Quebec City origins and residence, Taschereau acknowledged to be the metropolis, the key to province-wide prosperity.[5]

However, as Taschereau's manifesto admitted implicitly, as he already quietly appreciated, and as he would further discover in the severe economic recession which overtook all of Canada before the end of the year, the problems and responsibilities facing the new Quebec government were far more complex than terms like continuity and realization suggested. Momentarily at least, the very office of premier bore increased importance. With Laurier dead, Gouin temporarily retired to private affairs, and no credible French-Canadian minister at all in the federal government, Taschereau was the sole recognized political leader of French Canada. During the postwar reconciliation between French and English Canadians – if there was to be a reconciliation – his leadership would be critical. From the outset, newspapers treated Taschereau and Meighen as spokesmen for the two estranged communities, juxtaposing their respective appeals for understanding. Taschereau was not merely platitudinous on the subject. He suggested that French Canada could forgive but not likely forget the insults it had suffered during the war and that expressions of good will by the federal government must be palpable, not merely rhetorical. In addition to recognizing the specific economic needs of Quebec, this meant genuine respect for provincial autonomy in the administration of federal programs and for the French-Canadian viewpoint in external policy.[6] When the two leaders first shared a public platform, it was to dedicate a monument to George-Etienne Cartier. Taschereau attacked the idea of creating a Canadian national spirit through uniformity: "it is precisely in our [different] customs and traditions that the truest and best elements of the Canadian spirit are to be found." Unfortunately Meighen went ahead with a prepared English text and missed the opportunity for an impressive joint appeal.[7]

Beyond the sensitivity of spiritually and politically isolated French Canadians, the premier of Quebec had now to champion certain economic interests of his province against possibly damaging federal policies. This was a novel predicament for Quebec: since Confederation, major national trade and transportation policies had seldom been considered hostile. But now the CPR and related financial interests were insisting that nationalization of competing railways was going to injure Montreal, and proponents of a St Lawrence deep waterway, another threat to Montreal's trade and conceivably to industrial development as well, had recommenced lobbying on both sides of the Canadian-American border. On the tariff issue, Meighen seemed reliable enough. But within the Liberal party, which was expected to win the next federal election, Quebec business interests felt threatened by Mackenzie King's determination to recapture the allegiance of western farmers from the nascent Progressive party. That would probably involve promising tariff reductions which could severely damage mass-employment industries in Quebec. A further reason for Quebec's insecurity was that Ontario, traditionally Quebec's ally on the tariff policy, now had a United Farmers' government. Thus, as premier, Taschereau was carrying an unprecedented range of political responsibilities.

It was also evident to Taschereau that the administrative functions of the Quebec state must expand on several fronts. The latest eruption of the compulsory school attendance volcano had now largely subsided, Taschereau having sided again with the opponents of such legislation. But the educational system urgently required several political initiatives: flesh on the bones of Gouin's commercial and technical institutions (staff, equipment, qualified students), curriculum reform and improved teacher qualification throughout the primary system, solutions to the particular financial and administrative chaos which rapid growth had created for Montreal school boards, regularized support for the universities and *collèges classiques* of the province. Athanase David was also convinced that the state must help stimulate a French-Canadian artistic and literary revival. In the realm of public welfare, it was clear from staggering infant mortality rates and the prevalence of tuberculosis and smallpox that a major program of health education and disease prevention was overdue and that local authorities lacked the means to undertake it. Within months, moreover, the growing financial strain upon Quebec's charitable institutions (orphanages, crèches, adult refuges, and hospitals which took indigent patients) would reach crisis proportions, and existing provincial legislation would prove inadequate to cope with it. The liquor question needed to be settled again, because Gouin's 1919 legislation was being openly flouted, especially in Montreal. His commitment to private enterprise notwithstanding, Taschereau acknowledged several important governmental responsibilities in the management of Quebec's forest resources; these primarily involved protection against speculation, fires, and the instability of international markets.[8]

The problems demanded more than legislative enactments and financial generosity from the provincial government. They required expert administrative direction, "bureaucratic infrastructure," to use the jargon of a later age. Evidently, Taschereau was quite conscious of the need, for early in 1921 an aide would write to him that "You have already confided to me that you don't know any better way of improving your administrative machinery than by having at the head of each department and service a man thirty to forty years old who can bring to his tasks not only a vigorous intelligence and sound judgment but also the spirit of initiative and eagerness for work which are too often lacking in public servants who are encumbered by age and mired in an unchangeable routine."[9]

That the purpose of this letter was to solicit a job for the aide's brother points up one major obstacle in the way of modernizing the Quebec civil service and external institutions: the demands of patronage. There were others as well, perhaps more serious. One was finding highly competent personnel. During the Gouin regime, Quebec had begun paying for the European education of promising students of engineering, and had imported French and Belgian experts to fill a few important positions. To attract superior professionals, moreover, salaries and working conditions had to be competitive with those in private practice and employment; against that ran Taschereau's determination to keep the cost of government low. These priorities could only be reconciled by retiring or firing less skilled and less essential employees, and getting more efficient performances from those who remained. One such general trimming was actually undertaken in 1921,[10] but thereafter more buoyant revenues must have broken the government's resolve.

A further obstacle to the expansion of government activity was the certain hostility of the Roman Catholic Church. Religious authorities had revealed their sensitivity during the Gouin years, particularly in opposing the Ecole des hautes études commerciales. The HEC constituted a threat to the position of the church in French-Canadian society on several grounds. It conveyed the message that education had a vocational as well as a moral purpose; that the personnel and curriculum of religious institutions did not adequately prepare students to succeed in the world of commerce and industry; and that the state and educational reformers considered religious control an obstacle to the progress of new, vocationally oriented institutions. In the postwar period, this threat seemed all the more immediate. The increasing financial dependence of Catholic educational institutions on the state, the views of educational reformers as revealed in the compulsory attendance debate and in the drafting of a charter for the newly independent Université de Montréal, the victories of anticlericals in France, Poland, and Czechoslovakia, the spread of radical ideologies into Quebec through organized labour, and the continuing presence of anticlerical dissidents within the French-Canadian elite itself all combined to produce a siege mentality among some clergy and devout laymen. The fear of a secular, anticlerical onslaught carried out through the state was openly proclaimed in L'Action catholique and Le Devoir and in pastoral letters.

This outlook was easily transferred to the question of public assistance. The essentially preindustrial concept of indigence, stressing private responsibility and the moral quality of charity, was well suited to the institutional predominance of the church. The realities of industrial society challenged both the philosophy and the financial capacity of local and religious institutions. In this case, financial dependence upon the state had the effect of dividing clergy among themselves; ecclesiastical authorities and idealists resisted state intervention in principle, but religious orders actually involved with charitable work recognized that there was no real alternative to accepting provincial subsidies. There was, in fact, a third element to the division, urban parish priests who already felt threatened by the growth of specialized organizations within the church and now felt further threatened by any state organization which might diminish their leading role in charitable activity.[11] Understandably the specific fears of religious authorities concerning its two most important social functions, education and welfare, became generalized in all new government activity. And while there were no real anticlericals in the Taschereau government, "statism" was destined to become a most troublesome issue for it.[12]

A number of these factors – the recession, David's strong advocacy, religious sensitivity – combined to make the Taschereau government's first term better known for social legislation than for economic measures. The latter were by no means absent: in 1921 Caron introduced demonstration farms as models for the modernization of agricultural techniques; Mercier and Perrault satisfied a traditional *nationaliste* demand with bills to separate colonization land from the commercial forest domain; Mitchell brought in measures to restore order in municipal finances; and Galipeault responded to strikes by municipal workers by proposing compulsory arbitration for police, fire, waterworks, and incineration employees. In 1922 some vigorous forest protection regulations were enacted, J.-L. Perron established the administrative framework for major roadbuilding projects later in the decade, and a Royal Commission was appointed to modernize the system of workman's compensation.[13] But there was only one sign of the great industrial expansion Taschereau had envisioned, the signing of a contract with the Quebec Development Company to dam the headwaters of the Saguenay River at the Grande Décharge and produce 200,000 horsepower of electricity. This was also the only economic initiative to provoke controversy – less for its substance than for its alleged partisan implications. Taschereau is supposed to have demanded future editorial support from the Conservative *Quebec Chronicle* whose owner, Sir William Price, was a partner in the QDC along with American tobacco millionaire Benjamin Duke.[14]

The first social measure to attract public attention was the creation of the Quebec Liquor Commission. Taschereau rejected full prohibition as an unwarranted infringement on individual rights and, when imposed contrary to the will of many people, an unenforceable measure which taught disrespect for the law. Gouin's compromise of 1919, whereby wine and beer were sold under license and liquor was available for medicinal use, had also proven unsatisfactory. Partial prohibition still encouraged contempt for the law, and placed an unreasonable moral burden upon doctors and pharmacists. With total prohibition coming into force practically everywhere else in North America, the licensing of private firms to distribute beer and wine practically guaranteed an illicit interprovincial and international trade. So, Taschereau announced, the government would establish a commission to exercise monopoly control over the sale of liquor and most wines, to be the exclusive wholesaler of beer and light wines, to issue retail wine and beer licenses on a much more restricted basis than previously, and to police the entire system. Except in those districts where prohibition was in force through local option, Quebeckers could openly purchase a product of dependable quality. There would be less opportunity for Quebec entrepreneurs to flout the laws of neighbouring jurisdictions. And profits, instead of enriching a few individuals, could be put to constructive social use.[15]

Taschereau fully expected most of the criticism which followed. While the advocates of temperance generally approved on tactical grounds, hard-line prohibitionists were outraged because hard liquor was legally available once again and the government was "encouraging" rather than just tolerating drink. On the opposite flank, private distributors faced elimination by the government monopoly. Having no moral case to make, they responded by financing the political opposition and, Taschereau later claimed, by issuing anonymous death threats.[16] The official opposition attacked from various angles, blaming government corruption for the failure of Gouin's system, predicting shameless partisanship in the operation of the new one, insisting that the sale of liquor by the bottle would undermine fifteen years of temperance education, and denouncing the participation of a "Catholic government" in such a disreputable commerce. *Le Devoir* expanded the last point into a general warning against statism, and the inveterate *castor*, Abbé Georges Dugas, detected the work of freemasons. (In mock solemnity, a government newspaper assured him that sacramental wine would be inspected by a competent ecclesiastical authority.)[17]

What Taschereau did not anticipate was the encouragement of critics by the Roman Catholic hierarchy in Quebec City. He began to suspect this when *L'Action catholique* joined the battle, relentlessly pursuing the theme of statism. The new Liquor Act, Taschereau complained to Fitzpatrick, "was submitted to religious authorities prior to its introduction in the House ... [T]hat was the time to make representations to us."[18] Still, there were several Quebec bishops who had personally campaigned for temperance over the years, and Taschereau could appreciate the depth of their feeling on this issue. In isolation, he would not have regarded such a minor political intervention as a threat to harmony between the church and his government. Unfortunately, a similar pattern appeared almost immediately as the government tried to deal with an equally difficult social question, the crisis in public assistance. Once again, the hierarchy followed Taschereau's critics in the "Catholic press" into battle, and this time the dispute became extremely bitter.

The financial difficulties of private charitable institutions in the province were well known at the beginning of 1921, and the Throne Speech referred vaguely to some form of provincial relief. But virtually no one imagined that the government was contemplating as far-reaching a measure as the Public Charities Act which David introduced in March. To pay for the care of indigent hospital patients, orphaned or abandoned children, and destitute adults, the province proposed an equal sharing of costs among itself, the institution involved, and the municipality of residence. For this purpose, each municipality would collect a ten per cent amusement tax, depositing half the proceeds in a Public Charities Fund from which the provincial share would be paid. So far so good: the main effect of these provisions would be to redistribute funds in the direction of those municipalities suffering higher proportions of indigence and lower tax revenues. What drew vehement protests was the creation of a Bureau of Public Charities to oversee the operation. This new provincial authority would establish standard *per diem* costs for various categories of assistance, receive and adjudicate the applications of charitable institutions who wished to receive public assistance, and ascertain that funds were being properly disposed. The government also came under fire for its legislative procedure, having railroaded the bill through both Houses in a matter of hours and refused Opposition Leader Sauvé's demand, sound advice in retrospect, for hearings before the Public Bills Committee.[19]

The origins of this measure seem clear enough. An existing act, based on the English poor law tradition, was both unrealistic and unenforceable in requiring less affluent municipalities to assume the cost of these kinds of relief. Meanwhile the volume of appeals addressed directly to the provincial government by charitable institutions was becoming too great to continue being handled on an *ad hoc* basis. Finally, these appeals were for more than operating subsidies: many establishments were in desperate need of modernization and expansion. In the case of hospitals it was the medical profession as much as the directors of the institutions who stressed the need for large-scale capital expenditures, and hence provincial intervention. It is less clear why the government acted so precipitously. Part of the reason may have been the economic recession, which suddenly transformed a nagging problem into a critical emergency. Halfway through the session, in fact, Taschereau informed Fitzpatrick that the legislation was still being drafted.[20] Conceivably the government did not originally plan to bring such legislation forward until 1922. This theory is consistent with the fact that when first presented, the bill said nothing about provincial support for capital projects; only a later amendment authorized the bureau to undertake such commitments. A second possible explanation, by no means incompatible with the first, is that Taschereau and David anticipated a strongly negative reaction from "religious opinion" and feared that a long legislative debate would itself help mobilize opposition. Even moderate and discreet clergy might be persuaded that a government agency regulating charity was an invasion of the church's jurisdiction. But if Taschereau thought he could avoid confrontation by means of a *fait accompli* and a nine-month parliamentary recess, he miscalculated badly. The procedure only served to reinforce clerical suspicions, whereas committee hearings such as Sauvé recommended might have forced critics to state their alternatives and led the government to make minor changes whose value it would later concede anyway.

Henri Bourassa was the first to howl. This was so serious an invasion of the church's jurisdiction, he wrote, that it destroyed the existing equilibrium between civil and religious authority. To "secularize" charity in this way would be to deny the church one of its basic social functions, and provide a devastating precedent to anticlericals and atheists bent on a systematic erosion of religious authority. It would also deny the fundamental Catholic precept that private responsibility for charity was itself morally ad socially necessary, quite apart from the welfare of the recipients. On the practical level, if a provincial agency were to supervise charitable institutions operated by religious congregations, it would be usurping diocesan and ordinal authority – the internal discipline of the church. Moreover, the Bureau of Public Charities would almost inevitably become subject to the same partisan and personal chicanery which pervaded other state bureaucracies, affronting the dignity of religious institutions and the moral quality of charity itself. *L'Action catho-*

*lique* offered a similar analysis, although its writers could not match Bourassa's paranoid imaginings: legalized midnight harassment of religious orders by anticlerical government inspectors, seduction of the politically naïve Mother Superior by the smooth-talking "Môssieu L'Etat" with his promise of great riches, and so on. *L'Action catholique* could do no better than a pseudohistorical essay by Mgr L.-A. Pâquet on "les trois étapes de l'anti-cléricalisme."[21]

Although Taschereau considered these exaggerations foolish if not mischievous, he also recognized that there were legitimate fears to be allayed. He himself sincerely believed in the virtues of private charity and in preserving the social relevance of the church, and no doubt shuddered when David declared that charity had become a "scientific" and "technical" matter in the modern age.[22] Taschereau knew that David was referring only to the need for more efficient and rationalized administration of public assistance, but it sounded like a denial of the moral and religious aspect. Tachereau set out to make it clear that the Public Charities Act was intended to save, not destroy, the traditional welfare structure. "See for yourself all the frightful misery there is to relieve and tell me if the government does not have a supreme duty to come to the aid of our institutions so that they can accomplish their task." Tacitly conceding the validity of qualms about prevailing political and administrative practices in Quebec, he promised that only men of "high moral standing" would be appointed to the bureau. Finally, he denied that the bureau would use its powers of inspection to interfere with the operation of religious institutions. These provisions existed only because the government was constitutionally obliged to oversee the expenditure of public funds.[23] (*L'Action catholique* considered this a gratuitous insult to the church, but Taschereau genuinely feared that if the government failed to discharge its responsibility, it would reinforce the myth that French Canada was literally "priest-ridden." As he later reminded Mgr P.-E. Roy, "we live in a heterogeneous country. There are sensitivities we must live with and opinions we cannot ignore.")[24]

Realizing that the new law did raise serious and substantive issues in church-state relations, everyone involved acted as discreetly as possible during the remainder of 1921. Cardinal Bégin appointed a committee of bishops to study the act and formulate possible alternatives, but also agreed that, pending future amendments, Fitzpatrick should grant royal assent and allow the bureau to begin operation. The lieutenant-governor also tried to dispel the fears of Bourassa, with whom he had always managed to remain on speaking terms. Athanase David consulted unofficially with Mgr F.-X. Ross, a bishop known to favour the act at least in principle.[25] Although Taschereau was annoyed by Mgr Pâquet's treatise (republished in book form after its serialized appearance in *L'Action catholique*), he restrained his public utterances and contented himself with collecting written testimonials from the directors of religious institutions assisted by the bureau. Unfortunately, this truce was not able to survive another session of the legislature; in 1922 what began as a reasoned debate degenerated into a demeaning quarrel between the leader of the government and members of the Quebec hierarchy.

On 11 January the bishops confidentially but formally requested that Taschereau reconsider the Public Charities Act. While granting the innocence of government intentions, they insisted that the law would inhibit the "wondrous" daily achievements of private charity. Could the government not aid this work in a less obtrusive, more clearly subordinate manner? Could it not at least require religious institutions to obtain ecclesiastical permission before registering with the Bureau of Public Charities, thereby acknowledging the authority and jurisdiction of the church? To this letter Mgr P.-E. Roy, coadjutor of the Archdiocese of Quebec, appended an alternative draft bill which would create a body analogous to the Council of Public Instruction – politically independent and heavily influenced by the church. Taschereau mulled over the request, consulted the cabinet, and asked for a legal opinion on the draft bill. Then he issued a polite but stiff reply, protesting the bishops' implicit assumption that the government could not be trusted. Political life would become "impossible" if the government legislated without regard to non-Catholic sensitivities, whereas the existing law did not violate any (Catholic) principles and so far had furthered, not hindered, the work of private institutions. There was always room for improvement, of course, but the government would not contemplate any fundamental change in the new system. If the bishops could not accept it, Taschereau was "ready to ask my colleagues to repeal it, letting responsibility for the misery which would result fall upon the critics of this law." Finally, although he welcomed further discussion with the clergy, Taschereau confessed his annoyance with the church's approach to the problem. Why had religious authorities not raised their objections when consulted prior to first reading of the Public Charities Act? And what constructive purpose could possibly be served by Mgr Pâquet's articles, which accused the government of "paganism" and forced ministerial papers to respond?[26]

The substance of the bishops' letter quickly became an open secret in political and journalistic circles. Sauvé wanted the document tabled, in order to counteract the letters of gratitude from charitable

institutions which Taschereau was using to imply ecclesiastical
support for the act. Mgr Roy reaffirmed that the communication
had been private, and Taschereau could therefore refuse to table it.[27]
But by now Sauvé sensed the hardening of positions which was
occurring on both sides, and concluded that he could attack Taschereau's inflexibility while leaving outright condemnation of the act
to the Catholic press. That was his theme throughout the summer,
and by the time the legislature was recalled for a fall session, it
began to pay dividends. Clearly Taschereau could and should have
been far more conciliatory, for example,. by acceding immediately
to the bishop's request for an amendment protecing diocesan authority. Obviously the hierarchy was deeply divided over the basic
principle, and such an amendment would, by removing a legitimate
grievance, strengthen the position of those bishops who were sympathetic. Whether genuinely offended or just stubbornly determined
to establish his authority, Taschereau was helping to nourish and
prolong the very sort of controversy he had hoped to avoid as premier.

The Quebec Public Health Act of 1922 was a good deal less
controversial than the social legislation of 1921, but it was certainly
no less significant. David was a determined crusader against infant
mortality, of which the rate had climbed to nearly 20 per cent in
Montreal in 1919, and the epidemics which were practically com-
monplace among all age groups throughout the province. Quebec's
existing provincial health agency, the Council of Hygiene, fully
appreciated the problems and had begun planning an assault on
tuberculosis and infant disease. And under Metropolitan Commission
Chairman Décary's personal leadership, the Montreal Board of Health
had become considerably more proficient in recent years. But neither
body had sufficient legislative authority or resources to overcome
the immediate crisis, much less undertake the ambitious campaign
of health education, disease prevention, and medical research which
David envisaged. The new act therefore created a powerful new
agency, the Provincial Bureau of Health, whose director acquired
the rank of deputy minister in the Provincial Secretary's Department.
In the establishment and enforcement of sanitary regulations, the
bureau enjoyed much wider jurisdiction than the old council. It also
obtained the budget and staff to operate six specialized branches:
inspection, sanitary engineering, laboratories, tuberculosis, child
welfare, and venereal disease. Perhaps as important as the text of
the law was the identity of the first director, the determined and
energetic Dr Alphonse Lessard. Thanks to Lessard's political and
administrative skills as well as his medical knowledge, Quebec's
public health system improved dramatically during the 1920s.[28]

At the same session, David announced an impressive list of educational measures, beginning with a thorough restructuring of the primary school system. On the basis of a plan designed by the Catholic Committee, the existing three-tier program (four years "primary," two years "model," and two years "academy") was replaced by a six-year "primary-elementary" stage followed by two years of "primary-complementary" schooling. This change was designed to simplify administration and eliminate the first natural plateau, at which many parents felt their children had acquired sufficient education. This temptation had been especially strong in rural areas, because the model school was usually much further away than the primary school. At the same time, curricula became much more flexible than previously. Optional subjects could be taught in the primary schools according to local preference or needs, student aptitude, or the interests of the teacher. The complementary schools would offer four distinct vocational streams: commercial, industrial, agricultural, and (for girls) domestic. To help them institute the new program, both the Catholic and Protestant committees and the superintendent of public instruction received greater authority over local schools. The government also renewed its commitment to expand and upgrade teacher training, tied its financial support for independent commercial academies to observance of the new curriculum, and began to rationalize its own rapidly growing system of secondary technical and agricultural schools. The last process would culminate in the creation of a central administrative body, the Corporation des écoles techniques, in 1926.

David also celebrated the opening of schools of fine arts at Quebec and Montreal, announced a substantial increase in provincial support for the financially besieged *collèges classiques*, gave further attention to the Ecole des hautes études commerciales (still a pet provincial project despite its nominal affiliation with the Université de Montréal) and finally established provincial awards and European scholarships for writers and artists. While modestly declining to name the prizes after himself, he was persuaded to commemorate the literary exploits of his father. Hence Quebec's Prix David. Apparently some colleagues were sceptical regarding David's campaign to promote an artistic renaissance. "Christ!" Perron thundered in cabinet, "how many votes will this get us?" But Taschereau defended his provincial secretary, winning David's undying gratitude.[29]

David's announcements did not confirm the worst fears of the religious authorities with respect to education. The reorganization of the elementary school curriculum came from within the existing system, the promised financial support for improved teacher training did not imply any expansion of the state's role, and the creation of new secondary institutions outside religious control seemed to be proceeding on an ad hoc basis. With the compulsory education debate quieting down, politicians were not directly involved in such ideological controversies as the one over the teaching of English in elementary schools (although Taschereau and David declared themselves strongly in favour of bilingualism for French Canadians).[30] Vague misgivings about the continued political independence of the classical colleges were expressed only in the context of general warnings about "statism." On the other hand, it is fair to say that the Taschereau government had not yet addressed some of the more politically sensitive problems, especially the financial plight of local school boards, the status of Jewish students attending Protestant schools, and the pressure from Montreal reformers for the extension of French-Canadian public education beyond the eighth grade. Along with the need to coordinate the growing network of vocational schools, each of these issues contained some danger for the principle of denominational education and for the continued preeminence of the Council of Public Instruction. Taschereau and David would be forced to tackle these problems during their second term in office.

As premier, Taschereau was naturally invited to address a wide variety of audiences and expected to take a position on virtually every public issue or event. This remained true even after the federal election of 1921, which returned the Liberals to power and so placed other French-Canadian leaders, Gouin and Ernest Lapointe chief among them, in positions of authority. In addition to defending his government's legislation, Taschereau used these opportunities to maintain his reputation for candor. Referring to the financial obligations of both municipalities and individuals, he affirmed the absolute inviolability of contracts in Quebec. Governments must possess the "backbone and nerve" to resist momentary and unwise popular demands. English-Canadian schemes to standardize civil law, education, and other facets of culture were inimical to French-Canadian survival and hence totally unacceptable to Quebec. Appeals to the Imperial Privy Council must be retained in constitutional matters, for "the Canadian Confederation is a compromise ... [and] when so many conflicts of a racial, religious and ethical nature are liable to arise, have we not all a greater sense of security from the fact that the decisions to be rendered will come from ... men remote from our local strifes [sic] and disputes, unprejudiced by their surroundings?"[31] Disputing the claims of both radical farm groups which decried the Canadian tariff and Quebec traditionalists who charged that industrial development contributed to rural depopulation, Taschereau insisted that the interests of industry and agriculture were interdependent.[32] Taschereau hurled two challenges at young members of the traditional French-Canadian elite, calling for a more positive attitude toward careers in business and industry as an alternative to overcrowded and stagnating professions and inviting them to test their ideas in daily political battle instead of damning politics from the sidelines and leaving public life to career politicians.[33]

Hoping to prevent conflict with the church from spreading beyond the Public Charities dispute, Taschereau also seized opportunities to proclaim his devotion to traditional French-Canadian values. The Public Charities Act itself, he argued, would preserve the moral and religious basis of charity.[34] When the issue of women's suffrage arose, Taschereau privately declared it a complex question worthy of free discussion but in public emphasized his own implacable opposition.[35] Quebec's Catholic clergy had always opposed the suffragette movement, arguing that the "emancipation" of women would serve only to destroy the traditional bulwark of French-Canadian survival, the family. Until recently the invocation of both religious authority and national loyalty had effectively discouraged French Canadians of either sex from joining what was a strongly Protestant movement in Montreal. Not surprisingly, when bright and energetic young women like Mme Thérèse Casgrain finally did organize a French-Canadian branch and begin agitating, many clergy felt it was a blow to their own influence and yet another sign of the penetration of Protestant or materialist ideology into their society. Ignoring less sinister explanations of the phenomenon (such as the incongruity of women voting federally but not provincially), the church counterattacked: a pastoral letter from Cardinal Bégin, pontifical reinforcement of their position, a well-orchestrated series of resolutions and petitions by French-Canadian women's organizations, and finally a direct appeal to Taschereau.[36] By the time a suffragette delegation appeared in support of a private member's bill in 1922, Taschereau had already characterized the movement as "alien" to French Canada during a speech to the federation of St Jean Baptiste societies.[37] Now he reiterated this opinion and challenged the representativeness of the delegation. The bill was quickly defeated, and the French-Canadian feminists did not appeal again for four years. On this issue the clergy would have little cause for complaint for the remainder of Taschereau's career.[38]

A strike by the International Typographical Workers' Union in 1922 gave Taschereau another opportunity to placate clerical opinion.

Taschereau and his colleagues had been distinctly nervous about the postwar rise of the Catholic labour movement. Although endorsed in principle by Archbishop Bégin and by Henri Bourassa early in the century, Catholic labour had barely existed as an organizational force prior to the war. Now suddenly it was a province-wide organization, the Confédération des travailleurs catholiques du Canada, still supported by the church but also feeding upon the nationalistic sentiments of French-Canadian workers. Contrary to the image portrayed by later partisans of nonconfessional unionism, its leaders were far from pawns in a conspiracy among church, state, and business. And some of their fire had already been directed against the Taschereau government, notably a scathing attack on Caron delivered by Abbé Maxime Fortin in 1920. In contrast, Taschereau's experience in the Labour portfolio had placed him on fairly good terms with orthodox union leaders like Tom Moore, J.T. Foster, and Gustave Francq, the last a known Freemason. Moreover, the Liberals had absorbed three Labour deputies elected in 1919 into their caucus and promoted one to cabinet rank.

Early in February 1922, the ITWU struck for higher wages and shorter hours, forcing cancellation of a legislative sitting because necessary documents could not be printed. When Taschereau learned that the strike had been called by union leaders in Indianapolis without the knowledge of Canadian officials, he and Galipeault berated international unionism as a menace to Quebec's industrial development. "With national unions the government is prepared to negotiate and deal at any time," Taschereau promised. "International unions, on the other hand, should be allowed no power in Canada, and there will be no aid given by the government to assist men to achieve their ends if their demands are presented on the instigation of foreigners."[39] Strictly speaking, this was not an endorsement of confessional unionism over "neutral" labour organizations, and indeed Taschereau carefully avoided criticizing leaders of the Trades and Labour Congress of Canada. (In fact, one of the labour deputies belonged to the ITWU!) But he made a great show of temporarily turning over government printing work to L'Action sociale, a CTCC shop, and since there were very few independent Canadian unions left in Quebec at this time, his statements could certainly be interpreted as a positive gesture toward the church-sponsored unions. This was wisely followed by the inclusion of a Catholic labour representative on the commission examining workman's compensation.

By far the most celebrated act of deference to religious authority occurred in late April 1922, when Taschereau spoke to the Empire and Women's Canadian clubs in Toronto. In both addresses he emphasized the role of traditional classes, especially the farmers and the seigneurial elite, in preserving French Canada's distinct heritage. But he distinguished between traditional and retrograde, and in this connection challenged the image of Quebec as "priest-ridden." If that term referred to the active concern of a clergy for its people, then Quebec was indeed "priest-ridden." Quoting Parkman (but ignoring the historian's ultimately negative judgment of clerical influence), he reminded his listeners that the church had played a critical role in the birth and survival of New France. In 1776 and 1812, it was thanks to the clergy that Canada remained under the British flag. Most importantly, the continuing social influence of the clergy was proving a decided asset to French Canada in the modern age: less crime than in Ontario, a "sensible" working class which respected law and property, hardy colonists inspired and led by curés, profound social and religious harmony in Quebec. "If all that is a result of our being 'priest-ridden', we willingly plead guilty. And I need only add one point about the life of our people: it is a life of perfect independence and true liberty, free of any influences able to curtail our human dignity." Later he praised the philosophy and personnel of the church for the high quality of education which French Canadians received.[40]

Altogether the Toronto speeches were a highly exaggerated rhetorical exercise. Taschereau honestly subscribed to the version of French-Canadian history he was articulating, sincerely welcomed the social peace and ideological stability which attended Quebec's industrial revolution, and never hesitated to give religious influence credit for much of that stability. But seldom did he so minimize his enthusiasm for industrial development itself, so completely disguise his impatience with certain attitudes and customs still prevalent in French Canada, or imply such complete satisfaction with the institutional performance of the church. Undoubtedly part of the explanation for this aberration lies in the audience: Taschereau considered himself a missionary in Toronto, seeking to persuade English Canadians that national unity depended upon mutual respect between two different cultures. There were still, he knew, English Canadians who sincerely believed that unity could and should be achieved by having French Canadians adopt English Canadian values. It is obvious, however, that the speeches were also designed for home consumption – with or without a conscious memory of Taschereau's last Toronto speech in 1909! Almost immediately, *Le Canada* published a translation in pamphlet form, and the approving remarks of English papers all across the country were quoted in the Quebec Liberal press.[41]

The performance had its desired effect on religious opinion. *La Semaine religieuse* of Montreal termed his performance "one of the grand gestures of our recent history ... We do not customarily proclaim the merits and glories of politicians in our pages, no matter how worthy they may be. In all sincerity, we believe we are justified in making an exception this time." *L'Action catholique* proclaimed its favourite target to be "living proof of the value of the culture transmitted to successive generations behind the old walls of our colleges." Similar effusions were privately communicated by prominent members of the clergy.[42]

Unfortunately, most of Taschereau's efforts to establish the image of a prudent statesman were undone by his overreaction to a case of yellow journalism which arose later in 1922. This episode originated in the summer of 1920 when a young woman named Blanche Garneau was found raped and murdered in Victoria Park, Quebec City. No suspects were immediately apprehended, although two men were tried and acquitted in 1921 when one of them repudiated a confession in the witness box. Meanwhile malicious gossip began to circulate in the capital that members of prominent families were actually responsible, and that a cover-up had consequently been engineered by the Attorney General's Department. One rumour mentioned the sons of Liberal deputies Martin Madden and Joseph Paquette. Another accused Taschereau's son Robert, inspiring an anonymous pamphlet which, in the guise of fiction, contended that Garneau had been ritually slain by a sadistic group of young well-to-do's known as the Vampire Club. *La Non-Vengeance* concluded with an account of how the murderers' parents, prominent judges and politicians, had conspired to stifle police investigations.

The opportunity to exploit class prejudice and the universal dislike of Charles Lanctôt proved a greater temptation than Armand Lavergne could resist. During the 1921 federal election campaign, he actually accused Taschereau of interfering with the investigation. When *Le Devoir* printed this accusation, Taschereau successfully sued the paper for libel. There the matter could have rested except that on 27 October 1922, a weekly Montreal scandal sheet called *The Axe* offered $5,000 for the identity of the murderers. It also cited rumours concerning unnamed members of the legislature and high officials, and concluded by demanding that the lieutenant-governor launch a Royal Commission to investigate the murder and alleged cover-up. *The Axe's* editor was John H. Roberts, a fanatical prohibitionist furious with Taschereau's liquor legislation. In April, Léonide Perron had reported to Sir Lomer Gouin, now federal minister of justice, that Roberts regularly attempted to blackmail politicians and financiers, and asked if he could be deported as an undesirable (American) alien.[43] Roberts was also suspected by Taschereau of having been involved in the publication of *La Non-Vengeance*.[44] Hauling Roberts before the bar of the legislature on a Speaker's warrant, Taschereau demanded that he name the legislators and officials guilty of wrongdoing. On the advice of counsel, Armand Lavergne (who else?), Roberts refused. Asserting that this refusal placed all members of the legislature under suspicion, Taschereau introduced a bill sentencing Roberts to a year in prison. (Under existing laws, such an offender could be detained only until the end of the session.) The motion was quickly carried despite protests by Sauvé and by Thomas Chapais, one of two Conservatives left in the Legislative Council.

It would be an exaggeration to say that, once jailed, this contemptible "journalist" became a martyr. But Taschereau instead of Roberts became the object of criticism for usurping judicial functions and for administering justice undivorced from the passions. Sensing this shift in opinion, Sauvé not only condemned the procedure in harsh terms but endorsed Roberts's demand for a Royal Commission. When Taschereau eventually agreed to such an inquiry, Sauvé implied that the terms of reference were designed to perpetuate the obstruction of justice. Lavergne now abandoned all inhibitions, calling upon French Canadians to shake off their "excessive respect for authority" and rise up against tyranny. At the commission hearings, he gleefully summoned Taschereau and badgered him with irrelevancies and insinuations for an entire day. By now (20 December) Taschereau had regained his political senses, and did not let Lavergne provoke him. He had already agreed to let the commission hear evidence concerning the murder itself, not just the alleged obstruction of justice. And he had offered to pay the cost of a challenge to the constitutionality of the Roberts bill. But the damage was done: government tyranny and the need for stronger opposition became central themes in the election campaign which soon followed.[45]

The 1921 federal election had several important consequences in provincial politics. Naturally the Liberal victory changed the relationship between Taschereau and the federal government. It also forced a major cabinet change on Taschereau, because Walter Mitchell was persuaded by Montreal business interests to enter Parliament. Finally, the routing of the Union government signalled a possible restoration of serious political competition at the provincial level. With the external threat eliminated, French-Canadian voters were more likely to divide over "domestic" issues. This was doubly true in the context of an economic crisis and a nation-wide antigovernment trend. And with Quebec Conservatives in complete disarray with respect to federal politics, provincial leader Sauvé had a chance to build his own organization and attract much stronger candidates than the party had been able to field in many years.

It never occurred to Taschereau to regret sharing the political leadership of French Canada with Liberal colleagues in Ottawa. What mattered was to defeat, preferably humiliate, Arthur Meighen. "Quebec's day of revenge has arrived," he declared at the outset of the campaign, although he took a less active role in the anti-Meighen orgy than he would in two subsequent federal elections.[46] Meighen's biographer justly argues that the extreme language and distortions employed by Quebec Liberals to vilify Meighen served party interests more than they did the cause of national unity.[47] But it would be wrong to assume that Taschereau and others were just being cynical opportunists. Few had gone as far as Taschereau in respecting the aspirations of Canadian imperialists and ignoring the racial overtones of their movement. All, however, felt genuinely injured and betrayed after enduring *nationaliste* ridicule for nearly a decade, and measured against the capricious slandering of Laurier in 1917, any rhetorical excess seemed justified. Meighen's wartime role made him a legitimate as well as convenient target for their wrath, and his refusal even now to acknowledge and apologize for past insults and injustices merely strengthened their desire for revenge. Judging by his major campaign speech in Quebec City, Meighen appeared to believe that reconciliation would occur when French Canadians realized that neither he personally nor the Union government had ever caused them injury.[48]

The advent of the King government affected more the style than the substance of federal-provincial relations. There would still be conflicts, of course, and some forceful public statements would be required. In King's own presence, for example, Taschereau insisted that Ottawa join Quebec in opposing any scheme for international development of the St Lawrence River.[49] But as a general rule, mutual partisan interests dictated public harmony, and mutual confidence and familiarity made cooperation easier. Thus great celebration attended the final transfer of Gulf fisheries to provincial jurisdiction, and no one bothered to mention that the agreement had been largely concluded under the previous federal regime.[50] Taschereau and Gouin together helped orchestrate the campaign for an export embargo on

Canadian pulpwood, even though neither really favoured such a measure. (Taschereau correctly believed that cheaper power, labour, and delivery costs would soon induce American newsprint manufacturers to locate in Quebec anyway, and in the meantime an embargo would hurt Canadian woodlot owners and forest workers. The campaign was just a ploy to have an American tariff against Canadian pulpwood lifted, and when Taschereau finally came out against the embargo, Canadian newsprint manufacturers were dumbfounded.)[51] With difficulty, Taschereau stayed clear of the rivalry between Gouin and Lapointe, despite personal loyalty to the former and fear that the latter might be too accommodating toward low-tariff pressure from the West. (Mitchell angrily resigned his seat in protest against tariff reductions in the 1924 budget) Finally, Taschereau and Perrault hid their very real frustration with Charles Stewart, the federal minister of immigration, from public notice. Stewart refused aid to a provincial colonization scheme designed to repatriate French Canadians from New England and prevent still more farmers from emigrating. Taschereau finally wrote to King in confidence, warning of dire political consequences for the Liberals at both levels of government if this and other irritants were not removed.[52]

Taschereau had just completed a minor cabinet change when Mitchell resigned as provincial treasurer. Tessier and Séguin had retired, Perron had become minister of roads, and two ministers without portfolio had been appointed as token class representatives: Aurèle Lacombe for labour and Emile Moreau for the colonists. Moreau became a minor power through his responsibility for party oganization and patronage in the Lake St John region,[53] but Lacombe, the deputy who was compromised in the typographical workers' strike, did not survive the next provincial election. Replacing Mitchell was a somewhat delicate matter. Henry Miles, a member of the legislature and former president of the Montreal Board of Trade, seemed a logical choice but in fact was too closely identified with particular business enterprises (notably the National Hydroelectric Company) to inherit Mitchell's reputation for neutrality. Besides, at sixty-four he was not the sort of long-term prospect Taschereau preferred. On the other hand, Taschereau regarded the custom of having an English treasurer as a symbol of good will, not subservience or financial incompetence on the part of French Canadians, and he was loathe to violate it.[54] So, with no qualified Montrealer available to serve, he turned to an Eastern Townships entrepreneur and long-time acquaintance, Jacob Nicol. Nicol was in fact a 45-year-old French Canadian whose parents had been converted to Protestantism. But he moved with such ease among English and French Canadians of

Sherbrooke that both groups considered him one of their own. After articling with Taschereau and working briefly as the assistant to a former provincial treasurer, Nicol had become successful in business and a bulwark of Liberal party organization in the Townships. With a record of public service to Protestant education and to the Sherbrooke Board of Trade as well, he was more than an adequate replacement for Mitchell as treasurer and Protestant spokesman. Perron had to become the regional chief for Montreal, but Nicol was also a strong regional representative for the Townships. In many ways he resembled Taschereau. Both were given to brevity and precision despite the norms of Quebec political oratory, and spoke of running government like a business. Their political collaboration and friendship lasted well beyond Nicol's eight-year term as treasurer.[55]

The revival of provincial Conservative fortunes in the early 1920s was a credit to the determination of Arthur Sauvé. Chosen party leader virtually by default in 1919, he was confronted in the legislature by the greatest Liberal majority ever. Because of conscription, the Union government, and the railway nationalization issue, party organization was a complete shambles. Sauvé set out to take advantage of these conditions. He would build an entirely separate provincial organization, not only to escape the stigma of conscription but also to be free of all the factionalism and intrigue which was liable to plague the federal organization indefinitely. This would allow him to recruit prestigious Conservative politicians who knew there was no future in the federal arena. He hoped that it would also permit him to tap various sources of discontent within society – to make his party the vehicle of protest against general economic conditions as well as a focal point for groups with particular grievances. Labour and agrarian unrest were being politicized in many parts of Canada, and in Montreal there was a great deal of opposition to the Administrative Commission imposed by the province. The cry of municipal autonomy had already gone up, and there were many Liberals among the disaffected local politicians.

Sauvé's strategy and efforts began to look highly successful following the federal election, in which the Liberals captured all sixty-five Quebec seats. His energetic performance in the legislature from January to March of 1922, supported by a pathetic caucus of four nonentities, drew considerable admiration. In May his leadership and the principle of separate provincial organization were endorsed by a convention of delegates from eighty-one of the eighty-five constituencies. During the summer he and E.-L. Patenaude, the first notable refugee from federal politics, held a number of successful rallies. By fall he was able to appoint a full-time provincial organizer, and potential candidates were appearing in constituencies which the Conservatives had not even contested in recent elections.[56]

Ironically, Taschereau took a certain amount of comfort from these developments. This was not because of any great affection for Sauvé, who had called him a traitor during the naval debate. Nor was it because he regarded Sauvé as a weak opponent – legend has it that Gouin had "protected" Sauvé's riding, much as Taschereau sup-posedly discouraged Liberals in Three Rivers from defeating Maurice Duplessis in 1931 because the latter was a "gentleman" compared to his rival, Camillien Houde.[57] Rather, it was because Taschereau preferred an orthodox party opposition to organizations which appealed to class, ethnic, or other interests and prejudices and threatened social order and stability with their radical ideas. Such organizations were less likely to take root in the presence of a credible opposition party open to all segments of society. All this was more than a theoretical consideration. Several individual labour candidates, both Catholic and nonconfessional, had run strong campaigns in 1919. Catholic Action organizations had a reputation for hostility to the Liberal party, a reputation confirmed in Taschereau's mind by Abbé Fortin's performance in 1920. Fortin had proposed a temporary suspension of Canadian agricultural exports until such time as food prices fell back into line with working-class incomes. Accusing the priest of fomenting class division and of disparaging the noble French-Canadian farmer, Caron summoned him before the legislature's agriculture committee. Fortin refused to be intim-idated by Caron's mob of rural deputies, and lashed both his accuser and the rest of the government for their smug indifference to working-class hardship. This attack did not endear him to the former minister of labour.[58] In the realm of agrarian protest, an organization called the Fermiers unis de Québec had appeared in 1919, obviously inspired by the United Farmers' election victory in Ontario. Just after Taschereau became premier farmer candidates won two by-elections from official Liberals, and in Gouin's vacated constituency of Portneuf, Liberal organizers saved face by endorsing the farmer candidate.[59] The Fermiers unis suffered a loss of credibility during the 1921 federal election by running some disguised Conservatives, but Caron was convinced that a core of farm leaders were still committed to direct political action.

Naturally Sauvé's organizational successes impelled the Liberals to mend their political fences. In 1922 Perron virtually followed Sauvé around the province, promising new roads wherever he thought the opposition was making headway. Meanwhile, Caron worked to head off organized farm protest, persuading the Fermiers unis to abstain from direct political action, luring the three largest co-operative societies into a federation whose activities he could readily control, and reassuring Caisse Populaire leaders (who included many clergy) that the government would not usurp their role as the primary source of farm credit.[60] Things were more difficult in the cities, where the provincial government could do little to counteract rising unemployment and was meeting frustration on other issues as well. The Liquor Act was widely unpopular because the government monopoly was blamed for higher prices. Taschereau gave counter-arguments – the quality was higher and more dependable, the federal excise tax was to blame, smuggling had stopped and tourists were being drawn to Quebec, numerous states and provinces were copying Quebec's splendid system as they prepared to abandon prohibition[61] – but in vain. Worse still, while Sauvé denounced the Liquor Commission as a new source of Liberal patronage, Liberal organizers were complaining bitterly at the lack of "cooperation" they received from the chairman, Georges Simard. Meanwhile, Nicol, who had also assumed Mitchell's responsibility for Municipal Affairs, was getting nowhere with the problem of Montreal's civic administration.

Taschereau and Mitchell had hoped to defuse criticism of the Décary Commission by holding a referendum on the form which a new autonomous regime would take. Montreal ratepayers would choose between a highly centralized regime favoured by reformers and a virtual return to the ward system favoured by Mayor Médéric Martin and his cronies. Unfortunately for the reformers, a coalition of prominent businessmen, wealthy property-owners, and advocates of modern city planning, Martin's forces had won decisively on 16 May 1921. So when Nicol took office, the government was no closer to a formula for terminating the commission without restoring financial chaos and the neglect of serious problems in the city. The most immediate political danger, an open revolt by local Liberals, seemed to have been averted in 1922 when Martin accepted appointment to the Legislative Council. However, even this boomeranged when, as a councillor, Mayor Martin voted for a bill authorizing construction of a boulevard running the length of Montreal Island. This was a project recommended by the Décary Commission without consulting the municipalities which were to share the cost, and it therefore reignited the municipal autonomy issue. Patenaude took it up, and it became obvious that Martin had lost the ability to deliver Montreal votes.[62]

Against the background of a continuing economic crisis and Sauve's organizational progress, Taschereau properly regarded the fall 1922 legislative session as a political disaster. Lacking any attractive new bills (the Grande Décharge project was approved by order-in-council), the government had simply given Sauvé a platform to denounce the Liquor Board and stir the Public Charities controversy. Then came the Roberts affair, an opposition's dream in illustrating the danger of one-party domination. Not despite but because of this unhappy political situation, Taschereau and his colleagues decided to hold a surprise, midwinter election. Litle would be gained by waiting for spring or summer, a normal election period, and no Liberal government had ever taken the risk of waiting the legal maximum of five years. The advantage of an immediate vote was to preempt Conservative organizational work in the rural constituencies, which still dominated the membership of the legislature. Liberal incumbents were well known, and while formal constituency associations did not exist, most deputies had personal patronage networks which served for electioneering purposes. Challengers were usually unknown outside their local communities, and it was practically impossible for a candidate to traverse an entire county through the snow. Even where he could, few electors would know he was coming and fewer would risk frostbite to reach the site of his meeting. *Contradictoires* following Sunday mass might provide a few captive audiences, but even here the lack of local agents could spell disaster. A midwinter election did carry certain risks for the government: severe economic conditions might compound the problems of urban candidates, while Sauvé would inevitably charge (with considerable justification) that Taschereau was subverting the democratic process. Even if fully recognized, however, these dangers evidently seemed less significant than the advantage of striking before the Conservatives could launch a serious campaign in the countryside. The session was prorogued on 29 December, dissolution came twelve days later, and the election was called for 5 February.

Liberal organizers were certainly well prepared for the campaign. Taschereau's manifesto was published on 12 January as part of a lavish election handbook. Although booklets had been standard electoral fare since the late nineteenth century, this effort was unprecedented: 304 pages praising past performance, promising new initiatives, ridiculing Conservative proposals, rebutting anticipated criticisms, and quoting complimentary editorials in nonparty publications. For the first time, a substantial English edition was circulated. Examined closely, the party platform was actually quite devoid of new proposals. Taschereau merely promised to continue policies already in effect: financial aid to education at all levels, to colonization, and to private charity; a vigorous fight against infant mortality and tuberculosis; more provincial responsibility for road-building financed by revenue from the Liquor Commission; reduction of the provincial debt; forest conservation; and most importantly, the encouragement of further hydroelectric development. There were no specific commitments on the future of municipal government in Montreal, the creation of a permanent Workman's Compensation Commission, or farm loans, to cite three genuine issues of the day. In other words the government was running entirely on its record and personnel.[63]

However impressive the record may have looked on paper, the Liberals were quickly driven into a highly defensive public posture. Taschereau's oratorical style, still clipped and argumentative instead of flourishingly obfuscatory, merely accentuated the tendency. Only when expressing their indignation at Conservative scandal-mongering could government speakers excite the party faithful, and even this was a fundamentally defensive tactic. Taschereau's first major rally, held in the Liberal stronghold of Quebec East on 18 January, clearly indicated the direction of the campaign. The Quebec district seemed much safer for the government than Montreal. True, economic conditions and a strong Conservative candidate running with Catholic union support threatened the Liberal hold on working-class St Sauveur riding. In Quebec Centre, the Quebec Railway Light, Heat and Power Company was determined to oust Arthur Cannon, advocate of the rival Public Service Corporation. But there was no municipal autonomy question and, since Quebec City had until recently maintained prohibition under local option, no class of dispossessed liquor retailers. The closest thing to an issue was the King government's failure to appoint a Quebec City director to the Board of Canadian National Railways.[64] Moreover, the capital's two traditionally Conservative newspapers, the *Chronicle* and *L'Evéne-ment* were observing an attitude of highly benevolent neutrality vis-à-vis the government. Taschereau was a son of Quebec City, not loved but certainly respected for his demonstrated ability and trusted to defend the interests of the capital. The opening rally should therefore have been a spectacular success, but it was not.

Hecklers, who infiltrated the Salle Martineau despite precautions taken by Liberal organizers, listened patiently to the preliminary speakers like Ernest Lapointe and Adélard Turgeon. These were popular and effective orators, and in any case the hecklers did not want to be identified and expelled prematurely. They were waiting for Taschereau. Once introduced, he wisely ignored taunts concerning Blanche Garneau, trusting Turgeon's earlier tirade against such slander to hold the audience's sympathy. To the cry "we want cheap liquor," Taschereau replied, "It's obviously cheap enough for you now." Fairly effective for the moment, but there was little in his prepared speech to help Liberal partisans forget the hecklers. His excuse for the timing of the election – Sauvé had been claiming since 1920 that Taschereau lacked a mandate – was positively embarrassing. News that the Supreme Court had declared John Roberts's imprisonment legal was an equally unimpressive response to the charge of tyranny. As the *Toronto Telegram* correspondent reported with only slight exaggeration, even "this (mild) heckling of a Liberal Premier in Quebec East is regarded here as bordering on the sensational."[65]

This meeting notwithstanding, the Liberals thought they had a sound strategy for the Quebec district. They correctly assumed that as a Montrealer lacking orthodox newspaper support in the capital, Sauvé was not their real nemesis. The effective opposition were Taschereau's old friends the clerical nationalists. *L'Action catholique*, the only remaining critical voice, filtered the opposition campaign through its own interests and prejudices. Apparently the promise of its support induced Armand Lavergne to challenge Taschereau once again in Montmorency. After a ten-year respite, the *castors* seemed genuinely eager to do battle. As soon as the election was called, therefore, Taschereau and his colleagues launched a campaign to muffle *L'Action catholique*. Galipeault reactivated an old libel suit, claiming that the newspaper had destroyed the effect of its retraction by subsequent comments. Caron sued the publisher, L'Action sociale, on whose premises the weekly *L'Homme libre* was also printed. *L'Homme libre* was the organ of the anti-Cannon forces; knowing that Cannon was Taschereau's legal associate, it had begun attacking the entire government without too scrupulous a regard for personal reputations. When *L'Action catholique* accused the ministers of trying to intimidate the press (citing the Roberts case as further evidence), Caron privately asked Mgr Roy to intervene. Under the cover of religious and ecclesiastical authority, he complained, the editors of *L'Action catholique* conducted partisan and even personal vendettas. Referring to the Liquor and Public Charities controversies, *Le Soleil* denied *L'Action*'s right to question the collective religious fidelity of the government. Taschereau argued likewise in a public exchange of letters with Jules Dorion.[66]

Finally, with two weeks left in the campaign, Taschereau addressed a formal complaint to Cardinal Bégin. The immediate pretext was a Conservative party advertisement in *L'Action catholique*, barely designated as such, which declared that Quebec's liquor legislation "poisons and enslaves our race." But Taschereau confronted Bégin squarely with the broader issue. If religious authorities did not approve of the war being waged in their name against the government, then they must either control or repudiate the editors of *L'Action catholique*. If they did approve, "a conflict between them and us becomes inevitable, one which would be deeply regrettable from every point of view. Are we to witness ... a return to the violent conflicts of yesteryear? ... It will destroy one of my most cherished hopes [but] we are heading rapidly toward the formation of an anticlerical party in our province."[67] Forewarned about Taschereau's letter, *L'Action catholique* stopped carrying the objectionable advertisement "on its own initiative." Bégin praised this decision, and expressed his hope and confidence that the incident was now closed. But he also assured Taschereau that the hierarchy "wants neither war nor useless conflicts and will do everything possible to eliminate the causes which provoke them."[68] Apparently the cardinal was serious, so Taschereau had won a signal victory. Lavergne was publicly furious, Jules Dorion disappointed but obedient. Unfortunately Taschereau's letter reached the hands of Camillien Lockwell, founder of *L'Homme libre*, who accused the premier of intimidating Bégin. At Taschereau's request, the cardinal publicly denied that he had acted under duress.[69] Now Henri Bourassa pursued the matter in *Le Devoir*, citing disrespect for ecclesiastical authority as further evidence of government tyranny.

Meanwhile the Montreal situation had become nearly hopeless. Although Mayor Martin rallied to the cause, other Liberal municipal politicians supported Conservative candidates, accepted "opposition" nominations themselves, or launched independent campaigns. Patenaude challenged the mayor's prestige and influence far more effectively than Sauvé could ever have done personally. Patenaude first dared Martin to oppose him in Jacques Cartier, then lured him into an *assemblée contradictoire* and got much the better of him. The three Labour deputies also remained loyal and sought reelection, but Taschereau's threat to "break" international unions had destroyed their credibility completely: they were contemptuously labelled "the three sheep." As Perron had warned, the Liquor Commission was an electoral disaster. Prices had risen substantially, and no one cared whether a duty imposed by the Meighen government was primarily responsible. (Why had King not removed it?) The dispossessed retailers still wanted revenge, Simard refused to "cooperate" even temporarily with Liberal attempts to comfort the faithful, and all the while Sauvé continued to charge that commission profits were financing the Liberal campaign.[70]

The Liberals also faced a more critical press in Montreal. The *Star* and *Gazette*, both accustomed to supporting Gouin, leaned increasingly toward the Conservatives. Neither the business community nor the anglophone population confessed to any specific grievances against Taschereau, but he was less familiar to them than Gouin and had offended both liquor interests and outright prohibitionists. Gouin was even worried that some businessmen were mistaking Taschereau for a free spender, incredible as that seems. For its part, the Sauvé-Patenaude combination had a certain appeal. Anti-Meighen Tories respected their abstention from the 1921 federal election; the reliability of Patenaude and certain other Montreal candidates (Alfred Duranleau, for example) easily compensated for Sauvé's mildly nationalistic reputation; and the rebirth of conventional party competition would both serve the general public interest and remind the present administration of its commitment to "sound business government." As expected, *Le Devoir* also opposed the government, although for the first two weeks of the campaign it published the most balanced coverage of all French-language papers. It was apparently Taschereau's success in silencing *L'Action catholique* which provoked the direct intervention of Henri Bourassa. In a series of editorials beginning 24 January, he first argued that the government had simply become too powerful for anyone's good, including its own. Only a stronger opposition could check its autocratic tendencies and disturb the moral and intellectual slumber of its "mediocre" personnel.

Gradually, however, Bourassa's real preoccupation shone through. Both the Liquor and Public Charities legislation were inspired by the spirit of statism, the desire to impose direct authority over everything. To defend these measures on moral grounds, the good accomplished, was the road to socialism or even "soviétisme." In the case of liquor the argument was particularly insidious; no one would seek to justify arms sales to finance good provincial programs. Why then liquor, another destructive force? And how did Taschereau overcome resistance to his interference in the work of religious institutions, or answer sincere warnings about the "sabotage of our society"? With blackmail, lies, the gag, and finally the threat of religious warfare. The lesson, Bourassa concluded, was obvious. The public must protest this behaviour on 5 February, and elect an opposition strong enough to prevent it in future. Focusing on other issues, Bourassa's colleagues at *Le Devoir* reached a similar conclusion as election day approached and they gave Conservative arguments and rallies greater and greater coverage.

Perron, Irénée Vautrin, MLA, and Fernand Rinfret, MP, who were in charge of the Liberal campaign in Montreal, doubted whether Taschereau's presence there would help stem the antigovernment tide. In fact, it might be a positive danger, for a bad performance could have repercussions outside the city. For credibility's sake there had to be one major rally, but only after the most thorough preparations possible. Gouin, Mitchell, and other prominent Montrealers were recruited to share the platform with Taschereau and local candidates and ministers. Liberal partisans received tickets, so that infiltrators could be stopped at the door. For those who escaped the net, provincial police would be on hand to reinforce party bouncers. Despite these precautions, the meeting on 1 February justified the fears of the organizers. Forged tickets allowed adversaries to enter through a side door of the Monument National along with Liberals, filling the hall before the main doors could be opened to the public. In front of the building, "the public" had been gathering for two hours. By 8 P.M. 2,000 people had brought traffic on St Lawrence Boulevard to a standstill. The police riot squad was summoned in time for an announcement that there was no room inside for additional spectators. Despite the police, several hundred people piled into the stairways and corridors of the building, determined to make as much noise as possible throughout the evening. Taschereau, Gouin, Mitchell, and Perron arrived to find their special entrance padlocked against the mob; the whereabouts of the key being unknown, they had to wait while police smashed the lock.

Miraculously, the meeting began almost on time. Clement Munn, the candidate in Montreal-St Lawrence, spoke first but proved no match for the hecklers, whom police immediately began expelling. Taschereau was next, and fortunately rose to the occasion. Striding forward to the solid phalanx of Liberal partisans in the front rows, he exorted them to cheer more loudly, drowning out the catcalls from further back. After a few words, police broke up a fight at the back of the hall and removed the combatants. When he could be heard again, Taschereau raised the controversial issues before hecklers could: Montreal's autonomy, the Liquor Commission, the Public Charities Act, Perron's roadbuilding (under fire for partisan administration). With each salvo a chorus of boos went up, and Taschereau again urged his supporters to drown them in cheers. Then he stood with arms folded, often smiling, waiting for the din to subside.

Next he went after Bourassa, charging that the hecklers were all students sent by *Le Devoir* to break up this meeting. Most ungrateful, these university students, for the government's generous university grants and bursaries. Also immune to the civilizing effect of higher education. That provoked the biggest uproar of all, accompanied by more forcible ejections. But it seemed to exhaust the remaining hecklers, for Taschereau was able to recite his catalogue of Liberal accomplishments and even deny intimidating Cardinal Bégin without serious interruption. Subsequent speakers also enjoyed clear sailing.[71] By retaining his composure, Taschereau had admittedly not transformed the meeting into a triumph for the government. The determination of so many people to disrupt it reflected real popular hostility, and no one took seriously Vautrin's claim that they were all hired. When Sauvé received only cheers and applause from an equally large crowd the following night, the contrast did not escape anyone. But at least Taschereau had prevented a complete debacle, reassuring Liberal partisans that their leader was a capable political warrior who would rebound from inevitable election reverses in Montreal.

Taschereau then returned to Quebec for a final rally, taking heart from the fact that it was uneventful. On election night there were few real surprises, except possibly the size of the margins by which government candidates lost thirteen of the fifteen Montreal seats. Only the ethnic enclaves of St Louis (Jewish) and St Anne (Irish) voted Liberal. The heavily Jewish St Lawrence constituency might also have done so, had a dissident faction not split the government vote. No other race was close, whether the riding was French or English, working or middle class. Obviously, more had been involved than the influence of Bourassa, whom the Liberal press tried to pretend was the real enemy during the last days of the campaign. Outside Montreal the picture was much brighter, although Taschereau was personally disappointed to learn that the vendetta against Arthur Cannon in Quebec Centre had narrowly succeeded. Neighbouring St Sauveur fell to the Catholic Labour candidate, but otherwise the Quebec district remained solid. Only one seat east of the capital, Temiscouata, went to the Conservatives. Elsewhere the opposition won four seats, retaining Deux Montagnes and Joliette, regaining the swing constituency of Beauharnois, and capitalizing on labour discontent in Sherbrooke. The final count, including eight Liberal acclamations and deferred elections not seriously contested, was sixty-four to twenty-one.

Naturally Conservatives reacted by exaggerating their achievement. Sauvé declared that he would "not permit" Taschereau to resign until Conservatives could "have some fun" with him in the legislature. The *Gazette*, in equally blithe disregard of the government's three-to-one parliamentary majority, announced that Taschereau could not long remain in power without the support of Montreal.

For their part, Liberal papers offered predictable rationalizations. Urban losses were due to slander and appeals to prejudice; the "eternal good sense" of rural voters (not patronage or the timing of the election) had stemmed the tide. Taschereau didn't take any of this too seriously. He publicly regretted that Montreal would not be well represented in the government, but promised fair treatment nevertheless.[72] And he knew that in reality the Montreal losses were not crippling. Lacombe was the only minister defeated, for Montrealers David and Mercier had been reelected in outlying rural constituencies and Perron had never abandoned the security of the Legislative Council. Besides, there were plenty of channels through which the government maintained contact with Montreal; Taschereau himself spent one day a week in provincial offices there.

Generally, the government could be satisfied with having survived, with a popular vote of about 55 per cent, postwar discontents which toppled almost every other regime in Canada. The Conservatives had gained ground without articulating any coherent challenge to Liberal philosophy or policies. In four more years the economic crisis would be long forgotten, time would prove the wisdom of controversial legislation and recent embarrassments would meet the fate of all partisan commotions. Taschereau would again focus political life on what he considered its proper concern, material progress.[73]

## CHAPTER FIVE

# The Vindication of Liberal Policy

In accordance with his analysis of the election result, Taschereau decided to let the dust settle for as long as he could. Inevitably there were echoes of the campaign in subsequent months: the cabinet's election post-mortem featured violent denunciations of Simard, who eventually agreed to resign from the Liquor Commission in favour of a more cooperative party loyalist; Roberts was released from jail in mid-April on a promise of good behaviour, and promptly resumed his accusations; certain campaign pledges, including the financing of a provincial highway system, were honoured or confirmed.[1] But much to Sauvé's frustration, Taschereau waited almost as long as he was constitutionally permitted before calling the legislature into session. It finally opened on 17 December, just in time for a Christmas recess. Obviously the strategy was to deny the opposition a platform until the government had prepared important new measures.

Unfortunately the passage of time did not make all preelection grievances and issues disappear. Signs of the anticipated economic recovery were exceedingly faint in 1923, and instead of celebrating a period of renewed industrial expansion Taschereau found himself facing two crises caused by the lingering recession: the return to alarming rates of emigration from the countryside and the near-failure of a major French-Canadian bank. And just when Taschereau thought that the worst of the Public Charities controversy had passed, a new piece of social legislation further heightened tension between church and state and led ultimately to another Liberal appeal for papal intervention. Only in the second half of his new mandate did Taschereau feel liberated from the postwar crisis and able to concentrate on "managing" Quebec's golden age. This was the role he cherished; his delight in defending the Liberal policy of industrial development was obvious. Perhaps inevitably, it also made him somewhat complacent: not personally arrogant, but too confident of the strength of free enterprise, the stability of Quebec's economy, and the adequacy of reforms initiated during his first five years as premier.

Taschereau was well aware that the solidly progovernment vote of rural Quebec did not reflect the actual state of agriculture throughout the province. With the recession of 1921, rural depopulation had suddenly jumped back to nineteenth-century levels. Quebec's deputy minister of colonization suspected that official statistics, depressing as they were, understated the extent of the problem. "I know parishes," he wrote, "in the counties of Wolfe, Megantic and Arthabaska which are half-emptied. The inhabitants have crossed the border by car or carriage, without fanfare, and no statistical record of them exists."[2] Farmers slaughtered dairy cattle because they could not afford to maintain them. In many areas drought and low grain prices forced those who stayed on the land into subsistence. Taschereau rejected the absurd contention, most popular among reactionary ideologues and endorsed with manifest insincerity by Sauvé during the campaign, that industry was to blame for the crisis. But he fully shared the concern being expressed everywhere in the province, not only by farm organizations but by religious authorities, banks, merchants, trade unions, and school inspectors, regarding the long-term effects of this crisis. High emigration to the United States sapped the numerical strength of the French-Canadian nation with ultimate consequences for Quebec's political weight in Confederation as well as for the cultural identity of those who left. The desertion of farms for cities within Quebec aggravated the already severe unemployment, housing, and public health crisis. As those who departed were never likely to return to the land, and since abandoned farms were equally unlikely to fall into the possession of people willing to restore production, Quebec faced permanent dependence on imported staple foods. That meant a higher cost of living for workers and wealth draining out of Quebec – in Taschereau's eyes the decline of agriculture threatened the industrial progress of Quebec itself. Finally, rural depopulation created its own momentum: when enough farmers left to destroy the economic and social viability of a rural community, others were tempted or even compelled to follow.[3]

In the light of such grim prospects, Taschereau could not simply wait for a general economic upswing to alleviate rural distress. At a meeting with Prime Minister King and Immigration Minister Stewart soon after the election, he sought federal participation in a campaign to stem the tide. Unfortunately King and Stewart rejected

the logic of Taschereau's appeal, which was that Quebec derived
no benefit from federal spending on immigration. "No immigrant
farmer will settle in Quebec. We need no working men, who would
only increase the number of unemployed. But if Quebec would get
her [proportionate] share in cash ... we could very generously
supplement this grant, offer great advantages to our settlers, retain
them here and, I believe, get many to return." Nor was King
apparently impressed by the political dangers of which Taschereau
warned, for he refused even to reconsider the cancellation of Ottawa's
annual $270,000 grant for agriculture.[4]

Taschereau also urged King to repeal or extensively amend the
Bankruptcy Act. This legislation worked a double whammy on
French-Canadian farmers, according to Taschereau, Caron, and other
observers. During the wartime and immediate postwar agricultural
boom, many had gone blithely into debt. For the sake of pocketing
a fee, unscrupulous operators were persuading them to declare
bankruptcy and allow their farms to be sold by the liquidator, after
which the former owners often departed for the American border.
Such activity severely damaged the credit of all farmers. Often they
would have difficulty obtaining small advances to ride out the
depression; to establish a son on nearby land or to introduce the
machinery and techniques of Caron's demonstration farms became
impossible even for a moderately prosperous farmer.[5] Taschereau's
own policy and rhetoric, however, did little to improve the credit
rating of Quebec farmers. The government refused to extend credit
itself, arguing weakly that such a program would unfairly compete
with the Caisses Populaires. In actual fact there was ample room
for both, especially during the existing emergency. What the government really feared were the political dangers: the collection of debts
from voters, pressure on rural deputies to arrange innumerable (and
sometimes questionable) loans for constituents, and so on.[6] Perhaps
unwittingly, Taschereau also impugned the reliability of farmers
by attributing emigration to "wanderlust" and to the habits of luxury
acquired during the postwar boom.

Denied federal assistance and determined to resist participation
in a farms loans scheme, the government sought other means to
keep farmers on the land. Its ultimate opposition to a pulpwood
export embargo was clearly dictated by the desire to protect farmers'
major source of supplementary income. Caron received more and
more discretionary spending authority. Perrault's Department of
Colonization also spent more, and gave unprecedented recognition
and moral support to private colonization societies. In a time of
crisis, the Liberal government and the colonization movement thus

buried their historic mutual distrust and philosophical antipathy. (When a measure of prosperity returned in 1925, the knives came out again. Liberals insisted that "colonization" meant establishing local agricultural production near new industrial development sites, not sending farmers to a wilderness "uncontaminated" by the modern age. For their part, officials of the Ligue nationale de colonisation wrote articles critical of the government in *L'Action catholique*.) In addition, Taschereau and other ministers stressed the imminence of renewed economic opportunity in the countryside as a reason for farmers to hold on. Everywhere major hydroelectric power installations were nearing completion, with newsprint companies and other industrial concerns actively planning to take advantage. The government's ambitious roadbuilding plans would not only service these developments, but also encourage the burgeoning tourist traffic to go beyond the major cities and help farmers return from subsistence to market-oriented production. The geography of industrial development aside, general prosperity meant a stronger demand for food produced in Quebec.[7]

It was the Quebec City-based Banque Nationale which posed a serious problem for the provincial government in the fall of 1923. Strong during the war, the bank subsequently had risked its entire reserve and capital of nearly $5 million helping La Machine Agricole de Montmagny convert its production from munitions to farm implements. The recession of 1921 ruined Machine Agricole and would have brought down the bank itself had Taschereau not persuaded Georges-Elie Amyot, a wealthy Quebec City industrialist and legislative councillor, to preside over a reorganization. Despite lack of cooperation from W.S. Fielding, the federal finance minister,[8] Amyot raised or personally subscribed $1 million of new capital for the bank and devoted innumerable hours to the affairs of companies indebted to it: he even reopened Machine Agricole to finish work in progress and tried to market its products. In a depressed economy, however, these efforts could not restore the Banque Nationale's earlier prosperity. Now it was again on the brink of collapse, with Amyot bitterly disillusioned about his French-Canadian compatriots.

My present task ... is to persuade people to do business with us instead of the English banks. If we are to have a great bank, it is absolutely essential to favour it strongly by investing capital; in effect, every French Canadian in the city and district of Quebec must own one or more shares of the Banque Nationale, and everyone, big and small, must patronize it, without exception. But no, people come here to beg or collect: that they do regularly, always proclaiming "la Banque Nationale" and their French-Canadian names. And of course when they want a questionable loan, the Banque Nationale is sure to see them.

But look at Paquet Ltd, which could easily give us their business; they go to the Bank of Montreal, and it's the same way with others. How patriotic they are on St Jean Baptiste Day – or especially the night before. As the president of the St. Jean Baptiste Society where he does business, and if he is not too ashamed he will tell you that he patronizes the Canadian Bank of Commerce even though I personally asked him to purchase Banque Nationale shares and offered him every banking service he could possibly need.[9]

Amyot and Taschereau agreed that it was unthinkable to let the bank collapse.[10] Most of the 1,465 shareholders could probably survive the loss, unjust as that would be to Amyot and others who had poured in money knowing the institution was weak. But bankruptcy would mean discounting $6 million in notes and some $40 million deposited by 230,000 customers, as well as calling in all outstanding loans. The result would be unemployment and destitution. Approached in November, Fielding declared that the federal government would do nothing until Parliament assembled three months later. That was too long, for in the aftermath of the Home Bank failure, the mere rumour of collapse might fulfil itself by inducing a run on the Banque Nationale. Taschereau called in J.-A. Vaillancourt and Hormisdas Laporte, presidents of the Banque d'Hochelaga and Banque Provinciale respectively, and suggested the creation of a single, powerful French-Canadian bank. Laporte declined, cleverly evading Taschereau's patriotic appeal by arguing that French Canadians with biases or grievances against this single institution would be compelled to patronize English-Canadian banks. But Vaillancourt, whose bank was the larger and stronger of the two, accepted the idea of fusion as long as his shareholders were satisfactorily protected.[11]

The agreement was concluded on 3 January 1924. Hochelaga would absorb the assets and liabilities of the Banque Nationale, as well as about $600,000 in Machine Agricole debentures. To assure continued public confidence, it would receive a $15 million provincial loan repayable in forty years at five per cent interest. Vaillancourt and Senator F.-L. Béique would continue as chief executive officers, with Amyot becoming second vice-president and one or two Banque Nationale directors joining the new board. Ordinarily, the government need not have feared any "political" repercussions. Canadian bankers, still reeling from the Home Bank affair, were more relieved to see a second failure averted than alarmed to see the province risk its financial solidarity. It is highly doubtful that, as Robert Rumilly suggests, Senator Béique really had to "persuade" St James Street financiers. Many of the latter warmly congratulated Taschereau when the necessary legislation, a special bond issue to raise the $15 million, went through.[12] Equally, public opinion could easily comprehend the dire economic consequences which would result if the government did not act. French Canadians in particular appreciated the "national" dimension to this crisis: failure of the Banque Nationale meant not only immediate losses for its French Canadian shareholders and clientele, but destruction of a precious source of capital for small French-Canadian enterprises and a discouraging example of weak French-Canadian entrepreneurship.[13]

Unfortunately, however, the nature of Taschereau's initial salvage operation cast a shadow of suspicion over this more formal initiative. Amyot was a prominent Quebec City Liberal, as were the men who had contributed most of the new capital in 1922. Taschereau's brother Edmond had invested $25,000 and sat on the board, and later on Jacob Nicol had also become a director. The Hochelaga board was also predominantly Liberal. It could therefore be charged that the government was defending the interests of friends and relatives, not those of the general public. The government's otherwise understandable refusal to publish details of recent Banque Nationale affairs would undoubtedly reinforce any suspicion. For this reason there were reportedly some faint hearts in cabinet,[14] although when the decision was made no one dissented publicly.

Taschereau did everything possible to preempt insinuations in the legislature. He spelled out the full range of consequences should the Banque Nationale be permitted to fail. He acknowledged the participation of intimates, but justifiably pointed out that Amyot and others had invested in an obviously unsuitable enterprise; if profit rather than duty had been their prime motive, they could easily have found less risky ventures. He frankly admitted that unwise administration had been partly responsible for the bank's original difficulties. He announced provisions to ensure that the merged bank met its interest and amortization payments, that these obligations took precedence over dividends, and that at least one of the annual auditors had the approval of the government. He made sure that Nicol abstained from all votes on the loan. Finally and perhaps inevitably, he turned the issue of motivation into a question of his personal integrity.[15]

To the extent that it forced the opposition to tread warily, Taschereau's defence of the measure was successful. Neither Arthur

Sauvé nor E.-L. Patenaude, who emerged as the chief Conservative spokesman, wanted to appear irresponsibly partisan, let alone disloyal to a national undertaking on this first major issue since their electoral gains. They raised the patently phoney constitutional issue of whether the federal government's regulatory power over banking precluded a financial agreement between the Province of Quebec and the Banque d'Hochelaga. On motivation they resorted to subtle innuendo, demanding a legislative committee with full power to summon documents – without specifying what they expected the documents to reveal. Similarly, they refused to explain how a bank failure could be averted without "assisting" the shareholders and administrators, in addition to the depositors. But the opposition could afford to be subtle, for outside the legislature critics felt much less constrained. One anonymous pamphleteer representing the imaginary "Ligue de Protection des Epargnes de la Province de Québec" dismissed the entire effort as a corrupt scheme, implicating even Sir Lomer Gouin for having tried to arrange a federal loan to the Banque Nationale back in 1922.

Legislative approval was certainly the major hurdle. When it came, Gouin considered it a significant triumph for his successor. "He has shown himself to be highly energetic, and has performed one of the finest acts, perhaps the finest act of his entire political career. His opponents have succeeded only in discrediting themselves and have weakened their party in the eyes of all serious men ... I must say that I expected better from Patenaude in particular. He has missed a superb opportunity to raise himself in the estimation of businessmen in the Province, and if he doesn't understand that himself, he is not as smart as I thought he was."[16] There remained several formalities, however. The shareholders of the two banks had to approve the agreement, the government had to sanction the contract of fusion by order-in-council, and federal authorities had to charter the new institution. Taschereau had to intercede with both King and Lapointe at the last stage, in order to override the objection of Acting Finance Minister Robb to the proposed new name "Banque Canadienne Nationale." (Robb feared that foreigners might mistake it for a government central bank.) It is worth noting that Edmond Taschereau was excluded from the directorate of the new organization, Alexandre asking only that he be retained as the bank's notary. Now the operation was complete, but Taschereau believed firmly that "the future of the government rides with this legislation."[17] He therefore continued defending his actions at every opportunity, and on several occasions pressed Banque Canadienne Nationale interests before federal colleagues. Fortunately the new bank was a success: under the highly regarded management of Beaudry Leman, it took advantage of a combined clientele and an economic upswing to build assets which weathered the depression and even permitted repayment of its loan to the province in half the allotted time.[18]

Taschereau's third major problem, a renewal of tension in relations with the church, grew out of the Child Adoption Act of 1924. Controversy over this measure distressed and angered Taschereau for several reasons. First, the legislation was desperately needed. Quebec's orphanages and foundling homes were intolerably crowded, partly as the inevitable consequence of urbanization, with its greater incidence of unwanted or illegitimate children and the diminished capacity of families to care for such unfortunates. Existing law, however, further impeded the search for new homes. Adoption enjoyed no legal status whatsoever, and natural parents could reclaim their children at any time. Since an unwed mother could seldom exact financial support from the father of her child, she often surrendered the infant involuntarily. Potential adopting parents therefore knew that changed marital or economic circumstances might easily lead her to demand the return of her child. To protect the interests of children and to reassure potential adopters, David modelled a bill on Ontario legislation. It would secure permanent adoption for illegitimate children whose parents did not undertake to provide necessary care, for orphans or those totally abandoned for two years, and for children of the incurably insane. The fact of illegitimacy would be omitted from all documents.

Taschereau had some reason to expect support for the legislation from religious authorities. It was the religious orders in charge of orphanages who originally drew the severity of the problem to the government's attention. Charles Lanctôt had discussed the matter with Joseph Sirois, legal counsel for the Archdiocese of Quebec. There were precedents for provincial action to protect children, and, in contrast to the Public Charities Act, this legislation did not raise the spectre of a state bureaucracy challenging the role and prerogatives of religious institutions. Nevertheless Catholic militants seized on the legislation as fresh evidence of a conspiracy against their faith. Henri Bourassa complained that "this extraordinary legislation ... extends the list of attacks on everything which has given our social order its strength and vitality. They have multiplied noticeably in the last few years." Nor was it merely *Le Devoir* and *L'Action catholique* that protested; *La Semaine religieuse de Québec*, official spokesman for archdiocesan authority, quickly added its own denunciation.[19]

For all of Taschereau's self-righteous dismay at this reaction, his government invited trouble by its haste and carelessness. Like the Public Charities legislation, this bill was steamrollered through both Houses in the final hours of the session. Only later was it fully realized that Catholic children could be placed in non-Catholic homes, that no one would verify whether adopting parents were actually married and living together, and that the courts could decree adoption without the consent of mentally competent natural parents. While these loopholes were subsequently plugged to the satisfaction of episcopal authorities, the adoption controversy reopened hostilities just when Taschereau thought relations between church and state were improving. The bitter 1923 campaign was in the past, amendments to the Public Charities Act were being negotiated, and the government had twice recognized the status and special role of the Catholic labour movement. At the Quebec Eucharistic Congress in the previous September, Taschereau had made a highly conciliatory speech dwelling primarily on the necessity and validity of religious belief and on the immutability of Roman Catholic principles in the modern world. His brief allusion to recent controversies declared simply that the civil power, just like the religious authority, sought comprehensive, durable, and smooth cooperation between church and state. "Each of these powers, in the sphere belonging to it, has been the artisan of French and Catholic survival in this corner of the continent. We have too many difficulties to surmount, obstacles to conquer and outside influences to combat to forget what strength and courage this close cordial union can give us. Speaking for those I represent, we ask our colleagues of the other power, after assuring them of our cooperation, to apply to us those benign words of our Lord: Peace to all men of good will."[20]

While religious authorities became genuinely concerned about the adoption law, it is difficult to escape the impression that certain critics of the government were quite pleased to have a controversy which bolstered their cause. The *Action catholique* group hated Taschereau more than ever for the way he had outmanoeuvred them during the election campaign, and had rejoined the battle as soon as Bégin's order of political silence expired. In the transparent guise of a treatise on European anticlericalism, for example, Curé E.-V. Lavergne (cousin of Armand) intimated that the Public Charities Act belonged to the "second stage" of a classic anticlerical conspiracy, "the successful elimination and systematic displacement of the church's maternal influences." This sniping, which the Liberals reasonably felt must enjoy the approval of Coadjutor Archbishop Roy, continued throughout 1923 and into the first session of the new legislature. Here the government managed to slip through one social innovation, a Vital Statistics Act, without raising the cry of laicization, by formulating it in the context of health reform. But by the end of the session critics had both the Adoption Act and the absence of an amendment to the Public Charities Act to "prove" that the government was contemptuous of religious authority.

Although the adoption controversy set the stage, it was an incredibly petty and foolish incident which led directly to a new appeal to Rome. On 9 May 1924, L'Action catholique published an open letter from one of its junior staff members which questioned, among other things, Taschereau's religious fidelity. Already angry, Taschereau then learned that a priest in the Petit Séminaire had read the "Boulanger letter" approvingly to his class of thirteen-year-olds. Having received "little enough recognition in the past for what we have done for your institution," Taschereau informed the rector of Laval University, "we will learn our lesson ... Evidently we are not welcome at the Seminary."[21] (Taschereau may have recalled the earlier expulsion of two of his sons from the Petit Séminaire for trivial offences – smoking and attending a forbidden play.)[22] Cabinet ministers would therefore decline to attend the dedication of a new bell tower at the adjoining Quebec Basilica, which was to take place within a few days. One is tempted to agree with the anonymous seminary diarist that "this affair of the bells would be a fine subject for a comical epic poem," but the principals took it most seriously. Taschereau risked offending Mgr Eugène Laflamme, curé of the Basilica, who was one of his closest friends among the clergy. Both Laflamme and Cardinal Bégin seemed deeply distressed and tried to appease the government. Three teachers guilty of denouncing Taschereau in class were relieved of their teaching functions, and Arthur Maheux, a senior Laval University professor and administrator appeared personally before the classes to disavow the conduct of their teachers and explain their dismissal. Justly regarding L'Action catholique's retraction as equivocal and insincere, however, the Liberals followed through with their boycott of the Basilica ceremony. And as if to spite the editors of L'Action catholique, who were notorious antisemites, Taschereau used his free time to attend the sod-turning for a new synagogue several blocks away.[23]

There the matter did not rest. While L'Action catholique and Le Soleil traded insults publicly, Taschereau appealed to the apostolic delegate in Ottawa through Rodolphe Lemieux, now speaker of the House of Commons. Lemieux reported having informed His Excellency that "in the interests of religious peace, a strong intervention [might be necessary] against the insidious campaign of L'Action *catholique*. I gave him the article you sent me and explained the deplorable effect of these attacks against the civil power in Quebec, which has always been benevolent towards religious authority. H.E. seemed well apprised of the situation and expressed profound regret at recent events ... The Delegate would be pleased to receive you [in June] ... I can assure you that H.E. has the highest regard for you and your government and strongly wishes to put an end to the malaise which exists at Quebec." On the eve of the 7 June interview, Lemieux sent further encouragement. "I have reason to believe you will be delighted with the result of your initiative. Here as elsewhere, they deplore the lack of direction and authority at Quebec and real efforts are being made in high places to remedy this state of affairs as soon as possible."[24]

There is little indication of what precise undertakings, if any, Mgr Pietro de Maria and Premier Taschereau exchanged on this occasion. Indeed, the mere fact of their meeting went unreported at the time. But subsequent events suggest that Lemieux's confidence was justified. With apparent assurance, Taschereau returned to launch an immediate attack on "certain laymen who, under the pretext of having nothing but our eternal salvation in view, are ready to permit us to save our souls only if we pass under the Caudine Forks of their narrow intolerance."[25] Several weeks later he tried to force Archbishop Gauthier of Montreal to accept responsibility for a provocative article in *L'Action française* written by Abbé Lionel Groulx, a priest supposedly within his jurisdiction.[26] Back in Quebec City, the editors of *L'Action catholique* remained defiant but evidently felt pressured to assault the government with "pinpricks rather than thunderbolts."[27] Later in the year Camille Roy, a stronger man with liberal (if not Liberal) sympathies became rector of Laval University. This in itself helped cool one theatre of the war, but it also presaged a change at the very top of the Archdiocese of Quebec. When Cardinal Bégin died in 1925, he was succeeded by Mgr Roy, long the Liberals' real *bête noire*. But Roy himself was very ill, and when he died six months later a genuine housecleaning took place. Taschereau's original preference for a successor was Mgr O.-E. Mathieu, his philosophy professor, a former rector at Laval, and a close enough friend for Taschereau to have given dinner parties in his honour.[28] Mathieu had never sympathized with the *castor-nationaliste* element, and as archbishop of Regina for the last decade had avoided all the postwar Quebec controversies. Taschereau had little cause to complain, however, when Rome instead chose Mgr F.-R.-M. Rouleau, erstwhile bishop of Valleyfield.

Like Mathieu, Rouleau had more interest in theology and education than in exaggerated defences of religious prerogative and public morality. Unlike Mathieu, he was entirely new to the archdiocese and thus even more detached from the personal suspicions and animosities which underlay church-state tension. And at sixty years of age, he was considerably younger and more energetic than Mathieu, and more likely to succeed in restoring discipline among his subordinates. These advantages were fully exploited during Rouleau's five-year tenure. The petty sniping subsided, church and state cooperated fruitfully in several areas of mutual concern (particularly public health) and the government even won some applause from Catholic militants by resisting federal old age pensions and by questioning the "necessity" of Sunday work in the pulp and paper industry. Unfortunately, this reign of harmony would not long outlive Rouleau, who died suddenly in May 1931.

Only in the natural resource sector could Taschereau find any real signs of economic recovery before the end of 1925, confirming his belief that these resources were the key to Quebec's future prosperity. As early as 1923, considerable work was accomplished on major hydroelectric projects. The Quebec Development Corporation (Duke-Price) pressed ahead with its $12 million Grande Décharge development, while the government itself dammed outlets from nearby Lake Kenogami; the upper Saguenay Valley would soon have sufficient power to duplicate the industrial development which electric power had already brought to the St Maurice. In the Eastern Townships, the Southern Canada Power Company moved toward completion of its Hemming Falls plant at Drummondville on the St Francis River. By ending the region's dependence on small installations and on St Maurice power purchased from the Shawinigan Company, this development opened the way for more advanced manufacturing processes in several established centres. The hydroelectric potential of two new regions was also on the verge of development: various projects were being mooted in northwestern Quebec, while the Ontario Paper Company signed a contract to establish a capacity of at least 15,000 horsepower on the Outardes River on the north shore of the Gulf of St Lawrence. The pace of development slowed somewhat in 1924, but in 1925 the Aluminum Company of America acquired majority control of Duke-Price, and Shawinigan a minority share. This hastened completion of the generating station at Ile Maligne, and led quickly to the announcement of yet another project on the Saguenay, the harnessing of Chute à Caron to generate power for an aluminum mill at Arvida. Meanwhile the International Paper Company bought up hydroelectric installations and waterfall leases along the Ottawa and Gatineau rivers in preparation for a major expansion of its pulp and paper enterprises into the region. And in addition to its ongoing policy of absorbing existing companies around the province, Shawinigan added further generating capacity to its developments on the St Maurice. The result was that by 1927 Taschereau and his colleagues no longer had merely to boast of Quebec's potential hydroelectric capacity, for its developed capacity had doubled in four years and now surpassed that of Ontario.[29]

The reasons for the dramatic upsurge were obvious. The capital and technology were readily available and the market was absolutely certain. In fact, the capital was often raised by industrialists themselves, who preferred the speed and convenience of supplying power to their own mills. Even where hydroelectric development began without any particular industry in mind, the investors had no difficulty creating a strong demand for their power. Thus Southern Canada's directors promoted the establishment of the Canadian Celanese factory at Drummondville, and within a year 300 persons were employed producing artificial silk. But their project and ALCOA's aluminum plant at Arvida notwithstanding, by far the larger part of hydroelectric development occurred to supply the province's newsprint mills.

In terms of employment as well, it was the pulp and paper industry which led Quebec out of its postwar depression. Although a sudden and drastic fall in the price of newsprint spelled the ruin of one major operator in 1921, most companies saw the crisis as temporary and were already planning their expansion. In the age of mass circulation daily newspapers, the American and British thirst for newsprint must inevitably drive prices upward again. Three distinct types of enterprise characterized the industry during its spectacular period of expansion in the mid-twenties. There were the strong, independent producers, concentrated primarily along the St Maurice but also including the Saguenay-based Price Brothers and two companies in the Eastern Townships. There were new companies formed by major newspaper publishers in order to secure permanent supplies free of market competition and producer profits. While completion of the Ontario Paper Company project (*Chicago Tribune* and *New York News*) was still some years away, there was already such a company in the Gulf region linked to the London *Daily Mail* (Gulf Pulp and Paper at Clarke City). Eventually related interests, in the form of the Anglo-Canadian Pulp Company, built a newsprint mill right in the Quebec City suburb of Limoilou.

In a class by itself was the International Paper Company, whose

Canadian subsidiary had appeared in 1916. Originally interested in New Brunswick, International soon developed a vision of dominance over the industry in Quebec which, if successfully established, would give the parent firm virtual control over the price and supply of newsprint in the United States. In contrast to publishers who acquired mills, International acquired stock in at least fourteen daily newspapers and concluded long-term contracts for newsprint delivery. Its quest in Quebec began with the purchase of the Glen Falls Mills at Three Rivers, where by 1925 it had built four additonal highly efficient mills and could produce 7,000 tons a day. To feed these plants, it bought up vast timber tracts on the lower St Lawrence. Simultaneously it acquired various properties and timber limits in western Quebec, and also began developing what it lacked at Three Rivers – its own power sources. By 1927 it had invested over $100 million in Quebec, giving itself the volume and efficiency virtually to dictate the price of newsprint in eastern North America. Most competitors understood International's ambitions as early as 1925 and began groping their way toward some sort of collective resistance under the thinly disguised leadership of Montreal financier Herbert Holt. But with investors practically begging for a piece of the action, they expanded their own capacity as if the market for newsprint were infinite. Before the bubble burst, the industry was employing almost 18,000 men at wages considerably higher than those prevailing in older manufacturing industries.[30]

Quebec's mineral resources also contributed to the economic resurgence, albeit without such a direct and immediate impact upon employment. While the Eastern Townships continued to lead the world in asbestos production, it was the mining of precious metals which opened up a new region of Quebec, attracted substantial new investment, and swelled provincial revenues. The so-called "Rouyn District" of southern Abitibi and northern Temiscamingue counties was no Klondike. There was no chance discovery, but systematic surveying and testing of mineral deposits based on the assumption that northern Ontario's rich mineral belt must continue eastward. Nor was Rouyn a "poor man's camp" where individual prospectors could pan or dig their way to instant wealth. The depth, isolation, and low concentration of ore bodies ensured that only large, experienced companies would have the capital and technology to extract the deposits. Noranda Mines was the earliest and most successful of these companies, launching its exploration in 1922, discovering gold deposits later the same year, and then recognizing that copper was the more plentiful and profitable commodity to mine. By the end of 1927 it had acquired the necessary power and transportation facilities, built its copper smelter, and established a booming company town bearing its name. Overall, mining operations stimulated a growth of population from 26,571 to 44,301 in the two counties, tripled annual provincial royalties from $272,000 to $734,000 between 1925-6 and 1929-30, and incidentally opened up a new "colonization frontier" for Quebec.[31]

Traditional labour-intensive industries did not, unfortunately, enjoy the same speed or extent of development. Neither bitter strikes nor the improvement of general economic conditions appreciably raised the living standard of textile, clothing, and leather workers. Port activity in Montreal naturally rose in response to the western wheat boom of the mid-twenties, but most employment here continued to be seasonal. The one sector of Montreal's economy which did have a positive impact on working-class incomes in the later 1920s was construction, although even this boom had an ominous quality: the massive investment was in public facilities and office-buildings, not productive capacity.

The economic recovery was thus not only partial but deceptive as well, in the sense that traditional weaknesses in the Quebec economy remained. In fact, without denying that the massive capital investment of the mid-1920s brought fairly widespread immediate benefits, or pretending that Quebec's "reintegration into the North American economic mainstream" was unnecessary or undesirable in itself, it must be acknowledged that this stage of industrialization involved a dramatic extension of foreign ownership and control and an unprecedented degree of dependence (given the proportional decline in agriculture and the absence of strong, self-sustaining consumer goods and service sectors) upon external market conditions. Taschereau may well have perceived these dangers, at least vaguely, but if so he was not inclined to acknowledge them publicly. Instead he treated the growth of resource industries as a vindication of his policy and philosophy, and never tired of repeating his stock answer to nationalist critics. Neither in the legislature nor at the inauguration of new enterprises was there a hint of doubt in his mind. The opening of Canadian Celanese was a typical and widely publicized occasion.

We want to bring in new industries, and we are ready to do all that is possible in that direction. We are not afraid of foreign capital. We invite foreign capital to join with us in developing our natural resources and creating industries here. Let the capital of England and of the United States come here as much as it wishes and multiply our industries, so that our people will have work. Such capital is welcome. I am not afraid, and I never will be afraid, that our French Canadians will become Americanized because of an inflow of foreign capital. They have resisted other dangers and other trials, and as I have said many times, I prefer importing American dollars to exporting Canadian workmen.[32]

It was exceedingly difficult to mobilize public opinion against this philosophy, especially, for example, when striking underpaid shoe workers from Quebec City were finding relatively lucrative employment in the Saguenay-Lake St John developments.

Believing his philosophy vindicated, Taschereau felt little need to revise his views about the role of the state in economic development. The government must ensure that private enterprise did, in fact, use its natural resource concessions to create jobs within the province. Lomer Gouin's pulpwood export embargo of 1910 had been the first major exercise of this responsibility. In the 1920s the issue was hydroelectricity, for with the demand for power in Ontario and New York State extremely high, there were inevitably promoters interested in developing Quebec power sites primarily for an export market. In Taschereau's opinion this would be tantamount to "exporting French Canadians," for cheap and plentiful electricity was Quebec's trump card in attracting manufacturing industries.[33] Ordinarily the Quebec government could prevent the export of power simply by denying or cancelling the lease of an offending company, and in 1926 Taschereau finally enshrined such a policy in the statutes.[34] The matter was really far more complex, however, and required political and judicial initiatives as well as legislative action. The major reason was that Quebec did not have an exclusive claim to jurisdiction over sites which various interests wanted to develop for export.

Even before Taschereau became premier there were plans to harness the St Lawrence above Montreal as part of a Canada-u.s. deep waterway project, while at Carillon on the Ottawa River, the National Hydroelectric Company held a long-standing federal lease. In the first case, Taschereau estimated tht two-thirds of the 4,100,000 horsepower under consideration were entirely within Quebec. Yet if federal authority over navigation were allowed to take precedence over the province's control of resources, with the whole project placed under an international commission, then the Americans would receive at least half the power generated.[35] In the second case, even if provincial control were acknowleded, Ontario would have claims to power generated on the Ottawa. And legal considerations aside, it made little sense to treat Ontario as a foreign economic competitor rather than as a sister province. In any jurisdictional battle, it would be far wiser to overcome wartime bitterness and restore the provincial rights alliance between Quebec City and Toronto. Comparatively speaking, moreover, the waterway proposal threatened far greater damage to Quebec interests than the development of Ottawa Valley sites: it could permit ocean cargo to bypass Montreal and divert American investment capital towards manufacturing enterprises south of the border.[36] Now if Ontario could be assured of meeting its future power requirements through joint development or even purchases from Quebec companies established entirely on Quebec's side of the Ottawa River, then it would consider the waterway project far less urgent.[37] With Ontario thus neutralized, Taschereau would have a far better chance of blocking the more dangerous project. Moreover, Taschereau sensed that in the long run he might weaken his moral position by treating Ontario no differently than a foreign jurisdiction. "We are decidedly against allowing power to be exported to the United States," he therefore assured the premier of Ontario late in 1925, "but favourable, on the other hand, to supplying the sister provinces."[38]

The initial prospects for an alliance with the Ontario government were anything but bright. In 1922 politicians at all levels, Ontario Hydro officials, and private economic interests had welcomed the report of technical experts which declared the waterway proposal to be feasible, and had passed resolutions urging Ottawa to conclude a treaty with the Americans. In June 1924, the Conservative government of G. Howard Ferguson passed an order-in-council allowing Ontario Hydro to press ahead with plans for a dam at Morrisburg. Personally, Ferguson was less popular in Quebec than Arthur Meighen, if that were possible. A small-town Protestant Orangeman, he had argued even prior to Regulation XVII that English should be the sole language of instruction in Ontario schools. Then, as acting minister of education during the bitterest phase of the controversy, he had not only led the defence of Regulation XVII but also launched a malicious counteroffensive against Laurier and other French Canadians. Worse still, after more than a year as premier and at least two indications from Taschereau that Quebec opinion would demand a settlement of the schools issue prior to any interprovincial power agreement,[39] Ferguson resurrected his old claim that Regulation XVII did no harm to the French language in Ontario. And this during a Bonne Entente visit to Quebec City![40] Like Meighen on conscription, he seemed perversely determined to persuade French Canadians that they had no real grievance.

Fortunately the situation was really more hopeful than that. Ferguson was already under pressure from federal Conservatives to rescind Regulation XVII and had privately acknowledged that it had not achieved its proclaimed pupose of upgrading English skills. It is even possible that his Quebec speech was just a petulant reaction to warnings that Taschereau would try to "take credit" for a forthcoming change in Ontario's education policy.[41] On the power issue itself, moreover, the behaviour of the King government virtually forced Ontario into an alliance with Quebec. Ottawa appeared to be claiming future revenues from power development on the St Lawrence, in order to pay its share of the cost of the whole waterway project. It also appeared ready to put Ottawa River sites in the hands of political friends who could mercilessly exploit Ontario's need for electrical energy. Altogether, the federal position contained a dire threat to Ontario's economic development, to public ownership of power supplies, and to the constitutional rights of the province.

The federal attitude also caused Taschereau to overcome any lingering hesitation about dealing with Ferguson. The King government stalled agreeably on the waterway question by reviving the technical inquiry, but refused to withdraw or clarify its jurisdictional claims over the Ottawa River. Instead it tried to appease Taschereau with empty gestures like a promise to require the annual renewal of federal export licenses (as if that would safeguard Quebec interests), and an undertaking not to issue licenses without provincial consent. Politically desperate following the October 1925 federal election, King became more conciliatory in 1926.[42] But by then Taschereau was pretty well committed to the Ferguson alliance. "We have too many interests in common," he had written after Ferguson's provocative Quebec speech, "not to become closely united in community of ideas and unity of action." At the time of his assurance that Quebec would sell power to Ontario, Taschereau also agreed to Ferguson's request for a secret meeting early in the new year.[43] Although Taschereau's hard bargaining nearly drove Ontario Hydro officials back to the St Lawrence project,[44] a breakthrough occurred in the spring of 1926. International Paper was prepared to sell Ontario power generated by its new Gatineau River installation. And National Hydroelectric, which held a federal lease at Carillon on the Ottawa, came under the control of Shawinigan Water and Power. Here were two companies Taschereau knew would have to recognize and respect the policy and wishes of the Quebec government. With Ontario agreeing not to export any power purchased from Quebec to the United States,[45] the way was clear for a succession of agreements between Ontario Hydro and Quebec companies. By January 1927, Chairman Magrath of Hydro was proposing a formal interprovincial treaty governing development of the Ottawa River. Nothing came of it, but in response to a new Ottawa offensive the two provinces stood shoulder to shoulder and finally mounted a joint legal challenge to federal claims. By that time, Ferguson had found a way to set aside Regulation XVII.[46]

There was one other case where Taschereau felt obliged to defend Quebec interests against outside forces. Fearing that mining activity in Abitibi would be drawn into Toronto's rather than Montreal's economic orbit, he devised a legal pretext to delay the entry of an Ontario railway into the region and meanwhile arranged for the construction of a line to Montreal without a large provincial subsidy.[47] He also invoked the "manufacturing condition" on one occasion, warning asbestos producers of a possible export embargo if more of them did not follow the Johns Manville Company example and process the fibres within Quebec.[48] Generally speaking, however, the province was anxious to encourage resource developers. Financially its greatest contribution was in roadbuilding, where it spent more than $20 million between 1923 and the end of the decade. Highways became the largest single budgetary item at close to 25 per cent and the length of improved road nearly tripled to 12,464 miles. Several factors gave rise to this ambitious program, including the growing economic importance of truck and tourist traffic, the inability of most municipalities to afford the necessary expenditures, and conversely the dramatic increase in provincial revenues. (Recognizing that Liquor Commission profits alone were enough to finance all this construction, Roads Minister Perron reportedly began dreaming of what a provincial gasoline monopoly might accomplish!) But providing access to resource-rich districts of Quebec was clearly the central purpose. After a tour of the Abitibi region by launch and portage in 1923, for example, Perrault persuaded colleagues that "as we were dealing with responsible people who were spending their own money [Noranda Mines], the least we could do was provide them with or assist them to obtain every facility for opening up the country."[49]

At the same time that it built roads, the province was able to withdraw from the construction of storage dams. Previous strategy had been to amortize the cost of these dams by charging power companies which later used them, the Gouin and Mercier projects being prime examples. But with Shawinigan now having almost limitless financial resources and manufacturers like International Paper and ALCOA constructing their own power stations, the procedure changed radically. The companies built storage dams and turned them over to the province on completion.

A wider form of cooperation occurred in the forest industry, where the provincial Forestry Service conducted resource surveys, operated a tree nursery to aid reforestation, subsidized a school to train skilled pulp and paper workers, and shared the responsibility for preventing, sighting, and extinguishing forest fires. The chief of the Forestry Service, Gustave Piché, was also among the first to recognize looming dangers in the pulp and paper industry. Earlier Taschereau had admitted that only the state could ensure conservation and wise use of forest resources through a "long-term comprehensive policy."[50] But he moved too slowly and timidly to prevent disastrous over-production of newsprint. Whereas Piché recommended that companies diversify into other paper products, try to broaden their markets, limit production, and restrain competitive price cutting, Taschereau merely announced a moratorium on the auction of new timber limits at the beginning of 1927.[51] Since the major companies had recently acquired substantial leases, however, this gesture could have little immediate impact except as a signal. In view of Taschereau's inability to secure the cooperation of either the companies or the Ontario government, even when the inevitable crisis occurred,[52] it could be argued that he was powerless to control the industry anyway. But as an explanation for his behaviour that would be hindsight. It is more likely that like many investors and producers, he persuaded himself that the disaster could not really happen.

Besides providing transportation facilities, the government encouraged the mining industry through legislative and regulatory devices. A graduated profits tax replaced fixed production royalties on precious metals, both to ensure public benefit from rising prices and to induce companies to reinvest their earnings in further exploration. The enlarged Bureau of Mines conducted its own surveys, helped settle claims disputes, designed expedients to discourage speculators while bending certain rules for legitimate operators, and may have helped the latter raise capital by its publicity campaign against fraudulent stock promoters. Taschereau's only dissatisfaction with the mining industry during these years was directed toward the older sectors, for in addition to the asbestos processing issue he became aware of scandalous accident records in the open-pit mines and limestone quarries of the province. In response, the legislature enacted a series of new safety regulations – although there is strong evidence that the bureau lacked enough staff to ensure compliance.[53]

Critics then and later charged that Taschereau virtually "gave away" Quebec's natural resources during this period. To some extent this was obviously a nationalist argument, the real objection being to "foreign" (non-French Canadian) ownership *per se*, not the terms on which resources were developed. Taschereau and his colleagues had always rejected this line of thought, believing that it would

be irresponsible to delay industrial advancement until some hypothetical future time when French-Canadian entrepreneurs acquired
the necessary attitudes, skills, and capital to bring it about themselves.[54] The resource issue is also the most fertile ground for Fischer's
"furtive fallacy,"[55] with poker games and fishing camps the site and
legal retainers and campaign contributions the motive for concessions
to the foreign entrepreneurs. While motives (especially unconscious
ones) can seldom be proved conclusively, there is little evidence for
such an interpretation of Taschereau's policies. The poker games
were social occasions with a regular group of Montreal cronies; the
fishing conclaves were political strategy sessions which Taschereau
reluctantly allowed to impinge on his vacations. Contracts were
negotiated "like businessmen," with cabinet discussing the terms
and giving formal sanction when necessary. The practice of retaining
close friends of the government was neither unique to Quebec nor
very "furtive" at all; virtually no one claimed that legal patronage
determined the government's policies. Campaign contributions by
these companies were similarly part of a common system, and in
the Quebec Liberals' case there seems to have been a single fund
for both federal and provincial elections, raised by designated bagmen
who were closer to Ottawa than to Quebec City – Senator Raymond
being the prime example.[56] Where Taschereau actively contributed
to suspicion was in so openly retaining discretionary authority instead
of having agencies and procedures to regulate corporate behaviour
in accordance with these policies.

Legitimate questions nevertheless remain about the terms under
which resource development occurred. In particular, did the state
demand adequate compensation for the rights it granted to private
enterprise, and maintain sufficient control to protect the public
interest? While the profits and privileges enjoyed by some companies
certainly reflected little credit upon the Taschereau government, it
is easy to slip into a judgment of its conduct more appropriate to
our own era than the earlier one. At least one can try to understand
Taschereau's perspective, since he was sensitive to the issue and
addressed it on several occasions. In the first place, his government
did not feel the need for more revenue than it was actually deriving
from hydroelectric leases and licenses, timber auctions, stumpage
dues, and the mining profits tax. During the 1920s personal taxes
in Quebec remained low even though provincial responsibilities and
expenditures grew substantially.[57] Citing the obligations imposed
on International Paper for its dam on the Gatineau River and on
Shawinigan to link Quebec City with Lake St John by road as well
as by power lines, Taschereau pointed out that companies were also

relieving the state of some heavy expenditures.[58] Allowing private
interests to perform government functions could itself lead to abuses,
notably in the case of company towns. But Taschereau heard no
actual complaints of exploitation by company stores or the denial
of rights in these centres during the 1920s, and it is difficult to imagine
what other arrangements were practical in isolated areas. (Nor was
the misery of the 1930s demonstrably greater here than in other one-
industry towns where companies exercised less formal control.)
Moreover, Taschereau justly argued that in its contracts and lease
arrangements with private companies, the government never abdi-
cated its responsibilities or surrendered its ultimate control over
resources.[59] Of course, Taschereau would shudder at the idea of
altering, unilaterally and capriciously, an agreement with someone
who fulfilled his own obligations.[60] But there was no doubt about
the government's right to impose new regulations when necessary,
or the premier's willingness to demand compliance. The hydroelectric
embargo was ample evidence of the former, and Taschereau's investigation and ultimate curtailment of Sunday work in the pulp and
paper industry was a well-publicized demonstration of the latter.[61]

The case of Montreal Light, Heat and Power is the most frequently
cited in contentions that Taschereau allowed Quebec resources to
be exploited solely for the enrichment of a small corporate elite,
and it is indeed impossible to justify the enormous profits of Sir
Herbert Holt's enterprise. Nor did Taschereau ever attempt to do
so. While he praised J.E. Aldred and Julian Smith, the founders
of Shawinigan, for having shown "a big heart, a clear vision of
the future, and an indomitable will to succeed"[62] during the early
years, he never credited Holt with any great contribution to Quebec's
industrial development. On the contrary, by the mid-1920s Taschereau had apparently concluded that MLHP was an obstacle to progress
in Montreal. With profit his sole criterion, Holt refused either to
invest in new sources of electricity close to the city or to let others
develop them. Eventually, and to the amazement of local financiers,
Taschereau helped promote the establishment of Barclay's Bank in
Canada as a potentially strong independent source of capital on the
Montreal scene. And he supported the application of a new corporation, Beauharnois Light, Heat and Power, to harness the St
Lawrence River above Montreal – "primarily due to the fact that
I am satisfied that the Company will produce and sell power
materially cheaper [sic] than it is now available."[63] Unfortunately,
Taschereau felt himself limited to such indirect and ultimately futile
means. MLHP's privileged position did not stem primarily from a
provincial base or charter, but rather from a monopoly of urban

distribution and related services like public transportation. These were rights and properties legally acquired from other private interests and from municipal authorities. There did exist a provincial regulatory agency, the Public Service Commission, to which municipalities could appeal. But in the absence of strong local opposition to Holt during the 1920s, and having just suffered politically for "violating" the autonomy of Montreal, Taschereau was scarcely in a position to mount any direct challenge.

Taschereau continued to believe, as Gouin always had, that the place and well-being of French Canadians within the new industrial order depended more on education than on the Quebec government's resource policies. Within limits imposed by the tradition of local and religious control, the government was clearly willing to place its influence and more buoyant revenues behind the cause of educational reform. Creation of the Corporation des écoles techniques in 1926, for example, involved more than centralizing the financial operations of schools funded directly by the province, its declared purpose. The director, Dr Augustin Frigon specialized not in administration but in technical education itself. Predictably, he began by launching a new institution, a school for printers. Even before his appointment, however, the government had opened a major technical school at Hull, and increased the operating budgets of those at Quebec and Montreal in order to meet growing demand: although most were enrolled in night courses only, there were nearly 4,000 students in these technical schools by the end of the decade.[64] Gouin's cherished Ecole des hautes études commerciales finally became more than a legislative showpiece, acquiring full-time staff and students for its courses in accountancy and commerce. Although the HEC was formally affiliated with the University of Montreal, its curriculum and standards were directly controlled by the government and the business community. Even the schools of fine arts were now playing a vocational role by training professional architects.

Under the suspicious eye of Catholic militants, Taschereau and David could not intervene so directly in the traditional educational system. (Jules Dorion all but accused Taschereau of tyring to buy the political support of university and classical college authorities, simply because the premier had been reminding critics that provincial subsidies were unconditional!)[65] But the government actively supported implementation of the curricular reforms approved by the Catholic Committee in 1922. Provincial inspectors got the authority to ensure that local school boards complied with new curricula and with regulations concerning teachers' salaries and qualifications. Boards willing to upgrade their facilities and teaching corps got financial assistance, notably through the Rural Schools Assistance Act of 1927 and, for urban districts, loan guarantees. More money was allocated to normal schools, where the major priority was to train more men for the teaching profession, especially in commercial and industrial subjects. Finally, through a Commission of Inquiry chaired by Sir Lomer Gouin, Taschereau's cabinet gave Montreal reformers carte blanche to document their case for a complete overhaul of French-language Catholic education in Montreal. Gouin himself was actively interested, having become president of the University of Móntreal shortly after leaving the premiership. The two other driving forces were university professors Edouard Montpetit and Victor Doré, both personal friends of David. All their recommendations were subsequently accepted by the Taschereau government, despite protests from some priests and local politicians. The administration of primary schools was centralized, jurisdiction over secondary grades was transferred to a central board of school commissioners, and a pedagogical board and director-general (Doré) were appointed with immunity from political pressure.[66]

Once the economic crisis subsided, it became evident that Taschereau did not view social assistance in the same light as education – as something to be modernized in response to the realities of industrial society. In passing the Public Charities Act the government had "done its duty." If the state did more than subsidize private charitable institutions, it risked destroying the individual's sense of responsibility for himself and others. Even if Taschereau had been personally less wedded to these essentially preindustrial concepts of indigence and charity, and had questioned the adequacy of traditional means to combat the chronic economic vulnerability of a large urban working class, the bitterness of the Public Charities controversy would still have discouraged new initiatives. Thus, while he opposed the federal old age pensions legislation of 1927 for numerous reasons, he no doubt enjoyed the unaccustomed role of defending religious prerogatives.[67]

Fortunately, no such ideological and political restraints kept the Taschereau government from building on the Public Health Act of 1922. The crusade against tuberculosis and infant mortality, consisting of "dispensaries" (inoculation centres), extensive publicity campaigns called "Hygiene Weeks" in Montreal, and the improvement of sanatoria quickly brought positive results. It also captured the imagination of prominent Montrealers, whose pressure later in the decade forestalled any complacency which might have set in. The techniques developed during this crusade were successfully transferred to other health problems. Schools introduced separate, compulsory courses in health, and allowed dental as well as chest examinations. Montreal began the systematic immunization of babies against diphtheria and smallpox. The Bureau of Health inspection service received the funds to increase its size and effectiveness and was granted much additional authority in the wake of a typhoid epidemic which killed hundreds of Montrealers in 1927. The laboratory division grew comparably, with David now dreaming of an institute devoted to hygiene-related social problems and providing free services and drugs to the indigents of Montreal. This plan originated in the frustrations of combating venereal disease: the division was treating tens of thousands of people a year but having difficulty in retaining patients until they were cured and in overcoming ignorance and prejudice by its educational campaign. With urban health problems reasonably under control, the bureau then devoted some attention to small centres and to the countryside. Dr Lessard recommended the establishment of County Health Units consisting of full-time medical officers, public health nurses, and sanitary inspectors with powers of enforcement and the duty to train local agents of health education. The government swiftly obliged, and while it did not compel local authorities to establish health units, it did offer generous financial incentives, subject the units to the authority of the bureau once established, and require municipalities with more than 5,000 people to employ a full-time health officer if they were not part of a health unit.[68]

Taschereau's longstanding ambivalence toward labour did not change substantially during the mid-1920s, and it was reflected in government policy even though Galipeault was now the minister. He was more thoroughly convinced than ever that his policy of promoting industrialization and vocational education benefited the working man above all; the latter need not emigrate and could aspire to the modest affluence of a skilled worker in a modern industry. He believed that legislation protecting the health and safety of Quebec workers was as progressive as any in North America and was determined to maintain this leadership with appropriate reforms. And he accepted the right of workers to organize and treated their leaders as spokesmen for a legitimate interest group. His professed sympathy for workers ended abruptly, however, at the point of "disrupting" the operation of the labour market. A "just wage," if Taschereau thought in such terms, reflected the value of labour to the employer. To force higher pay, either directly or by increasing the power of unions, would "kill the goose that laid the golden egg" – destroy the viability of enterprise or surrender the competitive advantage vis-à-vis other regions offered by Quebec's "plentiful" labour supply. Given Taschereau's repeated references to "sane," "contented," and "responsible" labour, it is reasonable to assume that the perceived competition for capital investment, rather than a theoretical devotion to laissez-faire principles, really determined his attitude.[69] His single greatest fear about the trade union movement in Quebec was that it would import demands and expectations from abroad. Only months after his complaint about typographical workers' wage demands being dictated from Indianapolis, Taschereau privately confessed his misgivings about Canadian participation in the International Labour Organization: "Insofar as the Province of Quebec is concerned, these conferences give no good results. They give rise to problems which exist elsewhere but do not exist here, and induce our labouring class to press demands on which they would otherwise remain silent. Labour is remarkably quiet in the Province of Quebec, and it is perhaps a mistake to discuss new problems – Mr Galipeault came back [from Geneva] with the very strong impression that no good results derived therefrom."[70]

Two major developments illustrated the government's attitude to labour relations. One was passage of the Professional Syndicates Act of 1924. This legislation could hardly be described as antilabour, since it was virtually drafted by the Catholic labour confederation. It permitted labour organizations to incorporate themselves and thus enter into legal agreements, including collective agreements with employers. While thus providing an eventual framework for labour relations in Quebec, the law had a limited immediate impact. It did not require employers to recognize or bargain with unions, and in any case those unions which had won *de facto* recognition feared that as legal entities they could be sued for damage caused by their members during a conflict. Apparently the Catholic unions wanted this law for certain rhetorical purposes and to facilitate such internal activities as insurance and retirement plans and educational and social programs. Taschereau saw no harm in obliging the Catholic unions, as long as he compensated with a gesture toward the internationals. (The Women's Minimum Wage Commission was finally activated and Gustave Francq appointed chairman.) What was significant was the absence of any conscious move toward a code of labour relations, despite a bitter series of strikes in the clothing industry the same year and a recent Supreme Court ruling that the twenty-year-old federal Industrial Disputes Investigation Act was unconstitutional – industrial relations were a provincial responsibility![71]

The second revealing case arose from the proceedings of the Roy Commission reviewing workman's compensation, which reported in 1925. Compensation was, of course, Taschereau's favourite showpiece, his chief claim to be the friend of labour, and he made it clear to manufacturers that with the passage of time the system would become more and more generous to labour.[72] The commission unanimously recommended several measures to improve procedures, better define rights and responsibilities, and improve benefits, and Taschereau had these enacted in 1926 (though not in a manner entirely pleasing to the CTCC). Management and labour representatives could not agree, however, on whether to remove compensation cases from the courts entirely and create a permanent commission to administer the system. Such commissions existed in six other provinces and some Quebec employers favoured one on grounds of administrative efficiency, but Taschereau sided with the reluctant majority and refused the change. In all likelihood, he feared that a permanent commission might become too visible, a focus for politically embarrassing and economically "dangerous" demands from labour.[73]

Ironically, that very concern about the competitiveness of Quebec industry soon forced Taschereau to reverse himself. The 1926 legislation obliged employers to carry insurance against compensation claims, and suddenly insurance companies announced drastic increases in premiums for such coverage – in some cases, up to four times the rates prevailing in Ontario. Taschereau was not pleased, since this development forced him to suspend implementation of his latest improvements to the Compensation Act on the eve of a provincial election. However, employers did appear to be swinging over to the idea of a commission which could accept liability deposits in lieu of private insurance. Again, Taschereau was ready to accommodate them; he so warned the insurers, and asked Walter Mitchell to examine the details of other provincial systems.[74] Somehow the insurers managed to orchestrate a write-in campaign against creation of a commission, but this only enraged Taschereau. Assured publicly that the Quebec division of the Canadian Manufacturers' Association was not a party to the campaign, Taschereau had the legislation enacted in 1928. Under the chairmanship of Taschereau's nephew Robert, the Workman's Compensation Commission immediately exercised its authority to order and enforce accident prevention measures as well as make awards. By 1931, moreover, the threat of state competition brought private insurers into line. But Taschereau's foreboding also proved justified: almost immediately, organized labour called for the expansion of compensation into a much broader system of social insurance.[75]

It can be said on Taschereau's behalf that in most of Quebec's traditional, labour-intensive industries, there was little the government could do by way of legislation to raise workers' incomes. Its real failing with respect to labour was the poor use of such statutes and administrative agencies as existed to protect workers. The Women's Minimum Wage Commission, for example, calculated the living expenses of a workwoman in Montreal at $12.20 a week and then set $12.00 as a minimum wage for *experienced* female textile workers in the city.[76] Despite the good intentions expressed in 1919, the Department of Labour did not crack down fully on illegal child labour, and did not employ a staff large enough to allow proper inspection of industrial establishments. The bias of the Conciliation and Arbitration Service in favour of employers was so notorious that practically no workers asked for its services. In a bitter but reasoned minority report on the Quebec shoe workers' strike of 1925 and 1926, the labour appointee to an arbitration council rightfully denounced his management and government-appointed colleagues for their cynical misuse of statistical evidence and their extreme bias and lack of compassion. Naturally the workers rejected the majority report which defended wage-cutting and arbitrary downward reclassification by employers. But a renewed strike by 3,000 of them was broken within three months.[77]

By the beginning of 1927 Alexandre Taschereau's government was receiving criticism from several directions, but on balance its political position was far stronger than it had been four years earlier. The Liquor Commission and the Public Charities Bureau were widely accepted, higher religious authorities no longer protected or tacitly encouraged individual priests hostile to the Liberals, Montreal had recovered its autonomy, and municipal finances had improved generally throughout the province. Quebec had emerged dramatically from the postwar economic crisis, and even if the real incomes of urban workers were marginally higher at best, many appeared to share the myth or expectation of greater affluence and to embrace the first real wave of American mass culture to penetrate French Canada. To the chagrin of clerical and other moralists, English as well as French, "risqué" dances, films, and magazines grew increasingly popular. Radio programs and newspapers produced within Quebec naturally respected traditional standards of decency more carefully, but still faithfully transmitted most of the escapist ballyhoo being served up by their American counterparts. Even though they remained political party organs, mass circulation dailies like *La Presse* and *Le Soleil* had obviously decided that by glamorizing professional athletes and entertainers, aviators and stuntmen, gangsters and psychotic killers, they could increase both their readership and their advertising revenue.

Taschereau enjoyed high personal stature as well. Events were vindicating many controversial policies, and creating a situation in which his preferred role and image, that of chairman of the board, Province of Quebec, appeared singularly appropriate. He had learned to joke about his lack of oratorical flourish. During the liquor controversy he confessed that he was "not a poet [but] a total prohibitionist in matters literary," and often explained that spell-binding was David's responsibility.[78] Realizing also that his paternalistic bearing did not always inspire filial devotion, Taschereau was almost inadvertently developing a different kind of political appeal. He symbolized the necessary reconciliation between tradition and modernity in Quebec, the aristocrat who could master the dramatically altered realities of North American economic life and respond effectively to new administrative needs without abandoning the social and religious values which made French Canadians distinct. This was no image-maker's brainstorm. It is doubtful whether anyone in Taschereau's milieu even thought in terms of cultivating an image, and observers only began to identify the phenomenon explicitly in the 1930s.[79] It represented what Taschereau genuinely wanted to be rather than how he wanted to appear. But the elements were clearly presented as early as December 1925, when La Presse celebrated the twenty-fifth anniversary of his first election to the legislature with a 20-column panegyric. During Taschereau's trip to England and the continent in the following autumn, reports from abroad implied a recognition of these attributes by foreign political and social elites as well.[80]

In contrast to the political health of the government stood the feeble condition of the Conservative opposition. Taschereau himself remarked privately on their disarray at the close of the 1926 session.[81] At the first two sessions following their 1923 electoral gains, and in several by-elections as well, the Conservatives did seem well on the way to restoring serious party competition. Arthur Sauvé's hopes began to collapse, however, with the return of E.-L. Patenaude to federal politics in August 1925. Evidently no one had thought of consulting him during the long and tortured negotiations between Patenaude and Arthur Meighen, but this was hardly surprising. He had adamantly refused to reconsider his policy of separating federal and provincial politics, even at the backroom organizational level, without a condition Meighen could not fulfil, the repeal of Regulation XVII. Nor did Sauvé endorse Patenaude's "independent" Quebec campaign leading to the 29 October federal election, even when Taschereau intervened with the wild accusation that Meighen "with his conscription law, has filled the cemeteries of Flanders with

60,000 Canadians." Sauvé could certainly have criticized Taschereau and other Liberals for such excesses, for even their more accurate statements could only serve to reopen old wounds. Perhaps his refusal was a measure of French-Canadian hostility toward Meighen, who still would not acknowledge any wartime wrongdoing and now appeared to be conduct ng, with Patenaude's help, a reenactment of the Tories' 1911 election strategy. In any case, there seemed to be no possibility of an electoral backlash against Liberal tactics, no matter how unfair and irresponsible outsiders considered them.[82]

Sometime after the 1925 election, which saw the Conservatives gain significantly in the popular vote but fail to elect any French-Canadian members, Sauvé appeared to sense the need for a reconciliation. The separation of federal from provincial politics suddenly ceased being a matter of principle; the obstacles to cooperation were now Meighen's "misinterpretation" of his earlier conditions, Sauvé's resentment at the theft of Patenaude from the provincial caucus, and the factionalism of federal Conservatives in Quebec.[83] But he still refused to endorse Meighen publicly, even when Patenaude joined the short-lived Conservative administration in July 1926 and several provincial members took part in the 1926 federal campaign. Sauvé proved to be right on one count: French Canadians were no more ready to accept Meighen than they had been a year earlier. Unfortunately, however, the federal Conservative factions were now united and Sauvé was on the outside. He soon realized the full implications of that position: little financial or editorial support, and difficulty finding prestigious, "respectable" candidates for his own coming election campaign. Even some incumbents decided not to reoffer. Sauvé's tactics began to reflect a sense of desperation. St James Street and the *Gazette*, he charged, had deserted him as part of a corrupt bargain with Taschereau in which the latter would continue to favour vested and foreign interests.[84] Instead of formulating a reasoned critique of the Liberals' record and a coherent alternative to their philosophy, he simply identified the party with any grievance against the Taschereau regime. This offered possibilities in certain constituencies, especially where the recently founded Union catholique des cultivateurs was strong or an emotional local issue had arisen, but it did little to establish province-wide credibility for the opposition.

If the Conservatives did project one image consistently through 1926 and 1927, it was that of a party rejecting industrialization. Few Conservative deputies were so reactionary, but their criticism of excesses and abuses was filtered through the biases of *Le Devoir* and *L'Action catholique*, which were by now the only daily newspapers opposing Taschereau. The premier was naturally delighted to see industrialization and foreign investment shaping up as dominant election issues. He was always looking for a popular vindication of his philosophy and for a corresponding repudiation of *la bonne presse*, as he now contemptuously described his zealous nemeses. Economic circumstances more likely to produce such a result can scarcely be imagined, while a "referendum" on economic development would also conveniently obscure whatever real issues the opposition attempted to raise during an election campaign.[85]

The legislative session 11 January to 1 April 1927 became in most respects a dress rehearsal for the election everyone knew would follow. The Throne Speech celebrated the most recent examples of economic expansion and promised two major new spending programs: the Rural Schools Assistance Act and the province's assumption of complete responsibility for the construction and maintenance of highways. During subsequent debate, Taschereau gave such a comprehensive defence of the government's record that the Liberals could later publish it verbatim as their leading election pamphlet.[86] Although spirited, the opposition's attack seemed largely ineffectual and frequently cheap. More innuendo concerning the Banque Nationale sounded particularly spiteful, and only gave Taschereau the chance to crow about the success of the salvage operation. Impulsively, Conservatives tried to make political capital out of two terrible tragedies. The first occurred just two days before the opening of the legislature, when a blocked exit in Montreal's Laurier Palace Theatre caused seventy-eight children to be trampled to death escaping from a small fire. Here was another case where *la bonne presse* led the opposition astray, for they turned the issue from one of negligence by proprietors and building inspectors to the corrupting influence of the cinema. While this did force Taschereau to appoint a Royal Commission with terms wide enough to deal with the "moral" question, Conservatives should have realized that this kind of puritanical crusade would have as little popular appeal as earlier clerical causes of the decade. The second tragedy was the typhoid epidemic in March and April. The opposition blamed Caron's department for the outbreak, attributing it to contaminated milk which never should have reached the city. This serious accusation was based on no more than the fact that, as a precautionary measure, the United States had embargoed Quebec milk. But health officials discovered that the cause lay elsewhere, and Taschereau used diplomatic channels to have the embargo lifted quickly. He also won plaudits by expanding the authority of the provincial Department of Health, for municipal officials had been very slow and uncooperative once the epidemic began.[87]

There was yet another episode in Montreal, a scandal rather than a tragedy, in which opponents tried to implicate Taschereau. In 1926 a number of investors including Léonide Perron had purchased the Montreal Water and Power Company – just in time to sell it to the city at a hugh profit. Justifiably, a biracial hue and cry was raised locally, but at Quebec the Conservatives falsely alleged that Perron was the main instigator and that by failing to outlaw or rescind the transaction, his cabinet colleagues were accomplices. The latter was a strange argument, Taschereau countered, coming from deputies who had campaigned as defenders of Montreal's autonomy in 1923. If anything improper had occurred in Montreal, the courts had adequate remedies.[88] This answer did not remove the embarrassment caused by Perron's involvement, but even *Le Devoir* finally admitted that the scandal was a purely local affair. (Besides, Perron was already notorious for a far shadier association: being a director of the Canada Cement Company while minister of roads. If that didn't make him a political liability, nothing would.)

No session would have been complete without some attempt to exploit the unpopularity of Charles Lanctôt. The pretext in 1927 arose early in March, when the British Privy Council ruled in favour of Newfoundland in the Labrador boundary case. The loss of 102,000 square miles of potentially valuable territory was a serious matter for Quebec, and the decision sparked a pertinent debate about the abolition of references to the Privy Council. But the charges against Lanctôt – that Quebec had spent $1 million preparing the case and had taken it to court because he had overestimated the strength of Quebec's claims, and that the case had been lost partly because of his carelessness – were patent nonsense. The parties involved had been trying for decades to find a way of determining the boundary between Quebec and Newfoundland; Canada, not Quebec, was the formal litigant, and had retained excellent counsel in England; and Lanctôt had gone to England as little more than an observer. Blaming Lanctôt on this occasion was also rather insensitive, for his wife's illness had forced him to leave England before the case opened and she had died before he could reach her.[89]

The only issue which really put Taschereau on the defensive was the Lake St John affair, and ultimately the Conservatives misplayed that one as well. When the Aluminum Company acquired majority control of Duke-Price in 1925, its purpose was to increase the amount of power generated at the Grande Décharge. This involved raising the level of Lake St John higher, and consequently flooding more farmland, than authorized by the order-in-council in 1922. Under legislation introduced by Taschereau himself back in 1909, a hydroelectric company could expropriate land adjacent to its waterfall site. But because of the 1921 law separating colonization land from the commercial forest domain, in this instance cabinet approval was first required. Although such approval was a foregone conclusion, Duke-Price flooded the additional land in question before legally obtaining it and the government did not impose any penalty.

As long as Sauvé and his followers focused on the company's arrogant disregard for Quebec law, and on the government's indulgence thereof, their case was unanswerable. Athanase David gave them more ammunition when he belittled a protest movement organized by J.-N. Cabana, a Montreal journalist who had christened the affair "la tragédie du Lac Saint-Jean." David, pretending that farmers preferred generous *post facto* compensation to the possession of their land, claimed it was really a comedy for everyone except the government's opponents. Taschereau himself knew better than to be so flippant, and politely received several delegations. But his self-defence sounded more like a confession of impotence. The company had

committed a wrong, and knows it. For our part, we have told [the victims] many times that the company had acted illegally.

But how is the government at fault in all this? If a railway company takes over someone's land when it has a government charter, is that the government's fault? Don't the courts exist to permit this individual to have the work stopped and to claim damages? The government is not liable.

The victims ... came to us in great numbers to protest. The company paid all the delegates' expenses, coming and going. We told them to sue the company, and to stop the work by injunction. They refused. We offered to submit their claims to the Public Service Commission at our expense. Again refused. Finally we proposed to create a special tribunal composed of men they trusted who would determine compensation finally and without right of appeal, again at no cost to themselves. Many delegates declared satisfaction with such an arrangement, and that is the course we propose to follow.

The company has spent $37,000,000 up to now on its work. Are we going to have it demolish everything, and tell it to go away? That would be the end of foreign investment here. And because a neighbour wrongs you, should you cease being honest and just toward him?[90]

Predictably, however, the Conservatives and *la bonne presse* could not hold their sights on the unpunished illegality (Duke-Price would have paid compensation anyway), David's indiscretion, or even the government's apparent indifference to its own colonization law. They made an issue of the project itself, dragging out the hackneyed cry, "industry at the expense of agriculture." Now they were fighting on Taschereau's favourite territory, and it was not difficult for the premier to demonstrate that the interests of agriculture and colonization in the Saguenay-Lake St John district, as on the mining frontier of Abitibi, were best served by industrial development. Instead of an isolated, primitive, and marginal existence, colonists had a growing local market for their produce, rail and road connection with even larger urban markets, and opportunities to supplement their agricultural income. Few residents of the area were really opposed to such development, implied Taschereau. Despite local leadership, the Committee for the Defence of Lake St John was primarily a creation of urban utopians and habitual critics of his government.[91]

The legislature was dissolved on 19 April and a general election called for 16 May. Taschereau was obviously determined to restore Liberal fortunes in Montreal. He brought two Montrealers, one of them not yet an MLA, into the cabinet; his manifesto contained a special appeal for voters in the metropolis to end their "isolation" from provincial affairs; and through Perron, he made sure that party organization was much stronger than in 1923. Given control of nominations and patronage, Perron was to head off independent or dissident Liberal candidacies. Taschereau even made a lighthearted pitch for Westmount and Saint George, two English Protestant seats which the Liberals had more or less conceded in recent years. Mocking recent articles by Henri Bourassa, which criticized federal Liberals for supporting a "Tory" premier in the campaign, he told voters: "I am sometimes told that I am a kind of Tory, and that should be a good introduction to some of you. I do not object to the word. I am a Liberal, perhaps a bad Liberal, but perhaps there is nothing so near to a good Tory as a bad Liberal."[92]

The amount of Liberal campaign spending throughout the province was probably unmatched in Quebec's previous history, but the government's actual promises were far from extravagant. Taschereau asked in effect for a mandate to continue past programs and policies, with the implied guarantee that these would ensure continued prosperity. Little serious heckling, organized or otherwise, interrupted the flow of self-congratulation and righteous indignation at government rallies. Some of the indignation may well have been genuine on Taschereau's part, for if anything his criticism of Sauvé intensified after the ballots had been counted. During the campaign he merely observed that Sauvé was now

abandoned by all serious newspapers, even the Conservative press, supported by no citizens distinguished in industry, commerce, finance, or agriculture [and] has had to ally himself with a hundred petty opportunistic politicians more interested in settling scores than in serving the general interests of the province.[93]

But in the aftermath, he angrily ranked Conservative tactics ahead of Liberal policy in explaining the outcome, a government victory by seventy-five seats to ten.

Violent, hostile and unjust criticism has not been wasted ... the people have rendered prompt justice toward these calumnies. Their verdict consoles and avenges us for all that we will try to forget ... The Conservative party is stronger than is indicated by the ballot. But the people ... had enough of the campaign of personalities, of defamation and of minor incidents, which aid in no wise the development of a country ... This is the reason a large number of Conservatives rallied to our side. They see in our Party and our Government a programme which has the sense of reality, and a constant and determined movement toward practical, useful and progressive ends. Mr Sauvé ignored all of these and only offered a programme of denials to the people.[94]

Sauvé began the campaign with outward confidence and expressed surprise at the final result, a government landslide in which the Liberals recovered six Montreal seats and two more in Quebec City. Disappointment was understandable, for the Conservatives had certainly reinvigorated the legislature and had not let the recent depletion of their caucus discourage them during the campaign. Compensating for members who did not reoffer were several apparently strong new candidates and unofficial organizational support from local units of the UCC and the Catholic labour confederation. In Montreal, the opposition staged a closing rally as successful as the 1923 event. But Sauvé must have realized that this would not suffice. Such economic grievances as existed were not easily blamed on the Taschereau government. The nonconfessional labour movement supported Taschereau even more openly than the CTCC backed Sauvé, ignoring opposition attempts to exploit Taschereau's delay in proclaiming the new Compensation Act; evidently they agreed that "progress" was the issue.[95] General Smart, the Conservative member for Westmount, was so nervous about the anti-industrial bias of candidates like J.-N. Cabana that he dissociated himself from the party's campaign. In the countryside, the prospect of immediate government patronage proved more attractive than the long-term reforms advocated by the ucc. In fact the nomination of ucc founders Laurent Barré and Noé Ponton as Conservative candidates probably lent credence to Caron's charge that their organization existed for partisan purposes. And ultimately, Sauvé could not deny an element of truth in Taschereau's diatribe against him: the opposition was not united on serious alternatives to government policy and had relied heavily on personal attacks which were more than usually unfair.

Clearly, Liberal organizers in some Montreal ridings went overboard to ensure victory for their candidate. Equally, the distribution of seats was grossly out of line with the popular vote (61 to 39 per cent). But the decline of Conservative strength from 1923 was general across the province, and widely predicted by neutral observers from outside the province. Perhaps nothing better symbolized their failure than the loss of the Lake St John constituency by a substantial margin. Nor were Sauvé and his Conservatives the only ones demoralized by the result, for in the preceding months French-Canadian nationalists had been putting their case against large-scale foreign investment and rapid industrialization more clearly and strongly than ever. Filling the columns of *Le Devoir*, *L'Action catholique*, *L'Action française*, and the new *Progrès du Saguenay* with their message, and hearing it endorsed by several Conservative candidates during the campaign, they thought they were making progress with public opinion. Taschereau's undeniable triumph on "their" issue persuaded many of them that the cause was hopeless: American capital had achieved not only an economic but a moral conquest of French Canada. What Taschereau intended as innocent humour later in 1927, nationalists undoubtedly considered a painful reminder. For when Archbishop Rouleau attended ceremonies opening the new transmission line from Ile Maligne to Quebec, the premier remarked that until then, "the blessing of the church was the only thing Shawinigan did not have."[96]

## CHAPTER SIX

# *"The Summit Has Been Reached"*

During his early years as premier, Alexandre Taschereau had frequent occasion to state his views on Canadian constitutional issues and on the related question of French-English relations. Regarding the former, he placed himself firmly in the provincial rights tradition of Honoré Mercier and Lomer Gouin. In November 1920, he complained that the federal government was violating the Confederation agreement by failing to increase substantially its unconditional subsidies to the provinces. Having surrendered lucrative sources of revenue to the central authority in 1867, the provinces needed these subsidies to discharge their constitutional responsibilities. But instead of raising the subsidies in line with overall federal revenues and provincial requirements, Ottawa was offering grants for specific programs in agriculture, roads, housing, and other fields clearly under provincial jurisdiction, and also muscling unceremoniously into new fields of direct taxation.[1] The fact that a program was popular with Canadians throughout most of the country, he added in 1923, did not justify such interference.

Canadians do not constitute a homogeneous nation. Canada is a confederation of several separate provinces which, through a carefully studied contract, formed an association enabling them to put certain parts of their individual assets, rights and privileges at common disposal, while at the same time jealously retaining their sovereignty on subjects which, in their view, can only be dealt with by themselves.

... The Canadian Parliament should always exercise the greatest prudence when it is a question of promulgating laws repugnant to one or other of the provinces. Possibly that might suit other members of the Canadian family. But if only one of them is hurt, there results damage which time is not always able to heal. No province should ever be under the impression that Confederation is a burden to it, or an obstacle to its progress.[2]

However strongly Taschereau felt concerning the linguistic rights of French Canadians outside Quebec, this matter of provincial rights took precedence. He considered the Quebec government to be the only reliable guarantor of French-Canadian survival. That made him suspicious of virtually any proposal emanating from English Canada for amending or patriating the British North America Act. In 1922, for example, Clifford Sifton proposed that either a constituent assembly or a parliamentary committee be established to formulate constitutional amendment procedures, which would then be submitted to the Canadian electorate for approval in a referendum. Taschereau evidently agreed with Charles Fitzpatrick that "you know what would happen to our schools and our language if we were [so placed] at the mercy of the West and Ontario," for he rejected Sifton's plan at the first opportunity.[3] Pressure and persuasion should be used to defend and further French-Canadian cultural rights in other provinces, but Taschereau had never wanted the federal government to invade provincial jurisdiction even for this noble purpose.[4]

While his views were therefore well known, the defence of provincial rights never became a major preoccupation for Taschereau during the first half of the 1920s. For a variety of reasons, the King government began life far more respectful of provincial rights than its predecessor had seemed to be. Meanwhile, English-Canadian nationalists, whose postwar constitutional, legal, and educational projects initially disturbed French-Canadian leaders, carefully disclaimed any designs on Quebec institutions. The resulting sense of security proved temporary, however, and by the time of the 1927 provincial election Taschereau felt it necessary to make a rather pointed declaration: "As for our role in Confederation, there are certain matters on which we will not compromise, and in that we will be faithful to the Liberal party's past. We wish to live peacefully with our neighbours and contribute to the grandeur of our country. But we are determined to secure respect for the integrity of our laws, for the plenitude of our constitutional and religious liberties, for the full autonomy assured us by the federal pact, and for the traditions of our people."[5]

Two specific issues which alarmed Taschereau have already been referred to: control of hydroelectric resources on the Ottawa and St Lawrence rivers, and old age pensions. Equally important, however, was the general atmosphere in which these matters arose, for circumstances had opened the entire structure and operation of Canadian federalism to review. The three prairie provinces were about to achieve constitutional equality with the other six by gaining control of their public lands and natural resources from the federal government. Through the Maritime Rights Movement, meanwhile, the eastern-most provinces had enlisted considerable national sympathy for their declining status in Confederation and had extracted a promise from King to alleviate their severe economic problems by implementing the recommendations of a Royal Commission inquiry. Fundamental change in Canada's external relationships was also imminent, for at the 1926 Imperial Conference the self-governing members of the British Empire had agreed with Britain to remove the last vestiges of colonial subordination. For Canada this created almost as many problems as it solved: how would its constitution, an act of the British Parliament, be amended in future; and who, if not the Judicial Committee of the Privy Council, would impartially adjudicate federal-provincial constitutional disputes?

Taschereau had no objection to justice for Canada's two aggrieved regions, although many Quebeckers were chagrined to see the prairie provinces finally gain control of their resources without granting meaningful concessions to their French-Catholic minorities. In fact, he was originally disposed to help King settle these matters without a general provincial raid on the federal treasury. In 1926 he warned King that organizing such a raid seemed to be the main purpose of an interprovincial conference convened by Premier Ferguson, and on the eve of the 1927 Dominion-Provincial Conference he politely discouraged Ferguson from holding a preliminary meeting closed to the federal delegation.[6] His only real fear on this issue was of a precedent whereby Ottawa formally altered the terms of its relationship with several provinces without the knowledge and consent of all – in effect appropriating the right to amend the BNA Act unilaterally or bilaterally with one member of Confederation. Similarly, Taschereau at first welcomed the results of the Imperial Conference. He believed in Dominion autonomy, which he did not consider incompatible with continued use of the Privy Council as a constitutional arbiter. (This was not illogical, for fully sovereign states had just created an international tribunal to settle their legal disputes.) He also predicted a domestic political windfall for the Liberal party, for the inevitable Tory howl about dissolving the British Empire would consolidate Liberal support in most parts of the country. Again, all that seriously disturbed Taschereau was the prospect of a transfer of authority from Britain to Canada which gave the federal government more power to amend or interpret the constitution.[7]

All of these issues came sharply into focus at the Dominion-Provincial Conference held in Ottawa from 3 to 10 November 1927. With his officials apparently regarding all provinces including Quebec as adversaries, King had not seriously explored the possibility of enlisting Taschereau as a moderate ally. He had cancelled a 1926 agreement between Ferguson, Taschereau, and the ephemeral Meighen administration, by which National Hydroelectric would divide the annual rental for its Carillon site between the two levels of government. He had refused Taschereau's request to postpone implementation of the old age pensions scheme until it could be discussed by the conference.[8] Then, in July 1927, the federal government asserted a claim to power sites on the St Mary's River near Sault Sainte Marie, Ontario; this did not directly concern Quebec, but Taschereau agreed with Ferguson that it was a major offensive which both of them must resist.[9] Conversely, the Quebec and Ontario governments were drawing ever closer together. At the national Conservative leadership convention which chose R.B. Bennett to succeed Meighen, Ferguson pleased Quebec by sponsoring a resolution against international development of the St Lawrence waterway. In early September, legal advisers of the two provinces completed the formulation of a joint submission regarding Carillon. A week later the indispensable breakthrough occurred. The commission Ferguson had appointed in 1925 to review Regulation XVII recommended a wide range of substantial concessions to the French language in Ontario schools. Ferguson sent Taschereau a copy of the report just as the Ontario legislature was about to approve it, and the latter responded by congratulating Ferguson for "the very honest endeavour you have made to settle the school question."[10]

Only days later, Taschereau made the most of a happy coincidence: he had been invited to speak at celebrations marking the University of Toronto centenary. As an obviously pleased Ferguson presided, Taschereau defined the "essential elements" of the Confederation agreement. It had been "a generous compromise by men of differing language, differing creed and from different provinces, but of one country, who agreed to yield on some points in order to end racial animosity, religious antagonism, sectionalism and ruinous rivalries of trade and local interests." Thus had been created a powerful economic entity, capable of developing its resources and of attracting immigrants and capital. Problems which had arisen stemmed not from defective principles in the agreement but from misguided application.

Every Canadian must understand that sixty years ago we formed not a homogeneous country but a Confederation of different provinces for certain purposes, with the distinct understanding that each of these provinces should retain certain things which a people, like an individual, has no right to abdicate. There are some moral suicides which are every bit as repugnant to the soul of a collectivity as to that of any human being. Traditions, creed, laws, national aspirations, language and a heritage were abandoned by none of the contacting parties ... and to some extent were put in common only for their safeguard and protection.

... To live and endure, the spirit as well as the letter of the pact of Confederation must be respected ... If the recent steps just taken to settle the Ontario schools conflict give satisfaction, as I hope they will, to a minority which has considered itself aggrieved and has won much sympathy from the sister provinces, a great step will have been taken down the road which leads to unity of spirit and to bonne entente ... A hundred years from now, when the University of Toronto celebrates its 200th anniversary, the premier of Quebec will perhaps benefit from a similar invitation to say that the settlement of this difficult question marked a turning point in Canadian annals.[11]

Historically and even logically, this oration may have been somewhat fuzzy. But it dramatically symbolized a reconciliation between the two most powerful members of the Confederation, and implied that the two provincial premiers, representing the two major parties as well as the principal races and religions, held the key to national unity. There are more prosaic and more easily documented explanations, but this kind of moral authority may partly account for the power of the Ferguson-Taschereau alliance at the Dominion-Provincial Conference and thereafter.

The two played their role perfectly once the conference began. When Justice Minister Ernest Lapointe introduced the first agenda item, Senate reform, Taschereau quickly objected that there was no urgency about it which could justify opening the Pandora's box of constitutional amendment. Ferguson and then two Maritime premiers agreed, and the western delegates who most strongly wanted reform let the matter drop. Next came constitutional amendment itself, which King and Lapointe presented as a purely theoretical question: they had no actual amendments to propose, only a desire to conserve Canada's "self-respect as a nation" by giving Parliament the right to change at least those provisions of the BNA Act which did not affect the provinces. Here again, Taschereau denied the need and warned against the precedent. Canada's constitution, he argued, was a contract for which the Fathers of Confederation had in fact provided an appropriate amending procedure requiring the consent of all. It was probably a blessing that the procedure was cumbersome, for "even with a fixed constitution, rights have been infringed upon … Constitutional amending power in Canada would mean constant conflict with the provinces [whereas] men far removed from the battlefield are better qualified to pass an impartial judgement." Quebec, Taschereau argued, had special cause for concern. "If a majority can decide on an amendment, there is no security in our charter. If on the other hand, we require unanimity … on some questions Quebec would be alone and would be pointed out as a barrier to the progress of other provinces."[12] A few federal disclaimers later, the subject was smothered in a wordy deferment.

When the conference turned to the more substantive issue of subsidies, Ferguson and Taschereau wisely assented to federal grants for the smaller provinces without demanding more money for Ontario and Quebec. On the contrary, Taschereau argued that it was important for provincial governments to have enough revenue to discharge their responsibilities, for "the provinces are more in contact with the people, educating them, building their roads and looking after their health … and having control of their judicial machinery."[13] By inference, however, the larger provinces must not have their sources of revenue invaded by the federal government; and it was on this basis that the other provinces felt obliged to support Quebec and Ontario on the next issue, control of water-power on navigable streams. King simply could not rally the other premiers behind Lapointe's contention that Ottawa was entitled to such control, and hence presumably revenue. With the carefully prepared legal opinion in hand, Ferguson called for a judicial test. When no one objected to this procedure, King had either to agree or concede the provincial claim.[14]

There were other issues on which Ontario and Quebec did not agree so precisely, and not surprisingly Taschereau was less able to have his point of view accepted in these cases. Alone among the premiers, he was opposed to all conditional subsidies because this procedure merely encouraged Ottawa to invade provincial fields of taxation and policy making. Other provinces took a more pragmatic view and welcomed federal grants for road construction. The old age pensions question was more complex. Many premiers including Ferguson shared Taschereau's philosophical reservations about a measure which "displaced" filial responsibility. And they all had to agree, at least in principle, that it was "unjust and unfair for the Federal [sic] to make un beau geste and throw upon the provinces the odium of refusal."[15] But as practising politicians they had to consider the evident popularity of the act. And while poorer provinces might find their share burdensome, they also realized that the federal contribution would represent a net transfer of income to their people from wealthier areas. Only in Quebec were there special considerations strong enough to override the attractiveness of the scheme. The most obvious and compelling of these was an instinctive fear for the cultural autonomy of French Canada. The legislation apparently sprang from an alien ideology (the leading advocate was a socialist, J.S. Woodsworth), and had been enacted without any regard for the unique central role of the church in French-Canadian social organization. Provincial rights were a means to an end, but the right of French Canadians to control institutions according to their own social ideals was the very essence of the Confederation agreement. Even a French Canadian who was prepared to challenge the philosophical bias against state intervention would find it embarrassing to urge acquiescence in this external imposition; clearly this was the experience of labour leaders.[16]

Taschereau and Nicol argued, moreover, that Quebec would also pay a special financial penalty under the terms of the Old Age Pensions Act. If it refused to participate on principle, then its citizens would be taxed for the federal contribution in other provinces. If Quebec did submit, then it had to pay both its 50 per cent share and the cost of administration, whereas under existing arrangements the church collected voluntary donations and its personnel looked after the needy at no administrative expense to the province. Nicol estimated that the scheme would cost his treasury $2 million a year more than it currently spent through provisions of the Public Charities Act. Hence the federal contribution was a dubious blessing. Quebec also insisted that it would have proportionally more claimants than other provinces. It had more people over seventy years of age than Ontario and the West, whose large numbers of recent immigrants were still in their working years. More urbanized than all but Ontario (where incomes were higher), Quebec would have more of its aged qualify for assistance. These financial arguments may have been rationalizations, but no one challenged them. English-Canadian delegates probably felt like bystanders at a family quarrel between the French-Canadian Liberals, Taschereau and Lapointe. In any case, Taschereau could not persuade any other province to join him in outright opposition.[17] Even though he was later advised that a challenge to the constitutionality of the act might well succeed,[18]

Taschereau wisely dropped the issue. Since Quebec did not have to participate, there was really little to be gained by antagonizing English Canadians who strongly favoured federal pensions. Even the financial penalty was negligible unless and until Ontario entered the scheme.

On balance, Taschereau had reason to be pleased with the outcome of the conference. The water-power issue dwarfed others in importance, and here the Ferguson alliance had succeeded completely: after a short delay during which two Quebec ministers tried to discourage him, King announced a reference to the Supreme Court.[19] (The decision rendered early in 1929 was not quite as favourable to the provinces as Taschereau had expected, but he was right to assume that King would behave less aggressively on the matter. Only in 1930, when the St Lawrence waterway project resurfaced, did Taschereau fear a new federal offensive.)[20] If anyone felt himself a loser in the proceedings, it was clearly Lapointe. Outmanoeuvred on water-power and constitutional reform, he had also been embarrassed at having some of his previous statements on provincial rights thrown back at him during the discussion of pensions. Evidently he took out much of his frustration on Lomer Gouin, who was rather spitefully denied a senatorship amid rumours that Lapointe still had not forgiven "Gouin's pupil" for cooperating with Ferguson. (Growled Gouin, "Lapointe remains the large little man he was and will always be.")[21] In his capacity as justice minister, Lapointe prepared a one-sided federal submission to the Supreme Court on the water-power question. Taschereau rightly protested that the two levels of government invited nothing but confusion if they submitted different questions and elicited different judgments. King could only apologize and acknowledge the wisdom of a joint submission. Although he blamed unnamed bureaucrats for this deviation from "normal procedure," King betrayed a growing fear. "Very confidentially," he wrote, "I greatly deplore what on occasions has appeared to me to be a lack of whole-hearted confidence and, to some extent, a degree of estrangement between some of my Quebec colleagues and yourself. Just what the reasons for this may be I am at a loss to understand."[22]

Taschereau replied that he did not really understand either, but offered a guess along with the reassurance King obviously sought. Conflicts would always arise between the Dominion and the provinces, and government leaders at both levels had a duty to protect their respective rights and interests. "But I am afraid that some of our friends at Ottawa sometimes take it as a personal attack against them when we do not share their views on these important matters

... You can be assured of our entire co-operation, as we feel it is in the party's best interest." Evidently King still had doubts, however, for on the eve of the 1930 federal election he feared he would receive less than Taschereau's whole-hearted support.[23]

Despite his overwhelming mandate to continue traditional policies, Taschereau faced difficult problems on the home front following the 1927 election. One of these was growing pressure from the organized labour movement for some form of provincial social insurance scheme. As Taschereau had foreseen, many labour leaders felt free to urge Quebec's "grudging" participation in the old age pension scheme once it was a *fait accompli.*[24] Even Pierre Beaulé, lay president of the Catholic labour union, staggered his clerical patrons by calling publicly for implementation. And those who sided with Taschereau on philosophical or constitutional grounds still insisted that the province must recognize the problem of the needy aged. Abbé Fortin put this view as forcefully as anyone. "We must oppose statism, but we must also care for the destitute. And today we have come to the point where measures must be taken to aid the indigent." Ironically, his proposal was more radical than old age pensions: government must force industry to provide wages and benefits which would permit workers to support aged parents and save for their own retirement.[25]

At exactly the same time as the old age pensions controversy, the Quebec government had suffered its embarrassment concerning amendments to the Workman's Compensation Act. Labour was generally pleased with the commission created at the session of 1928, since its existence solved the immediate problem of employer insurance and allowed the rest of the legislation enacted in 1926 to take effect. Also, the commission was accorded unexpectedly wide powers. Under sufficient political scrutiny it could provide substantial protection to workers, and there were Liberals as well as Conservatives who took its work seriously. But labour spokesmen also recognized that once a permanent commission existed, they had a much better chance of overcoming ideological taboos against state intervention. They had simply to represent state social insurance as a logical extension of the principle of compensation for industrial accidents. Unemployment in working years and financial hardship in retirement were occupational hazards of working class life in Quebec, just like injury and illness. Workers were therefore entitled to protection. Individual employers obviously could not carry the entire burden, but the commission could function as the instrument of collective responsibility, administering a single fund subsidized by the province.[26]

Taschereau defended his refusal to implement old age pensions frequently in 1928 and early 1929,[27] but support for the scheme continued to grow. He himself admitted that pensions *per se* did not violate the principles of self-reliance and family responsibility, as long as the individual contributed during his working years; indeed, provincial employees had a contributory pension plan. Meanwhile, he and Galipeault had almost despaired of persuading insurance companies to lower their premiums for employer liability. It was not entirely surprising, therefore, when Galipeault informed delegates to the 1929 CTCC Convention that the government was prepared to create a provincial insurance fund.[28] Shortly thereafter the government promised a formal inquiry into the possible scope of such a system, with Taschereau indicating that the idea of contributory social insurance was acceptable.[29] In April 1930 Edouard Montpetit, French Canada's foremost economist, agreed to chair a Royal Commission on Social Insurance, charged with recommending a system based on Quebec needs and upon the experience of Catholic European states. The mandate was probably more elaborate than necessary, and Taschereau may be suspected of wishing to postpone the evil day when government actually had to supplement worker and employer contributions. It is more likely, however, that Taschereau was taking out some insurance of his own – against a repetition of the Public Charities fiasco. This time, social legislation would be based on Catholic precedents and the Quebec hierarchy would participate in its formulation. Thus one of the province's most conservative bishops, Mgr Courchesne, became one of the commissioners. What Taschereau failed to anticipate was how quickly and thoroughly the Great Depression would expose the inadequacy of Quebec's traditional ideology and institutions in the field of social welfare. Ultimately the Montpetit Commission would recommend what were, in the Quebec context, almost revolutionary innovations.[30]

A second major problem, agriculture, was all the more delicate because it involved the declining effectiveness of the veteran minister, Edouard Caron. Caron's health was poor, and Taschereau first tried to reduce his burdens by appointing him to the Legislative Council. But the trouble lay deeper, in Caron's outdated approach to his portfolio. Trained as an agronomist, he saw the Agriculture Department's role solely in terms of encouraging better husbandry. This he did well through innumerable pamphlets, demonstration farms, short courses, and a network of specialists in scientific agriculture. Unfortunately, by the mid-1920s there were many, including some of his younger employees, who felt that there should be other priorities such as a more sophisticated approach to marketing and greater mechanization. Caron resisted this advice, reportedly because he took it as an implied criticism of previous accomplishments and because he was too insecure to let the department move into areas where his personal expertise was limited. Caron's war with the Union catholique des cultivateurs was undoubtedly related to this; one can see it in the annual ucc resolutions, which were often based on serious and thorough inquiries. Some partisan motives may have been present, but most ucc leaders were genuine reformers frustrated by the failure of existing farm organizations (tightly controlled by Caron) to press for the modernization of Quebec agriculture.[31]

For a while loyalty and convenience led Taschereau to ignore reality. Politically Caron's patronage system, along with Perron's roadbuilding program and Perrault's colonization grants, was still delivering a solid bloc of rural Liberal deputies, whereas the proposals of his critics contained major financial implications for the government. Mechanization, for example, would require much more elaborate farm credit arrangements – substantial long-term loans rather than annual advances against production. But Taschereau still sensed numerous dangers here: the government could become a collector of debts from voters and a competitor for the clergy-supported Caisses Populaires, and there would be pressure on and from Liberal backbenchers to arrange unwise loans. For a time he resisted participation in a federal farm loans program, fearing that statutory criteria would impose uncontrollable financial commitments on the province. On one occasion, he even declared that he would rather give than lend money to farmers.[32] But when it was pointed out that Quebec agriculture was not even meeting the needs of the domestic market – the province was importing foods which it could produce, while exporting comparatively little – Taschereau and his cabinet colleagues finally recognized the need for change. His health unimproved, Caron was retired to the vice-chairmanship of the Liquor Commission following the 1929 session. This was generally expected; what stunned observers was the identity of his replacement. Taschereau passed over the two ambitious backbenchers frequently mentioned for the post, J.-C.-E. Ouellet and Elisée Thériault, and gave the responsibility to Léonide Perron.[33]

Perron wasted little time living up to his reputation for toughness and efficiency. He issued a manifesto proclaiming his goals, with provincial self-sufficiency in agriculture high among them, and also his confidence that Quebec farmers understood "the necessity of a complete change in the methods of marketing and production now in use." His department would initiate change by supporting local marketing and purchasing co-operatives, by transforming the Coopérative fédérée into a province-wide marketing and exporting agency, and by circulating "the most recent and reliable information on market prices and on the probable demand for different products."[34] Establishing contact with the UCC leadership, committing himself to long-term modernization projects such as rural electrification and putting an end to political control of the Co-opérative fédérée, Perron quickly pacified the province's most progressive agricultural organization. Within a year, a remarkable amount of legislative and administrative reform had been accomplished.[35] Caron wrote pathetic letters to Taschereau, complaining that his many years of service were already being denigrated and forgotten.[36] But the story turned out to be tragic not only for Caron. Perron's heart was not as strong as his determination, and Taschereau's most capable and energetic minister died on 20 November 1930, at the age of fifty-seven. And although Taschereau found a highly promising replacement in the person of Adélard Godbout, the depression now made it virtually impossible for the government to support agricultural modernization in a serious way.

Taschereau's third major domestic problem was the pulp and paper industry, whose overexpansion could no longer be denied. In his 1927 report, Gustave Piché had warned that the danger was imminent: in order to avert a disastrous fall in the price of newsprint, producers must restrain their output and try to reach a pricing agreement. In 1928, Piché reported that the inevitable had occurred despite a belated attempt by some manufacturers to form a marketing cartel: "First of all the selling price fell from $70 to $65 a ton, then the daily output, of some at least, was reduced to 80% of the normal. Lastly the association to sell newsprint was dissolved in the spring of 1928, with the result that several of the members ... sold paper on prices and conditions equivalent to not over $55.00 gross per ton ... If an independent group does not undertake to unite the various manufacturers to have them adopt a policy in common, all the ground gained in the industry since 1917 will be lost irreparably."[37]

Belatedly the government began heeding its official. It held fast to the policy of not granting more timber limits despite some attractive new offers in 1928, and announced a moratorium on new plant construction. The latter represented a painful admission for Taschereau, who had been especially active promoting expansion in his own Quebec City district.[38] And whereas he had long defended large-scale American investment against nationalist criticism, it was now the International Paper Company whose very efficiency and market power threatened the stability of the industry as a whole. After the failure of a voluntary pricing and production agreement among ten Quebec and four Ontario companies in 1927, Taschereau and Ferguson in the following year instigated the founding of a stronger marketing cartel, the Newsprint Institute, among International's rivals. In November, Taschereau heard rumours that International had violated its undertaking to respect the cartel price of $65 a ton for 1929 deliveries, by signing a contract with the Hearst newspaper chain at $57. This would spell ruin for many institute members, who had long-term contracts to deliver fixed quantities of newsprint each year at a price no higher than that prevailing elsewhere in the industry. Taschereau immediately summoned A.R. Graustein, president of Canadian International's parent firm, to a week-long conference in Montreal. Under threat of government reprisals, Graustein agreed to renegotiate with Hearst. Stability was momentarily restored when the two giants signed a new contract for $62 in February 1929.[39] But no basic problem had been solved, and immediately following the October 1929 stock market crash, cut-throat competition resumed and plunged the indusry into a long and deep crisis. During the 1930s this crisis would become Taschereau's heaviest and most frustrating preoccupation, and his willingness to take personal responsibility for managing it a monument to his sense of public duty.[40]

Much to his eventual displeasure, Taschereau also had to intervene in a dispute concerning the education of Jewish children in Montreal. The problem seemed fairly simple when it first appeared in 1922, but before it was finally settled ten years later leading religious authorities and politicians had displayed staggering prejudice and irresponsibility. In a province whose laws provided only for Catholic and Protestant schools, the Jewish issue naturally arose as soon as significant numbers of Jews came to Quebec and concentrated themselves in central and western Montreal. Most Jewish parents sent their children to Protestant schools in order to have them learn English and to avoid the heavier religious content of the Catholic curriculum. But as a 1902 court decision revealed, these children attended on sufferance and had no rights. For its part, the Protestant School Board suffered under a tax-sharing system which did not compensate it for educating practically all of the 3,000 non-Protestant, non-Catholic students in the city. In 1903 the legislature declared Jews to be Protestants for educational purposes with all attendant rights and obligations; the Protestant Board thereby received tax revenue in proportion to its actual share of the student population.

Within two decades, however, new financial anomalies and other grounds for dissatisfaction had arisen. Jews complained that while paying equal taxes they had not received equal rights. They had no representation on the Protestant School Board and there was a strict quota for the number of Jewish teachers who could be employed; none at all were permitted in the high schools. Jewish children were also being segregated on the pretext that their absence on religious holidays disrupted the progress of Christian students. Some of the more recent Jewish immigrants, who were generally Orthodox, hoped not for equal rights within the Protestant system but for the establishment of a separate Jewish system. A corresponding division existed on the Protestant side, where most leaders only wanted to solve the financial problems and were prepared to make concessions to Jews within their system.[41] But a minority used the occasion to express their hostility to the growing Jewish presence in Protestant schools, now about 40 per cent. According to the Reverend E.I. Rexford, a member of the Protestant committee of the provincial Council of Public Instruction, Jewish requests for representation and/ or an end to discrimination against Jewish teachers were "attacks on ... the constitutional and religious rights" of Protestants. The basis of this division probably lay deeper than the attitude toward Jews. The educational ideas of the moderates were quite secular, in line with most North American Protestant thinking. The Protestant system in Quebec already accommodated many denominations and really existed because the Catholic majority insisted upon sectarian education for itself. Rexford and his sympathizers (who included J.J. Creelman, chairman of the Montreal Protestant Board) were thus fighting a rearguard action. But to use the Jews as scapegoats in this manner was all the more odious, and it thoroughly embarrassed Protestant moderates such as Herbert Marler. The zealots, he insisted, did not speak for all Protestants, and board members "acted like a lot of docile sheep" when they supported Creelman's "view of intolerance towards the Jews in Montreal."[42]

Taschereau hoped the two minorities would settle matters among themselves, but he was far from indifferent to the outcome and constantly favoured Protestant moderates and Jewish integrationists. In 1922 he blocked a one-sided bill presented by Creelman and substituted legislation which simply granted financial relief. He blocked another unfair proposal in 1923, and in the election of that year supported the nomination of Peter Bercovitch against Louis Fitch, an advocate of separate Jewish schools, in the Jewish con-

stituency of St Louis.[43] When private negotiations did not resolve
the noneconomic issues, Taschereau referred them along with other
problems to a commission chaired by Sir Lomer Gouin. All three
Protestant commissioners and two of the three Jews appointed were
moderates. Unfortunately this did not really expedite matters, because
the focus of attention quickly shifted from substantive to legal and
constitutional issues. What did the legislation of 1903 mean when
it accorded to Jews "the same rights and privileges" as Protestants,
and was it *intra vires*? These and related questions were pursued
all the way to the Judicial Committee of the Privy Council, which
handed down its judgment in February 1928. The 1903 statute was
largely *intra vires* in so far as it concerned the cities of Montreal
and Quebec City, with one major exception: it could not enable
Jews to be appointed to the Protestant Board of School Commissioners. The statute did imply this, and therefore violated Section
93 of the British North America Act. The board was not obliged
to appoint Jewish teachers, only to admit Jewish children to its
schools. The Provincial Legislature did not have the right to pass
new laws providing for the appointment of Jews to the board or
to the Protestant Committee, or requiring the appointment of Jewish
teachers. All it could really do without infringing the constitutional
rights of Protestants and Catholics was to create a separate Jewish
school system.[44]

This decision appeared to favour the extremists. If the Protestants
could not be persuaded to make voluntary concessions which satisfied
Jewish integrationists, then the government would face an intolerable
dilemma. Either it must permit discrimination against Jewish students and teachers, or else it must create a tax-supported Jewish
school system. Immoral in itself, the former course of action could
force parents to establish private schools and so perpetuate in Quebec
the same financial injustice suffered by Catholic minorities in western
Canada. The latter course, it soon became obvious, risked a confrontation with Catholic authorities fearful that the same privilege
could be demanded in future "by other religious groups or even
by anti-religious sects." Taschereau and David could only hope that
the unpleasant alternatives might facilitate a compromise among
moderates, and the outlines of a settlement did actually appear early
in 1929. But it provoked objections on all sides and Bercovitch, to
preserve his credibility with the Jewish community, introduced a
bill in 1930 calling for the creation of a separate system. This he
soon withdrew in favour of a government bill calling only for the
creation of a Jewish school commission in Montreal. Ignoring the
important distinction, both Cardinal Rouleau and Coadjutor Arch-

bishop Gauthier of Montreal protested to Taschereau against the alleged departure from a Christian system of education. As if on cue, other bishops soon followed. Gauthier was the least discreet, claiming that the Jews had been "wrapped in absolutely unjustifiable sympathy" and accusing David (the bill's sponsor) of anticlerical motives. "Some are clearly hostile to our traditional faith; others, more numerous, let themselves be taken in by words they misunderstand: liberty, broadmindedness, tolerance. Pronouncing them with just the right emphasis, they enjoy the vanity of believing themselves to be intellectuals. It is an old story, the one who considers himself a free spirit vis-à-vis the Catholic faith accepting the most humiliating servitude in other domains."[45] The Catholic faith was in danger, and the Jews were now to blame!

Still on good terms with Rouleau, Taschereau tried to be conciliatory. He attributed the Catholic authorities' worst fears to a misunderstanding of the bill and of the situation, and proposed a meeting to clear the air. This meeting occurred on 21 March, with David accompanying Taschereau and Rouleau joined by Gauthier and two other bishops. Taschereau explained why the legislation was necessary and hinted that separate Jewish schools might not actually come into existence: there would be tremendous expense and difficulty, and most Jewish leaders still preferred a compromise with the Protestants. Then he dispelled several misapprehensions: the bill applied only to Montreal, it did not involve "neutral" schools, and it would not alter the dual, Christian structure of the Council of Public Instruction. Finally a face-saving communiqué was composed, indicating that the bill would be "amended" in a manner satisfactory to the church. A second controversy erupted over the wording of one clause, which Rouleau feared would increase the authority of the Provincial Superintendent at the expense of the council – "a step towards the creation of a Minister of Public Instruction." This was resolved, and the Jewish School Commission of Montreal came into existence.[46]

As Taschereau had predicted and hoped, and much to the chagrin of the Orthodox Jewish faction, moderate Jews and Protestants soon reached an agreement which made the creation of separate Jewish schools unnecessary. In the meantime, however, Taschereau had one more cause for anger and sorrow about the affair. As if inspired by Archbishop Gauthier's display of bigotry, the premier's political opponents criticized his handling of the issue with blatant appeals to antisemitic prejudice. The new Conservative leader, Camillien Houde, had second thoughts about the campaign once Taschereau called him to account.[47] But the outburst heralded a sad chapter in Quebec's history, in which Jews were scapegoats for all manner of fears and frustrations during the 1930s. This was by no means confined to the lunatic fringe of the self-proclaimed Fascist leader Adrien Arcand, whose newspaper *Le Goglu* first captured public attention during the Jewish school controversy. Overt antisemitism became positively respectable in student and young nationalist circles, especially in Montreal. The *achat chez nous* movement (a thinly disguised call to boycott Jewish merchants and professionals) and the campaign to bar Jewish interns from Catholic hospitals were two of the worst examples, but hardly isolated cases. With some brave and honourable exceptions, the older generation made no effort to discourage it even after Hitler's rise to power. *Le Devoir* itself engaged in Jew-baiting under Bourassa's successor Georges Pelletier; when Montreal Jews organized a protest rally against Hitler's anti-semitism in 1933, the Jesuits gave their meeting hall for a counter-demonstration held by protégés of Abbé Groulx, who had emerged as the spiritual leader of postwar French Canadian nationalism. Groulx himself wrote or published scurrilous assaults on Quebec and world Jewry in *L'Action nationale*, his recently founded successor to *L'Action française*.[48]

Taschereau denounced this phenomenon at every opportunity, but also seemed a bit intimidated by its growing force. When Peter Bercovitch introduced a bill in 1932 to permit civil action against group libel, Taschereau's first impulse was to support at least a watered-down version of it. From personal experience he despised the venomous prejudice which habitually infected the nationalist press in Quebec, and he considered the writings of Arcand an especially dark blot on the reputation of his province. But he was forced to change his mind, not so much because such a law could conceivably be used against legitimate expressions of opinion but because *Le Devoir* had succeeded in portraying the Bercovitch bill as a Jewish demand for undue special privilege. Sealing its doom with a classic bit of understatement, Taschereau conceded that "public opinion is not ready for such a radical measure."[49] Evidently the matter did not rest easily on Taschereau's conscience, however. After the session a test case clearly demonstrated that Jews did not have adequate recourse under existing laws, as Bercovitch's opponents had pretended. As a result Taschereau prepared his own amendment to the Civil Code, introduced in 1933 despite heavy criticism, and only withdrew it when all three of Adrien Arcand's rags suddenly and unexpectedly ceased operation.[50]

Unfortunately Quebec antisemitism did not require Arcand's pen to thrive; only Auschwitz drove it underground. Even then echoes of the 1930s could be heard and read. Robert Rumilly, for example, implied that the root of the Jewish school problem was a conspiracy between Jewish leaders and federal Liberals to smuggle illegal Jewish immigrants into Quebec – an ironic fabrication in the light of recent research, but accepted uncritically by the leading historian of Quebec education.[51]

Whereas Taschereau's first two terms as premier were marked by stability in the *personae* of Quebec political life, his third witnessed a flurry of important changes. By the force of circumstance rather than by design, and amidst constant press speculation which seemed to annoy Taschereau,[52] the cabinet underwent a modest rejuvenation. In addition to losing Caron and Perron, he had to accept (and conceivably urge) the resignation of two much closer friends, Jacob Nicol and Antonin Galipeault. Nicol's growing business interests made it questionable whether he could devote all the necessary attention to his responsibilities as provincial treasurer, especially when a young Conservative MLA named Aldéric Blain was campaigning energetically to revive meaningful legislative scrutiny of the public accounts. Moreover, Nicol now owned *Le Soleil*, the largest single recipient of government printing contracts, and other favoured newspapers. Conflict of interest charges were growing louder, and Nicol went to his reward in the Legislative Council. Galipeault had his own conflict of interest storm brewing: legal advice to a firm bidding on public works contracts. In any case he was tired of public life after more than a quarter of a century, and like most veteran political players did not really mind being relegated to the bench. Rumours that Athanase David would also retire were actually well founded, even though they never materialized. For years the provincial secretary had wished to be the provincial agent in Paris, and now Montreal party organizers were complaining that David was neglecting political duties. If Taschereau persuaded him to remain, he may later have regretted the advice. For David became increasingly distracted by personal problems over the next few years.[53]

Initially there did not appear to be any major problem in replacing the departed ministers. Both J.-N. Francoeur (Labour and Public Works) and Hector Laferté (Colonization) were respected and experienced politicians, although still in their mid-forties. Godbout was thirty-eight, and though a political neophyte was obviously an outstanding orator and persuasive diplomat. He shared Perron and Taschereau's view of agriculture as a vital element in the Quebec economy, not some metaphysical basis of French-Canadian nationality. And he had the professional background, as an agronomist and professor of agriculture with personal contacts among reform-minded farm leaders, to continue Perron's work.[54] The new treasurer, Andrew R. McMaster, was a curious but equally promising choice. To maintain the tradition of having an English Protestant in the post, Taschereau once again had to reach outside the provincial Liberal caucus. McMaster was a veteran member of Parliament who had embarrassed the King government early in the 1920s with calls for strong conflict of interest legislation, and had never received an opportunity to advance from the back benches. There is no evidence that Taschereau enticed him to Quebec City with promises of political reform, but McMaster did come with a healthy reputation and quickly reinforced it by abandoning customary mumbo jumbo in favour of a clear, forthright budget presentation. Instead of pandering to the popular prejudice against public debt, McMaster explicitly defended the citizens' right to know the real financial state of the province and the government's true expectations concerning revenue and expenditure for the coming year.[55]

Two serious problems did eventually result from these cabinet changes, however. McMaster served only through the 1930 session before falling seriously ill. His successor, a capable Montreal accountant named Gordon Scott, was defeated in his attempt to enter the legislature through a by-election. Now Taschereau took on the treasurer's portfolio himself, hoping Scott could win in the next general election. This arrangement had one noteworthy consequence, presentation of the 1931 budget in French for the first time in anyone's memory. The other difficulty was the reaction of disappointed aspirants for cabinet rank. Both Ernest Ouellet and Elisée Thériault had now been passed over twice for the Agriculture portfolio, and both received seats in the Legislative Council as consolation. Far from showing the gratitude Taschereau expected, they immediately began using their safe haven to criticize the government and later encouraged younger Liberals to rebel against Taschereau's leadership.

Changes in the enemy camp were considerably more dramatic following the 1927 election, and most of the excitement surrounded the meteoric rise of the new Conservative leader, Camillien Houde. Humble of origin but not in self-estimation, Houde had won the provincial constituency of Ste Marie during the Conservatives' Montreal sweep in 1923. Despite a determined effort to portray himself as champion of the workingman, he was narrowly defeated in 1927 by Joseph Gauthier, a Liberal trade unionist. But polling irregularities were so blatant that the election was annulled, and in October 1928 Houde recaptured Ste Marie. (At the next session, a practical joker unknowingly presaged Houde's impact on the political atmosphere by placing a stick of dynamite, its fuse lit but then extinguished, outside Taschereau's office.) By the time of his reelection, Houde had achieved an even more prominent office, the mayoralty of Montreal, as a last-minute candidate capitalizing on the waterworks scandal. In July 1929 he was virtually unopposed for the provincial Conservative leadership, vacated as promised by Sauvé. Houde performed aggressively in the 1930 legislative session, and easily won reelection as mayor even though he had done nothing to punish the perpetrators of the waterworks scheme.[56]

Personally, Taschereau had no use for this man of no culture and fewer manners, and despised Houde's stock-in-trade, the appeal to class and racial prejudices. In fact, Taschereau never revealed the social prejudices of a seigneur more clearly than during Houde's first months as opposition leader. During a by-election campaign he described Houde as "the chief of a group of bobolinks, little birds that eat what they can when the horses have passed" as well as a "nonentity." At Laval University he warned students against "arrivistes," and expanded on the theme "Elites and Democracy" at Queen's University. On balance democracy had probably added to the welfare of western societies, but

in some respects, it is still in the experimental stage. This being so, a restraining power, a guiding hand may be necessary to direct the world in its process of evolution. Democracy is international, and clever leaders, by more or less wise appeals to classes, may shake foundations built on ages of experience, thought and statesmanship ... The task rests with a certain class of aristocracy. Not the aristocracy of blood, lineage, or money, but the aristocracy of learning, science and knowledge [which] is open to every democrat however obscure his origin [but] must realize its responsibilities.[57]

In private, he described the opposition leader as "a bit of a scoundrel and a vulgar fellow."[58] He was determined not only to withstand the challenge of a revitalized opposition, but to destroy Houde's political career entirely. Such determination appeared all the more necessary following the federal election of July 1930. Not only did the new Conservative leader, R.B. Bennett, score a convincing national victory, but without Arthur Meighen to kick around, Liberals saw even their Quebec base eroded. Largely on the strength of Bennett's promise of higher tariff protection for the dairy industry, the Conservatives won nearly twenty farming constituencies and twenty-four seats in the province overall. Philosophically Taschereau probably had more in common with the new prime minister than he had with Mackenzie King, a thought which occurred very early to their mutual nemesis, Henri Bourassa.[59] But that did not alter the new political reality, which was that Taschereau's opponents now controlled the federal government. In fact two of Bennett's three French-Canadian cabinet ministers, Arthur Sauvé and Alfred Duranleau, had just graduated from the ranks of the provincial opposition. Unless the Bennett government became very unpopular very quickly in Quebec, Houde's Conservatives would enjoy unfamiliar rhetorical and material advantages in the coming provincial election.

By 1931, of course, the economic context of Quebec politics had changed even more radically than the cast of characters. As the depression settled upon Canada, the special weaknesses of the Quebec economy were quickly and dramatically revealed. The boom of the 1920s had been dependent upon external investment capital, world demand for Quebec's forest and mineral resources, and the prosperity of western Canadian farmers, whose exports of wheat through the ports of Montreal and Quebec City and whose purchase of goods manufactured in Quebec were responsible for tens of thousands of jobs. Except for the price of precious metals, all these external stimuli disintegrated quickly following the Wall Street crash. Wheat and newsprint prices, in fact, presaged the collapse of the stock market. For one-industry towns throughout Quebec, for workers whose port-related employment was already highly seasonal, for employees in the dozens of small clothing and other manufacturing concerns which were marginal at the best of times, and even for employees of bigger firms which had never paid more than subsistence wages, the impact was swift, brutal, and highly visible. For those in the construction trades, and for small merchants, professionals, and landlords with a working-class clientele, hardship was only slightly mitigated and delayed.[60]

Nor was Quebec institutionally or philosophically equipped to cope with a prolonged economic crisis. The Montpetit Commission was just beginning to deal with the problems of social insurance and social assistance on the provincial level. Major cities, including Montreal, had no mechanism for organizing relief and had to call in local, voluntary charitable agencies like the St Vincent de Paul societies. Municipalities big and small lacked the financial resources to meet their one-third share of relief costs, under the terms of Bennett's 1930 Unemployment Relief Act. Provincial finances, and thus the province's borrowing capacity, were strong after years of reducing the provincial debt. But these assets would be quickly depleted as soon as the province was forced to assume municipal obligations.[61]

Observers generally assumed that the depression further increased the possibility of a change in government at Quebec. A party in power is the obvious target for economic discontent and frustration, and Camillien Houde lost no time identifying Taschereau with Quebec's privileged business and industrial elite and condemning him for failure to implement a wide range of social and economic reforms.[62] For his part, Taschereau occasionally hinted that the day of his retirement might not be too far in the future. Departing from a text released earlier to newspapers, he told his first election rally of 1931: "I can credit myself with the fact that when my political career is finished, and you will admit that after 31 years the summit has been reached and I am descending the slope, I will be able to hold my head high despite all the insults that have been hurled at me and will be hurled at me."[63]

There were personal as well as political reasons why Taschereau might sense and even welcome the end of his era. He turned sixty-four in 1931, and was several times a grandfather. All five children were now married, and the three boys were becoming well established professionally. Paul had assumed *de facto* leadership of the law firm. Robert had launched a political career of his own by winning Galipeault's constituency in a by-election, and Charles had joined Shawinigan Water and Power as an engineer. The demise of two long-time colleagues was a less happy reminder of time's passage. Lomer Gouin had returned to Quebec as lieutenant-governor in January 1929, only to die of a heart attack two months later. Adélard Turgeon's death the following year ended a friendship dating back nearly half a century to the happy innocence of the Union libérale. Despite advancing years and an insatiable desire for travel, Turgeon had served throughout Taschereau's premiership as Speaker of the Legislative Council.[64]

Thoughts of retirement did not, however, make Taschereau indifferent to the outcome of the coming election. Party loyalty, contempt for Houde, and personal pride all provided strong motives to resist the Conservative challenge. He refused to be intimidated by Houde within the legislature, and avoided Mackenzie King's disastrous mistake of appearing to minimize the responsibility of his government to help those hardest hit by the depression.[65] On the level of party organization, he took federal Conservative inroads into Quebec as evidence that all was not well within the Liberal camp. To the utter astonishment of French-Canadian nationalists, he persuaded Olivar Asselin to assume editorship of *Le Canada*, the Liberal mouthpiece in Montreal. Taschereau's one-time assailant was still a nationalist, but he had no patience with the reactionary idealism of the organized nationalist movement or with the "racketeers" attached to Houde's

Montreal administration. He was preoccupied with more meaningful causes like Les Oeuvres de Notre Dame de la Merci, a personal charitable undertaking, and urban reform. In poor physical and financial health, working long hours for a brokerage firm, and forbidden political activity by his employer, Asselin was ripe for Taschereau's generous offer.[66] It quickly became apparent that age had not diluted Asselin's vitriolic resources. In tandem with Jean-Charles Harvey at Le Soleil, Asselin unleashed a devastating assault on the reformist pretensions of Camillien Houde.

In shoring up the Liberal electoral machine, Taschereau enjoyed the active cooperation of federal colleagues. Some of the latter were grumbling (unjustifiably and after the fact) that Taschereau had let them down during the federal campaign. Others wanted him to match Houde's more attractive promises, such as family allowances and cheaper farm credit; at least he should bring Quebec into the old age pension scheme.[67] But King, Lapointe, and the Quebec caucus were too terrified of losing the last and most important bastion of Canadian Liberalism to seek revenge or set conditions. They would spare no effort to ensure Taschereau's reelection.[68] This undoubtedly explains why Taschereau was able to persuade C.G. ("Chubby") Power, the MP for Quebec South, to become chief provincial organizer in June 1931. For years the post had been occupied by Philippe Paradis, like Taschereau a "Parentiste" whose talents saved him from political oblivion following the coup of 1905. His chief asset was close contact with rural constituencies which he originally established as a travelling salesman. Under both Gouin and Taschereau he was a prominent member of the inner circle, attending the poker parties and fishing expeditions at which political strategies were devised. Viewing the 1930 federal results, especially in the Quebec district where he ran the show personally, Paradis himself acknowledged the need for a younger, more energetic successor. Power was initially surprised that Taschereau and Paradis would choose a non-French Canadian who had little knowledge of rural constituencies, but he was reassured by the appointment of a representative advisory committee and by a carte blanche from the provincial cabinet.[69]

Taschereau and Power differed slightly over what was required to reinvigorate local organization. Power objected, for example, to the automatic renomination of incumbent deputies. This discouraged local Liberals from weeding out weak candidates, because it forced them to sponsor an independent candidate and thereby risk an opposition victory at the polls. But Taschereau refused to abandon the traditional procedure, which generally spared him troublesome members and involvement in local disputes. Taschereau did agree, however, to an innovation whereby strong but financially straitened candidates could be subsidized by the provincial war chest. Fortunately, the two men scrupulously observed their agreement making Power the final authority in the allocation of resources and cabinet the sole author of policy announcements. Power was among those favouring generous promises, whereas Taschereau seemed prepared to risk defeat rather than make "irresponsible" commitments. According to Power's memoirs, Taschereau told Godbout this in so many words when the issue of farm loans at two per cent interest became central to the campaign in rural constituencies.[70]

Taschereau's determination to win without such concessions was clear from the outset of the 1931 election campaign, which began officially on 30 July. He vaguely committed himself to future recommendations of the Montpetit Commission, which "will show us how to deal with these questions of social insurance, old age pensions, etc." But he emphasized the need "to avoid foolish and unrealizable promises; they won't solve anything." All relief and reform measures must be undertaken "while maintaining stability in our finances – that is the first condition of a good administration." Agricultural grants and road construction would maintain the rural economy during the expected difficult winter ahead. Public works, incentives to private industry, and colonization would be the chief weapons against urban unemployment.[71] To demonstrate the effectiveness of this approach (not to mention the advantages of supporting the party in power), the Liberals poured enormous amounts of money into relief projects during the three-week campaign. Conservatives later complained that these funds were "borrowed" from federal grants destined for relief during the fall and winter, but it was a difficult charge to prove. In order to avoid constitutional difficulties, Bennett had entrusted the administration of federal contributions to the provinces without any procedure for monitoring expenditures.[72] Only in Quebec did this hurt the Conservatives in partisan terms, for they controlled six provincial governments and the other two were nonpartisan administrations.

On polling day, 24 August, Taschereau swept to his biggest election victory ever, seventy-nine seats to eleven. The conventional explanation, originating with the same observers who had predicted a close fight or a Conservative triumph as late as ten days before voting, was that Houde had destroyed his own chances. He spoke too often in a voice that became rasping when he addressed thousands of radio listeners who were not strongly enough committed to attend partisan rallies. The tone and substance of his remarks became similarly irritating. He questioned the personal honesty of Taschereau and several colleagues, and even attacked Canada's most prestigious auditors, Price Waterhouse, whose examination of provincial accounts had just verified Liberal claims. On the basis of no evidence whatever, Houde tried to implicate Taschereau in the Beauharnois scandal which had just exploded in Ottawa.[73] A number of federal Liberal politicians including Mackenzie King had accepted or offered improper benefits in connection with the Beauharnois project, but Taschereau was if anything slightly duped in the affair. In 1928 he had come to the support of a financially strengthened Beauharnois Power syndicate managed by R.O. Sweezey, an experienced engineer well known in business circles. Besides hoping that the project would increase the supply and lower the price of electric power in Montreal, Taschereau saw provincial licensing of the company as an important precedent in his jurisdictional battle with Ottawa. All the improprieties occurred in the process of financing the venture and obtaining the necessary federal approval for development on a navigable waterway. Moreover, none of Taschereau's political "friends" in Ottawa bothered to tell him when Herbert Holt insinuated himself into the Beauharnois organization.[74]

Since there were no polls to track a rapid shift in public opinion, it is difficult to prove or disprove the hypothesis that Houde snatched defeat from the jaws of victory. Certainly there is another credible interpretation, that Houde's behaviour was a sign rather than a cause of his declining fortunes. He may have become so reckless and vindictive only after sensing that government patronage, divisions in his own ranks, and Bennett's sagging popularity had turned the tide against him. The Liberals obviously felt they would gain by associating Houde with Bennett, for they referred increasingly to federal issues and gave Lapointe and other prominent MPs the centre of the stage at party rallies. Taschereau himself emphasized the lesson of the 1930 election: that wild promises were no cure for the depression. And while other Liberals were highly pessimistic early in the campaign, the leader never lost faith in the voters' "good sense."[75] Without referring specifically to the recent campaign, one commentator explained to the "outside world" in 1932 that "the *canadien* ... prefers to be represented by someone whom he considers, to quote the Chinese, "a superior person." He thinks Mr Taschereau is a "superior person," he has not been so sure about some of Mr Taschereau's opponents, and in consequence, when the elections have come around, Mr Taschereau has had the majorities. It has not only been because he was a superior person, but that has been one of the reasons."[76] One could be less patronizing toward French Canadians and still agree that Taschereau's image of responsibility and competence outshone promises of radical reform from an upstart. Voting for established authority is a common first reaction to a crisis. Bennett himself had benefited from the tendency in 1930, not of course as the incumbent prime minister but as an individual who had achieved brilliant personal success in the economic world.

Regardless of just when the public mood began to change, it appears that Houde lost ground most rapidly where he should have been strongest – in the cities, especially Montreal. In rural Quebec, where farm loans never ceased being the dominant issue and where few people heard Houde's radio appeals, the Conservative popular vote rose substantially. Only the size of previous Liberal majorities prevented the opposition from translating these gains into seats. The Liberals gained among urban English voters, although not sufficiently to elect Gordon Scott in St George or defeat General Smart, who once again dissociated himself from the Conservative leadership in order to retain Westmount. Conservatives gained marginally in some urban French-speaking constituencies, but lost ground in others. Houde himself was defeated in two working-class Montreal ridings, and Maurice Duplessis, his eventual successor as leader, clung to Three Rivers by less than 100 votes.[77] Nor was the swing against Houde and towards "respectable" leadership a temporary phenomenon, even in working-class Montreal: in the spring of 1932 Houde was swept out of city hall by a federal Liberal MP, Fernand Rinfret, who also ran on a platform of sane, responsible administration.

Even allowing for the usual electoral shenanigans by Liberal organizers, the 1931 election was a surprisingly impressive vote of confidence in Taschereau's administration. If he had chosen to retire shortly thereafter, history would have recorded it as a crowning achievement and a fitting recognition of many years' public service. But despite his preelection musings Taschereau did not consider the vote a mandate to retire. Rather, it conferred upon him his most onerous responsibility yet, that of guiding Quebec through its gravest economic crisis in a century.

## CHAPTER SEVEN

# "Obedience to Authority, Respect for Law and Property"

On the morrow of his stunning electoral triumph, Alexandre Taschereau stood as the unchallenged political master of Quebec. Resisting a tide which seemed to be running in the opposition's favour, not to speak of pressure from within the Liberal party, the premier had won on his own terms. Despite his refusal to promise "financially irresponsible" but attractive measures, and whatever their doubts about a regime so long in power, the majority of voters evidently retained enough confidence in Taschereau's ability that they did not feel compelled to take a chance on the volatile Houde. Although the overwhelming Liberal majority grossly exaggerated the government's actual popularity, there was no doubting the legitimacy of Taschereau's mandate to continue governing according to his best judgment. Having been shown that their prescriptions for electoral victory were unnecessary, young and reform-minded Liberals were now in a weak position to urge new directions upon the party leadership. According to Chubby Power, Taschereau made this clear in rejecting his advice that younger, more active Liberals be recruited for the legislature. "I prefer to have these older men who ... are not unduly ambitious and so cause us no great difficulty."[1] Out of office and deep in the valley of humiliation on account of the Beauharnois scandal, federal Liberals had scarcely more influence. On the contrary, they were so excessively dependent on the provincial government to protect and restore their national power base, that on at least one occasion they urged Taschereau to obstruct R.B. Bennett's relief efforts, just for the sake of partisan advantage.[2] And the official opposition, its leader and other strong candidates having suffered personal defeat, was in nearly total disarray.

It therefore seems almost incredible that Taschereau should have begun his new term with a measure as arbitrary, reckless, and totally unnecessary as the so-called Dillon Act. This legislation was a gross overreaction to a scheme concocted by Houde and Thomas Maher, a leading Conservative organizer, to contest the election of all seventy-nine Liberals in the new legislature. Eventually sixty-three defeated Conservatives agreed to play along, many of them persuaded by the offer of a single party supporter to furnish the necessary $1,000 in each constituency. The Dillon Act was designed to thwart this scheme, first by requiring defeated candidates to put up the money themselves and second by declaring that the time for civil actions against elected candidates had expired. These provisions were arbitrary because they denied justice to any genuinely aggrieved candidate who lacked the necessary funds, and because they were retroactive: the government was using its legislative majority to block established judicial procedure in cases involving its own supporters. The strategy was reckless because it forced warring Conservative factions into a show of unity, gave opponents an example of arrogance they could use far into the future, and even caused many Liberals to wonder what had possessed Taschereau. Petitioned by Conservatives to withhold royal assent, Lieutenant-Governor Carroll, a faithful party man, evidently wished he could explain publicly that he was constitutionally obliged to sign it – and thus imply his personal distaste.[3]

The whole exercise was unnecessary because Houde's scheme was already dying of its own inanity. Led by Maurice Duplessis, a rival of Houde for the party leadership, most elected Conservatives dissociated themselves from it. Petitions heard in court before passage of the Dillon Act were unsuccessful and seemed likely to establish a precedent for the others. They were dismissed because the complainants had practically no knowledge of most of the offences alleged to have occurred within their constituencies.[4] And in public opinion generally, Houde lacked enough credibility to launch a crusade against long-tolerated campaign skulduggery. This was too obviously a ploy to save his own leadership of the party, and to avenge a clever case of organizational one-upmanship achieved by the Liberals prior to the election – transferring electoral lists in Montreal from municipal to provincial control.

Taschereau's motives can be surmised easily enough. There was an element of genuine indignation, with which Duplessis openly sympathized. "This is an insult to the province of Quebec and to our race," the premier complained, "and I resent it strongly."[5] In challenging the election of all Liberals, moreover, Houde was questioning the legitimacy of the government – not exactly an inducement to public order during perilous economic times. And Taschereau was undoubtedly determined to make sure that Houde did not escape the fate he so richly deserved: political oblivion. The problem is to explain Taschereau's failure of judgment. Did the election result persuade him that he was politically invincible? Were the streaks of authoritarianism and self-righteousness he had always exhibited getting out of control? After so many years, was his vaunted political sense simply deserting him? If they pertained only to the Dillon Act, these would not be terribly important speculations. But similar questions seem applicable to later, more disastrous failures in retaining public confidence. In other words, while the Dillon Act was hardly a major contributing factor to Taschereau's decline and fall,[6] it can fairly be considered an early sympton of the fatal weaknesses.

The problem certainly did not arise from any lack of personal effort or dedication on Taschereau's part. With Scott no longer treasurer following two electoral defeats, and with no qualified successor at hand, Taschereau had to retain the additional portfolio himself. The intention was to keep Scott's accounting expertise at hand by reappointing him to the Legislative Council, and observe the potential of Ralph Stockwell, a successful lawyer and businessman from Cowansville just elected for the first time. Stockwell proved suitable and was sworn in as treasurer in October 1932, but in the interval Taschereau had been carrying four major portfolios as premier, treasurer, minister of municipal affairs, and attorney general. (Asked later why he retained the last, he answered seriously that this opportunity to "practise law" was his "diversion" from the economic crisis.)[7] And although Mercier was an increasingly knowledgeable and respected minister of lands and forests, Taschereau was forced by circumstances into an almost singlehanded attempt to save the pulp and paper industry. About the only development which indirectly eased Taschereau's burden was the surprise victory of Charles-Joseph Arcand, a veteran Railway Workers' Union official and lately a Montreal alderman, in working-class Maisonneuve constituency. During the campaign Taschereau had promised to give labour its own minister, drawn from the ranks of organized labour, if a union representative were elected on the government side. Arcand's appointment, carefully accompanied by the hiring of a Catholic unionist as deputy minister, freed J.-N. Francoeur to concentrate solely on the Public Works portfolio. He thus became the minister in charge of relief projects, and except for Taschereau's leadership in the annual renegotiation of relief agreements with Ottawa, he took full personal charge of the operation.

Although Taschereau responded with great personal dedication to the difficult administrative challenge, his approach to the depression was fundamentally conservative and defensive. Fluctuations in the world business cycle he considered inevitable or at least beyond the control of a Canadian provincial regime. Even in regard to federal policies, Taschereau never adopted the Keynesian belief that governments could counteract the economic slump itself. The responsibility of political leaders was to cope with the effects of the depression until a more prosperous phase of the cycle returned. With respect to individual livelihoods, this meant encouraging personal restraint and private charity, and when these virtues proved inadequate, undertaking direct relief and public works. For the province as a whole, it meant preserving the basis of Quebec's recent development and future prosperity against permanent damage: opposing the slaughter of forest resources in a buyers' market; helping companies keep their productive capacity in operation, lest it not be reactivated following the crisis; avoiding for as long as possible a drastic increase in public debt, lest subsequent taxation discourage new investment; enabling farmers' sons to remain on the land, not only to prevent them from swelling urban relief rolls, but also to forestall a permanent desertion which would increase Quebec's dependence on agricultural imports; defending the principle of individual self-reliance and resisting proposals which implied the perpetual reliance of individuals upon the state. This approach extended even to federal-provincial relations, where Taschereau welcomed federal spending on emergency relief but resisted any permanent shift in the constitutional balance toward Ottawa.[8]

Throughout the autumn of 1931, Taschereau used every possible occasion to urge government economy, cooperation between workers and employers, colonization, and "the kindness and charitable spirit" of private citizens as solutions to the unemployment crisis. He even predicted that a scheme under which affluent people "adopted" several destitute families would relieve "half the unemployment problem of the province," and he set a generous personal example.[9] The sentiment behind this proposal was widely applauded, since it reminded the wealthy and reassured the poor that they belonged to the same community. But Taschereau recognized as clearly as anyone that the provincial government would have to carry an increasingly heavy burden of relief. Gone from his speeches were confident assertions that the recession would end momentarily; instead, there were subtle intimations that Quebec's proud succession of budgetary surpluses was nearing an end. As he would have to confess openly by 1933, it was meaningless to proclaim balanced budgets or a low "provincial" debt when municipalities were exhausting their credit with loans they could never repay. The province must at last make use of the excellent credit rating which he and Gouin had so carefully established; the depression had created a burden which had to be shared by future generations.[10]

Agreements with the Dominion government continued to form the basis of relief administration. A few weeks after the provincial election, Taschereau, Francoeur, Mercier, and Perrault journeyed to Ottawa to negotiate Quebec's participation under the Unemployment and Farm Relief Act. Bennett and Labour Minister Gideon Robertson were under considerable pressure from Quebec Conservatives to halt the allegedly partisan distribution of federal relief funds by provincial authorities. The matter was more awkward for Bennett than for Taschereau because his followers had furnished no evidence and Taschereau had already denied the charge publicly.[11] Eventually the two governments agreed to a system of bipartisan control. Otherwise, the terms of the new agreement were similar to those of 1930. The theoretical ceiling on federal contributions was removed, allowing them to rise with municipal and provincial expenditures. In addition, there was a broader definition of "Trans-Canada Highway" work, where the federal share was higher than for "provincial" roads and bridges, and a new feature, settlement of unemployed workers on the land. This "colonization" idea became a major bone of contention in subsequent years' negotiations, because Quebec wanted it expanded to include sons of farmers who had not yet gravitated to the city breadlines. Such men, Taschereau argued, were far more likely to succeed in opening or restoring farmland than were men with urban backgrounds. Ottawa did increase its support for resettlement under the so-called Gordon Plan of 1932, but would not go beyond what was demonstrably "unemployment relief." Colonization *per se* was still a provincial responsibility.[12]

In 1932 there was a further serious deterioration in economic conditions. Lumber and paper companies curtailed cutting operations by nearly half, putting 6,000 of 10,000 Chicoutimi residents on direct relief and raising the spectre of actual starvation in the Gaspé, whose fisheries were also in trouble. Henri Bourassa estimated that there were 75,000 people living a subhuman existence in Montreal, and further reports of misery emanated from Verdun and Valleyfield. By now destitution was threatening the lower middle class as well. Laid-off whitecollar workers and professionals and storekeepers deprived of a paying clientele exhausted their savings. Landlords could extract little rent, and even if they were heartless enough to evict their tenants, there was no guarantee of finding new ones who could pay. Farmers had practically no cash income and faced foreclosure on their mortgages. There were happy exceptions to this bleak picture. The mining industry of western Quebec continued to thrive, and certain towns with a well-diversified industrial base, such as Sherbrooke and St Hyacinthe, could afford sufficient public works to keep almost everyone employed. But the overall circumstances were so desperate that Taschereau agreed to a shift in federal assistance from public works to direct relief. Although the former was infinitely preferable in terms of morale, it meant diverting a substantial proportion of funds toward equipment and materials. For Taschereau there was an additional consideration involved: those municipalities most in need of relief were precisely the ones least able to match federal and provincial contributions as required under existing arrangements. When the danger posed by concentrations of idle men dictated a return to some public works activity, Taschereau made certain that the state of municipal finances was taken more realistically into account. The 1933 Relief Agreement provided that Quebec and the Dominion divide evenly the responsibility for both unorganized territories (as before) and bankrupt municipalities. Increasingly frustrated by partisan wrangling and an unwieldy system of accounting, Bennett ultimately scrapped cost-sharing in favour of monthly payments to each province. Taschereau naturally protested that Quebec's allotment of $600,000 a month was inadequate, and was genuinely dismayed when this preliminary figure was adjusted to $500,000.[13]

Still, the new system enormously simplified relief administration, since by the time it came into effect in late 1934 Quebec's Municipal Commission had assumed financial control of most municipalities in the province. Taschereau created the commission shortly after the 1931 election, in response to appeals from two sources: local governments already overwhelmed by their relief burdens, and financial institutions uneasy about extending further credit even to solvent municipalities. Special concern arose from uncertainty about the legal responsibility for debts contracted by the *fabriques*, or parish councils, which served as municipal authorities in some localities. Under the direction of Oscar Morin (deputy minister of municipal affairs), the commission was empowered to investigate and judge all municipal loan applications, to manage the finances of any council or school corporation declared in default by the courts, and to assume entirely the functions of any local administration judged guilty of bad faith. Predictable howls on behalf of local autonomy, leading in one case to an unsuccessful judicial challenge, had a distinctly hollow ring: most municipal leaders recognized the necessity, especially after the Union des Municipalités led by T.-D. Bouchard pledged its coop-

eration. Within two years, seventy-five municipal or school corporations fell under commission control, and most of the others were
to all intents and purposes borrowing on the credit of the provincial
government.[14]

Whether or not they had retained their autonomy, the larger towns
and cities were dealt another severe blow in the spring of 1933. When
the depression began, practically all relief of poverty in Quebec was
*intra mures*, that is, there was no established legal or institutional
framework for direct, "outdoor" relief. A legislative amendment
permitted the Public Charities Bureau to subsidize municipal and
private agencies which became engaged in outdoor relief, but Taschereau had no desire to create a new state bureaucracy. That would
mean an extra charge on the Treasury, and probably the displeasure
of episcopal authorities as well. Hence the responsibility for distributing relief was undertaken by local chapters of the St Vincent
de Paul Society, with Protestant and Jewish organizations caring
for minorities in Montreal. Very quickly, however, the society found
its clergy and lay volunteers being blamed for every delay or
inadequacy. In assuming a role elsewhere fulfilled by the state, it
shared the fate of civil authorities and became a target for outbursts
of frustration. Fearing that their reputation and future effectiveness
were in grave peril, officers of the society gave notice of intent to
withdraw their services. So just when the need for direct relief was
reaching its peak, solvent municipalities and the commission were
faced with increased administrative costs.[15]

Montreal was a special case. Taschereau excluded it from the
jurisdiction of the Municipal Commission, not only for political
reasons urged by local Liberals (autonomy was an issue on which
Houde might escape defeat in the April 1932 elections), but also
because its problems were highly complex and its burden was heavier
than that of all other municipalities combined. In fact, while the
victory of Fernand Rinfret over Houde may have smoothed relations
between provincial and municipal authorities, it did not solve any
fundamental problems. Montreal relief and works programs still
served as a mirage for the destitute elsewhere in the province;
wagecutting and layoffs continued in the clothing industries as
marginal operators drove each other out of business; railway and
port employment shrank as the western drought starved Canada's
transportation system still further; private construction was practically nil; major educational institutions became insolvent. Ratepayers, far from being able or willing to bear the mounting cost
of the relief, were demanding a tax reduction to reflect decreased
property values. Some landlords even argued that the rent of their

unemployed tenants should be paid out of relief funds. At the time of the St Vincent de Paul Society's bombshell announcement, over 280,000 Montrealers, one quarter of the population, were on direct relief.[16]

Rinfret and Taschereau realized that Houde's Unemployment Committee, comprised of aldermen and assisted by a volunteer advisory board, would no longer suffice. It had functioned only as a coordinator of public works projects and makeshift employment bureau, simply channelling funds for direct relief to the religious agencies. Rinfret therefore appointed a full-time Unemployment Commission (the Tétrault Commission) to set up a system of relief administration and begin a thorough reorganization of Montreal's welfare services. Freed from what had become an unmanageable task, St Vincent de Paul and other agencies organized the first federated appeal ever made by Montreal Catholic charities, and were better able to finance their traditional, more specialized works. Unfortunately, that did not solve the city's financial woes. By 1934, bankers were urging Taschereau to place Montreal's finances under the control of the Municipal Commission or some other provincial agency. This would mean, in effect, attaching the credit of Montreal to that of the province as a whole, a risk the premier preferred to avoid. Politically it seemed more dangerous than ever, for in addition to reopening the autonomy issue, Taschereau would expose himself to criticism that his allegedly handpicked candidate (Rinfret) had failed to provide the "responsible" leadership promised in 1932. That could damage his own reputation for wise administration. With Houde preparing a new challenge for the mayoralty, Taschereau had to contemplate an even worse possibility: that in the charged atmosphere of Montreal, even if the candidate did not intend it, Houde's traditional populist appeal would turn into a racial one. Provincial control meant government to protect the interests of the financiers and large property owners, who were English; autonomy meant a local government free to raise money to assist the poor, mostly French-Canadian. There would be no attack on Montreal's autonomy in 1934.[17]

Even so, Rinfret did not bother seeking reelection and Houde was swept back into office. This led to one of the few pleasant surprises Taschereau experienced during these years. It was a different Camillien Houde, at least in his attitude to the provincial government. The former Conservative leader had abandoned provincial aspirations, and was far more hostile towards his successor, Duplessis, than he ever had been towards Taschereau. Houde now utilized his populist appeal to maintain social peace in Montreal, something Taschereau with his aristocratic image could never hope to achieve. His major aim was to protect his own authority against the demands of the bankers, and this he pursued with unprecedented discretion. On a number of issues, publicly and privately, he evinced a clear desire to cooperate with the provincial government. Conversely, he spurned invitations to lead new political movements and, when Duplessis became premier in 1936, he temporarily resigned the mayoralty lest Montreal be penalized for his incompatibility with the new regime.[18] Naturally the city's debt continued to mount as long as major relief expenditures remained necessary.[19] But otherwise Taschereau felt that the worst was over by the spring of 1934: a viable structure for the administration of relief was taking shape, economic conditions were improving slightly, and the flood of migrants into the city appeared to be slowing. The greatest political threat in Montreal ceased to lie in municipal politics, in the Conservative party, or even in the extremist movements tapping the discontent of the unemployed. It lay rather within the ranks of the Liberal party itself.

One solution to the economic crisis which never impressed Taschereau very much was colonization. He continued paying lip service to the ideal, since if anything its popularity was growing. If colonization projects could squeeze more money out of Ottawa, and if the mirage of successful settlement on marginal farmland would temporarily ease the pressure on Montreal, so much the better. But Taschereau knew that even in the 1920s, when forest and mining companies had furnished a local demand for food, wood, and seasonal labour in the interior of Quebec, few settlements had prospered. Now it was absurd to expect that unemployed city workers who signed up under the Gordon Plan would succeed, even though the first groups reportedly set out with great enthusiasm for the promised land where no one paid rent and every family had $600 in government vouchers. They should have attached greater significance to the name of their destination in the Abitibi district: it was called Rivière Solitaire.[20] Predictably, most colonists found that they lacked sufficient farming skills and that the pulp and paper industry was too depressed to purchase their wood or labour. Many drifted back to the cities once their credits expired, while those who remained became dependent upon permanent government subsidies. "We have created a horrible mentality," complained Taschereau,[21] and again he urged Ottawa to transform the Gordon Plan into a preventative program: help farmers settle their sons on nearby land rather than send them off to the city. But he was reluctant to promote even this sort of colonization entirely at provincial expense, despite the urgings of Godbout and Laferté.[22]

What changed his mind in 1934 was undoubtedly political pressure. There were still traditional nationalists, mostly clergy whose biases against urban life were reinforced by the depression. To their ranks were added greater numbers of sincere middle-class humanitarians who simply believed that, for the moment at least, anywhere was healthier than Montreal for the unemployed, physically and psychologically. The UCC leadership, anxious for the broadest possible program of rural recovery and perhaps with an eye to broadening its own somewhat elitist membership, lent its voice to the call for a major province-wide intitiative.[23] When Lomer Gouin's son Paul, whose Action libérale movement had just formalized its defection from the Taschereau regime, agreed to be president of a new provincial colonization society, a political response was obviously necessary. A Montreal rebel named Gouin was harnessing discontent over Quebec's colonization policy in order to help him challenge the party leader – *déjà vu?* At its first meeting in August, the cabinet therefore agreed to supplement normal colonization expenditures by $10 million. His campaign having succeeded, Laferté resigned to become speaker of the Legislative Council and bequeathed to an ambitious colleague, Irénée Vautrin, the task of designing a politically effective and economically sensible plan for spending the money.[24]

Taschereau announced the broad outlines on 8 August: the figure of $10 million was a minimum commitment; colonists would be grouped to establish viable communities, most of whose facilities and services would be paid for by the government; lands would be exchanged with forestry companies so that new settlements could be established close to older ones; government would assist in the revival of abandoned farmland in existing parishes; finally, a colonization congress would be held in October to secure the advice of interested individuals and organizations.[25] Although Gouin, Duplessis, and some clergy boycotted what they contemptuously (and somewhat justifiably) called "le congrès électoral de colonisation," the convention at Quebec City was a notable success. Taschereau joined other political and ecclesiastical dignitaries in praising the holy cause, but it was Vautrin, a worldly Montreal architect, who delivered the political tour de force. First he warmed the traditionalists' hearts by proclaiming greed to be responsible for tempting men to abandon their farms, often for the "vitiated air of the city factory. The lesson is terrible, but surely will be beneficial. Distress is great but let us hope that it will open our eyes and bring us back to a calmer philosophy of life and better principles of education." Next, he used the pretext of a historical perspective to praise the Taschereau government's previous contributions to colonization.

Then he damned the Gordon Plan for its unsuitability to Quebec conditions and argued that Ottawa had a moral obligation to support his new initiative. After spelling out some of the details, he promised that the colonization society and clergy in each diocese would be assigned an important role in the selection and preparation of colonists. (The intended implication was that partisan considerations would be excluded; cynics concluded that Vautrin was trying to bring the societies themselves under Liberal control.) Finally, he served notice that private capital and industry would be required to cooperate with the venture, and sat back to receive further suggestions, confident that he had preempted any possible criticism.[26]

Vautrin was almost too convincing. Not only did the delegates endorse his plan enthusiastically, but on the morrow of the congress more than fifty heads of families declared themselves ready to depart immediately. In fact few legislative or administrative arrangements had been completed, and no formal proposal had been dispatched to Ottawa. The cabinet hurriedly passed an order-in-council abolishing statutory restrictions on the number of farmers in each county eligible for assistance in resettling their sons, and Vautrin sent Gordon a summary of his speech to the congress as notice of a formal proposal. It was December before he specified how the proposed $2 million federal contribution would be spent. Gordon still doubted whether aid to farmers could be considered unemployment relief, while Bennett's Quebec supporters warned that Taschereau would use the money to oil the Liberal election machine. In these circumstances, the federal cabinet not surprisingly refused to participate, and the Vautrin Plan went into operation as a purely provincial scheme in time for the 1935 election.[27] Despite all the Taschereau government's troubles during that campaign, it must be said that colonization had disappeared as an issue for the opposition. As a stimulus to the rural economy in certain regions, it probably even saved a crucial few seats for the government.

Of all employment problems, the one which taxed Taschereau's patience and energy most heavily was the state of the pulp and paper industry. Given the tremendous number of jobs at stake, this was an understandable preoccupation. But there were other industries, clothing and textiles for example, which also employed tens of thousands of people, and Taschereau paid them little attention. The difference was that newsprint production suffered as much from irresponsible management as from the depression. Human failure created and perpetuated the problems, so human effort (his own) must try to overcome them. In explaining the orgy of overexpansion which overtook the industry in the late 1920s despite government warnings, and led to bankruptcy in the 1930s, Taschereau did not mince words.

There is only one answer, and that is through the promoters' passion to "get" – and this is no abuse of language. Abundant illustration of the mischief already done in this direction [ruining a basically sound industry] is easily available, and through it all runs excessive overcapitalization of the industry carried out within the past few years. "Future profits" have been capitalized, and the overcapitalization converted, it may be presumed, to the benefit of the enterprising promoters, and as a result this basic industry has been hopelessly overloaded to the crack of doom. This proficiency in clapping a crushing mortgage [$58 million in 1929 alone] on an essential basic industry seems to come as easily to our promoters as falling off a log.[28]

He continued to utter audible curses about the presence of "too many financiers and not enough manufacturers" in the newsprint industry, and was led finally to a public denunciation of the companies for refusing to curtail their suicidal price war voluntarily.[29]

Actually, the origins of the newsprint crisis were a little more complex than Taschereau allowed in his 1931 statement, which came in reply to charges that his government was largely to blame. It was true that promoters had been unable to resist quenching a public thirst for pulp and paper securities with heavily watered stock. But there were other reasons why the industry failed to secure its foundations during the 1920s, and especially why an ominous decline in the price of newsprint after 1927 was not taken more seriously throughout the industry. The most powerful and rapidly expanding company, Canadian International, did not suffer from moderate declines in price. Its economies of scale and superior technology were lowering the cost of production far more rapidly than the price was falling. A few other companies were owned directly by major American newspaper publishers, and therefore market conditions were only a matter of bookkeeping. Smaller and less efficient companies had little choice but to follow the price leadership of International in spite of a measure of consolidation among them. Even when marketing cartels were organized to try and break International's dominance, mutual suspicion and the inability to operate profitably at less than full capacity drove these companies to violate the spirit if not the letter of their agreements. As noted, Taschereau made some early efforts to control the situation. But cooperation from Ontario and other jurisdictions was irregular, expansion was based on limits previously conceded, and Taschereau was reluctant to penalize the most efficient and progressive company for the sake of others, even though he did finally threaten Graustein.[30] In the long term, International would continue its quest for dominance of the industry by investing elsewhere, and Quebec producers would still have to meet its price.

The depression lost no time delivering its inevitable blow to the industry, with newsprint prices collapsing at the first sign of softening demand. Even International and the publisher-owned companies claimed the need for tax concessions if they were to pay living wages to a full complement of employees. The less efficient mills were of course the least able to withstand drastic price reductions, and where these were located in one-industry towns closure meant not only economic disaster but the destruction of entire communities. Taschereau intervened personally in two such cases. The Ontario-based Abitibi Power and Paper Company closed its Ste Anne de Beaupré mill in 1931 despite Taschereau's appeal to consider the social consequences of its action and its moral obligation to reciprocate earlier government cooperation. The mill did have a major efficiency problem, high power costs compared to competitors who owned their sources of electricity, and the parent company was in deep financial trouble. But Taschereau felt that Abitibi was sacrificing its lone Quebec mill because it had more to fear from Ontario authorities, and his angry suspicion was reinforced by the company's refusal to consider operations on a reduced scale, or to accept any financial responsibility for releif – as many other companies did in communities where they had to suspend or curtail production. International, which later helped other mills by subcontracting portions of its work, refused in this case because it believed Abitibi could keep Ste Anne in operation if it really wanted to.[31] Clarke City was a happier story. This was an isolated company town established in Charlevoix County by the English-owned Gulf Pulp and Paper Company, of which Sir Charles Fitzpatrick was a director. Forewarned that the company could not long survive cutthroat competition, Taschereau arranged for financial and marketing supprt from the Imperial Paper Mills in England. In return he promised material assistance for the operation and particularly for the town. Although the agreement was strained by a reorganization of the company and by delays in government school and hospital grants, Clarke City remained in production.[32]

Taschereau's most persistent headache regarding the affairs of a single company arose from the bankruptcy of Price Brothers in April 1933. To cease production would undermine the economy not of a single town but of the entire Saguenay Valley, an unthinkable prospect. More than half the population of Chicoutimi was already on direct relief because mills there were closed. Fortunately the company did function in bankruptcy under the trusteeship of Gordon Scott, but even so was chronically in arrears paying wages, could not guarantee the livelihood of its woodcutters, and proved to be one of the less cooperative companies in the attempt to stabilize newsprint prices. Price Brothers' Donnacona subsidiary was reorganized as a separate company and there were offers to assume the remaining assets and liabilities: it was the financial rather than operational structure of the firm which had been weak. But Taschereau was very concerned about the terms of any takeover. For one thing, he was anxious to protect the interests of stock and bondholders, most of whom were Quebeckers. For another, he was growing wary of American companies. Because of its major responsibility for declining newsprint prices, International had ceased to be his model of good corporate citizenship. The Aluminum Company of Canada, subsidiary of the Aluminum Corporation of America and already connected with Price through their joint control of Duke-Price power company, was suspect because there might be a conflict of interest between profitable power sales and the efficient operation of pulp and paper mills. Finally, there was the Hearst Corporation, which Taschereau felt would have no interest whatsoever in high prices and which continually tried to sabotage his attempts at stabilizing the market. Any American company, moreover, would be vulnerable to the political clout of the u.s. Newspaper Publishers' Association.

Taschereau therefore tried to arrange for Canadian and/or British control. He communicated frequently with Anglo-Canadian Pulp and Paper but he really preferred to attract Eric Bowater as head of a consortium which would include Anglo's Lord Rothermere and also Lord Beaverbrook. The trouble with Anglo was that it was thought to be conspiring through Scott with the Aluminum group; later, it concocted flimsy pretexts to evade pricing agreements assented to by the others, even International. When Taschereau left office in June 1936, the future control of Price Brothers was still up in the air, though thankfully most of its mills were back in production.[33]

The basic cause of all these difficulties was, of course, the price of newsprint. What outraged Taschereau was that there existed an obvious solution to the crisis, if only the industry and other governments would agree to it. Demand for newsprint had not really fallen that much; rather it had ceased to expand. In other words there was enough work to keep almost all mills operating at about 75 per cent of capacity, a level which the Quebec Forestry Service had declared sensible as far back as 1926. The trouble was the unrestrained competition, arising mostly from International's drive to dominate the industry. This company would take orders which committed its mills to operate at more than full capacity, while others starved at 25 per cent. In theory it could be argued that those companies unable to match International's efficiency should fall by the wayside, and that once fully in control of supplies, International could arbitrarily raise prices. But theory meant little when entire communities were being destroyed, when woodcutters were nearing starvation or, in one case, rioting, and when many Quebec institutions and individuals were threatened with the loss of their invested savings. Nor was there much point in allowing the depletion of Quebec's forest resources at prices so low that the province, burdened with the growing cost of relief, could collect only token royalties. Even the theory was dubious, for American publishers were already looking to their own southern states for alternative sources of supply in case International did gain a stranglehold on northern supplies.

Taschereau therefore continued to seek marketing agreements, even though the Newsprint Institute had fallen apart in 1929. Abitibi and Canada Power and Paper (a Quebec holding company recently formed to unite several St Maurice Valley mills) were on the verge of concluding contracts at $67 a ton for 1930. No sooner had Taschereau and Ferguson persuaded International to follow suit, than Price Brothers and the St Lawrence Company renewed contracts at the 1929 price. The latter claimed, with considerable validity, that Canada Power and Paper was itself cheating by offering kickbacks to publishers in the form of stock. International followed Price Brothers and St Lawrence, so the price for 1930 deliveries remained at $62, and the Institute was dissolved soon afterwards. For 1931 deliveries, the price dropped to $57, sending inefficient and over-capitalized companies into receivership. For 1932, the financiers whose banks administered these companies organized some tonnage pools on a voluntary basis, but this could not stop the price from hitting $48 and overall Canadian production from falling below 2 million tons for the first time since 1925. Pooling continued in 1933 and 1934 under the auspices of a new cartel, the Newsprint Export Manufacturers' Association, with production recovering slightly. But the price continued to fall, reaching $40 per ton for 1934 deliveries.[34] With demand apparently turning upward along with general economic conditions in North America, Taschereau's patience finally expired. Patience with the contempt of producers who ignored his pleas for voluntary cooperation. Patience with American publishers who with equal contempt threatened retaliation against his attempts at "price-fixing." Patience with Ontario, which despite brave talk evaded strong joint action. There was, he proclaimed, no longer any excuse for denying "an equitable wage for forest and mill workers and also ... a just return to Quebec for the exploitation of its resources."[35]

The showdown began in October 1934, after producers had agreed to demand \$42.50 for deliveries in the first half of 1935 and \$45 in the second half. When it was revealed that St Lawrence had contracted for \$40, Taschereau ordered the company to renegotiate. However, the buyers refused and all Taschereau could do was penalize the company by raising its stumpage dues and cancelling a portion of its cutting rights. Anglo-Canadian then claimed it had a contractual obligation to match the St Lawrence price, and the entire industry appeared on the verge of following suit. Taschereau was further infuriated when American publishers threatened to seek other sources of supply "should [he] and certain Canadian banks ... succeed in establishing a precedent whereby contracts between Quebec mills and u.s. publishers may be arbitrarily vitiated." Dismissing the threat as "pure bluff," he summoned the producers to Quebec City in December.[36] He now demanded an end to the cutthroat competition. If the industry was finally prepared to regulate itself, he informed the company presidents, it would be allowed one more opportunity. Otherwise the government would require the registration of all contracts and the reporting of all details. Either way, he would now introduce legislation empowering the government to take harsh punitive action against any company guilty of undercutting the rest.[37]

Taschereau did a great deal of preparatory work to ensure the credibility of his ultimatum, and hence the success of the meeting. He won assurances from the new Hepburn administration that Ontario would support Quebec's action by enacting similar legislation.[38] More importantly, he reached a prior understanding with Graustein and with the powerful Hearst purchasing bloc. Graustein then informed the assembled rival producers that he supported the government's intention to compel good faith and integrity and vouched for Taschereau's claim that consumers would accept a slightly increased common price, with no secret stock options or kickbacks. Finally, Taschereau made sure that Charles Vining, president of the Newsprint Export Manufacturers' Association, attended the meeting to argue for "prorating" as the basic principle of self-regulation by the industry. Prorating simply meant the sharing of newsprint tonnage according to the relative capacities of the mills. If a company owned 5 per cent of the total production capacity of the industry, it would be assigned 5 per cent of the market. In other words, if there was enough demand to employ 75 per cent of the entire industry's capacity, then each individual would operate at 75 per cent. Partial and informal systems of prorating had been tried since 1931 to keep weaker mills in production, but had contained severe limitations. Aside from the fact that they were voluntary and depended on the generosity of the "longs," these transfers of tonnage were not arranged until after sales contracts had been signed. Hence they could not serve to reduce the deadly price competition. Furthermore, there was never an agreed formula or neutral authority to determine the genuine or "efficient" capacity of each mill. Vining proposed that the industry delegate a technical committee to rate the capacity of the mills and coordinate the negotiation of sales contracts. With each company guaranteed an equitable share of the market, none would have a legitimate reason to undersell its competitors. The role of the province would be to act as final arbiter in case of disputes over rated capacity, and to penalize companies violating the system.[39]

Taschereau favoured not only Vining's plan for self-regulation by the industry, but also his suggestions for precise legislative action. The new act should be predicated, Vining wrote, on a government's responsibility to protect the public domain against irresponsible exploitation. It should do so by adjusting stumpage dues, so that any sale below the common price could be made immediately unprofitable to the defiant company. Both the rationale and the means would free the provincial government from any formal involvement in either price-fixing or international trade, thus avoiding conflict with American law or Canadian federal jurisdiction. It was while drafting this legislation that Taschereau delivered his most bitter public denunciation of the industry's lack of cooperation and loyalty. Frustrated by his failure to restore the 1935 price increase, and informed that the producers still had not accepted prorating or any other plan, Taschereau was not merely being theatrical. As letters exchanged in retirement make clear, he felt a genuine sense of betrayal, and his frank expression of it should be recalled by those who characterize Taschereau as no more than a willing tool of private capital. So should his courage in proceeding with the tough legislation in April, for not only did American publishers respond with their anticipated threats, but at the last minute Hepburn decided against concurrent legislation. This would mean, in effect, that Ontario companies could violate pricing agreements with impunity. Prorating in Quebec alone would be a futile exercise.[40]

Fortunately, Hepburn changed his mind by early 1936. The connection is uncertain, but in 1935 Taschereau encouraged the *Chicago Tribune*'s Ontario Paper Company to exploit its long unused timber and power concessions in the North Shore wilderness area later known as Baie Comeau. Taschereau's association with this company was long and cordial: it had bid high for its original Manicouagan limits in 1923, given its legal business to the family firm, and observed all price agreements. As a long-term project, the development of this region would not aggravate the present crisis. In fact since the *Tribune*'s policy was to produce its own newsprint, Baie Comeau would never take business away from another Quebec mill. Hepburn, who knew that the company was intending to expand but expected it would so in the troubled Lakehead region, likely concluded that cooperation with Quebec rather than competition would maximize Ontario's share of the newsprint market. Reopening discussions with Taschereau in February, Ontario Lands and Forests Minister Peter Heenan committed his province to joint action which would assure equitable distribution of tonnage between provinces as well as among companies. In March the producers were reconvened and instructed to devise a plan based on the principle of prorating while Hepburn announced that Ontario would now duplicate Quebec's year-old Forest Resources Protection Act. The companies then created a Newsprint Association of Canada, with Vining as chairman, to establish the efficient capacity of all mills and to act as an interprovincial liaison. Ironically it was in June, precisely at the time of Taschereau's resignation from the premiership, that the rating process was completed to everyone's satisfaction. Politically speaking, he did not live to enjoy the fruit of his personal efforts.[41]

Taschereau never received much credit for the long, often frustrating hours he devoted personally to the prevention of relief of unemployment. The general public was perhaps not fully aware, especially of his efforts in the pulp and paper industry. To family and close associates, the increasingly arduous work schedule was perfectly in character, though in the worst year of the depression Ralph Benoît, his nephew and private secretary, did appreciate the strain. "Mr Taschereau is leaving at noon for his yearly pilgrimage to the Moisie River, and I noticed on his face this morning a smile that I have not seen there for a long time. The premiership is getting more and more onerous, and you can easily understand what it means to him to be able to free himself for a week from all the worries incidental to the administration."[42] It took a relatively new acquaintance, Charles Vining, to observe that Taschereau's pace ought to kill a man in his late sixties.[43] But Taschereau never complained and even his rare allusions to retirement contained no sense of immediacy. He showed no signs of real physical or mental exhaustion, and in fact boasted that he had still not seen a doctor during his adult life. As far as he was concerned, there was nothing mysterious about either his physical durability or his psychological equanimity. They were products of an approach to work cultivated since school days: devote one's full effort to the task at hand, and let the results care for themselves. "Later, I found this method of working ... a great benefit to me. Now I can keep my worries separated, and when the occasion arises, put them all away to enjoy my family life."[44]

It was highly doubtful, of course, whether even a fully informed public would have been any more appreciative. Nowhere in Canada were the unemployed inclined to be grateful for the meagre subsistence they and their families were apportioned. More often they shared the resentment felt and expressed by those working for equally meagre rewards, and by educated young people whose families could maintain them but who could not establish or advance their careers. The mere fact that Quebec workers were stricken more harshly by the depression than those of any other region was enough to ensure that resentment would be deepest and most pervasive there. But control of Quebec's major industries and financial institutions by cultural aliens, revelations before a parliamentary inquiry that the worst exploitation of workers and consumers by large corporations was taking place in Quebec,[45] and the conspicuous ability of some Anglo-Quebeckers to insulate themselves from the hardship of the depression all sharpened the anger of French Canadians still further. Although the explosive potential of this racial animosity was fortunately never realized, a great deal of hostility became focused upon Taschereau, personally affluent and closely identified with the corporate elite. There was no way in which he could escape this fate entirely, even if he had renounced, sincerely or not, principles he had defended publicly for more than thirty years. R.B. Bennett, whose indignation at the social irresponsibility of Canadian capitalists was probably genuine, could not convince Canadians of his sincerity even on the strength of his New Deal legislation.[46] Taschereau had been developing his authoritarian and aristocratic image far longer than the Dominion prime minister.

Yet without feigning any miraculous conversion, or actually undergoing one in the midst of his dealings with newsprint manufacturers, Taschereau still had opportunties to restore confidence in his willingness and ability to govern in the public interest. On two issues in particular, hydroelectricity and social security, he could have displayed much greater flexibility and sensitivity in the face of changing public expectations of government. Instead, he defended traditional policies and practices with such uncompromising self-assurance that opponents could successfully portray him as "un trustard," not merely a tool but a full-fledged member of the "economic dictatorship" which enslaved Quebec. Once established, this image proved immune to all contrary evidence, including substantial though belated concessions, and long discouraged balanced historical assessments of his career.

Antitrust sentiment and rhetoric were present in Quebec long before the Great Depression. They had come, naturally enough, in the age of great industrial enterprises and mergers around the turn of the century. Like American Progressives, members of the Ligue nationaliste warned and protested against the growing concentration of wealth and power. While they sometimes acknowledged the need to mobilize capital on a massive scale or the advantage of "rationalizing" the manufacture and distribution of goods, these critics called upon political authorities to protect the public interest against the natural greed of great capitalists. Lomer Gouin satisfied some of the demands for protective legislation, while the *nationalistes* often weakened their argument by appearing to oppose industrial development itself and eventually turned their attention away towards the issues of imperialism and linguistic rights. Immediately after the war, however, Arthur Sauvé tried to revive the theme by charging that Gouin had become the protector of the trusts. During the 1920s, French-Canadian nationalists deflected the cause slightly by focusing on foreign domination rather than on corporate concentration *per se* – an understandable reaction to the flood of American investment and of accompanying cultural influences. Even so, the growth of powerful and interlocking trusts and mergers was clearly perceived by critics toward the end of the decade.[47] Thus roots for the wider and more emotional antitrust crusade of the 1930s had been well established.

This crusade began with an apparently innocuous billing dispute between the Quebec Power Company and one of its customers, a prominent dentist named Philippe Hamel. Dr Hamel was in fact predisposed to widen the issue, for he was among those conservative Catholics who feared the social destruction greedy capitalists could wreak. He began to scrutinize company claims about its rates in comparison with other Canadian cities, and about its profits. He also became aware of evidence presented to the United States Federal Trade Commission concerning the National Electric Light Association, an elaborate propaganda agency operated by the major private power interests in North America. The NELA, to which Quebec Power's parent firm, Shawinigan Water and Power, belonged, unashamedly advised its members how to plant false or misleading information discrediting public ownership, how to disguise or justify their profits, how to appear socially concerned and beneficent, how to corrupt universities and their individual business and economics professors, and how, if the need finally arose, to crush dangerous opponents. The Trade Commission also heard and published damning evidence concerning the structure and business practices of the industry itself.[48]

To Hamel, these revelations seemed perfectly consistent with the structure and ambitions of the hydroelectric industry in Quebec and with the experiences of municipalities who tried to resist the domination of "the trust." And the more he spoke out during the early 1930s, the more his opponents resorted to the propaganda tactics already familiar to the south. In fact the Canadian Electrical Association, a regional component of the NELA, was quickly able to furnish statistics purporting to demonstrate the inefficiency of Ontario Hydro. Hamel's first clash with the industry occurred in 1930, when he was appointed to a civic committee investigating complaints against Quebec Power, sole distributor of electricity in Quebec City. The company refused to cooperate, but thanks to Hamel's energetic collection of external evidence, the committee's report was still a well-documented indictment. Quebec Power first responded by offering minor reductions to domestic and commercial customers, but public opinion was now being led by Hamel to demand either rates comparable to those charged by Ontario Hydro or else municipalization of the company's distribution facilities. Though not personally nominated in 1931, Hamel pursued his campaign at the side of Conservative candidates, charging that the Taschereau government was the creature of a province-wide trust to which Quebec Power belonged. The Conservative platform itself contained a vague promise "to guarantee both countryside and cities the use of electricity at reasonable rates."[49]

With municipal elections due in February 1932, and in trouble on other issues, Mayor H.-E. Lavigueur and several aldermen continued riding the electricity issue after the provincial campaign had ended. In January they petitioned the legislature to amend Quebec City's charter to permit municipalization. Quebec Power presented a counter-petition urging that, in the event of municipalization, the city be required to purchase its entire operation, not just the most lucrative distribution component. The city retained Ernest Lapointe as counsel, while its strongest advocate among members of the Private Bills Committee was Lapointe's protégé, Oscar Drouin. The company hired Louis St Laurent and Lucien Cannon to argue its case, but in the course of debate Taschereau himself became irrevocably associated with the defence of Quebec Power's interests. Prior to the session his brother Edmond had informed him of Quebec Power's diminished 1930 profits.[50] Now he personally advanced the argument, designed to sway rural deputies, that only the profitability of city operations would permit the hydroelectric industry to expand service into the countryside. Unwisely and unnecessarily, Robert Taschereau also spoke in the company's defence. Lapointe clearly got the best of the arguments, which made matters worse. The premier tried to save face by urging the rejection of both petitions, noting the city's admission that it considered municipalization a last resort and was really just trying to strengthen its bargaining position in future negotiations with Quebec Power. Taschereau also promised an investigation of Quebec Power's rates by the Public Service Commission, but the commission's effectiveness and good faith as a regulatory body were already highly suspect. It had refused to force open Quebec Power's books in 1930, and more recently had failed to take seriously a complaint by Chicoutimi against that city's distributor. When votes were taken, all of the Quebec City members followed Drouin in breaking Liberal party ranks. Drouin was now well on the road to a complete repudiation of the Taschereau regime.[51]

It is very doubtful whether Taschereau yet realized the extent of his vulnerability on this issue. Several friends and family members were known to be associated with the company: brother Edmond and Georges Parent were directors, Paul and Robert held a retainer from the parent firm (as did Lanctôt, according to rumour), and of course Charles was a Shawinigan employee. Taschereau might rationalize that he had no right or obligation to interfere with these associations, and that they did not influence his decisions. But he himself was compromised in more than one respect. Since 1927 he had accepted invitations to join the boards of directors of several major financial institutions, including North American Life, Barclay's Bank, the Royal Trust Company, the Sun Life Assurance Company, the Title Guarantee and Trust Corporation, and the Royal Liverpool Insurance group. In 1932 he joined Canadian Investment Funds and in 1935 he was elected to the board of Metropolitan Life. His motives were an admitted mixture of personal and public advantage, with heavy emphasis naturally on the latter. Directors' fees and dividends were, he claimed, a legitimate source of investment income, especially for the day he retired. On the public's behalf, he would understand the workings of a financial world in which French Canadians no longer participated, would influence important investment decisions, and would secure favourable consideration for a variety of French-Canadian institutions whose plight would otherwise escape the attention of the great financiers.[52]

Though perhaps initially surprised by Taschereau's willingness to be formally associated, the financiers were obviously happy, even anxious, to have a prominent French Canadian among them.[53] Many of the invitations followed the death of Sir Lomer Gouin, whom they had previously welcomed to their councils as a gesture of good faith. Neither side considered this practice a conflict of interest, since the provincial government did not license or regulate such financial institutions. Unfortunately matters were not that simple. These institutions invested heavily in hydroelectric, newsprint, and other industrial corporations which *did* treat with the provincial government, and which were themselves owned or controlled by Taschereau's fellow directors. When Philippe Hamel's attack broadened from Quebec Power to the entire hydroelectric industry and thence to the whole system of interlocking directorates – his magnum opus was aptly titled *The Electricity Trust: Source of Corruption and Domination* – Taschereau would find it impossible to deny a direct connection.

Originally, Taschereau's regular Tuesday visits to Montreal had been accepted as the normal duty of a government and party leader. Legends even developed concerning his skill at poker and his being robbed of $1,200 while sleeping at the Hotel Viger.[54] But now these visits attracted sinister attention, since Taschereau used part of the time to attend directors' meetings. In a more subtle way, Taschereau's reputation for integrity was also undermined by his highly personal method of dealing with the major agents of economic development. Despite his confidence in the ability of individuals like Mercier, Piché, and Arthur Amos, chief engineer in the Hydraulic Service, he believed that developments in key industries were too important to be left under the control of any single department or agency of government. There needed to be flexibility and mutural confidence between business and government which could only be derived from the discretionary and overriding authority of the premier. This was the meaning of Taschereau's original promise to deal with businessmen "like businessmen." As Wilfred Bovey described it, "you can transact business with the Quebec Government as quickly as you can with any private company," without the bureaucratic delays and complications which usually characterize governments.[55] The need for Taschereau to spend so much time on the newsprint crisis was one result of this informal system. The industrialists were simply not accustomed to accepting the authority of any subordinate,[56] even though Mercier and Piché were perfectly capable of sharing much of the burden. Where regulations did exist, for example concerning payment of wages to forest and mill workers, the first impulse of employers was to appeal directly to Taschereau for exemptions.[57]

Only in the Forest Resources Protection Act of 1935 can one find
a recognition of the value of statutory procedures.

The effect of informal communication was even more profound
in the case of hydroelectricity, because Taschereau was so enamoured
of the earlier performance of Shawinigan Water and Power. To him
Julian Smith, its vice-president and general manager, who was also
president of Quebec Power, remained the very model of beneficent
capitalism.[58] Privately informed of the difficulties faced by both the
parent and the subsidiary firm during the depression, he could not
seem to deal objectively with complaints and warnings. Instead he
forwarded packaged rebuttals to Liberal newspapers, and replied
personally to other critics of Quebec Power. "You are very wrong,"
he told a Quebec city priest, "to say that electricity rates benefit
the big shareholders who are the enemies of the poor. If you knew
what losses these companies and their shareholders had suffered
[recently], perhaps you wouldn't speak in such a manner."[59] On
technical matters, Taschereau would often have Charles explain the
problems during a visit home before discussing it with government
engineers.[60] Even after he had been forced to appoint a Commission
of Inquiry into the hydroelectric industry, Taschereau still accepted
Shawinigan's viewpoint quite uncritically. A genuine regulatory
agency – an independent Public Service Commission with teeth –
could well have done what Taschereau, in his personal admiration
and loyalty towards Shawinigan, could not do. In the process it would
have saved Taschereau from the folly of refusing so openly and
defiantly to adjudicate sincere, widespread complaints against a
corporate giant. His conscience was evidently clear, but not his
judgment. Shawinigan symbolized "the trusts," and he allowed
himself to become its chief defender.

In 1933 the hydroelectric dispute was transformed from a local
to a volatile province-wide political issue. Reelected mayor on the
strength of his promise to extract better terms from Quebec Power,
Lavigueur again demanded that the legislature grant his city the
right to municipalize the company. Taschereau spoke forcefully and
at length against both the principle of public ownership and the
tactics of Quebec City. Municipalities could not possibly afford to
buy out private distributors in the foreseeable future, and the threat
Lavigueur wanted to brandish over Quebec Power would therefore
be empty.[61] Ironically, Hamel was beginning to agree with Taschereau about the futility of municipalization. But of course his conclusion was that to root out the evil, the provincial government must
nationalize the giant companies who controlled the generation of
electric power. This impression was powerfully confirmed in late

autumn, when in the absence of two members of Quebec City's Executive Council, Lavigueur was authorized to accept a new twelve-year contract with Quebec Power. The next day, before Hamel could protest the terms, this procedure was sanctioned by City Council. The mayor and his supporters on council were trounced at the next municipal election, but the opportunity to rein in Quebec Power had escaped its opponents. Hamel directed as much of his fury at Taschereau as at Lavigueur. The premier's sons, he charged without being contradicted, had drawn up the insidious contract. The provincial government was merely being cynical when it promised, in the January 1934 Throne Speech, to permit the acquisition of electrical distribution facilities by municipalities once existing contracts expired. Provincial action, he warned ominously, might require the rise of a new political party free of the corrupting financial control of the trusts.[62]

Hamel's crusade for public ownership had won important converts outside Quebec City by the end of 1933. The Union catholique des cultivateurs had long considered rural electrification as the key to modernizing Quebec agriculture. Now Hamel had convinced many of its leaders that "the trust" would never do voluntarily what was not immediately profitable to itself. The annual Catholic union delegation urged Taschereau to create a provincial system similar to Ontario Hydro.[63] Several smaller municipalities had their suspicions and their courage raised by events at Quebec, and began challenging the private distributors. Père Archambault invited Hamel to publish his critique of "Trusts et Finance" under the auspices of the Ecole sociale populaire, a twenty-year-old think tank on social issues sponsored by the Jesuit order.[64]

Within the Liberal party, Drouin was only the first to threaten rebellion over the issue. Elisée Theriault, a lawyer for the City of Quebec who also happened to be Hamel's brother-in-law, denounced high power rates from his seat in the Legislative Council. Ernest Ouellet used the same platform to criticize the industry's failure to serve rural Quebec.[65] In Montreal Paul Gouin's group of young Liberals, driven primarily by other grievances against Taschereau (their inability to advance within the party, his refusal to countenance progressive social legislation), gradually seized upon "the trusts" as the explanation for all their frustrations. They too were soon calling for state ownership.[66] One Liberal no one had to convince was T.-D. Bouchard, who as mayor of St Hyacinthe and chairman of the Union des municipalités du Québec had long advocated municipal control of electrical distribution. He was so knowledgeable on the subject and so influential throughout the province that both Hamel and the Liberal rebels sought him as their leader. Fortunately for Taschereau, Bouchard had several reasons to hesitate. He was speaker of the legislature, and thus not really in a position to campaign on a provincial issue. He could resign this post, but in the circumstances that would be a declaration of war against the government. He still retained a good deal of personal respect for Taschereau and a firm loyalty to the Liberal party, in both cases because of their longstanding opposition to clericalism. And while he favoured provincial nationalization in theory, he did not believe it was immediately practicable. It made more sense to pursue what might be won: tighter regulation of private interests, and legislation to facilitate municipalization.[67]

Not until June 1934 did Taschereau fully recognize the political damage he had suffered and think seriously about how to repair it. For in addition to defending the hydroelectric industry, he had earlier been content to lecture or threaten his critics. "Don't ask anything more from me," he snarled at Drouin after the first Quebec Power episode. "If you would like me to provide you with a seat opposite among the Bleus, I am ready to give you one." Spurning Drouin's offer to discuss the issue more thoroughly, Taschereau simply invoked the need for party discipline.[68] When *L'Action catholique* joined in criticizing Quebec Power and its political allies, Taschereau complained to Archbishop Villeneuve that the paper was undermining respect for authority.[69] Taschereau's more serious response was undoubtedly triggered by the formal defection of young Montreal Liberals led by Gouin and by the tone and result of the municipal elections in Quebec City. Having despaired of reforming their party from within, the Montrealers constituted themselves the Action libérale, a new party dedicated to defeating the Taschereau regime. Prominent in their platform was the promise to end control of the hydroelectric industry by the trusts.[70]

As Gouin's group began sponsoring public meetings and radio broadcasts throughout the province, Ernest Lapointe, Jacob Nicol, and T.-D. Bouchard all warned that further delay could be politically disastrous and offered their cooperation. On 25 July Nicol rejoined the cabinet and soon afterwards the ministers agreed upon a broad public inquiry into the hydroelectric industry, to be followed immediately by legislation based on its recommendations. Even if, as Taschereau still believed, the companies were contributing to Quebec's well-being, this had to be publicly demonstrated by impartial investigators.[71] Similarly, only legislation bearing such independent authority could possibly escape the accusation of election gimmickry. For a chairman of the commission of inquiry, Taschereau first approached Henry George Carroll, the recently retired lieutenant-governor. But Carroll declined for lack of personal expertise in the field, a reasonable claim in view of the fact that the government expected a final report by the end of the year.[72] So Taschereau turned to Lapointe, obviously an active party man but nevertheless above suspicion of links with or undue sympathy for "the trust." On the contrary, he had ably represented Quebec City in its battle against Quebec Power. Lapointe may have been reluctant to appear closely associated with the Taschereau government, but ultimately it was in his own and the federal Liberals' interest to help the regime restore its popularity. Assuming that Taschereau was sincere in his commitment to implement the recommendations – and despite past differences Lapointe considered Taschereau a man of his word[73] – this was an excellent opportunity to restore unity in party ranks. If the Action libérale remained opposed to the provincial leadership, there could be severe organizational headaches in the coming federal election campaign. Worse yet, if the provincial government did not improve its image, it might lose office to the Conservatives and thus permanently undermine the national power base of the Liberal party.

So Lapointe agreed to serve, along with Montreal accountant George C. McDonald and Augustin Frigon, who was now head of the Polytechnical School in Montreal. Their commission of 23 August 1934 specified three distinct subjects: the costs and benefits of nationalization or municipalization; prevailing electricity rates and the possibility of reductions; and the prospects for rural electrification. They were free to go beyond these, but were asked to report by 1 January 1935. Naturally Taschereau hoped that the investigation would endorse his views, and he was not above drawing Lapointe's attention to articles and documents critical of public ownership. But he never went back on his promise of "carte blanche to conduct your inquiry in whatever manner you judge the most suitable," and on 29 August assured the commissioners that they would be granted any additional authority (to swear witnesses, for example) which they required.[74] Nor did the commission lack voluminous testimony for the other side. Hamel was not about to waste his long-awaited day in court, and on 13 November presented such a devastating "brief" (206 pages) that Taschereau felt obliged to assure panicky share and bondholders that their rights would be protected in any government action.[75] Focusing more narrowly on the conflict between Quebec City and Quebec Power, newly elected Mayor J.-E. Grégoire came to heap scorn on the company's "counter-proposals" of 1931–3, upon the contract negotiated by Lavigueur, and upon Taschereau's stalling tactics in defence of the company.[76]

The decisive presentation, however, was a confidential memorandum from Bouchard to Lapointe. Setting out the results of his eighteen-month survey of municipal leaders, Bouchard reported universal complaints against domestic and commercial rates and a rapidly growing faith in municipalization as the only escape. Not only Conservatives and nationalists but also loyal Liberals strongly resented the behaviour of the hydroelectric industry, and with this in mind Bouchard designed a moderate set of reforms to protect both the political interests of the Liberal party and the long-term economic interests of the province. In sum, Bouchard recommended that the province enable local councils to take over distribution facilities, to expand and operate them efficiently, and to purchase their electricity from the private suppliers at rates comparable to those charged by Ontario Hydro. The companies would retain valid titles and leases on developed power sources but no further resources should be alienated to them and undeveloped sites should be reintegrated into the public domain at the original price – possibly for future public projects which could compete with private interests. Bouchard did not expect that many municipalities would take advantage of such legislation immediately, given their current financial burdens. What he did hope was that the threat would be sufficient to induce reductions by private distributors.[77]

The Lapointe Commission fell somewhat short of recommending Bouchard's precise scheme, emphasizing tight regulatory control rather than the reacquisition and development of power sites by the province.[78] With Bouchard publicly critical, Taschereau recognized that his credibility rested less on implementing Lapointe's exact recommendations (his original promise) than on securing Bouchard's adherence. For this reason a rather formal negotiating process occurred between Nicol on the government's behalf and Bouchard as spokesman for the Union des municipalités – an organization of mayors who were mostly Liberals. Bouchard's letter to Taschereau at the successful conclusion of these negotiations speaks for itself.

You can be sure than no one in the world wants more than I do to preserve the friendly relations and good fellowship we have enjoyed together for better than twenty years. I have no doubt that men of ill-will either toward you or toward me have spread·all kinds of falsehoods about my sentiments toward you [Bouchard had reportedly called Taschereau "the biggest thief in the province"], but I know that you have too much experience in politics to attach undue importance to gossip designed to make straws into pillars. In the campaign I have waged to popularize my views on this question, I have had no difficulty refraining from personal allusions against you, for I have always hoped to find that basis of understanding which would allow me to fight the next election under your leadership as in the past.

Having spoken in eighteen cities on this subject, I am convinced that people want a radical change in our laws which will force the companies to stop their uncontrolled speculation on electrical securities and to give reasonable rates to all categories of customers. We can attain these ends without compromising the legitimate rights of the companies and without tying up the province's funds.

But we must give ourselves the means to fight and assure the people that our attitude is not just an election gimmick and that we have laws on the books which will permit us, if the companies refuse to give reasonable rates, to sell power ourselves to municipalities wishing to resell it to the public at a fair price.

I made several concessions to Mr Nicol and I think we have found a solution which by leaving the cabinet in absolute control of the situation, should satisfy you since you are and will remain the undisputed leader of the government. On the other hand, our essential principles having been inscribed in the law, my group and I will be satisfied ... we will have no difficulty assuring the reelection of the government.

With that Bouchard submitted a draft bill fairly close to the Lapointe recommendations.[79]

The much awaited legislation was introduced in April. As minister of municipal affairs, Taschereau sponsored the bill which enabled any municipality to take control of local services. Mercier moved the creation of an Electricity Commission, a permanent, three-member regulatory body with wide control over the production, transmission, and distribution of hydroelectric power. These included the authority to fix rates and to order the extension and upgrading of services. The most remarkable feature of this bill was its preamble, whose language raises the possibility that Taschereau had finally taken some of the evidence against the industry seriously. The control and distribution of electricity "constitute economic problems having a widespread social effect and the electricity industry is essentially of public interest." The industry must therefore "be subject to strict control ... [and] the mistakes and abuses of the past must be rectified and a repetition of them be prevented." Every private electrical interest "becomes the mandatory of the State and must use [its] privilege in the general interest." The government also accepted Bouchard's compromise on nationalization with "an Act respecting the exploitation of falls and rapids on watercourses in the public domain and their concession in future."[80]

Oscar Drouin announced that this legislation was insufficient,

and used it somewhat falsely to justify his formal defection from
the Taschereau Liberals – he had to all intents and purposes joined
the Montreal rebels months earlier.[81] But Bouchard welcomed it, and
soon after joined the cabinet as minister of municipal affairs, trade
and commerce. Municipal Affairs was an obvious assignment, and
Taschereau was also pleased to remove it from his own shoulders.
The creation of a Trade and Commerce portfolio for Bouchard was
undoubtedly meant as a positive response to calls for both regulation
and encouragement of business activity. If this legislation and
appointment had come a year earlier, they might have decisively
affected the course of political events in Quebec. As it was, they
probably spelled the difference between heavy losses and total defeat
for Taschereau during the election which followed in November.

Taschereau's problems with the issue of social security were both
analogous and closely related to those he suffered over hydroelectricity. The early 1930s saw a rapid and substantial change in the
climate of opinion in Quebec, away from laissez-faire and towards
state intervention. Taschereau refused to accept either the validity
of this change – a conclusion drawn from evidence furnished by
the depression – or the political reality of heightened public expectation. Many of those who urged statutory payments to the needy
and legislation ensuring just wages could find only one possible
explanation for Taschereau's resistance: that he had become the
protector of a wealthy corporate elite and indifferent to the needs
of the majority. There is also a tragic irony in the way Taschereau
handled these two issues. He could have avoided such a close personal
identification with the hydroelectricity trust and if he had done so
he might conceivably have maintained the unity of the Liberal party
and received much more credit for the legislation of 1935. Yet such
discretion alone would not have calmed the antitrust movement,
whose essential appeal was to nationalist rather than reformist
sentiment. It stirred and channelled deeply rooted French-Canadian
resentment against foreign economic domination. No step short of
nationalizing the hydroelectric industry could have soothed the
popular anger and frustration toward this mighty symbol of foreign
exploitation. In marked contrast, Taschereau could fairly easily have
satisfied demands for social security legislation, which were quite
modest compared with some being heard elsewhere in Canada. But
apart from a last-minute promise to implement the federal old age
pension scheme, Taschereau refused to concede even the hypothetical
case (if the province could afford it) for such measures.

Although Taschereau successfully skirted the issue during his 1931
election campaign, the shift away from traditional ideas about public

assistance was already in evidence. Looking at the hardship immediately created by the depression, and guided unofficially by a McGill
University economist, Leonard Marsh, the Royal Commission on
Social Insurance appointed by Taschereau himself was rapidly
exceeding its original terms of reference. In a series of reports
submitted during 1931 and 1932, the Montpetit Commission formulated dozens of recommendations involving regulatory laws, wider
provincial support for private charitable institutions, and such direct
support programs as needy mothers' and family allowances, old age
pensions, unemployment insurance, and subsidized health insurance.
Some of the latter were guarded as to timing and detail, but there
was no mistaking the overall thrust. Even Mgr Courchesne was
reconciled to a contributory, provincial pension system.[82] For 1931
had also brought the papal encyclical *Quadragesimo Anno*, which
unequivocally declared the state responsible for protecting the economically weak members of industrial society. No longer, rejoiced
Father Archambault, need priests fear that in demanding social
reforms they would be "meddling in politics" without the authority
of their church. The Jesuit-sponsored Semaines sociales of 1932 were
devoted to the "social question," and out of this came publication
of the first *Programme de restauration sociale*. This document called
upon the state "to ensure, through a better distribution of wealth,
the relief of the common people," to protect workers against dep-
rivation due to accident, sickness, old age, and unemployment, to
insure farmers against their unique occupational hazards, to require
salaries high enough to support average-sized families, to supplement
the income of large families, and to subsidize medical and hospital
care for the poor.[83] A second *Programme de restauration sociale*,
the publication to which Hamel contributed his attack on the trusts,
specified some means of achieving these goals. A section on labour
and social legislation, written by a Catholic Union official, Alfred
Charpentier, called for general minimum wages, a requirement that
companies pay wages before dividends, and stronger bargaining rights
for unions in addition to direct payments of the kind urged by
Montpetit.

Even before the more definitive *Programme* appeared, proposals
for income security had reached the political arena. At the October
1933 convention which chose Duplessis as their new leader, provincial
Conservatives also endorsed an impressive list of social reforms. Then
in 1934, Paul Gouin's new political party adopted the *Programme
de restauration sociale* almost verbatim as its platform.[84] Taschereau
was certainly aware of the widening call for social reform measures,
but his determination to resist seemed only to stiffen. Partly redeeming

an election pledge, he accepted those of the Montpetit recommendations which did not involve statutory payments to individuals. That meant new regulations concerning child protection and public health, and major amendments to the Public Charities Act. Previously, the Public Charities Bureau could only draw upon special taxes collected by municipalities and a $1,000,000 annual transfer from Liquor Commission profits. Now aid given to indigents outside of charitable institutions became eligible for provincial subsidies, and the bureau itself was given access to ordinary provincial revenues.[85] But beyond this Taschereau would not go, and in 1933, the worst year of the depression, he began to reject the philosophy and denounce the proponents of income security without any apology or qualification.

Pensions and family allowances, he stormed in January, were "pernicious remedies which will compromise the future" both financially and in terms of the moral fibre of society.[86] In November he charged that the bourgeois proponents of such laws were inviting "social revolution" by encouraging the masses to expect "everything" from the government.[87] The substance of his message did not change during calmer moments. At a banquet honouring Archbishop Villeneuve on his elevation to the cardinalate, Taschereau insisted that Christian virtue and the duty of the church both lay in defending peace and the social order. This they accomplished by teaching "obedience to authority, respect for law and property, the sanctity of the home, the sovereignty of the father of the family in his little kingdom [and] the assurance that death is not an end but a beginning."[88] And while Taschereau never denied the state's obligation to provide emergency relief to the unemployed, he later bemoaned the psychological effect. Confusing the recipients of unemployment relief with rebellious middle-class youth who "seem to feel that the state or their families owe them a living," Taschereau concluded that "the dole ... is the worst evil that ever afflicted Canada."[89] On this issue there was certainly no deathbed conversion, old age pensions notwithstanding.

By 1934 there were numerous groups agitating against the Taschereau government, each ready to exploit antitrust sentiment for its own purposes. From these, Gouin's Action libérale emerged as the principal vehicle of protest. Although Hamel himself hesitated, most of his nationalistically inclined followers joined the new party within weeks. So did several participants in two new nationalist enterprises inspired by Abbé Groulx in Montreal, the Jeune Canada movement and the journal L'Action nationale. Fittingly, the name of Gouin's party was lengthened to Action libérale nationale. Having embraced the *Programme de restauration sociale*, the ALN also readily attracted UCC, CTCC, and other Catholic Action leaders whose previous political associations had been distinctly Bleu. *L'Action catholique* gave full and sympathetic coverage to party rallies. Ernest Laforce, Quebec's high priest of colonization and a personal friend of Duplessis, prudently guarded his formal political neutrality. But he could scarcely hide his sympathy for a party whose program declared colonization a major priority and whose leader served as president of the Quebec Colonization Society. Few older Liberals joined the young rebels, but those who did played an important role. Thériault, Ouellet, and Edouard Lacroix, MP, ensured the success of the ALN's first major public rally held on 12 August in Lacroix's constituency of Beauce. A self-made millionaire in the lumber business with a reputation for treating employees generously, Lacroix was the ALN's first and most reliable financial supporter. The only other substantial contributor, Quebec City merchant L.-J. Demers, was also a Liberal. And when Drouin finally declared himself, he took on the job of chief organizer for the Quebec district. Apart from inconsequential fringe groups, the only anti-Taschereau faction still outside ALN ranks was the official Conservative opposition. And it was not long before supporters of both Gouin and Duplessis began to realize that in the coming elections, competition between their two parties would only serve the common enemy.[90]

Until the young Liberal reformers actually defected, Taschereau was complacently tolerant. They seemed like innocent idealists, much like the Union libérale of his own youth, for whom the Liberal party must always have room. Their turn to lead the party and govern the province would come, at which time they would implement some of their advanced ideas and recognize the impracticability of others.[91] He knew that some federal MPs, including Lacroix and Lapointe, were encouraging them to speak out on certain issues, and that there was a certain admiration for them even among several provincial deputies, ministers, and senior civil servants. But this was all to be expected, and in the final analysis he could allow it because the group posed no real danger. Gouin himself was far from ambitious, comparing poorly with both his father and his older brother, Léon-Mercier. Taschereau's own nephew, Gérald Coote, was involved, as was Lapointe's son-in-law Roger Ouimet. What else would such a group do but talk to each other, wait for him to retire, and faithfully support their party? What else could they do?[92]

When the break came, Taschereau could only confess to being stupefied and take some comfort from the fact that not all the reformers were prepared to go along.[93] But Gouin and his colleagues were clearly determined to carry their message to constituencies all over the province and to the public at large. An immediate counter-offensive was necessary. The Lapointe Commission and the Colonization Congress, both announced on the eve of the Beauce rally, were part of it. Laferté went to the Legislative Council partly to help Nicol counter the rhetoric of Thériault and Ouellet. A major effort was launched to shore up party organization well in advance of the next election. By having *Le Soleil* make a premature announcement in mid-August 1934, Taschereau first attempted to steamroller Chubby Power into becoming chairman of a new, largely honorary provincial organizing committee. If successful, this ploy would have taken considerable wind out of ALN sails, for Power was known to sympathize with Gouin. But Power delivered a polite but firm rebuke, which Taschereau then hurled back as evidence of ill-will on the part of federal Liberals.[94] (Power privately revealed that this was true, explaining to a non-Quebec colleague that "there are Liberals in this province who look upon Taschereau as a reactionary ... This [rift] is perhaps accentuated by the dictatorial system of administration ... and a fairly well-founded suspicion that only two classes may expect favours ... relatives of the premier and the big interests." Jimmy Valentine, who was neither a relative nor a big interest but received lots of favours, put it a little differently: with the Liberals out of power federally, Taschereau lacked enough patronage to satisfy all the party claimants.)[95]

Taschereau had in fact already persuaded a more devoted ally, Jacob Nicol, to be his real chief organizer. Nicol had done a preliminary and not terribly encouraging survey in the spring, and by autumn he had regional agents visiting worrisome constituencies.[96] Organizers for the Montreal district were the intriguing combination of Edouard Tellier, general manager of the Liquor Commission, and Victor Marchand, president of Melcher's Distillery. Olivar Asselin's illness and depression caused him to leave *Le Canada*, but he left the able Edmond Turcotte to carry on.[97] Valentine, a great personal admirer of Taschereau, agreed to take charge at Quebec. The initial strategy for dealing with the ALN at the local level was apparently to be passive and not antagonize every Liberal who flirted with the new party. Watch and listen carefully and be ready to attack when the time comes, Valentine told his contact in Chicoutimi. Taschereau and Nicol were confidently assuming that once the futility of the exercise became apparent, all but a hard core would return to the governing party.[98] In his public statements Taschereau took the same calm approach during the fall of 1934. He cited the long-term record, particularly of labour legislation, to prove that he was no "Tory reactionary." Against the charge that he was a friend of the trusts, he distinguished between entrepreneurs who risked their capital and sacrificed their health to create jobs, and those who hoarded capital and exploited the poor. The former he had encouraged, the latter he was fighting "more than ever." He had prosecuted the "coal trust," passed the Collective Agreements Extension Act (which allowed the government to extend the terms of a labour agreement to an entire industry and thus protect the employer and union from unfair competition), and promised to implement the recommendations of the Lapointe Commission regardless of company objections.[99] Finally, Taschereau ridiculed the "curious" strategy of a movement which sought to reliberalize the Liberal Party by allying itself with "Tories," and still appeared to believe that this argument could win Paul Gouin back if it were put to him by his brother.[100]

Taschereau soon discovered, however, that neither organizational work nor protestations nor important legislation nor even the ALN's failure to recruit a prestigious and experienced leader (Lapointe, Bouchard, and David were all courted) could stem the growing force of the "trustard" accusation. He had waited too long on electricity, and still had not budged on social legislation. It would have been quite reasonable for him to step aside early in 1935, and it is fair to speculate that had he done so, he would still have secured a much happier retirement and a more positive historical reputation. But as the attacks mounted and became increasingly personal, Taschereau's honour and pride demanded that he seek vindication through yet another electoral victory. Tolerance toward Liberal dissidents now ended, except where he had to appease federal leaders. There were private "warnings" to provincial employees, and personal accusations were returned in kind in the press and on the platform. Predictably, these tactics served more often than not to stiffen ALN resolve.[101]

"Down with the trusts! Down with Taschereau!" intoned Edouard Lacroix in the same breath at St Georges de Beauce. How these two slogans became inseparable is no mystery, for Taschereau was a visible, accessible, and apparently willing target for the antitrust movement. Why Taschereau allowed this to happen is quite a different question. The most obvious answer involves the tenacity of his beliefs about hydroelectricity and social security. In both cases he sincerely believed that the principles underlying reform proposals were false and destructive. Since 1897 the key to material progress had been large-scale private initiative operating in an atmosphere of respect for property and rights legally acquired. Hydroelectric development had been the model and spearhead and would be again once the depression ended. Government could always protect public interests within this existing framework, whereas to abandon a successful formula and to dismantle strong economic institutions would be a disastrous overreaction to the temporary crisis. It would mean renouncing progress even when prosperity returned, and would only make current problems more severe. With the province's financial resources and credit already strained to capacity, nationalization (or for that matter piecemeal municipalization) was totally impractical. Moreover – and here Taschereau was unwittingly testifying to the efficacy of tactics encouraged by the National Electric Light Association – the first victims of arbitrary or punitive government action would be the many individuals and social institutions in Quebec who had invested in the hydroelectric industry. Reacting to the charge that only he and his friends stood to suffer, Taschereau even had Mercier compile a list of shares held by religious communities, which he then invited Olivar Asselin to publish in *Le Canada*.[102]

To Taschereau it was even more obvious that the state should not and could not afford to weaken the principle of self-reliance and the institution of private charity, and he was confident that a strong societal consensus still supported his personal philosophy. Despite its expressions of concern about economic conditions, the church still had not renounced the jurisdiction its spokesmen had claimed during the Public Charities and old age pensions controversies; and no one had contradicted his claims about financial impracticability or suggested that government spending would help cure the depression – no Canadian political leader had yet absorbed Keynesian economic theory. On both issues, one can readily understand Taschereau's rigid adherence to traditional beliefs just in terms of age and the burdens of office. A man approaching seventy seldom abandons the convictions of a lifetime, especially after having espoused them publicly. In Taschereau's case, there was hardly the time to rethink and modify old assumptions, or to concede the validity of new principles in a changing world. Precisely because he was so closely involved in fighting the effects of the depression, Taschereau could not accept any "lessons" on the reality of the situation.[103]

There was, however, a major external factor in Taschereau's blindness to the possible validity of reform proposals, and in his apparently supreme confidence that he could survive politically without major concessions. This was his grave doubt about the motives and sincerity of the advocates. The significance of the Conservatives' Sherbrooke policy resolutions he could dismiss out of hand, especially with Duplessis as leader. Confirming Taschereau's initial assessment, Duplessis was proving to be an able and ambitious politician. A graceful and witty speaker, he could outshine the premier on any public platform and occasionally outpoint him in legislative debates. But he observed all the traditional rules of the electoral and parliamentary game, indulging in none of Houde's undignified demagoguery or inflammatory appeals to prejudice, for example. And in the tradition of his father, a politician close to the ultramontane Bishop Laflèche, he was at least as conservative as Taschereau on substantive issues. Of all the Sherbrooke reforms, Duplessis stressed only farm assistance – the time-honoured device of extolling rural values and appealing to the overrepresented rural electorate. So on those rare occasions when Duplessis did mention social assistance or attack free enterprise, Taschereau concluded that he was playing traditional politics, battering the government with any convenient weapon. It was no proof that "radical" legislation was really necessary.

Among Paul Gouin's followers there were undoubtedly a number of genuine reformers, such as Jean Martineau. But this minority, Taschereau believed, was being led astray by friends who were primarily interested in advancing their own careers. Almost all had some wealth and a good education, but they were not prepared to achieve status and influence through patient hard work. They expected to be handed these immediately through political and family connections. The worst example was Gouin, whose relations with Taschereau had been uneasy almost since Sir Lomer's death in 1929. Despite his excellent mind and legal training, he aspired to no more than a virtual sinecure (as assistant curator of the Quebec Museum), which would free him to write poetry and give dinner parties. Taschereau considered this an insult to the memory of Paul's father and grandfather and a sad contrast to his brother Léon-Mercier, already a highly respected lawyer and constitutional authority. If Paul's social concerns had been serious, he might well have accepted the juvenile court judgeship Taschereau offered him. Instead, the highlight of his legal career turned out to be the unsuccessful defence of J.J. Harpell, a Hamel-like crusader against the insurance industry who was finally sued for libel by the president of Sun Life.[104]

Even before their formal alliance with assorted Catholic Action and nationalist elements, these Liberal rebels were already keeping what Taschereau considered strange company. In particular, Taschereau was disturbed by their mutual sympathy with the Jeune Canada group inspired by Abbé Lionel Groulx. As professor of Canadian history at the University of Montreal since the end of the war, and editor of *L'Action française* during the 1920s, Groulx had been preaching the inevitability of racial conflict in Canada, flirting with separatist ideas, formulating increasingly reactionary critiques of the industrial age, and on occasion attacking the provincial government directly. The founders of Jeune Canada were his former students, as were a number of admiring *actionnistes*, including Paul Gouin. The original Jeune Canada manifesto proclaimed that "the unseating of Mr. Taschereau [was] the first item" on their agenda.[105] A large rally several months later, in November 1933, was told by one of Groulx's protégés that "it is no longer the time for moderate means ... it is not with rose water that we will purify our social system; if we need acid to deliver us from these organisms of speculation and the trust, let's use it." Another speaker indicated just where the real concern lay: "Look at the foreigners who implant themselves among us, who grab our waterfalls, our forests, our mines, who use them for their own benefit and who, not satisfied to live at our expense, outrageously exploit the people they have dispossessed: even more, for these *trustards* (American or "British") our natural resources are engines by which they subdue us without pity, machines for robbing us ... Either established authority will defend us, or else the people will usurp that authority."[106] Taschereau scoffed at this rhetoric, which merely reminded him of his own youth, "when we used to settle the most prickly and complex questions in a single evening."[107] It was also disturbingly similar, however, to the rhetoric of earlier generations of nationalists who sought to discredit industrialization by attacking its agents. With the help of the economic crisis, this retrograde message was penetrating "tomorrow's leading class."[108] In Taschereau's mind demands for reform became, like those of the prewar *nationalistes*, a disguise for opposition to material progress.

Taschereau was even more suspicious about the motives of "Catholic" reformers, refusing to believe that after years of unremitting hostility to state intervention, these activists really wanted the government to nationalize the hydroelectric industry or secularize social assistance. Around Quebec City, the critics were simply too familiar and too personally hostile towards him for their sudden concern about social justice to be taken seriously. *L'Action catholique* had reverted to form immediately after the death of Cardinal Rouleau; Curé Lavergne became a virtual mouthpiece for Philippe Hamel in his parish newsletter, *La Bonne Nouvelle*; Abbé Pierre Gravel, one of the teachers removed from the Petit Séminaire in 1924, denounced Taschereau openly from his post in Thetford Mines. Archbishop Villeneuve did nothing to discourage any of this activity;

on the contrary, Rouleau's successor openly associated himself with some of Taschereau's critics.[109]

The premier's distrust of clerical activists in Montreal was not based on a history of personal antagonism, but he did attribute their behaviour to a partisan bias. This was particularly true of the Jesuits, whose support and encouragement of Jeune Canada he could explain in no other way. "I cannot comprehend why the Reverend Jesuit Fathers make themselves the protectors of these young people who – I am not afraid to say it – are becoming the destroyers of public order and authority ... At the request of the highest religious authorities, we have fought actively against communists and disturbers of order; the disappearance of the Université Ouvrière is proof of it. And yet these young people went as far as many communists [at their meeting the other night]."[110] Father Archambault, who had published Hamel's latest diatribe on the trusts (along with an equally damning political tract by Wilfrid Guérin) as part of the *Programme de restauration sociale*, also belonged to the Jesuit Order. Archambault himself evidently recognized the partisan quality of the *Programme*, for he was most anxious to have at least one Liberal sign it. "It will be a great disappointment for us," he wrote to Paul Gouin before the latter's repudiation of Taschereau, "if your name does not appear. It will have less effect on public opinion. And it seems to me that with the modifications which were accepted at your request, the disadvantages you foresee are considerably reduced."[111]

It would have been considerably more difficult for Taschereau to ignore reform proposals if they had been urged more strongly by trusted political allies. Senator Raoul Dandurand had politely supported labour's call for the acceptance of old age pensions in the late 1920s, but had then given up. Federal Liberals led by Lapointe undoubtedly hoped Taschereau would make concessions that would reunify the party and restore its popularity. But while Taschereau genuinely admired Lapointe's political talents, he felt that the Quebec MPs were too much wedded to expediency for their views to be considered a guide to "right" action. Their own opportunistic response to R.B. Bennett's New Deal could only confirm Taschereau's view.[112] It is of course difficult to know what was said in private by members of the cabinet. It appears, however, as if several veteran ministers shared Taschereau's opinion that in the midst of crisis the government's duty was to resist "false doctrines." Laferté and Godbout were insistent only about rural issues. Vautrin did raise the old age pensions question at the first cabinet meeting of 1935, but nothing followed.[113] David, the sponsor of so many progressive initiatives in the 1920s - and the author of a book urging yet more

– had become the victim of personal problems so severe that Taschereau's compassion alone kept him in his portfolio. But he also shared his leader's antagonism toward the clerical nationalists, labelling Father Archambault "the most active and most extreme ... of those who inspire Jeune Canada."[114]

Nor was David the only progressive Liberal who reinforced Taschereau's prejudice. Olivar Asselin dismissed the *Programme* as "a weapon of war directed against the Liberal party by the Jesuits."[115] Jean-Charles Harvey, whom Taschereau protected against clerical censorship, believed that the premier's critics "included in their fold every extreme-right Laurentian, supernationalists, fascists, anglophobes, isolationists, separatists and clericals." Harvey sympathized with Paul Gouin, but warned him about the allies he had chosen.[116] In the last analysis T.-D. Bouchard probably rallied to Taschereau because he feared that the alternative was a regime of clerical reaction. He was satisfied with the government's hydroelectric legislation, but in his memoirs he also commented negatively on the reformist potential of the eventual alliance between the ALN and Duplessis. The latter "belonged to the ranks of traditional Conservatives while his allies of the moment consisted on the one hand of Liberals discontented with the Taschereau regime and on the other of clericals with fascist tendencies. The only thing which had brought them together was their desire to overturn the government. Now [1936] that they had achieved their objective, one could expect the crumbling of this political bloc at any moment."[117] And with Taschereau finally gone, Lapointe too became distressed at the growing force of clerical nationalism.[118] All of this suggests that Taschereau's essentially *ad hominem* arguments against reform proposals contained a fatal half-truth capable of seducing many genuine liberals younger and more progressive than the premier himself.[119]

## CHAPTER EIGHT

# "Still the Premier of Quebec"

Although his government was the target of shrill, unrelenting criticism by the summer of 1935, Alexandre Taschereau considered his political fortunes quite buoyant. Strange as it may seem in retrospect, he had some reason to suppose that as in 1931, voters would ultimately reject inflammatory appeals in favour of experienced, responsible leadership. The ministry was not displaying outward signs of political arteriosclerosis. The two newest members, Bouchard and Vautrin, personified with considerable flair and energy the government's response to popular concern over hydroelectricity and colonization. With a federal election imminent, Ottawa Liberals were beginning to rally. They feared too close an association with an unpopular premier, especially since they planned to vilify R.B. Bennett with rhetoric very similar to that being directed against Taschereau. But the Action libérale now contained so many Bleus and *cléricaux* that they could no longer regard it as a vehicle for "reliberalizing the Liberal party"; only the Taschereau Liberals could be relied upon for crucial organizational support. For his part, Taschereau considered their actual sympathy for the rebels misguided. But he could appreciate the strategic reasons behind their desire to maintain good relations with certain Liberal *actionnistes*, and therefore agreed that "we don't excommunicate anyone."[1] As Chubby Power had sensed in 1934, all Taschereau really wanted was a show of public solidarity. So Lapointe and his colleagues obliged, swallowing Taschereau's dictum that for true Liberals there was only one party, operating at both levels of government.[2]

Taschereau could even believe that the tide was already turning. True, Bouchard's entry into the cabinet did not spark a mad rush of dissidents back into the fold – just an orgy of sour grapes within the ALN and sighs of relief among Taschereau loyalists.[3] But the stream of defectors had basically dried up: few Liberals were crossing the line drawn in mid-1935, and Drouin's formal declaration in July was a foregone conclusion. Since most new ALN adherents came from traditionally Conservative elements, Taschereau felt that Duplessis had as much to worry about as he did. Despite Power's embarrassing refusal to resume the role of chief organizer, Jimmy Valentine, John Hall Kelly, and Jacob Nicol had been shoring up the rural Liberal machine since late 1934. And in Montreal, where defections most damaged the party apparatus, Conservatives also had a serious problem: many of their agents looked primarily to Mayor Houde for direction, and His Honour was not disposed to cooperate with Duplessis. Finally, his control of the next election date gave Taschereau important strategic options. If the ALN seemed to be spending its force or suffering from internal divisions, he could wait as long as the fall of 1936. If there was no hope of winning back any important rebels, he could capitalize on the expected Liberal sweep in the federal contest and call a snap election immediately afterwards.

For a while, events bore out Taschereau's optimism. Even the economic situation looked a little brighter that summer. Employment was rising at least marginally in most sectors, and in August Quebec trade unions reported the lowest unemployment rate among their members (18.3 per cent) in four years. Wages and the value of trade also crept upward without a corresponding increase in the cost of living. Bad weather would ultimately cause a slight decline in gross agricultural revenue for 1935, but for the moment it was the spectacular 1934 increase (to $182 million from $139 million in 1933) which determined the outlook of many farmers. Newsprint production rose for the second consecutive year, this time without another fall in price.[4] It also looked as if solvent and trustworthy British interests would finally take control of Price Brothers' operations. With Price Brothers able to observe pricing agreements, Charles Vining reported, "the industry will stand together in resisting further bribes by Hearst." In other words, the price of newsprint might rise for the first time in a decade the following year.[5] As Honoré Mercier had predicted, moreover, most companies could pay forest workers the wages decreed by his Forestry Commission, provided that the government did not start granting exemptions.[6]

The state of Montreal's economy did remain gloomy. Whereas in September the province as a whole had climbed back to its 1926 employment level, Montreal had not yet reached 90 per cent of that job figure.[7] But with an adequate system of relief administration finally taking shape, and Houde determined to cooperate, there was some comfort even here. In a late June meeting with Nicol, Houde made a series of proposals which were both specific and fairly reasonable: he needed $600,000 to complete current relief projects; he wanted the city and province to pay medical bills for the unemployed, as was done in Toronto and other major cities; relief should include the rent of the unemployed; the financial crisis of the University of Montreal must be resolved. Houde was ready to cooperate with Vautrin's colonization program, and he was anxious to "square accounts" between the two levels of government. Grateful to Taschereau for supporting the city's right to levy a sales tax, Houde insisted only on continued respect for municipal autonomy.[8]

Parliament was dissolved on 15 August, and the ensuing federal election campaign could hardly have unfolded in a manner more favourable to Taschereau. At a luncheon for Young Liberal leaders early in September, both King and Lapointe endorsed Taschereau's call for party unity and declared their solidarity with the provincial government.[9] At nominations and assemblies throughout Quebec, Liberal candidates, provincial deputies (including ministers), and organizers supported their leaders without any apparent reservation. Sensing the futility of a direct attack on Lapointe, Conservatives tried to ignore him or damage his credibility by association with Taschereau. Their slogan became "A vote for King is a vote for Taschereau," and their rhetoric in denouncing him was obviously designed to resemble that which Liberals were using against Bennett. It is difficult to fault the federal Conservatives for adopting this strategy – no better one comes to mind. But for provincial purposes it played into Taschereau's hands. In the first place, reporters let him respond to charges from the sanctity of his own office, and thereby avoid tumultuous public gatherings where opponents would surely try to arrange demonstrations of his unpopularity. Thus on 13 September he could chide Quebec City Conservatives, led by Solicitor General Maurice Dupré, for ignoring Bennett and federal issues.[10] Ten days later he blamed Bennett for two major inadequacies in Quebec's system of relief: the prime minister had broken his promise to assume the full cost of old age pensions, and had rejected the province's offer to share with Ottawa the unrealistic burden which existing legislation imposed on municipalities. At a press conference at his Montreal office on 8 October, he denied Bennett's charge that he had made his own recent promise to implement old age pensions conditional upon a Liberal victory. "I am surprised to see such an important man economize on the truth ... I announced that in [*sic*] the advent of either Mr Bennett or Mr King to power, the province would pay the balance of the pension fund if the total was not paid by the federal government."[11] Taschereau did not campaign formally until two weeks before polling day, 14 October, and even then his appearances were all relatively safe: several in Montmorency on Wilfrid Lacroix's behalf, and one on a national radio hookup featuring the eight Liberal premiers.[12]

Conservatives were not the only ones to focus their attacks on Taschereau. For the candidates of H.H. Stevens' Reconstruction party, many of whom were ALN sympathizers, it was natural to exploit antitrust sentiment. Stevens himself set the example at rallies in Sherbrooke and Quebec City. This gave Taschereau an even better opportunity to defend himself. He would not be dragged into a full scale debate with Stevens, Taschereau told reporters on 21 September, but since the issue evidently preoccupied many Quebeckers, he would demonstrate that he was not a "protector of the trusts." He had destroyed the liquor trust, reformed workman's compensation and collective bargaining legislation over strong opposition from industrialists, created a dairy commission to protect milk producers and a fair wage commission for forest workers, and raised taxes on banks and other financial institutions. The new Hydroelectric Commission had tight regulatory control over the so-called electricity trust, and he had successfully prosecuted the coal trust despite a lack of cooperation from the federal Department of Trade and Commerce, H.H. Stevens, minister.[13]

If the Liberals had not swept Quebec on 14 October, their failure would almost certainly have been attributed to Taschereau's unpopularity. But as they did win sixty seats, and Taschereau was not an issue in the five constituencies where Conservative MPs survived, he could claim that the result was a personal vindication. He attached special significance to the victory of Charles Parent, his legal associate, over Dupré in the partly working class constituency of Quebec Southwest. Following this successful demonstration of Liberal party unity, moreover, Taschereau could point to the future benefits of cooperation between the two levels of government. Turning the Tories' slogan against them, provincial Liberals could enter their next election proclaiming "a vote for Taschereau is a vote for King." The dismal showing of Reconstruction candidates was also rhetorically useful: voters had evidently not taken the "trustard" accusation very seriously, at least following Taschereau's rebuttal; moreover, their unsuccessful venture demonstrated the futility of third parties in an "old province."[14]

In various ways Taschereau's opponents acknowledged his apparently advantageous position. *Le Devoir* credited rumours of an immediate dissolution, with voting as early as 4 November. Its Quebec correspondent played down the alternative scenario, a fall session and spring election, even though Taschereau had playfully achieved perfect ambiguity with "It's unfair to hit a man while he's down" and "strike while the iron is hot."[15] Paul Gouin hastened to assure radio listeners that the ALN was not a third party, but rather the true Liberal party. Most importantly, supporters of both the ALN and the provincial Conservatives admitted at least privately that Taschereau could not be overthrown in a three-cornered contest. Despite the reluctance of Gouin and Duplessis, their followers were now actively exploring the possibility of an electoral alliance.[16]

Quebec's paper mills may still have been operating at only 75 per cent of capacity, but for the next two weeks her political rumour mills worked overtime. In contrast to *Le Devoir*, the *Montreal Star* did not expect a provincial election in 1935: the government would need at least a brief session to implement agreements reached at the Dominion-Provincial Conference which King had promised to hold as soon as he took office.[17] Cabinet shuffles were freely predicted, variously involving the retirements of Vautrin, Arcand, Bouchard, David, and even Taschereau, the addition of Hector Authier, Deputy Labour Minister Gérald Tremblay, and Robert Taschereau to the ministry, and the accession of either Francoeur or Perrault to the premier's office. The chances of an opposition coalition were reported slim: Conservatives supposedly believed that they could simply absorb *actionnistes* who really wanted a change of regime, that mere Liberal malcontents would drift back to their own party, and that Duplessis could win a majority by himself with only a small swing in the 1931 popular vote. In contrast, some Taschereau Liberals were said to be hoping for an opposition alliance, since this would "prove" that the *actionnistes* were nothing but opportunists.[18]

Taschereau's exact thoughts during the last half of October remain a matter for speculation. It is almost inconceivable that he considered retiring without the vindication of a final provincial campaign, and the rumours concerning other ministers were scarcely more plausible. Bouchard was crucial to the government's credibility throughout the province, and the retirement of Arcand or Vautrin (let alone both) would be a demoralizing confession of Liberal weakness in Montreal constituencies. With opponents already charging that the cabinet was extravagantly large, Authier, Edgar Rochette, and other promising aspirants would have to wait for post-election vacancies. Only the timing of the election was really problematic, with Taschereau apparently leaning toward an early vote and Jacob Nicol speaking for the contrary view.[19] Taschereau evidently saw no serious risk, however, in a short delay: the rhetorical and organizational advantages afforded by the federal result would not disappear overnight. It was more important to examine the validity of Nicol's objections, to let King's new administration get organized before calling upon the Quebec ministers for support, and to plan campaign strategy in minute detail.

The final decision must have been reached shortly after 22 October. On that day Taschereau met briefly with Houde, no doubt to confirm the mayor's indication of benevolent neutrality. Then he disappeared for what his office called a "brief vacation" – more likely a secluded meeting of the brain trust in the Laurentians. Within a week David, Bouchard, and Godbout were out rehearsing campaign rhetoric while King, sworn in on 23 October, had agreed to postpone his Dominion-Provincial Conference. The cabinet meeting which preceded dissolution on 30 October was brief and devoted mostly to housekeeping: evidently the ministers already knew that the election would be held on 25 November. A single minor cabinet change accompanied the election announcement: John Hall Kelly became the "Irish" representative in place of Joseph Dillon, who had won a seat in the House of Commons. A more significant appointment was that of Augustin Frigon as chairman of the Hydroelectric Commission. Highly respected as Quebec's director of technical education for more than a decade, and originally trained as an electrical engineer, Frigon would, it was hoped, lend further credibility to the government's recent electricity legislation. Also significant were the appointments Taschereau did not have to announce: the predicted rush of Liberals-in-trouble to the bench or bureaucracy did not materialize.[20]

Taschereau's apparent confidence still seemed justified as the campaign opened. His first rally in Victoriaville was actually an All Saints' Day celebration which J.-E. Perrault's local organizers had been planning for some time. Mild weather, band music, and the presentation of roses to Adine created a relaxed and friendly atmosphere in which heckling could not be effective. Perrault and Godbout adopted positive themes, extolling the work of their departments. Taschereau's address was similarly appropriate to the mood of the large crowd. In fact, it was probably one of his best-delivered campaign speeches ever, somewhat plaintive in his own defence yet not strident in attacking his opponents. "You read in Conservative and Gouinist papers that I am a tyrant, an autocrat, a veteran whose time has passed, a man in politics to get rich, a man who should disappear ... [But] I am not the black sheep they describe. I am a Canadian like you, who loves his country, his province and his race, who gives the best of himself to preserve Quebec's place at the head of the Canadian Confederation. And despite the burden which grows heavier every day, I still have the heart and the will and my health remains strong." Reading telegrams of support from King and Lapointe, Taschereau dismissed reports that his regime could not cooperate with Ottawa. On the contrary, it would make no sense for Quebec voters to reject the party they had just supported federally and to place a Conservative government amidst the Liberal administrations which now ruled seven of the other eight provinces. As expected, Taschereau actually did invert the Conservative slogan, declaring that a vote for him was a vote for King.

After reviewing the government's initiatives on farm credit and colonization, Taschereau resumed his self-defence.

They say ... [we] are the friends of the trusts. I don't like the trusts any more than you do. Ask those who say it which trusts the government has protected or assisted. You won't get an answer. Let's see if the government has aided them or has brought them under control.

Formerly ... the liquor trade was in the hands of a few barons of finance. If we had been their friend, the machine and tool of the trusts, do you think we would have said: "Out?"

When we enacted the workman's compensation law, do you think the employers, the trusts, were favourable to a law requiring them to pay an indemnity even when the worker was at fault? ... Was that bowing our heads to the trusts? When M. Arcand introduced the Collective Agreements Act, do you think the employers were favourable?

They say the provincial government is the friend of the coal trust and does nothing. The Ottawa government led by Mr Bennett conducted a coal inquiry; though it has the right to prosecute the companies it didn't, and it passed the buck to us. The Quebec government, if it is the friend of the coal trust, did its duty. It prosecuted the companies and had them fined $40,000.

... At the last session we created a commission whose members were named yesterday. We have told them: You will be the Electricity Commission, you have complete control of the companies, you will be able to oblige them to serve such and such a municipality, you will set the price, you will even have the right to take existing contracts and reduce rates in the public interest. Is that siding with the trusts, being their machine, bowing down before them? That is my reply to our friends who say we are at the mercy of the trusts.

After once again blaming Bennett for his own refusal to introduce old age pensions, Taschereau reiterated his earlier promise to bring them in whether or not King agreed to assume the full burden. He hastened to add that his government had not ignored the aged during the dispute with Bennett, paying millions of dollars to charitable insitutions which cared for them.

Then Taschereau dealt with the fundamental challenge to his integrity and performance, the question of directorships. He challenged Paul Gouin to cite a case where his membership on a board had led to a decision harmful to the public interest. On the contrary, he could show Gouin a list of French-Canadian individuals and institutions helped because of his influence with the financial community. Taschereau could not close without an attack on Gouin's motives, but at least managed to sound more condescending than vindictive. Reading aloud the now celebrated correspondence concerning Gouin's job requests, Taschereau suggested that the ALN leader finally enter the Quebec Museum and deposit his program among the articles of antiquity.[21]

Obviously these were not brilliant arguments; Bouchard refuted Gouin's charges far more convincingly in a speech elsewhere the same day.[22] What encouraged the Liberals was the receptiveness of the audience. Taschereau had apparently succeeded in projecting the image of a senior statesman whose ability and integrity were the prime election issues. If he could repeat that performance throughout the campaign, diverting public attention from the opposition's more substantive criticisms and proposals, the inevitable government losses might be held to a minimum. While ALN spokesmen lamely tried to play down the Victoriaville rally, Liberal spirits remained high throughout the weekend. Their organizational preparedness was paying off in a spate of well-attended nominations, whereas the ALN and Conservatives were both moving very slowly. The number of mayors who participated in Liberal nomination meetings indicated, moreover, that Bouchard had largely delivered his colleagues in the Union des municipalités. Aware that high-level negotiations were in progress between the two opposition groups, Taschereau told a press conference that "our opponents must have all gone to Geneva, or somewhere – I don't see too many of them rising against us."[23] Liberals were also somewhat amused by Edouard Lacroix's vain effort to become an ALN candidate: by law MP could not run for a provincial seat, and Lacroix could not resign from the House of Commons until his 14 October election was officially reported.[24]

The direction of campaign momentum changed abruptly, however, on Thursday night, 7 November, when Gouin and Duplessis announced they were forming "a common front against the common enemy: the Taschereau regime." Radio listeners learned that there would be a single "Union Nationale" candidate in each constituency (a secret provision accorded sixty to sixty-five of the ninety nominations to the ALN), that the platform of the alliance would be the ALN program, and that following the expected victory Duplessis would become premier with Gouin choosing a majority of the cabinet ministers.[25] The news did not really catch Taschereau and his followers by surprise. In fact Liberal intelligence was so good that *Le Canada* published a fairly accurate version several hours before the opposition leaders made their electoral alliance official.[26] Nevertheless, conclusion of the alliance provoked a more realistic assessment of the political situation by the Liberals. The slow start on nominations turned out to be an asset for the opposition, since there were not many constituencies where the ALN and Conservatives had both selected candidates. Taschereau's belief that genuine Liberals would abandon the ALN rather than fight alongside Conservatives proved false. With the sole exception of his nephew, Coote, they had all become so obsessed with defeating Taschereau that they ignored the dangers inherent in an alliance with Duplessis. The medium chosen by Gouin and Duplessis for their declaration was also significant, for by 1935 radio had severely reduced the extent to which the Taschereau Liberals could, through their virtual newspaper monopoly, control political information and debate.

The Gouin-Duplessis alliance was not the only campaign development to dampen Liberal optimism as the deadline for nominations approached. Another was the number of threatened independent Liberal candidacies, mostly rebellions against sitting members who would not submit to a nomination meeting. In 1931 Taschereau had rejected Chubby Power's advice that they be required to do so, preferring not to interfere in local squabbles.[27] The time-honoured practice was for dissidents to run as independent Liberals and, if elected, to be accepted into the Liberal caucus. The obvious risk of handing the opposition a seat by splitting the Liberal vote was not considered serious when large government majorities were expected. Now that the province-wide result was uncertain, however, Liberal organizers had few means to deal with the situation. Taschereau had not even used the patronage at his disposal to induce the retirement of weak MLAs.

The development which surprised Taschereau most of all was the unrestrained intervention of clerical opponents. He had, of course, been sparring with certain Montreal priests since 1933, the year of Jeune Canada and the *Programme de restauration sociale.* He also knew the futility of formal complaints to the Archbishop of Quebec about *L'Action catholique,* and had even conceded to Cardinal Villeneuve that Curé Lavergne was uncontrollable.[28] However, he did expect Villeneuve and Archbishop Gauthier of Montreal to moderate rather than encourage open partisanship among their subordinates, and to preserve the dignity of their high office by suppressing their personal partisan preferences. But Villeneuve apparently committed himself to the opposition cause several months prior to the election, giving Philippe Hamel "good news" and causing Paul Gouin to rejoice that "contrary to what our opponents claim ... we can win our elections with prayers."[29] At the end of July, in the guise of a neutral directive on political morality, Villeneuve ordered his clergy to warn parishioners against "blind" party allegiance and to condemn electoral shenanigans traditionally practised by parties in power. This message was to be read on the Sunday preceding any federal or provincial election.[30] In case that invitation was too subtle, he then arranged to be out of the country during the probable election period. Amid delicate negotiations to save the financially distressed Séminaire de Saint Sulpice in Montreal, Gauthier was considerably more discreet. But here the Liberals' clerical antagonists were less in need of licence, for the lay movements which they advised and sponsored already knew their "patriotic duty" and Le Devoir (unlike L'Action catholique) was formally independent of ecclesiastical authority. Only an explicit order to control their followers would have caused these priests any embarrassment, and Gauthier issued nothing of the kind.[31]

Taschereau greeted the formation of the Union Nationale with outward calm. The alliance, he told reporters, would be "profoundly laughable if it were not, from the standpoint of political principles, deeply saddening. The contract read last night does not speak at all of political principles, but is content with a distribution of honours and offices ... I have never heard of anything more childish. There is something clownlike in the fact that a man consents to be premier but with the condition that someone else will choose his colleagues. That is contrary to all principles of constitutional law ... But we can remain undisturbed. Mr Duplessis will not be premier and Paul Gouin will have nothing to say in the choice of members of the government."[32] Nor did Taschereau and his advisers betray their concern by altering campaign plans. The premier's itinerary was set: the North Shore on 9 and 10 November, Rivière du Loup on the 11th, and a swing through the Eastern Townships made up his first tour; the following week would be devoted to large rallies in Three Rivers, Quebec, and finally Montreal. In between, he would canvass Montmorency for the twenty-third time, including federal elections. With appropriate variations according to locale, his speeches contained essentially the same material as the one he gave in Victoriaville. With federal ministers and deputies at his side, he emphasized the importance of future cooperation with Ottawa.[33] Then he reviewed his vigilance in controlling the trusts, and repeated the familiar defence of his directorships. If an orgy of promises signify panic in a leader, Taschereau was certainly not in such a state: he never exceeded his two original commitments, old age pensions and higher subsidies for the interest on farm loans, plus financial relief for municipalities if Ottawa would share the cost. The legislative record of 1934 and 1935, along with traditional electoral porkbar-relling, he apparently believed, would satisfy reasonable people.

However, the tone of Taschereau's campaign changed markedly after 7 November. Attacks on the sincerity and integrity of his opponents, especially Gouin, grew daily more violent. Duplessis had betrayed party and principle out of sheer opportunism. But far worse than political ambition were Gouin's despicably petty motives. To avenge the museum affair, Gouin was repudiating the party and principles of his own father and grandfather, "usurping the right of the first-born" to speak in Sir Lomer's name, and slandering his father's long-time intimate colleague and faithful successor. As if in court, Taschereau then summoned Honoré Mercier II and Léon-Mercier Gouin to verify his version of the Liberal tradition. This attack sounds desperate enough, but it may equally have expressed the kind of angry self-righteousness Taschereau had displayed many times before. Having entertained "no higher ambition than to be worthy of the name [his ancestors] had left him and to pass it on to his descendants as clean and respected as he had received it," he could hardly ignore Paul Gouin's accusation that he had "sold out to vested interests." And Paul was indeed stretching the truth when he contrasted the "happiness, peace, prosperity and economic independence [sic]" of his father's era with the misery he now blamed on Taschereau's policies.[34]

Whatever caused Taschereau to adopt this more strident tone, his ministers and the Liberal press quickly followed suit, aggressively defending the integrity of their leader and unleashing a hail of *ad hominems* against ALN leaders. Ouellet was disgruntled because he had not become minister of agriculture; a man of real conviction would surrender his seat in the Legislative Council and become an opposition candidate. (Of course, other Liberals were traitors for running against the government.) Hamel was out to discredit the hydroelectric industry just because he had once lost money spec-ulating on it. Mayor Grégoire was a hypocrite, having broken his promise to cooperate with Taschereau for the welfare of Quebec City even though new legislation had granted Quebec its long-sought authority over power distribution. Drouin had lied to colleagues about his political intentions, keeping a foot in the Liberal camp while actively promoting the ALN cause.[35]

To be fair, the Liberals did not exactly monopolize the art of denigration. In fact, some of their opponents sank considerably lower. Hamel claimed that Taschereau (not some mischievous hack, but the premier himself) had sent women to tempt him. Curé Lavergne asserted that Taschereau "kept a crowd of young girls at the legislature occupying positions which should have gone to men, and what is more, 78 per cent of these girls were having relations with ministers and deputy ministers." In a sermon whose text the Union Nationale circulated widely, Lavergne also charged that Taschereau's policies were dictated by personal avarice and that the government habitually intimidated and blackmailed the clergy. Not to let Montreal be outdone by these Quebeckers, Calixte Cormier accused Taschereau of criminal conspiracy and accepting a bribe in connection with the Harpell suit, and another candidate declared that Taschereau had never been elected, but had "stolen and bought his way into office."[36]

With a week left in the campaign, the "issues," such as they were, had been entirely submerged in a sea of mud. It was so bad that Léon-Mercier Gouin, while continuing to support the government "in the name of Sir Lomer," had appealed privately to Taschereau to restrain *Le Soleil*'s attacks on his brother.[37] The sole redeeming feature was that most of the violence remained verbal. A few rocks and vegetables were hurled outside Taschereau's Montreal rally, but a rumoured demonstration blocking his return to Windsor Station never materialized. John Hall Kelly was rumoured shot in Gaspé, but it turned out that he had been hit by a snowball. The only serious disturbance occurred in Chicoutimi, where Hector Laferté's speech had to be cancelled. If anything significant happened during the final days, it was that the Liberals appreciated the full extent of clerical intervention and began reacting to it. Lavergne was in full flight – physically as well as oratorically. Campaigning for Grégoire in Montmagny, he had to keep one jump ahead of a "desist" order issued by Bishop Plante. Lavergne's friend Pierre Gravel, now a Catholic union chaplain in Thetford Mines, was working frantically for the Union Nationale candidate in Megantic. At least two priests were planning to use religious broadcasts to berate the government. In both cases Taschereau found out, requested their superiors to check the contents in advance, and was falsely but predictably accused of intimidation. From all over the province came reports of priests telling students and parishioners that Liberals were godless, or non-

Catholics and Freemasons, that the defeat of the government was morally imperative, that the premier was a criminal who would be electrocuted in America and hanged in England, and so on.[38]

The Liberals wisely refrained from a direct public counter-attack which would only have served to validate the charge of anticlericalism. Instead, they condemned or ridiculed political opponents who campaigned in the name of religion. Lapointe, for example, sounded rather apologetic throughout most of his speech on the government's behalf. Acknowledging past differences with Taschereau, he argued that parties (and thus party loyalty) were essential to the democratic system, and that "total conformity is not demanded in our party. This is the basis on which we have cooperated and will cooperate fruitfully." But then, with far greater conviction, he angrily insisted that he could not abstain from taking part in a contest between Taschereau and those who had unfairly attacked him during the federal campaign. "Where are they, the ones who insulted and disparaged me on radio and elsewhere, calling me a communist or nonbeliever? If they are all on the same side, you cannot go far wrong lining up on the other side." At the same Quebec City rally, Taschereau tore into "the calumny trust ... These people who pretend to be so much holier than their neighbours may have faith but they have no works to show for it, and faith without works is dead. They pretend that Liberalism is opposed to religion. Have they forgotten [all the contrary evidence]?"[39] And no single opponent infuriated Taschereau by his smug piety more than Grégoire. Grégoire had endorsed the *Programme de restauration sociale* and Hamel's anti-trust crusade in 1933, captured the mayoralty of Quebec using anti-Taschereau slogans devised by Hamel and Curé Lavergne in 1934, and chaired an ALN rally in January 1935. Then he had had the audacity to feign political neutrality until "discovering" on the very eve of the provincial election that Taschereau had no commitment to economic reform or social justice as defined by papal teaching. Paying an unscheduled visit to Montmagny three days before the election, Taschereau did his best to puncture the conceit of "a holy man who performs his own canonization before dying ... who proclaims all his own qualities and virtues except one, the inability to administer his city ... [who] offers you encyclicals [whereas] my friend M. Choquette offers you bread."[40] Naturally Curé Lavergne charged that the last phrase was a promise of patronage, but in context it is clear that Taschereau was comparing his administrative experience and concrete relief proposals to Grégoire's record as mayor and his vague economic panaceas.

T.-D. Bouchard also joined in, seizing upon the ridiculous claim that French Canadians' faith would be undermined by his scheme to barter Quebec produce for Russian coal. It was a good excuse, he pointed out, for opponents to ignore the fact that such a deal would undercut the Canadian "coal trust." But the accusation that he was sympathetic to communism "does not surprise me or anyone else who knows the activities of these organizations."[41] It probably did not occur to either Bouchard or Taschereau, at least in the heat of battle, that the new minister's sudden prominence may itself have contributed to Villeneuve's attitude. Although highly intolerant of criticism from priests and *la bonne presse*, Taschereau had never supported traditional Rouge causes. Yet some clergy had always believed he was an anticlerical at heart,[42] and some of his recent complaints to Villeneuve could easily have reinforced that suspicion. At the beginning of 1935, for example, Villeneuve was alarmed about the revival of pressure to end tax exemptions for ecclesiastical property. Taschereau replied that while he remained personally opposed, support for this longstanding Rouge ambition was growing. This sentiment he attributed not to the desperate state of municipal revenues, but to the Liberals' exasperation with the constant moralizing of *L'Action catholique* and Curé Lavergne's *La Bonne Nouvelle* on nonreligious issues. If so concerned about social justice, he intimated, religious authorities should first examine "the acquisition by communities of princely residences which thereby escape taxation while our people bear a crushing burden." In closing, Taschereau raised the spectre of an anticlerical backlash – his first warning of that kind since the celebrated Bégin incident of 1921. "My own career is nearing an end; I draw the danger to your attention and pray to God that this danger will not strike us when others, perhaps less well disposed than the men of today, have replaced them."[43] At the time, Villeneuve acknowledged the "serenely melancholic" rather than threatening tone of Taschereau's letter.[44] But when Bouchard joined the cabinet less than five months later, the threat became immediate and vividly personified. As saviour of the government's credibility, the most notorious Rouge since Godfroy Langlois would have a strong claim to succeed Taschereau.[45]

Election day found Taschereau and other leading Liberals reconciled to the loss of several seats, a consequence of economic discontent and of scattered ALN organizational accomplishments. They were at least outwardly confident, however, that their campaign strategy had worked well enough to ensure a comfortable survival. Some of Tellier's crew were actually talking about a sweep of Montreal until the first returns showed city Liberals being swept out instead of in.[46] Gloom also pervaded Taschereau's Quebec City office when the opposition took an early province-wide lead, although the premier himself was either less surprised or more philosophical than others present. The experience may have been more embarrassing for his close friends and relatives, who must have feared that, since his integrity had been an issue, he would be personally humiliated by defeat. But only the announcement of Ernest Grégoire's election visibly upset him, and everyone finally relaxed when favourable returns from the lower St Lawrence put the government ahead , forty-eight seats to forty-two.[47] Clearly, the Liberals had been saved by their rural base. They were virtually wiped out in Montreal, Quebec City, Sherbrooke, and the industrial towns of the St Maurice and Saguenay Valleys. Only the Jewish and Irish vote preserved four seats on the Island, while the English of Quebec West and suburban Quebec County gave them two more in the capital. Nicol had completely lost control of the Sherbrooke area, with only Stockwell surviving. The Montreal cabinet members were less fortunate than their Eastern Townships colleague: Arcand was trounced in Maisonneuve and Vautrin edged out in St Jacques.

To the Action libérale nationale apparently belonged the great moral victory. They had captured twenty-six seats from the Liberals, including five on Montreal Island, three in Quebec City (including Lévis), an arc of five vast northern constituencies stretching from St Maurice to Chicoutimi, and a cluster of four rural counties centred on Edouard Lacroix's Beauce stronghold. Conservatives naturally joined in celebrating the government's reverses, but in reality they had little to crow about. They actually lost three seats they had won in 1931, made most of their eight gains in constituencies where they had always run strongly, and gained surprisingly little in popular vote over 1931. Several long-time Conservatives and Duplessis loyalists who ran under the ALN banner won considerably more impressive victories. The ALN, therefore, deserved most of the credit for shattering the dominance of the Taschereau regime. History has generally acknowledged this fact, even while recording that, within a year, Duplessis and his Conservatives had managed to turn the achievement to their own advantage. There is, however, an important aspect of the election which hindsight has obscured. In describing this bitter campaign as the beginning of the Taschereau regime's destruction, analysts have not stopped to consider how or why the government survived the 1935 election even temporarily. The only "explanation" amounts to the uncritical acceptance of opposition claims that "in an election honestly conducted the government would be out."[48] This partisan assertion is far from indisputable, and even if it could be proved there would still be a need to explain the government's strong performance. As Taschereau himself remarked on election night, governments elsewhere in Canada had been decisively repudiated throughout 1934 and 1935.[49]

Despite opposition insistence that "inconceivably fraudulent manoeuvres" determined the outcome, no one has ever demonstrated that this election was unusually corrupt. Against a stronger, more vigilant opposition than they had faced for decades, the Liberals probably got away with less chicanery than usual. Opposition charges must also be considered in the light of the Union Nationale's post-election strategy, which was to erase the government's majority prior to the opening of the legislature by means of annulments, recounts, and conversions.[50] In any case, ridings where the opposition documented major irregularities were not those narrowly won by the government. In St Jacques where Vautrin lost by forty-six votes, and L'Assomption, which Gouin won by sixty-two, Liberal tricks were wasted. In St Lawrence (more ballots than voters) and St Louis (opposition candidate unable to find returning officer on nomination day), Jewish electors were not going to support a French-Canadian nationalist campaign. Even the attention afterwards focused by opposition spokesmen on these cases reeked of antisemitism, as did their comments about Mercier, a riding whose substantial Jewish minority saved Dr Anatole Plante against Calixte Cormier.[51] In Gaspé North and South, where some Liberal organizers cruelly used relief cheques as government largesse, the Union Nationale finished a poor third behind independent candidates. And in Terrebonne, Athanase David was well ahead when a judge declared him elected by the single vote of the returning officer. The opposition was simply hoping that a technical error in the printing of ballots would result in a new election. The most dubious Liberal victor was Hector Authier, who trailed in settled portions of Abitibi but compiled a huge majority in the temporary polls circulating among newer colonists in the wilderness. *Le Devoir* justly wondered how many spruce trees had voted.[52] The Liberals did win several close races, and in each of these the loser naturally sought a judicial recount. But recounts are not contested elections, and do not require evidence of corruption.

Far more decisive than election day skulduggery was the role of independent Liberal candidates, especially in the two largest cities. In Laurier, St Henri, Verdun, and Lévis, the Union Nationale won with substantially fewer votes than the combined total of two Liberals. In Laval and Saint Sauveur (and also the rural constituency of Temiscaming), division in the Liberal organization undoubtedly helped opposition candidates edge past 50 per cent of the vote. In contrast, no independent candidate appears to have cost the opposition a seat. Thus, had Taschereau's organizers been able to reconcile local personalities and factions, the government would almost certainly have achieved a more comfortable majority – and the mystery of its success would have been that much greater. Undoubtedly there were many poor rural counties in which the sheer power of patronage prevailed. This was especially true where the opposition presence was not strong enough to persuade voters that the government might actually be defeated with their help – in the lower St Lawrence region, for example. But elsewhere, it is not unreasonable to suppose that the Liberal campaign actually convinced substantial numbers of people. Taschereau had never been personally popular; his appeal had always rested upon a reputation for sound administration and a strong sense of public duty. By concentrating on the defence of this image, and by contrasting it with evidence of opportunism on the part of his opponents, the Liberals were actually quite shrewd. Taschereau was not just whistling in the dark when he claimed that many traditional Conservatives would resent the "morganatic marriage" of opposition parties.[53]

But more than the alliance itself made this Liberal strategy effective. The obvious personal antagonism of many ALN leaders toward Taschereau may also have backfired, once men like Bouchard and Lapointe had testified that most legitimate causes for complaint had been removed, and that the remainder could be resolved within the Liberal party. Finally, even the opposition's call for more advanced social legislation may have rung hollow by election day, the sincerity of Martineau and other Action libérale originals notwithstanding. Later adherents to the ALN were known to be more nationalist than reformist, their Conservative allies were dubious proponents of state intervention, and most clergy who campaigned had previously denounced government interference with the social prerogatives of the church. Much as they disliked the regime in power, voters had good reason to be wary of the opposition as well.[54]

The torrent of personal recrimination which increasingly dominated the campaign was no mere contrivance to inspire the troops or entertain the masses. For senior cabinet ministers and ALN leaders especially, the fury was all too genuine, often approaching the fanaticism of civil war. Literally, brother turned against brother and a generation against its elders. Through the crust of civility for which elite society in Quebec City was renowned burst venomous prejudice and repressed hatreds. Here as elsewhere in the province, allies were considered patriots and opponents were labelled traitors. With the votes counted, however, the strategic interests of the two sides began to exert more control over their public behaviour. The Liberals' prime interest was to establish political calm, emphasizing their authority and capacity to continue governing. It also happened to be in the public interest, of course, to assure Quebeckers that someone was effectively administering the province. But clearly the Liberals were hoping to retain power for themselves, first by ensuring the continued loyalty of partisans who might jump ship if they thought it was sinking, then by gracefully retiring Taschereau in favour of a successor who could rally some of the dissidents and restore public confidence. The Union Nationale, in contrast, had a definite interest in maintaining the turbulent atmosphere of the campaign. It was not just a case of foiling Liberal strategy but of preserving its own cohesion and credibility as well. For while the terms of the 7 November alliance governed the formation of a Gouin-Duplessis administration, they did not stipulate what should happen following an electoral defeat. Without a formal understanding, the precarious unity of the opposition was at the mercy of latent suspicions, divergent priorities, and Liberal manoeuvring. The solution was to deny that the opposition really had been defeated, both by contesting the formal result and by interpreting the election as a crucial but not final step toward the destruction of the Taschereau regime. This would keep the Liberals on the defensive, sustain and hopefully increase public support for the opposition cause, and bind the various factions both morally and tactically to a continuation of the alliance.

These rival strategies may not have been explicitly formulated or consciously pursued by all participants, but they do accurately describe the actual behaviour of Quebec politicians following the election. Within twenty-four hours, Duplessis, Gouin, and Drouin all challenged the validity of the result and vowed to continue the fight. Within a week rallies were organized across the province and judicial proceedings launched in several constituencies. In Montreal the nationalist youth organizations, including the brand-new Jeunesse patriote formed just for the purpose, ensured that all rallies were boisterous and well attended. Around Quebec the ALN refused to be intimidated by thugs who broke up a meeting in Montmorency, planning bigger assemblies and pointedly reminding Charles Lanctôt of their right to be protected by the provincial police. Rightly crediting much of their recent success to the influence of radio, Gouin and Duplessis continued broadcasting election-style appeals. They even tried to record public meetings for this purpose, but the rhetoric was so inflammatory that stations refused to play the recordings. In a similar incident, advertising for a Jeune Canada demonstration was so provocative that the Jesuits withdrew permission for the use of their hall. Offering some unintentional comic relief, ALN deputy-elect Zenon Lesage uncovered a Taschereau-Houde plot to "kill or cripple" opposition members in a forthcoming benefit hockey game between MLAS and Montreal city councillors. The game was cancelled.[55]

Taschereau launched the Liberal appeal for calm and reconciliation just as quickly, asserting his continued authority but emphasizing the sense of public responsibility which would animate his government. "This is Taschereau, still premier of Quebec," he told radio listeners on election night. "We will deal with the facts which have diminished our majority ... seek to forget the fight which was waged against us ... [and] give to the people of the province the best of ourselves so as to ride over the crisis which still exists and which requires the support of all of good will, and of everyone, to be vanquished."[56] The message was similar at press conferences in Quebec and Montreal, and even when hung in effigy by the Jeunesse patriote, Taschereau substituted mild condescension for his customary indignation. "They are so enraged because of the government victory that their effervescence must vent itself in some way. It doesn't offend me. It amuses me."[57] At the Dominion-Provincial Conference which opened on 9 December, Taschereau was determined to fulfil his election promise of fruitful cooperation with other Liberal governments. When Ottawa rejected his scheme for the financial relief of municipalities, he left severe public protest to Camillien Houde. Indulging in some humour at his own expense, itself an unusual occurrence, he surprised many observers by acknowledging the need for constitutional reform. "Confederation is pretty old now. It is about my own age ... and although I am told that I never amend myself, probably the Canadian Constitution does require some amendments."[58] Taschereau's New Year message similarly combined a call for "patience, devotion and collaboration ... to accomplish lasting reforms" with a humble statement of his personal dedication.[59]

There were two immediate threats to Taschereau's program of sweet harmony. The more ironic was a serious dispute with the premier of Ontario, traditional ally of Quebec leaders at Dominion-Provincial conferences. At issue was Ontario's repudiation of agreements by its Hydro Electric Commission to purchase electrical power from four Quebec companies. Signed during the 1920s in anticipation of growing demand, these contracts had since become an enormous financial burden to Hydro. In March 1935, after the companies spurned his initial requests to renegotiate the contracts, Premier Hepburn introduced a bill declaring them "illegal, void and unenforceable." Taschereau and the companies immediately sent emissaries to protest, and dire consequences were predicted for Ontario in the financial world. But Hepburn drove the bill through, partly to enhance his populist image and partly in the hope that the companies would become more reasonable and make proclamation of the act unnecessary. Unfortunately, he and Taschereau never got together to thrash out the problem. First they could not find a mutually convenient date in June. Then, not wishing to embarrass federal Liberals with a public dispute, they postponed their meeting until after the federal election. In late October, illness forced Hepburn to take a southern vacation. Some of his colleagues, notably Acting Premier Nixon, gave Honoré Mercier a cordial reception during his absence, but undertook only to delay proclamation until after the Quebec provincial election. As predicted by J.L. Ralston, who advised Taschereau throughout this affair, Hepburn returned on 3 December and proclaimed his legislation the same day. Thus Taschereau had been given no real opportunity to dissuade Hepburn and he apparently displayed considerable anger once the two met privately in Ottawa. But news of this fruitless confrontation did not leak out for more than a year, and since journalists failed to report how little had actually been agreed upon at the conference itself, the Quebec delegates could return home brimming with pretended enthusiasm.[60]

Taschereau's second and more complicated problem concerned the political agitation conducted by priests during the election campaign. On tactical grounds, he was almost compelled to pursue the issue forcefully. For in extending its agitation beyond election day, the political opposition would certainly continue invoking the moral authority of the church. And if Lavergne, Gravel, and other priests were not silenced by the hierarchy, then it might appear as if the church really did consider the government evil or illegitimate. Clerical intervention was also a convenient diversion for Taschereau. Outside Montmagny it was practically irrelevant as an explanation of Liberal reverses, but among Liberals it remained a highly serviceable rallying cry. Moreover, alleged cases of undue influence gave the Liberals ammunition for a judicial counter-offensive against the Union Nationale. If every proceeding stemmed from accusations against the government, this would contribute to the impression that the election had been stolen. (Party organizers and lawyers on both sides admitted privately that most contestations were being pursued primarily for their "moral" effect.)[61] Yet Taschereau had reason to be cautious. A practising Catholic all his life and a strong believer in the church as a guardian of social stability, he had always been basically honest in fighting *castorisme*. That is, he opposed exaggerated jurisdictional claims, stifling philosophies, political partisanship, and personal antagonism masquerading as the universal teaching of the church. As he had clumsily warned religious authorities, however, not all Liberals were as sympathetic as he was to the true interests of religion. In response to a resurgent clericalism evident even prior to the election campaign, genuine anticlericals could enlist the support of moderates for an attack on the church's influence and prerogatives.[62] The polls were not even closed when signs of such a reaction appeared. In the absence of his superiors, *Le Soleil*'s editor, Joseph Barnard, published dire threats on 25, 26, and 27 November. Reading this kind of material in the Liberals' official organ, *Le Devoir* understandably credited rumours that an openly anticlerical party would rise from the ashes of Taschereau liberalism.[63]

Taschereau the politician could happily exploit these prophecies, but Taschereau the Catholic, nephew of a cardinal-archbishop, had no desire to see them fulfilled. He solved the dilemma by urging his own followers to restrain their public utterances while he himself privately insisted that Villeneuve acknowledge and terminate the improprieties of his clergy. Thus Henri Gagnon, general manager of *Le Soleil*, apologized on his own behalf and that of the owner (Jacob Nicol) for Barnard's offensive editorials.[64] When Villeneuve returned to Quebec City on 5 December, *Le Soleil* simply predicted that he would restore ecclesiastical discipline and Taschereau withheld any formal complaint. Preoccupied in any case with Hepburn and the upcoming Ottawa conference, Taschereau probably hoped the archbishop would act on his own initiative. Meanwhile, he was content to amass further information, affidavits, and legal advice concerning the intimidation of voters.[65] During the next couple of weeks Villeneuve did try to cool the situation, asking all priests to be silent on political matters. When Lavergne and Gravel defied him, he sent the former on a southern vacation and brought the latter under his immediate supervision in Quebec City.[66] While in Ottawa Taschereau received further assurances from Mgr Cassulo, the apostolic delegate, that Villeneuve would deal fairly with Liberal grievances.[67] As a result of these hopeful signs, Taschereau's first approach to Villeneuve was highly conciliatory. He promised not to summon priests before civil courts, even though the evidence of slander by Lavergne was overwhelming. He gave Villeneuve the opportunity to deny rumours current in Liberal circles about the cardinal's own complicity – that his absence from Quebec had been purposely timed to coincide with the election, and that he had concluded a private understanding with Grégoire in New York on his way home. Finally Taschereau provided details of clerical intervention, especially Lavergne's, which Villeneuve could verify to his own satisfaction.[68]

Predictably, Villeneuve dismissed the accusations concerning his own conduct out of hand. He had honestly expected a spring election and besides, had given appropriate instructions to subordinates he left in charge. Grégoire had been received as mayor of Quebec and promised nothing. More discouraging for Taschereau was that, after two weeks, Villeneuve had done little more than obtain a blanket (and absurd) denial from Lavergne regarding his behaviour during the campaign.[69] Taschereau immediately forwarded a more comprehensive dossier citing the specific transgressions of thirty-four clergy in schools and hospitals as well as in the pulpit and on political platforms. He also reminded Villeneuve that previous ecclesiastical directives in Quebec limited clerical intervention in politics to the defence of religion. Taschereau doubted that the Liberals had ever acted against religion, and challenged Villeneuve particularly to explain why it had been necessary for priests to intervene in 1935 but not in 1931.[70] Only at this point did Villeneuve show signs of launching a serious investigation, and still he characterized many complaints as imprecise or hearsay. Finally, on 24 January, he replied in detail. Ecclesiastical discipline, he allowed, had been breached and would henceforth be tightened, with recent excesses condemned by implication.[71] Villeneuve even granted that priests should be more discreet than laymen in making political accusations and that ecclesiastical tribunals would deal seriously with real cases of slander. With unusual frankness, however, he then revealed his scepticism about the Liberals' evidence and motives. Not all the evidence of slander was impartial or first-hand, and as long as priests were allowed political expression, naturally some of them would repeat charges that were in the air. In suggesting that priests were primarily responsible for the prevalence of these charges, he implied, the Liberals were looking for scapegoats rather than a real explanation for their difficulties. The clergy were hardly taking sides, moreover, by urging honest elections and praying for good government. In fact it might help if "political leaders declared themselves formally opposed to corrupt electoral manoeuvres and clearly supported the Ligue de moralité publique." Villeneuve also objected to Taschereau's habit of confusing party and state: criticism of a party during elections did not constitute an attack on civil authority and the church was grateful to the institution of government, not the Liberal party, for financial assistance to religious institutions. Finally, he noted, the Liberals were not entirely innocent of provocation against the clergy. Police types who took notes in church and questioned parishioners about their priests were themselves guilty of intimidation.[72]

Taschereau had no real answer for these remarks, which deflated several Liberal pretensions while satisfying legitimate demands. He could only dispute some of the more flimsy excuses and denials of individual clergy, whose declarations were appended to Villeneuve's letter, and here the matter rested.[73] There was a brief flurry of accusations in March, when the Quebec bishops' confidential directive to their clergy, unequivócally forbidding further political pronouncements, became public.[74] But by then the religious question had lost most of its strategic importance for Taschereau, and there is no evidence that he pursued Lavergne, Gravel, and the Reverend Archange before ecclesiastical tribunals, as his legal adviser had recommended.[75]

Beneath all this dramatic posturing, of course, lay the real political manoeuvring. Most Liberals agreed that only federal politicians could effect a reconciliation between Taschereau loyalists and rebels, so it was natural that the active search for a successor to Taschereau began during the Dominion-Provincial Conference. Ernest Lapointe was extremely tired and somewhat reluctant to become involved in these negotiations, perhaps fearing that they would result in pressure to assume the premiership himself. "Very singular," Mackenzie King would note at a slightly later stage, "that with a crisis such as this in Quebec, Lapointe should go off on a trip to Bermuda."[76] But like King, who had initially celebrated the election result as the reassertion of a "real liberal sentiment," Lapointe feared the advent of a Quebec government hostile to the federal administration.[77] So, along with Chubby Power, they undertook to be discreet fixers. The key to their strategy was Edouard Lacroix, who had managed to combine unswerving loyalty to Lapointe with critical financial and moral support for the ALN. No one believed he could adequately administer the affairs of Quebec on a permanent basis, but he alone had immediate prospects of winning the allegiance of opposition members and restoring public trust in the provincial Liberals.

Taschereau pledged his full cooperation. He had already persuaded Vautrin and Arcand to postpone their resignations, so that if any leading *actionnistes* did rejoin the Liberals, two portfolios could quickly be made available. At lunch with King and Nicol on the first day of the conference, he was so agreeable that King observed a "fine nature" not visible during the previous fifteen years of their association. Taschereau readily admitted that the opposition had successfully campaigned against him personally, and that he must now retire. Perrault was his preferred successor, but he recognized that Mercier was more acceptable to others. He even conceded Lacroix's temporary importance, and urged King to transmit the assurance that he bore the Beauce MP no grudge. For himself, Taschereau sought only the honourable exit and the minor continuing role in public life which a Senate appointment would afford.[78] Three separate initiatives grew out of this hopeful beginning: King summoned Lacroix to Ottawa, Power was dispatched to determine the conditions under which Paul Gouin might support a Liberal administration, and Nicol tried to sound out Oscar Drouin through a mutual friend. The federal Liberals soon learned, however, that the task of saving Quebec for their party was highly complex, if not impossible.

Power met Gouin in Quebec City on 15 December. Gouin insisted that there must be a new "national" government fully committed to the ALN program. Godbout, Francoeur, and perhaps Mercier might take part, but Duplessis must be premier unless prepared to renounce his claim to the office. The inclusion of Taschereau Liberals could not, moreover, forestall prosecutions under the Elections Act or the resignation of fraudulently elected Liberal members. Eventually Conservative representation in cabinet might be reduced from three to two in a ministry of seven or eight, but for the moment Duplessis' group commanded greater consideration and status than their numerical strength suggested. Power left this meeting sensing that Gouin was talking off the top of his head – he had no mandate to negotiate any sort of agreement with the Liberals.[79] However, Lacroix professed much the same view of what was possible when he met Power, King, Lapointe, and L.-J. Demers in Ottawa on 19 December. After expelling his daily quota of anti-Taschereau venom and predicting civil war if Taschereau did not soon leave office, Lacroix declared that events were too far advanced for the Liberals simply to reunite and retain power. The Gouin-Duplessis agreement, the Conservative ties of many ALN deputies, and a decline in Honoré Mercier's standing meant that there had to be a Duplessis-led national government. Like Gouin, Lacroix believed that the best Liberal hopes lay in a long-term decline of Conservative influence within the coalition.[80]

While King and Lapointe reluctantly accepted this analysis, Oscar Drouin furiously rejected the idea of sharing power with any Taschereau Liberals. Knowing that many ALN adherents in Montreal still preferred a "reliberalized" Liberal party to continued association with Duplessis, he immediately sent Gouin a forceful and detailed counter-argument. In the Quebec district (and elsewhere, he suspected), most ALN deputies owed their election to Conservative

organizational support and to voters who wanted Taschereau overthrown. It would therefore be tactically dangerous and a betrayal
of public trust to dissolve the alliance before the regime was finally
and completely buried. The inclusion of Francoeur, Godbout, or
Mercier could prevent the investigation of past government misconduct and block important reforms. Drouin also confessed a strong
personal revulsion toward the various schemes. As Godbout and
Francoeur both represented the Quebec district, patronage would
still reach the same parasites he so thoroughly despised. And he
equally resented the federal Liberals who had supported Taschereau
during the campaign and now shamelessly plotted the eventual or
immediate exclusion of Duplessis from office. In both cases their
own partisan advantage took precedence over the public interest.
Drouin's letters served their purpose, for despite his own sympathy
for Lacroix and Lapointe, Gouin realized that his hands were tied.
He might continue listening to federal emissaries,but he could not
accept any of their schemes on behalf of the ALN.[81]

Taschereau had never consented to the idea of an all-party coalition
in the first place. On principle he could not voluntarily have made
way for a government headed by Duplessis, for only victory at the
polls entitled a party leader to govern. And personal pride would
have prevented his acquiescence in a ministry containing Hamel
and Grégoire, whom he perceived as spokesmen for resurgent clerical
reaction as well as slanderers. Now it was clear that his resignation
would not instantly reunite the Liberal party; on the contrary, his
own immediate retirement and that of senior colleagues had become
highly impractical. Younger loyalists would still have to defend their
predecessors, probably could not control the legislature, and would
thus be forced into another election at a tremendous disadvantage.
Mutter as some did about Taschereau "clinging to office" (King
would later use this as an excuse to deny him a senatorship), a new
strategy pretty well imposed itself upon him. And for all the rumours
of a palace revolt, no one in the cabinet or caucus had any better
suggestions. Following minor cabinet changes, the government
would bring forward an agenda of popular legislative measures. After
the session, Taschereau would announce his retirement and invite
all Liberals to a truly open leadership and policy convention. The
precarious unity of the Union Nationale would by then, it was hoped,
be shattered, but in any case individual Liberals within the ALN could
rejoin their party without submitting to the authority of the outgoing
administration. The new regime would be far better equipped for
an election, and might even call one on its own initiative.[82]

Taschereau's belief that the Union Nationale might disintegrate was more than an exercise in wishful thinking, for acute paranoia had infected the opposition soon after the election. While Liberal newspapers exploited, exaggerated, and even fabricated signs of dissension, the actual behaviour of the various factions more than sufficed to sustain mutual suspicion. Without any authorization by the ALN, for example, the chief Conservative organizer announced a permanent fusion of the two groups. Gouin's followers could not easily deny this without appearing to substantiate Liberal claims that a divorce was imminent. Proponents of Liberal reunification under Lacroix then floated the argument that since the Union Nationale had not won at the polls, the terms of the alliance were no longer binding. Ultimately, Duplessis would appropriate this argument to justify his personal domination of the Union Nationale, but first he quietly and systematically cultivated the loyalty of individual *actionnistes*. Some of the latter accepted his financial assistance, some were alarmed or angered by Gouin's contact with Ottawa fixers and others simply concluded that in Duplessis' superior ability lay the best hope of achieving their own cherished goals – hydro nationalization, Taschereau's political demise, or whatever. Symbolic of Gouin's fading control over the ALN was Drouin's decision, communicated on 10 February, no longer to clear the content of speeches with his leader. In contrast, numerous people appear to have been spying for Duplessis on their own initiative. Opposite them stood the original Liberal rebels, men who feared "l'aile trustarde conservatrice" and were determined not to "free ourselves from Taschereau only to be delivered into the hands of Webster, L'Espérance and Co." By late February they distrusted even Drouin. Hamel considered the whole situation so desperate that when Taschereau finally set a date for the opening of the legislature, he undertook to organize a peace conference. What few Quebec Liberals – Gouin's, Taschereau's, or Lapointe's – yet understood was that their opponents' "disunity" was really a process of consolidation under Duplessis, whose skill and force they seriously underestimated.[83]

By mid-February, it was clear that the Ottawa fixers had failed in their endeavour. And after seeing Grégoire reelected mayor of Quebec City by a huge majority on 17 February, no individual *actionniste* would dare rejoin the Liberals. Grégoire's entire campaign had been an attack on Taschereau,[84] so the result indicated that momentum remained with the Union Nationale. Meanwhile, the government's excuses for not convening the legislature were starting to wear thin. Ottawa had announced its decision on relief grants – Quebec would receive an additional $350,000 a month – and it was not practical to postpone action until the constitutionality of Bennett's New Deal legislation had finally been determined. Further delay would only feed rumours that the government was paralysed by fear and dissension. In reality, the political turbulence had not caused any cabinet members to neglect their individual responsibilities. Perrault and Francoeur took on additional burdens, administering the departments of Colonization and Labour respectively when the defeated ministers finally resigned. Taschereau's own schedule was extremely taxing, even for him. In addition to dealing personally with religious and legal complications resulting from the election, he took a direct hand in the work of financial and constitutional committees established by the Dominion-Provincial Conference. With Houde, he devoted more hours to Montreal's seemingly endless financial crisis. The mayor was still cooperative, but for that very reason he was now being harassed by Union Nationale partisans on City Council. In line with his election-night pledge, Taschereau received an unprecedented flood of delegations in person and demonstrated unusual sympathy and tact in deflating the unrealizable expectations of labour and municipal spokesmen.[85] It was now time, however, for cabinet to plan collectively for the legislative session at which the fate of the government would be determined and the real outcome of the election would become known.

By the time the cabinet met on 19 February, all ministers had accepted that Taschereau must last out one session, then make way for a successor chosen by an open convention.[86] The first real order of business was therefore to set a date for the opening of the legislature. Taschereau stepped out to tell reporters that 24 March had been selected, then returned to attack an agenda so long that it had to be completed the next day. On the appointment of new ministers, Taschereau still preferred to wait. The UCC veteran, Laurent Barré, a supporter of the Vautrin Plan and no admirer of Duplessis, might yet be enticed from Conservative ranks into the Colonization portfolio. And if there was any possibility of attracting one of the Montreal rebels for Labour, the door should be left open. Turning to matters of policy, Taschereau had at least one piece of encouraging news. Quebec and Ontario were again close to coordinated action on newsprint production, with the Ontario minister, Peter Heenan, expected shortly in Montreal to conclude the details. The path to an agreement was a little smoother now that Quebec power companies were trying to solve the repudiation issue without further intervention by their government. But improvement in one industry would not solve the overwhelming problem of unemployment, and the government had no hope of regaining public support without more relief for the poor. On the other hand, no substantial new program could be financed through the increased federal contribution alone, and the modest economic recovery of the past year had generated no appreciable rise in ordinary provincial revenues. With tax increases unthinkable, only further borrowing could allow the government to be more generous.[87]

Grudgingly accepting this imperative, ministers dealt first with election promises. There was no way to avoid the introduction of old age pensions, for Taschereau's campaign to have Ottawa assume the full cost had stalled at the Dominion-Provincial Conference, and now he was receiving a flood of letters, some demanding that he honour his pledge, some inquiring almost pathetically when payments would begin, and the inevitable few seeking jobs administering the program.[88] Taschereau had one more rather desperate proposal for Finance Minister C.A. Dunning (Ottawa should reduce the size of the pension to little more than its existing 80 per cent share), but obviously Stockwell had to allow for this new burden in planning his budget.[89] There was more room to manoeuvre on the farm credit promise, and Godbout still had reservations about competing with the Caisses Populaires. But here again, unless federal legislation could be altered to suit Quebec's needs, some provincial scheme was essential to retain the loyalty of rural electors.[90] Fortunately there was a third promise which did not require new expenditures, extension of the three-year-old moratorium on collection of mortgage debts. Beyond these specific issues, the general system of relief required its annual review. Minor changes would be necessary to meet the criteria and procedures of the new federal relief commission, and where the province retained discretion, relief money had to be apportioned among hungry competing projects. In terms of revenue, there was apparently some suggestion that a provincial income tax would be more effective and equitable than property-based municipal assessments. Houde's cooperation notwithstanding, cabinet also had to prepare for a politically inspired row with Montreal City Council over the sharing of both revenues and expenditures.[91] Finally, Athanase David, recovering some of his long-lost energy and enthusiasm, outlined an imaginative solution to the financial crises of the University of Montreal and the Saint Sulpice seminary. Basically it involved fusing the two .institutions and refinancing their debts over a provincial guarantee.[92]

Either the ministers were fine actors, or else this gruelling session had the effect of restoring their confidence. Arriving in Montreal, Perrault and David issued good-humoured assurances that the cabinet was united on both policy and leadership for the approaching session.

Concerning rumours of his imminent retirement, Taschereau told reporters that "the wish is father to the thought." He gave no hints about forthcoming legislation, except to reaffirm the commitment to pensions. But as if to emphasize his government's will to survive, he announced that the cabinet would now meet twice weekly until the session opened and predicted a doubling of his majority by that day.[93] And while long-term speculation naturally continued, this show of confidence appeared to stifle talk of a palace coup or a forced retirement. Taschereau's only real disappointment, as 24 March approached, was his failure to draw Barré or any *actionniste* into the fold. Cabinet reconstruction could wait no longer, so on 13 March he surrendered his own post of attorney general to Perrault, combined Mines with Public Works under Francoeur, and brought in four veteran backbenchers. Hector Authier took Colonization, Edgar Rochette of Charlevoix-Saguenay assumed Labour along with Game and Fish, and Paul-Emile Côté of Bonaventure was given Roads, doubtless in gratitude to the loyal voters of the lower St Lawrence.[94] Cléophas Bastien became a minister without portfolio. These were not objectionable choices. Rochette and Côté would in fact serve with distinction in a later administration. But neither did they have the youth (at forty-three, Adélard Godbout was still the youngest minister) or the reputation to make the government any more palatable to the rebels. For all the sound and fury since 25 November, the legislature would open without a single shift from opposition to government ranks, or vice-versa.

The expected fireworks did not materialize during the first few days of the session, much to the disappointment of Union Nationale partisans who packed the galleries. Following a bland Throne Speech, Duplessis quietly assented to government nominations for Speaker and Deputy Speaker. "We're not out to punish anyone," he proclaimed magnanimously. In reality, he was not out to force a vote which would merely demonstrate that Taschereau controlled the House. Opening the Throne Speech debate on 26 March, he was equally reserved. He flattered his allies, belittled the government's legislative program as well as its chances of survival, and offered to suspend normal procedure so that an old age pensions bill could be introduced immediately. But he carefully avoided extravagant charges and ignored most positive features of the ALN manifesto, to which he was still supposedly committed. There was no hint, if indeed Duplessis knew it himself at this point, that his strategy for the session would consist of obstruction and scandalous revelations.[95]

Taschereau's hour-long reply had a distinctly valedictorian quality, though it implied an honourable retirement, not a humiliating defeat. With considerable feeling, he proclaimed his religious fidelity and rehearsed his government's record of benevolent support for the church. Then came the inevitable but cleverly devised pitch for ALN support. First, to give Liberal rebels the courage to return to the fold, he tried to minimize Duplessis' stature. Purely to further personal ambition, the Conservative leader had sacrificed the historic identity of his party and latched on to Gouin's movement. "He [Gouin] is the real victor among the redoubled opposition, and deserves and shall receive from the government, for himself and for his colleagues, the respect and consideration the electorate has chosen to accord them." Then he recalled their original purpose, "to reliberalize the Liberal Party," and argued that this was still the best way to achieve reform. Reliberalization was already under way. Moreover, "when the session is over, we wish to bring all Liberal deputies together, no matter what their faction or shading, and ask them if necessary to remake the Liberal Party program so that it satisfies the aspirations of everyone." Implying that he might already have retired except for the need to answer personal accusations, Taschereau thus left the door completely open to the rebels without either conceding defeat or demanding a surrender.[96]

As if fearing that Taschereau had struck a responsive chord, Drouin jumped up to remind Gouin what corrupt villains the ministers were. With that the seconds joined in, and gradually the anticipated insults and accusations began to fly. The continuing surprise was that Taschereau's colleagues more than held their own and even seemed to enjoy the battle. With brawlers like Godbout and Bouchard in the ring, Taschereau was even prepared to let opposition supporters in the gallery cheer their favourites. Whether or not this performance impressed the general public, it visibly boosted the morale of government backbenchers.[97] Taschereau occasionally taunted Duplessis by asking "Who has the majority?" but more often he fixed his gaze upon Gouin, silent amidst the uproar. By now both men were sensing regret, even if neither would admit it even to himself. In retrospect Taschereau recognized how easily Gouin's allegiance could have been retained two years earlier. For his part, Gouin already knew that he had ceded far more than parliamentary leadership to Duplessis. The fate of his entire idealistic national crusade rested with an ambitious professional politician. Consumed by their hatred of Taschereau or overwhelmed by the scent of power, few erstwhile followers shared his concern.[98] His maiden speech to the legislature, when it finally occurred on 28 April, was almost mournful. The ALN, he pledged, would never be the saviour of the present regime no matter what eleventh-hour concessions were offered. Neither would it help install a "Tory-Conservative" regime. By pretending that the Union Nationale was still a bipartisan movement committed to national objectives, he could ignore the question of what role the ALN would play.[99]

A few days later Duplessis' real strategy began to unfold. The Throne Speech debate had concluded after five weeks, and now the opposition was filibustering every government bill including Stockwell's budget. The object was to force an election before Taschereau's post-session plan for Liberal reunification could be achieved. Since the government's previous spending authority expired on 30 June, Duplessis thought he could succeed by preventing a vote until that date. With no closure provision in the rules of the Quebec legislature, Taschereau began looking for other expedients. At the beginning of June he suggested one of these to Ernest Lapointe: "There is a way to deal with the situation and disarm the opposition. Ottawa had advanced money [relief grants] to other [bankrupt] provinces. If we applied to your government for a loan of less than $5,000,000 we could go on until September 1, when another session could be held. The moment we could announce that Ottawa was going to advance us $5,000,000, I believe the opposition would lift its blockade."[100] The scheme was clever, since if it worked Ottawa would not really have to advance the money. But before Lapointe had much time to consider it, his reaction no longer mattered. For the second, more devastating weapon in Duplessis' arsenal had forced both an election and Taschereau's resignation.

That weapon was the mass of evidence which informers in and outside the government had given Duplessis concerning the unauthorized or extravagant personal use of public funds by members and friends of the regime. Announcing in advance that there would be damaging revelations, Duplessis exercised his prerogative as opposition leader to summon the long-dormant Public Accounts Committee of the legislature for 7 May. The proceedings immediately became those of a spectacular criminal trial. The government stood accused of systematic corruption on an unimaginable scale. The prosecutor was Duplessis alone, for he had not shared his information with any colleagues. The chief defence attorney was Peter Bercovitch, who doggedly kept Duplessis from straying beyond the committee's mandate but suffered from a major tactical disadvantage: he never knew in advance what specific admissions Duplessis would try to extract from his long list of witnesses. Most of the latter were senior public servants, forced to implicate themselves or their superiors.

Nominally the judge was Deputy Speaker Léon Casgrain, but even with a Liberal majority to sustain his rulings, he exercised little control over proceedings. The jury were of course the public, and the Union Nationale made full use of radio, newspapers, and public rallies to keep the province informed.

Day by day the evidence mounted: sinecures and inflated salaries for relatives and retired candidates; distribution of statutory grants, especially for colonization, at the whim of Liberal deputies; fradulent invoicing; huge printing contracts for government newspapers, especially Nicol's; a minister (Vautrin) charging exorbitant personal expenses. No single revelation was serious enough to excite or even surprise public opinion. It was the enormity, the pervasiveness, and the brazenness of abuse which first staggered, then enraged the people of Quebec. In the midst of unprecedented poverty and suffering, while leaders preached the virtues of self-reliance, family responsibility, private charity, and "fiscal responsibility," this behaviour was regarded as positively obscene. No civilized society could freely tolerate such a regime while preserving its self-respect. The government must go, and it was irrelevant who the opposition were and what they stood for.[101]

But Duplessis' assault was far from finished. To focus public indignation more sharply, and to satisfy the bloodlust of certain followers, he must personalize the villainy. Thanks to Dr Hamel, the links between Taschereau's immediate family and "the trusts" were already well known. Testimony concerning Le Soleil's contracts revealed that the premier's brother Edmond was a shareholder and director of the newspaper, thus profiting from government patronage.[102] Now Duplessis could further blacken the premier's name by indicting Charles Lanctôt, his despised protégé, and Antoine Taschereau, his less-than-brilliant older brother. Eventually it would be discovered that Lanctôt had long been pocketing annual surpluses in the budget of the attorney general. At this point all Duplessis needed was the hint of irregularity in his expense reports as an excuse to summon him before the committee and review his corporate ties. As accountant of the Legislative Assembly, Antoine had custody of funds used to pay members' salaries and other expenses. He had been depositing these in personal accounts – including one in a bank twenty-five miles from Quebec where his son was manager – and keeping the interest. He did the same thing, evidently, as secretary of the Quebec City Catholic School Board. When bank officials questioned the propriety of this procedure, he threatened to take the deposits to their competitors. He even led people to believe that he was acting with Alexandre's knowledge and consent, for his account cards read "Antoine Taschereau, brother of the Prime Minister." As if he were not already in enough trouble, Antoine then perjured himself by denying these facts when first summoned before the committee. Confronted with the truth at a later session, he then lied about the amounts involved.[103]

These revelations cannot have taken Taschereau totally by surprise. Prior to the session, the deputy colonization minister, L.-A. Richard, had documented at least one case where a Liberal candidate had authorized public works on his own initiative, then presented him with a bill for payment.[104] The provincial auditor, Edgar Vézina, had been warning Taschereau and Stockwell at least since 1933 that provincial finances could not stand so much discretionary spending.[105] (Undoubtedly someone in Vézina's office was a major Duplessis informant.) Lanctôt had been a walking time-bomb for the Liberals since the day Lomer Gouin hired him, and Taschereau had freely chosen to risk their close association. He probably did not suspect Lanctôt's financial shenanigans, though as his superior for sixteen years he should have. But he would not deny Lanctôt the potential conflicts of interest he and his own family maintained, or seek substantive reasons for Lanctôt's unpopularity. Apparently he learned of Antoine's operation early in 1935, and suggested only that his brother quietly start making restitution.[106] What did surprise Taschereau was that Duplessis, whom he had formerly considered a gentleman, would go so far as to humiliate the Taschereau family purely for partisan gain. But the deed was done. At Taschereau's request both Antoine and Lanctôt resigned, implicitly confessing their guilt. On 8 June he told his cabinet what they already knew, that he and his leading colleagues must follow. He would not subject his family's name to further public degradation, nor could he expect the entire Liberal party to bear the burden of Duplessis' accusations.[107]

Only the question of the succession remained, and contrary to legend it really wasn't much of an issue.[108] Though federal emissaries had never ceased trying to arrange it, no *actionniste* would jump aboard a sinking ship. Neither cabinet nor caucus would tolerate Lacroix, who acknowledged the fact by renouncing all ambition on 10 June.[109] Taschereau's choice, endorsed enthusiastically by the many rural deputies who felt they owed their election to him, was Adélard Godbout. Only Godbout himself had reservations, which his colleagues' assurances overcame.[110] So on 11 June, accompanied by Honoré Mercier, Taschereau called upon Lieutenant-Governor Patenaude. First, he asked for the dissolution which Duplessis would soon force anyway, and thereby halted the work of the Public Accounts

Committee. Then he submitted his resignation, recommended his successor, and walked the short distance to his home on the Grande Allée.

# Conclusion

"I can keep my worries separated," Taschereau told an interviewer on the eve of his resignation, "and when the occasion arises put them all away to enjoy family life."[1] This casual remark, intended no doubt to explain past successes in his career, turned out to be prophetic as well. For only Taschereau's ability to compartmentalize his concerns allowed him to enjoy his declining years. It was a remarkably long retirement, equal to his tenure as premier. While sudden idleness often destroys the health of men accustomed to strenuous activity quite rapidly, Taschereau remained physically active and mentally alert until Adine's death in January 1952. A few weeks later he collapsed following a dinner at Paul's celebrating his eighty-fifth birthday, and died at home on 6 July.

In one sense his endurance was no accident. He impressed residents of Quebec City by his habit of striding briskly along the Grande Allée, and occasionally he walked to or from his law office in the Lower Town. During the summer he continued to hike, fish, and play tennis (of a sort) with grandchildren at the summer home in Pointe Rivière-du-Loup. He kept his mind active by following provincial politics on a daily basis, by attending to legal and business affairs (mostly the latter, since former clients feared offending Duplessis and sought Taschereau's assistance only when the Liberals returned to office in 1939), and by participating in charitable activities.[2] In his last years he began to engage in stimulating and often amusing correspondence, more often than not with former opponents. At the invitation of the priests, he wrote articles recalling his days at the Petit Séminaire de Québec, "when we were happy without knowing it ... only realizing it later when bumps along the road of real life shook us up a little."[3] He even joked about nineteenth-century religious warfare after Duplessis had invited him to dedicate a monument to Bishop LaFlèche of Three Rivers, his uncle's major ultramontane nemesis. Fearing that LaFlèche might take offence, "I believed it my duty to write to him, and naturally addressed my letter to heaven. To my great surprise the letter was returned, stamped 'addressee unknown'." (Not to be outdone, Duplessis explained that "if Mgr LaFlèche is not in heaven, it is because his love of the Cardinal was such that he desired to make the greatest sacrifice in order to be able to spend eternity with your uncle in the place where he is.")[4]

Taschereau's real joy seemed to be the time he could spend in the company of family and friends. There were elements of tragedy here. Adine was bedridden for most of her last ten years, and daughter Gabrielle was widowed in early middle age. His brother Antoine and Charles Lanctôt were hounded by Duplessis long after their resignations, and Robert Taschereau, the Montreal nephew who had given up a flourishing legal practice to chair the Compensation Board, became an innocent but equally destitute victim of Duplessis' partisanship.[5] But events long past had prepared Alexandre to accept philosophically the obligations imposed by events he could not control. He sold the family home and moved into the nearby Claridge Apartments, where he and Gabrielle amused and cared for Adine and made it possible to continue entertaining visitors. And he gave the political casualties and their families what protection he could – the Godbout regime was naturally more merciful than its predecessor. Lanctôt, a professed atheist throughout his life, accepted the last rites – very likely as much for Taschereau's peace of mind as his own – before his death in 1947. The family remained closely knit under its patriarch, even with Charles and Robert (appointed to the Supreme Court in 1940) not residing in Quebec City. Alexandre and Edmond were never closer than in retirement until the latter's death in 1946, and the accomplishments of his son André were a continuing source of satisfaction for Alexandre. Among cabinet colleagues, Galipeault proved a long and faithful friend and David an amiable host whenever Taschereau went to Montreal.[6]

That part of Taschereau which suffered through retirement was the one requiring some sort of public vindication, at least symbolic. At first Taschereau was philosophical about this, too. He understood why Liberals could not immediately repeat the outpouring of gratitude and praise which had marked Gouin's retirement from the premiership. The cabinet Godbout swore in to fight the 1936 election could hope to escape annihilation only by dissociating itself from Taschereau, and Godbout had the courtesy to assure his predecessor privately that "your name will go down in our province's history as that of the greatest statesman Canada has produced and who has done the most for his country and his compatriots." One of the new ministers, Césare Gervais, was equally considerate in thanking Taschereau and his sons for remaining silent and invisible while Duplessis ran his campaign entirely against their name.[7] Taschereau also understood the predicament of the federal Liberals, who wanted to support Godbout but also win back or maintain the allegiance of young Liberals at the federal level. "I have been too long in office to ignore the realities of political life," he replied when Mackenzie King denied him an immediate Senate appointment on grounds of "internal strife and public discussion."[8]

Yet at some point there had to be some recognition that Taschereau had upheld the family's honour and tradition of public service, an assurance that the Public Accounts scandal was soon to be a forgotten incident of partisan politics while Taschereau's record of successful leadership and administration would long endure. Although the passions of 1935 and 1936 did indeed fade away, Taschereau became obsessed with a Senate appointment as the symbol of his vindication or personal rehabilitation within Liberal ranks. And, for reasons which are much more difficult to understand, King became absolutely determined that he should not have it. In 1937 he again informed Taschereau that the Quebec ministers were still afraid of alienating the "so-called Liberal nationalists" (Taschereau's phrase), but this excuse rapidly wore thin as these Liberals returned to the fold and began directing all their fire at Duplessis. And it was soon clear that the Quebec Liberals themselves had stopped worrying about it. They welcomed Taschereau warmly at a testimonial dinner for Ernest Lapointe early in 1939 and encouraged him to find personal vindication in Godbout's election victory later that year. Ralston invited him to represent Quebec on the National War Loan Committee, and the Taschereaus were frequently asked to entertain European royalty and other official wartime guests of the Canadian government who were accustomed to elegant hospitality. Quebec ministers did not object to David's Senate appointment in 1940, or even Nicol's in 1944. Lapointe put Robert in the Supreme Court primarily, it was said, to console the father. And when Lapointe died in 1941, there were even Quebec Liberals prepared to consider Taschereau as a stop-gap minister of justice.[9]

Yet King persisted. Eventually he told David that Taschereau had "missed his chance," implying that he had clung to office following the 1935 election contrary to party interests. David took violent exception to that fantasy and was probably the only person who ever challenged King directly on Taschereau's behalf. "I would be the most astonished man in the world if this was your conception of the gratitude due to those who for years have held up the flag of the party.''[10] After a few more years King simply let it be known that Taschereau was too old for the vigorous demands of Senate membership.[11] King's eccentricities continue to fascinate historians, and all are entitled to their speculations. In this case he possibly bore Taschereau a permanent grudge arising out of the 1919 leadership convention, or believed nonsense about Taschereau's role in the 1930 federal election. One entry in his diary compared Taschereau's regime to the Family Compact of Upper Canada: perhaps King was subconsciously punishing the persecutors of his grandfather, William Lyon Mackenzie.[12] Two things are certain. One is that King was a colossal hypocrite if he thought the Public Accounts scandal justified his treatment of Taschereau. His own indiscretion concerning Beauharnois had been quickly forgiven, and he had previously rewarded one of his own scandal-rocked Quebec ministers with a senatorship. The other certainty is that Taschereau humiliated himself unnecessarily by persisting in his quest for the appointment, very nearly begging whenever a vacancy occurred and having friends plead on his behalf. He continued even after Adine's illness made moving or commuting to Ottawa unthinkable in practice and pressed St Laurent after King's retirement, though he must have realized that the new prime minister was not going to appoint an octogenarian.[13]

In a far more rational way, Taschereau made some effort during the last years to defend his political record in the court of history. He was generally complimentary toward the early volumes of Rumilly's *Histoire de la Province de Québec*, and in fact tried to help the author with his research. (And though Duplessis became Rumilly's hero and patron, Taschereau got high praise for his defence of provincial rights.) But Taschereau had one major and predictable complaint.

Why make Bourassa's place so large and accord him the leading role in every event? I admire his oratorical talent, his cultivation, his knowledge, his consuming activity. But where will it leave him? Has he not been like a meteor in the Canadian sky? ... If he had employed the gifts which I freely admit he possessed to play the role of builder rather than wrecker, what accomplishments he could have left behind. [But] no one achieved grace in his eyes. He spared neither Liberals nor Conservatives, Laurier nor Gouin, who nevertheless live on in the works they achieve. He did not hesitate to criticize, sometimes harshly, the bishops and the clergy. I myself was struck by the Master's blows; I remember them with amusement, for they did not prevent me from being premier for sixteen years and a minister for twenty-nine.[14]

Then, in April 1949, the journalist Eugène L'Heureux wrote a series of articles condemning the Duplessis government's iron ore concessions in the Ungava region. He argued that Duplessis was now proven a hypocrite for having labelled Taschereau "un trustard" in 1935, and that this deal was qualitatively worse for Quebec than any made by previous Liberal governments. He even acknowledged that Parent, Gouin, and Taschereau had been in a relatively weaker bargaining position, in terms of the need for jobs and the availability of indigenous capital to develop Quebec resources.[15]

Taschereau wrote and L'Heureux published a long letter expanding on this theme. "Several concessions were made," Taschereau recalled. "Consider those I believe most important: on the St Maurice, the Saguenay and at Baie Comeau. All three gave rise to violent criticism. Let's see if these criticisms were justified or if the future has not demonstrated the wisdom of what we did." All the jobs created paid higher wages than those in existing Quebec industries, and in the long term more jobs were created because new industries increased government revenues, created prosperous towns and cities, and helped nearby agricultural economies. Nor, Taschereau insisted, were foreign capitalists indifferent to the welfare of the community, for they supported educational, charitable and conservation projects.[16]

L'Heureux had been a savage critic of the Taschereau regime from the time of the Lake St John affair, and one of the first nationalists to charge that foreign capitalists were turning French Canadians into the "white niggers of America."[17] In 1949 he would not join Taschereau in making folk heroes out of these same capitalists, but he did repeat that anyone who considered Ungava to be nothing less than a gross scandal would have to revise his harsh judgment of previous regimes. He also hinted that while sincere, his own earlier criticisms might have been exaggerated. Most importantly, he seemed to regret the personal abuse Taschereau had suffered during the mid-1930s. By his letter, he wrote, "Mr Taschereau shows himself to be so dignified in retirement that all his former adversaries can forget the blows exchanged with him and admire this octogenarian whose heart and spirit remain young after so much time and labour. The more thoughtful among them will explain this remarkable twilight serenity by a greatness of spirit which must have existed even before his retirement but which the smoke of battle hid from the impassioned spectators that we all were in politics."[18]

L'Heureux's generosity and his willingness to put Taschereau's record in perspective sound considerably more genuine than the "consideration" shown by Duplessis in later years. The latter consisted of private jokes and pious admonitions, probably intended as jibes at Liberals, not to forget Taschereau in his old age.[19] Duplessis never gave a hint of apology for attacking Taschereau's family during the 1936 campaign when he knew they couldn't reply, or for thrice reviving the Public Accounts inquisition when he had little to gain politically by prolonging the agony suffered by Antoine, Lanctôt, and hence Alexandre.[20] Most of his complimentary references to Taschereau were really self-serving attempts to justify his own political practices – he had learned them from the master. When Taschereau died, Duplessis could not interrupt his election campaign long enough to attend the funeral.

L'Heureux was not alone in modifying his judgment of Taschereau in the light of Duplessis. This became common among veteran nationalists who had fought against both of them. René Chaloult, for example, made this interesting comparison after Duplessis too had passed from the scene:

Several of our ministers, from whose number I exclude Honoré Mercier and Alexandre Taschereau, were stricken with a sense of inferiority vis-à-vis the English [business elite]. Despite his bravado this reflex characterized Maurice Duplessis. Reminded that a powerful English-speaking capitalist was waiting impatiently in his antechamber, he would bark with a false assurance, "Let him wait!" A meaningful pose which denotes weakness. In contrast Alexandre Taschereau did not play at being an important person; he was one, and he knew it. In the same circumstances, he would simply have replied: "Tell him I will see him in a moment."[21]

In all likelihood, the new-found respect of L'Heureux and Chaloult for Taschereau owed much to their contempt for the newer villain, Duplessis. Nevertheless, it is unfortunate that the themes they suggested were never really pursued, and that important differences between Taschereau and Duplessis disappeared into the *grande noirceur* of the pre-1960 era. For such a comparison provides an excellent basis for a balanced judgment of Taschereau's historical record. The similarities are undeniable. Both men believed strongly that private enterprise as a system and foreign capital as an instrument were essential to economic progress in Quebec. It was therefore the duty of political leaders to defend their philosophy and the agents of industrial development against what they considered mischievous or misguided attacks. Yet both were slow to alter their conceptions of the role of the state in response to conditions created by industrial expansion, particularly in the realm of social security. Neither Taschereau nor Duplessis had great faith in the basic assumptions of liberal democracy, particularly the wisdom and the rights of a universal electorate. They therefore made no effort to reform abuses in the electoral system: the lack of female suffrage, the gross over-representation of rural constituencies, ruthless partisanship in distributing government largesse between elections, and the absence of a sense of proportion or fair play at the polls. In a broader sense, both feared organizations which were immune to political influence or control. Finally, both Taschereau and Duplessis vigilantly defended provincial rights against federal encroachments on the grounds of constitutional integrity in general and French Canada's right to cultural autonomy in particular.

Similarity must not be confused with identity, however, and each of these points of comparison bears closer scrutiny. Moreover, it would be wrong to apply the same standard of judgment to two men or two political regimes which were essentially a generation apart. Duplessis was twenty-three years younger than Taschereau and entered the legislature twenty-seven years later; the economic, social, and intellectual context of post-World War I Quebec differed markedly from that in which Duplessis operated after his return to power in 1944. No valid comparative assessment can ignore radically different circumstances.

Taschereau came to maturity during Quebec's period of severe economic stagnation, the early benefits of the National Policy notwithstanding. Industrial development through the large-scale exploitation of natural resources appeared as a form of deliverance from the rural poverty and massive emigration which threatened the very survival of French-Canadian nationality, for only within Quebec could the institutional basis of that nationality be fully maintained. Taschereau and his mentors, Parent and Gouin, rightly considered themselves allied to the forces of progress, acting in the intellectual tradition of Etienne Parent, Arthur Buies, L.-O. David, and most recently Errol Bouchette.[22] Facing honestly the dilemma posed by the absence of a strong French-Canadian entrepreneurial class, they consciously accepted the dominance of foreign capital. French Canada's traditional elite, the legal establishment, could insist upon a role and a share of the immediate benefits, but in the long run French-Canadian ownership and control of great enterprises depended upon changes in formal education and social attitudes. Opposition to this course was not widespread but it could certainly make itself heard. Generally speaking, this opposition did not come from a victimized entrepreneurial class aspiring to develop Quebec's resources itself, but from a clerical-petit bourgeois alliance which fundamentally rejected the industrial age. (The debate about whether Henri Bourassa accepted or rejected industrialization rests on an equivocal use of the word "accept."[23] He eventually conceded its inevitability and therefore proposed reforms, but he never approved of it.) Even though the opponents never proposed a serious economic alternative, they were well placed institutionally and possessed formidable rhetorical weapons: church control of education and social welfare had been invested with national as well as religious justifications, while the close and often self-interested cooperation of political elites with non-French Canadian capitalists exposed the former to accusations which obscured the real issue. Although they had patronage and a party press at their disposal, the Liberals of Taschereau's era fought an uphill battle for the legitimacy of their philosophy within French-Canadian society.

French-Canadian nationalism of the mid-1930s, when Duplessis first won power, contained a streak of anti-industrialism. But this was a last gasp, and during his second regime industrialization was an established fact, not an issue. Clearly this was the time to evaluate the success of past policy. Was private capital functioning in the public interest? Was there satisfactory progress toward the participation of French Canadians in ownership and management? In many ways conditions were ideal for a government to do this: strong demand for Quebec's resources during a period of sustained economic growth put provincial authorities in a strong bargaining position, as did heightened public expectation and the emergence of a more highly skilled and ambitious generation of French Canadians. The criticism and pressure for reform, in other words, now came from the left. Yet Duplessis refused to question old formulae, or to defend them in open debate in the manner of Taschereau in the mid-1920s. Nor were there any interventions comparable to Taschereau's actions when corporations violated or threatened to violate his concept of the public good: the hydroelectric export embargo, the promotion of a rival to Montreal Light Heat and Power, the Forest Resources Protection Act, even the Dominion Coal prosecutions. Instead, Duplessis waged war against labour unions and other sources of reformist criticism, invariably substituting force, intimidation, or smear for argument.

The case of social legislation is analogous. Taschereau's reputation as a reactionary rests primarily on his rejection of federal old age pensions and his opposition to other forms of permanent income security in the worst years of the depression. But this assessment ignores a great deal. Neither present-mindedness nor conspiracy theories should be allowed to obscure his initiatives in labour legislation. Clearly Quebec did not trail other jurisdictions in the letter of its laws: most complaints concerned their enforcement, and while they could scarcely be satisfied with the rate of progress, union leaders appeared to understand that Taschereau's liberal philosophy included the gradual amelioration of labour's condition. He treated them respectfully even when fearing the consequences of their demands, and they regarded him less as an enemy than as someone to be convinced. Certainly they never described any legislation as "antilabour," and this includes the Collective Agreements Extension Act of 1934. (Although it was requested by the CTCC as a means of limiting competitive wage-cutting among employers and was introduced by C.-J. Arcand, a nonconfessional trade unionist, this law has for no apparent reason been characterized as hostile in intent and even "fascist."[24]

The image of Taschereau as a reactionary pure and simple also ignores the substance of social and institutional reforms in the 1920s. The Public Charities, Public Health, and Adoption acts and various educational initiatives come quickly to mind. So does the ferocity of clerical opposition to state intervention – again, the question of context arises. At least in terms of the ability to generate public controversy, conservative forces within French-Canadian society exerted more political pressure than did progressive thinkers in the trade unions and the Union catholique des cultivateurs. Perron's agricultural "manifesto" and the appointment of the Montpetit Commission probably indicate that this was beginning to change and that Taschereau was preparing to respond when the depression struck. Nor did he ever deny the social responsibility of either government or capital in the midst of the economic crisis. What he could not overcome was the fear of financially "impossible" expectations and of permanent "dependency" of individuals on the state. That is not to excuse his rigidity, but to attribute it to something other than a reactionary philosophy. Nearing seventy years of age, conditioned throughout his long career to suspect the motives and sincerity of clerically inspired reformers, and convinced of a duty to protect Quebec's economy and society from permanent damage, Taschereau was just not capable of such a radical advance in his thinking.

Duplessis governed in an entirely different atmosphere following World War II. Like other Canadians, Quebeckers were determined never to relive the poverty, insecurity, and humiliation of the depression. It was still prudent not to defy clerical authority and welcome the beginnings of the welfare state too openly, but clearly the climate of opinion had changed. The Godbout regime enacted reforms of its own and accepted both a constitutional amendment and precedent-setting federal legislation in the realm of social security. The King and St Laurent governments began implementing the welfare state with the support of virtually all Quebec members of Parliament. Even some clergy were warning that the church courted disaster by trying to maintain its traditional monopoly of social services. Throughout the province, and particularly in urban centres, specialists were identifying and articulating the needs of a modern industrial society and acquiring the skills to provide appropriate services.[25]

Duplessis' reaction to all this was entirely negative and hostile, even though buoyant provincial revenues could easily have supported popular reforms. His war against organized labour, which has no parallel in the Taschereau era, involved more than the attempt to suppress the demands of workers as employees. Union leaders figured prominently in a widening progressive alliance whose demands for a variety of social reforms challenged vested economic and institutional interests. Whatever his motives (and lengthy biographies still have not explained them satisfactorily), Duplessis sided unequivocally with the resistance to the modernization of Quebec institutions and practices.[26] He was a vicious partisan of capital in industrial disputes, he discouraged the resumption of educational reforms set in motion during the 1920s (although Godbout's school legislation had opened the door), he propped up antiquated institutional structures (making private social agencies virtually into patronage-dispensing organisms of the Union Nationale),[27] and he even appears to have taken sides in the church's internal debate.[28] Duplessis' defenders might imagine that, like Taschereau in the 1930s, their hero was trying to maintain stability during a temporary crisis. Unfortunately, there is no evidence that Duplessis considered the old system viable. "You will have trouble when I am gone," he predicted with complete accuracy.[29] Après moi, la déluge.

Taschereau's record as a liberal democrat is far from inspiring. Beyond modest increases in urban representation in the legislature, he took no interest in reforming traditional electoral abuses. On the contrary, the midwinter election of 1923 and the use of federal relief money in 1931 (even allowing for some exaggeration in Conservative complaints) were unconscionably partisan manoeuvres. Nor was the dignity of the legislature a valid excuse for measures as arbitrary as the jailing of John Roberts or the Dillon Act. Even if it was the exception proving the rule, and too personal to be construed as anti-English, Taschereau's vendetta against Arthur

Meighen bordered on demagoguery. And he made no secret of his willingness, as attorney general, to act against Communists and others who threatened social order during the depression. Nevertheless, Taschereau was a genuine Whig. He accepted the idea of popular government, but feared the influence of political opportunists who were not fit to govern. It is fair to say that many of Taschereau's critics, such as Arthur Sauvé's clerical allies in the 1920s and Abbé Groulx's nationalist followers in the 1930s, were far more fundamentally opposed to democracy than he was. Taschereau's abhorrence of racial and religious prejudice was a lifelong characteristic, and he had the political courage to denounce it inspite of prevailing sentiment. When it came to antisemitism, there were other Liberals who either shared the prejudice or were reluctant to challenge it.[30]

In post-World War II Quebec the democratic forces grew much stronger, not because the population suddenly embraced the principles of popular sovereignty but because numerous interest groups became anxious to participate in the making of decisions which affected them.[31] In other words, the real challenge was to paternalistic and arbitrary government and came from organizations rather than individuals. Duplessis was absolutely determined to resist this sort of "political modernization," which he saw only as a threat to his own power. Thus patronage ceased to be merely a tool for securing and rewarding party allegiance or enriching friends and relations. It was used to ensure the dependency of major provincial institutions and local agencies (which ironically is what Bourassa had predicted would occur under an anticlerical administration). Duplessis almost never discussed an issue seriously in the legislature or in public, often avoiding it by appealing to popular fears and prejudices.[32] The more determined or courageous the challenger, the more extreme Duplessis' methods became: in the case of labour leaders and Jehovah's Witnesses, he obviously did not stop at rhetoric. Electoral reform may not have been a major priority of Duplessis' critics, at least initially, but a growing number of French Canadians were beginning to regard continuing abuses of this nature as a blot on their society.[33] But if anything the system grew worse, largely because the means of corruption – the sheer size of the Union Nationale war chest and the pervasiveness of its patronage system – were much more extensive than in Taschereau's era.[34] Without whitewashing the Taschereau record with respect to democracy, it is therefore reasonable to distinguish it from that of Duplessis. The context and the nature of political abuses differed substantially, and while both men may have been highly paternalistic in their political philosophy, there was a critical difference in their attitude to power. For Taschereau it was a means to a higher end, public service. For Duplessis it was an end in itself.

Finally, in the realm of federal-provincial relations, it is worth noting that Taschereau never attempted to turn provincial rights or French Canada's right to cultural autonomy into a nationalist ideology, complete with alien bogeymen. He merely insisted upon respect for what he considered the letter and spirit of the BNA Act. While properly objecting to the constitutional precedent of the Old Age Pensions Act, he did not challenge it in court (where he might well have succeeded) and he did not use the constitution as an excuse for refusing to let it take effect in Quebec. Rather, he had the honesty and courage to argue against the substance of the legislation. His real battle with Ottawa was over control of hydroelectric development, an issue with enormous economic implications for Quebec.

For all Taschereau's failings, then, he must be given some credit for a genuine sense of public duty, for the purposeful exercise of power beyond his own aggrandizement, and for courage in resisting forces in French-Canadian society which were far less progressive and open-minded than he was. Taschereau consistently challenged traditional nationalist ideology and prejudices, risked clerical hostility with social reforms he considered necessary, and confronted powerful business interests when their behaviour threatened Quebec's economic well-being. In all this he was far more than a "Duplessis with manners."

Taschereau's funeral at Saint-Coeur de Marie Church and the procession to Belmont cemetery were attended by many civil and ecclesiastical dignitaries as well as several hundred ordinary citizens of Quebec City. The obituaries recited family accomplishments along with his own, just as Taschereau would have wished. Yet, for the province as a whole, the event seemed no more than a reminder of some distant past. Even in the capital, many young people had been unaware that Taschereau was still alive during the late forties and early fifties; for them, the Taschereau era was already ancient history. No one took the occasion to observe what Taschereau himself had sensed during the final years: that social and economic forces encouraged by his own political leadership had already virtually ended the day when Quebec could be governed by a tiny professional elite drawn from a few great families. The end of the 200-year-old Taschereau judicial tradition, marked by the retirement of Robert and André from the highest courts of Canada and Quebec respectively, would coincide appropriately with the Quiet Revolution, the funeral of Old Quebec.

# ABBREVIATIONS

ANQ  Archives Nationales du Québec
ASQ  Archives du Séminaire de Québec
AUL  Archives de l'Université Laval
CAR  *Canadian Annual Review of Public Affairs*
CHR  *Canadian Historical Review*
CJEPS *Canadian Journal of Economics and Political Science*
FLAT  Fonds Louis-Alexandre Taschereau
HPQ  Robert Rumilly, *Histoire de la Province de Québec*
PAC  Public Archives of Canada
QSY  *Quebec Statistical Yearbook*
QUA  Queen's University Archives
RHAF  *Revue d'histoire de l'Amérique française*

# Notes

NOTE REGARDING TRANSLATION

With a few exceptions, all quotations originally in French have been translated into English by the author. If drawn from dated correspondence or periodicals, such passages are indicated in the note by leaving the name of the month in French. Otherwise the title of the document or publication indicates the original language.

## PREFACE

1 PAC, W.L.M. King Papers, L.-A. Taschereau to King, 20 July 1936 and 13 January 1937; ANQ, FLAT, Taschereau to Louis S. St Laurent, 2 mars 1944.
2 B.L. Vigod, "Alexandre Taschereau and the Negro King Hypothesis," *Journal of Canadian Studies* 13 (Summer 1978): 4–10. A similar case, unfortunately never expanded, was made for Taschereau's predecessor in Bernard Weilbrenner, "Les idées politiques de Lomer Gouin," *Canadian Historical Association Report*, 1965.
3 *Histoire de la Province de Québec (HPQ)*, 41 vols. (various publishers, 1940–69)
4 E.g., John Dales, *Hydroelectricity and Economic Development in Quebec 1898–1940.*
5 Mason Wade, *The French Canadians 1760–1967*, chap. 14; Susan Mann Trofimenkoff, *Action Française: French Canadian Nationalism in the 1920s*; Herbert Quin, *The Union Nationale: A Study in Quebec Nationalism*, chaps. 2–4.
6 Antonin Dupont, *Les relations entre l'Eglise et l'Etat sous Louis-Alexandre Taschereau, 1920–1936*; Yves Roby, *Les Québécois et les investissements américains (1918–1927)*.
7 P.-A. Linteau, René Durocher, et J.-C. Robert, *Histoire du Québec*

*contemporain: De la Confédération à la crise 1867–1929.* A second volume is in preparation.

8 *Le pouvoir dans la société canadienne-française,* numéro spécial de *Recherches sociographiques* (Québec 1966); Richard Desrosiers, ed., *Le personnel politique québécois;* Paul Cliche, "Les élections provinciales dans le Québec de 1927 à 1960" (MA thesis, Université Laval, 1960); Blair Neatby, *Laurier and a Liberal Quebec;* Joseph Schull, *Laurier* (Toronto 1965); Dale Thomson, *Louis St. Laurent: Canadian* (Toronto 1967); Brian Young, *George-Etienne Cartier: Montreal Bourgeois* (Kingston and Montreal 1981).

9 Electoral data in Jean-Louis Roy, ed., *Les programmes électoraux du Québec,* 2 vols., and Jean Hamelin, Jacques Letarte, and Marcel Hamelin, "Les élections provinciales dans le Québec," in *Cahiers de géographie de Québec* 4 (octobre 1959–mars 1960). On the twentieth century see Marc La Terreur, *Les tribulations des Conservateurs au Québec de Bennett à Diefenbaker,* and Réal Bélanger, *L'impossible défi: Albert Sévigny et les Conservateurs fédéraux 1902–1918.* One hopes for the publication of Jean-Guy Genest, "Vie et oeuvre d'Adélard Godbout 1892–1956" (Thèse de D. ès L., Université Laval, 1977). On the late nineteenth century, see Andrée Désilets, *Hector-Louis Langevin: Un père de la Confédération canadienne 1826–1906,* and Marcel Hamelin, *Les premières années du parlementarisme québécois 1867–1878* (Québec 1974).

10 Coined originally by André Laurendeau in connection with a particular episode involving Duplessis (*Le Devoir,* 4 juillet 1958), "Negro King" quickly became a catchword for the portrayal of French Canadians as a "colonized people," e.g., Léandre Bergeron, *The History of Quebec: A Patriot's Handbook,* especially pp. 171–80. On the longevity of Quebec regimes, see the application of Quinn's theory in the thesis of his student, Harold Angell, "Quebec Provincial Politics in the 1920s" (MA, McGill University, 1960); Michel Brunet, "Trois dominantes de la pensée canadienne-française" in *La présence anglaise et les Canadiens* (Montréal 1964); Pierre-Elliott Trudeau, "Some Obstacles to Democracy in Quebec," *CJEPS* 24 (August 1958); Jean et Marcel Hamelin, *Les moeurs électorales dans le Québec,* chap. 6; René Durocher, "Le long règne de Duplessis: un essai d'explication," *RHAF* 25 (décembre 1971).

11 Ralph Heintzman, "Image and Consequence," *Journal of Canadian Studies* 13 (Summer 1978): 2.

12 Sheilagh Hodgins Milner and Henry Milner, *The Decolonization of Quebec.*

13 *Le Soleil,* 28 Juillet 1920 (his "manifesto" upon assuming the

premiership); Wilfrid Bovey, *Canadien*, 130, 134-5.

14 David Hackett Fischer, *Historians' Fallacies* (New York 1970), 74-5.

15 Liberals never disguised the fact that *Le Soleil* (Quebec City) and *Le Canada* (Montreal) were strictly party newspapers. *L'Action catholique* (Quebec) and *Le Devoir* (Montreal) were certainly not Conservative party organs, but functioned as an opposition press by inclination and by default. While they represented special interests of their own, it was the English papers (*Quebec Chronicle* and *Telegraph*, *Montreal Star* and *Gazette*) which were least partisan in their coverage of daily political events.

16 The interviewees are identified in the bibliography. The most directly relevant memoirs are Norman Ward, ed., *A Party Politician: The Memoirs of Chubby Power*, and T.-D. Bouchard, *Mémoires*. Others important for the period include those of Abbé Lionel Groulx, Alfred Charpentier (ed. G. Dion), Thérèse Casgrain, and Senator Raoul Dandurand.

17 See particularly Albert Faucher, "Le caractère continental de l'industrialisation au Québec" and "Pouvoir politique et pouvoir économique dans l'évolution du Canada français," in *Histoire economique et unité canadienne*.

CHAPTER ONE

1 Cited in *Le Soleil*, 10 décembre 1925.

2 P.G. Roy, *La famille Taschereau*, passim; Honorius Provost, *Sainte Marie de la Nouvelle Beauce: Histoire civile* (Québec 1970), passim; W.A. Craik, "The Romance of the Taschereaus," *Maclean's*, April 1914; Charles-Marie Boissonnault, *Histoire Politique de la Province de Québec*, 234-39.

3 ASQ, "Bulletins du Séminaire," 1878-9 to 1883-4 (ms.); *Annuaire de l'Université Laval* (1881-2 to 1885-6).

4 L.-A. Taschereau, "Du temps que j'étais écolier," *La Nouvelle Abeille* 5 (novembre 1948): 2; his conduct is consistently judged "excellent" or "bon" in the "Bulletins du Séminaire."

5 Joseph-Edmond Roy, *Souvenirs d'une classe au Séminaire de Québec 1867-1877* (Lévis 1905), 248-320; Marc Lebel, Pierre Savard et Raymond Vezina, *Aspects de l'enseignement au Petit Séminaire de Québec 1765-1945* (Québec 1968), 61-77, 103-43.

6 L.-A. Taschereau, "Trois Confrères," *La Nouvelle Abeille* 7 (novembre-décembre 1950).

7 *Annuaire de l'Universite Laval* (1889–90): 71.

8 Henri Têtu, *Histoire des familles Têtu, Bonenfant, Dionne et Perrault* (Québec 1898), 547–69.

9 Mme Gabrielle (Taschereau) Fages, interview, 3 November 1976; *Le Soleil*, 11 décembre 1925; *Le Devoir*, 2 novembre 1935. A biographical sketch of Adine prepared while Alexandre was premier is in FLAT, vol. 33, dossier d.

10 *L'Electeur*, 21 juillet 1891, cited in Roy, *Famille Taschereau*, 145–47; FLAT, vol. 34 (re: testament of Jean-Thomas); Craik, "Romance."

11 Boissonnault, *Histoire politique*, 237–39.

12 The Catholic Programme is in Roy, *Programmes électoraux* 1: 14–18. Judge Taschereau's verdict is in Supreme Court of Canada *Reports* (1876–7), 1: 213, and the entire conflict is described from many angles in Neatby, *Laurier*, chaps. 1 and 2; Désilets, *Langevin*, especially chap. 9; Roy C. Dalton, *The Jesuit Estates Question* (Toronto 1968), chap. 9; Nive Voisine, *Louis-François Laflèche: Deuxième évêque de Trois-Rivières*, vol. 1 (St Hyacinthe, 1980); and Roberto Perin, "Troppo Ardenti Sacerdoti: The Conroy Mission Revisited," *CHR* 61 (September 1980).

13 *Castorisme* and *castors* were epithets conferred on the philosophy and practitioners of the Catholic Programme beginning in the 1880s. For two of Taschereau's later allusions, see *Le Soleil*, 27 mai 1909 and 13 juin 1924.

14 Turpin, "Pêle-Mêle," *L'Union libérale*, 25 mai 1888. For measured analyses of Tardivel and his journal, see Pierre Savard, *Jules-Paul Tardivel, La France et les Etats-Unis* (Québec 1967), and Mathieu Girard, "La pensée politique de Jules-Paul Tardivel," *RHAF* 21 (décembre 1967).

15 *L'Union libérale*, 27 septembre, 2 novembre, 27 décembre 1889; 3, 31 janvier, 7 février, 25 avril 1890; 3 janvier 1891; 29 décembre 1892; 12, 19 janvier, 4, 11 février, 4 mars, 7 octobre 1893. Some of the later articles appear under an alternative pseudonym, "Frollo."

16 *HPQ* 2: 280–81; *L'Electeur* (pro-Taschereau) and *L'Evénement* (pro-Pelletier), 2 janvier–10 mars 1892; Boissonnault, *Histoire politique*, 243–45.

17 *L'Union libérale*, 19 juillet, 2 août 1889.

18 Ibid., 1 juin, 27 juillet 1888, 27 septembre, 2 novembre 1889, 8 août 1890.

19 Ibid., 18 juillet 1890, 18 mars 1893.

20 Ward, ed., *Power*, 323.

21 Fitzpatrick acquired a reputation for "treachery" by standing as an independent Liberal in 1892, rather than supporting Mercier to be

bitter end as Taschereau did. But this is somewhat unfair since many Liberals including Laurier felt obliged to dissociate themselves, in the light of the charges of political corruption brought against the Mercier government. Neither partner seems to have resented the other's course of action.

22 For example, a series of articles in May and June 1893, saluting French-Canadian industrialists.

23 Copy of agreement dated 31 décembre 1898 in FLAT, vol. 31.

24 Bernard Chevrier, "Le ministère de Félix-Gabriel Marchand (1897)," *RHAF* (juin 1966): 41–6; *Quebec Chronicle*, 2 March, 1 October 1900.

25 See below, pp. 23–4.

26 Criminal and charity cases were reported frequently in the *Chronicle*, and Taschereau's growing reputation as a criminal lawyer drew comment in *Le Soleil*, 18 février 1901. Notable corporate clients included the Bank of Montreal, Ernest Pacaud (owner of *Le Soleil*), lumber baron William Price, and the Canadian Northern Railway, as well as the Quebec government itself. Sources: Supreme Court of Canada *Reports*, 1899–1901, and *Le Soleil*, 11 janvier 1906.

27 Cf. *Le Soleil*, 18 février 1901 and 5 mars 1936.

## CHAPTER TWO

1 For a comprehensive account of Quebec economic history in the latter half of the nineteenth century, see Jean Hamelin and Yves Roby, *Histoire économique du Québec 1851–1896.*

2 The "location" interpretation of Quebec's industrial development was launched by Albert Faucher and Maurice Lamontagne in "History of Industrial Development in Quebec," in J.-C. Falardeau, ed., *Essais sur le Québec contemporain / Essays on Contemporary Quebec* (Québec 1953).

3 See Bishop Laflèche and Mgr Pâquet, cited in William F. Ryan, *The Clergy and Economic Growth in Quebec*, 91–6, 247–49 (although the author attempts to explain away these quotations).

4 Neatby, *Laurier*, 143–4.

5 *Le Soleil*, 11 décembre 1925 (reminiscence).

6 Far from being a chance misfortune, the catastrophic defeats suffered by the Conservatives federally in 1896 and provincially in 1897 were the culmination of two decades of bitter feuding between *castors* and moderates. No process of reconstruction had begun by 1900. Bélanger, *Sévigny*, 13.

7 *Quebec Chronicle*, 24 November 1900; reminiscence in *Le Soleil* 5 mars 1936.

8 *Le Soleil*, 11 décembre 1925; *Chronicle*, 24 November–8 December 1900.

9 The subsequent account is drawn from the *Chronicle* (16 May 1902 et seq.) and from the Supreme Court of Canada *Reports* 36 (1905): 247–50.

10 14 August 1902.

11 FLAT, Taschereau to A. Cannon, 23 juillet 1903.

12 Joseph Levitt, *Henri Bourassa and the Golden Calf*, 60–3; Robert Rumilly, *Henri Bourassa: La vie publique d'un grand canadien*, chap. 9.

13 Neatby, *Laurier*, 171–3; *CAR* 1904, 310–15.

14 P.-A. Choquette, *Un demi-siècle de vie politique* 113–32, 162–3.

15 Parent drafted, but may not have sent, a letter to Laurier supporting the Quebec and Lake Huron Railway Company, which Choquette and Adélard Turgeon (one of his ministers) were promoting. Original copy in ANQ, Papiers S.-N. Parent, Parent to Laurier, 10 novembre 1904.

16 Choquette, *Vie politique*, 161.

17 *Chronicle*, 5 November 1904.

18 Choquette, *Vie politique*, 165–74; *CAR* 1904, 318–25; Papiers Parent, circular letter from Choquette to deputies, 30 novembre 1904 (copy).

19 *CAR* 1904, 310, 318–26; *Chronicle*, 1, 29 December 1904.

20 PAC, Laurier Papers, Laurier to Choquette, 2 janvier 1905; Choquette, *Vie politique*, 174–5; Papiers Parent, Dominique Monet to Parent, 19 janvier 1905.

21 Papiers Parent, Lomer Gouin, Adélard Turgeon, and William Weir to Parent, 3 février 1905; Parent to Sir Alphonse Pelletier, 22 février 1905; conditions of agreement recorded by A. Girard, member for Rouville, 23 février 1905; *Chronicle*, 8–10 February 1905.

22 *HPQ* 11: 216–17; *CAR* 1905, 307.

23 *Chronicle*, 6–10 February 1906. Good general account in *CAR* 1905, 305–8 and 1906, 363–4.

24 Laurier Papers, Taschereau to Laurier, 5 décembre 1905, 5 janvier 1906; Choquette, *Vie politique*, 164.

25 See *Chronicle* and *Le Soleil*, 10 January–10 February 1906. Taschereau's personal campaign journal, *L'Eclair*, made its appearance on 16 January.

26 *L'Eclair*, 18 janvier, *Le Soleil*, 20 janvier, 10 février, *Chronicle*, 12–13 February 1906; PAC, Lomer Gouin Papers, Gouin to Laurier, 10 février, and Laurier to Gouin, 15 février 1906.

27 PAC, Charles Fitzpatrick Papers, Fitzpatrick to Laurier, 30 March 1906.

28 Levitt, *Golden Calf*, 121-4; Neatby, *Laurier*, 177-8.

29 *CAR* 1907, 548-55.

30 *Le Nationaliste*, 25 novembre 1906 and 27 janvier-19 mai 1907.

31 *Chronicle*, 24 January 1906.

32 *L'Action sociale*, 18 mars 1910.

33 *Chronicle*, 4, 12 October 1907.

34 Parent was, in fact, among the first to offer congratulations when Taschereau entered the Gouin cabinet. FLAT, Parent to Taschereau (telegram), 17 octobre 1907.

35 Laurier Papers, Taschereau to Laurier, 12 février 1907 and reply, 13 février.

36 *Discours-Programme prononcé par l'Hon. M. Lomer Gouin, 5 avril, 1905*, esp. 4-5, 11, 15; Weilbrenner, "Gouin," 49-54.

37 Laurier Papers, Laurier to Henri d'Hellencourt, 27 avril 1907; *Le Soleil*, 30 octobre 1907; *HPQ* 13: 50, 118.

38 André Beaulieu and Jean Hamelin, *Les journaux du Québec de 1764 à 1964* (Québec 1965), 226.

39 Levitt, *Golden Calf*, 136-45.

40 *Le Soleil*, 6 novembre 1907 (speech of 5 November, cited below). Taschereau evidently expressed similar sentiments in private, for when he entered the cabinet a Montreal legal associate referred to their common desire to reunite the Liberal party against the *castors*. FLAT, Charles Archer to Taschereau, 17 October 1907. T.-D. Bouchard, who supported Taschereau in his final battle against *castorisme*, also recalled the epoch in these terms (*Mémoires* 2: 158-9).

41 Best account in *Chronicle*, 17 May 1907 et seq. Court proceedings also cited in *Politique provinciale: Trois discours de l'Hon. Lomer Gouin*, 43-52.

42 *CAR* 1907, 552-5.

43 J.C. McGee, *Histoire politique de Québec-Est*, 130-3; Bouchard, *Mémoires* 2: 158-9. Regarding *La Patrie*, see *CAR* 1908, 356 and *HPQ* 13: 79.

44 Turgeon to Choquette, 15 octobre 1907, cited in Choquette, *Vie politique*, 247; *Chronicle*, 12, 14 October 1907.

45 *Chronicle*, 22, 25 February 1902.

46 Ibid., 18 October 1907.

47 FLAT, Archambault, Monet, and Casgrain to Taschereau, all 18 octobre 1907.

48 17-25 October 1907; *CAR* 1907, 553-4.

49 *CAR* 1907, 558-9.

50 *Le Soleil*, 30 octobre, 1 novembre 1907.

51 *Chronicle* and *Le Soleil*, 19 October-4 November 1907. Regarding

the Bellechasse campaign, even Bourassa later admitted that *natio-naliste* accusations had stretched the limits of truth and fair play. *HPQ* 13: 88.

52 *Le Soleil*, 6 novembre 1907.

53 *HPQ* 13: 125-6; *CAR* 1908, 358-65.

54 *Le Soleil*, 5 mai-9 juin 1908; *CAR* 1908, 366-78.

55 Regarding internal Conservative divisions, see Bélanger, *Sévigny*, 43-6.

56 *Trois discours de Lomer Gouin*, passim; "Programme d'Henri Bourassa," in Roy, *Programmes électoraux* 1: 137-41.

### CHAPTER THREE

1 *CAR* 1908, 238-60.

2 *Le Nationaliste*, 26 juillet 1908.

3 *Le Soleil*, 4 mars 1909.

4 *HPQ* 14: 25-8; *Le Soleil*, 5 mars 1909; *Chronicle*, 13 May 1909.

5 *Chronicle*, 21 April 1909.

6 Michel Pelletier and Yves Vaillancourt, *Les politiques sociales et les travailleurs*, Cahier 1 (Montréal 1974), 86-9.

7 Violette Allaire, *Louis Guyon* (Montréal 1953), passim; Terry Copp, *The Anatomy of Poverty*, 49-56, 123-5.

8 *Montreal Star*, 24 March and 15 April, *Chronicle*, 6 May 1909. *The Report of the Commission on Labour Accidents* (Quebec 1907), which underlay the legislation, is summarized in the *Star*, 19 March 1909.

9 *Chronicle*, 29 April and 13 May 1910; *CAR* 1911, 489 and 1912, 402.

10 *Chronicle*, 24 March, *Montreal Star*, 27 and 31 March 1909; *HPQ* 14: 52.

11 *HPQ* 14: 42-3, 17: 213; *Le Canada*, 4 mars 1907. Taschereau's impression, it should be noted, was long shared even by sympathetic observers of Bourassa. See Roland Parenteau, "Les idées économiques et sociales de Bourassa," in F.-A. Angers, ed., *La pensée de Henri Bourassa*, 170-1.

12 *Le Nationaliste*, 25 septembre 1906 and 31 mai 1908; Levitt, *Golden Calf*, 50; *Discours Programme ... 1905*, 7.

13 Marcel-A. Gagnon, *La vie orageuse d'Olivar Asselin* 1: 110-111; *Le Soleil*, 19 mai 1909. Rumilly's version is that Asselin simply fled before Taschereau could retaliate. *HPQ* 14: 52.

14 *HPQ* 14: 52-6; *Chronicle*, 20-21 May 1909.

15 *L'Action sociale*, 26 mai 1909.

16 *Le Soleil*, 27, 29 mai 1909.

17 Account based on FLAT, vol. 16, dossier a ("Affaire Trudel").

18 *HPQ* 14: 41, 66.

19 Ibid., 102.

20 O.D. Skelton, *The Life and Letters of Sir Wilfrid Laurier* 2: 122.

21 Neatby, *Laurier*, 188.

22 FLAT Discours (vol. 20); *Toronto Globe*, 16 December 1909.

23 Laurier acknowledged the need to sway French-Canadian opinion even at the time of his 1909 resolution. Skelton, *Laurier*, 2: 122.

24 Ibid., 129.

25 Brig. John A. Price, interview, 12 June 1972; Charles Taschereau, interview, 19 November 1976.

26 *Le Soleil*, 15 janvier 1915.

27 *Le Canada*, 13 décembre 1909. See also pp. 50-2 and notes 34-5 below.

28 *HPQ* 14: 101 and 15: 13, 58-9.

29 *L'Action sociale*, 18 mars 1910. See also *Le Devoir* and *Le Soleil*, 23 mars 1910.

30 *HPQ* 15: 60.

31 Ibid., 106, 174-6.

32 *Montreal Star*, 18 March 1910. He was forced to repeat the same admission in 1919.

33 *HPQ* 15: 55-7.

34 Taschereau's authorship is established by the drafts in his handwriting, FLAT, vol. 17, dossier j. The pastoral letter, issued 15 February 1911, is printed in *Mandements, lettres pastorales et circulaires des évêques de Québec* (1912) 10: 357-68.

35 Complete text published in *HPQ* 16: 28-36.

36 *CAR* 1912, 397-8; *Chronicle*, 25 January, 13 March 1912.

37 According to Rumilly (*HPQ* 17: 34-5), the friendship was established well before this first controversy. The witnesses include Brig. John A. Price (interview, 12 June 1972), Joseph Couture (interview, 28 October 1976), and Hon. Antoine Rivard (interview, 2 November 1976).

38 *Chronicle*, 9 April-12 May 1912; *HPQ* 16: 73, 17: 215-18.

39 Roy, *Programmes électoraux* 1: 144-53; *CAR* 1912, 408-16; *HPQ* 17: 97-100.

40 *Le Soleil*, 6 mai 1912.

41 Michael Oliver, "The Social and Political Ideas of French Canadian Nationalists 1920-1945" (PHD thesis, McGill University 1956), 87-9; Copp, *Poverty*, passim; Levitt, *Golden Calf*, chap. 5.

42 *CAR* 1914, 487-97; J.-C. Bonenfant, "La première table d'écoute au Québec," in *Les Cahiers de Dix* 40 (1975).

43 Robert Choquette, *Language and Religion*, 161-73; Marilyn Barber, "The Ontario Bilingual Schools Issue: Sources of Conflict," *CHR* 47 (September 1966); Peter Oliver, *G. Howard Ferguson, Ontario Tory*

39–50. The courts subsequently upheld Whitney's contention that no such right existed.

44 Joseph Levitt, ed., *Henri Bourassa on Imperaialism and Biculturalism 1900–1918* (Toronto 1970), esp. 130–53.

45 René Durocher, "Henri Bourassa, les évêques et la guerre de 1914–1918," *Historical Papers/Communications historiques* (1971).

46 *Le Soleil*, 15 janvier 1915.

47 *Le Devoir*, 14 janvier 1916. Rumilly (*HPQ* 21: 33–4) has Landry present on 25 January, in which case Taschereau made similar speeches on two occasions.

48 *Le Devoir* and *Le Soleil*, 23 février 1916.

49 *CAR* 1915, 291; *HPQ* 20: 105–6; *Le Soleil*, 9 septembre 1915, 20 février 1917.

50 *HPQ* 19: 74; *Le Soleil*, 16 février 1915.

51 The sorry tale of deterioration and provocation is fully recounted in Elizabeth Armstrong, *The Crisis of Quebec 1914–1918*, chaps. 5, 6, and Wade, *French Canadians*, 2: 658–710.

52 *Le Devoir*, 16 mai 1916.

53 See note 59.

54 *Le Soleil*, 9 décembre 1916 (editorial endorsing the mood of a rally addressed by Taschereau).

55 Armstrong, *Crisis*, 166.

56 Ibid., 166–72; Wade, *French Canadians* 2: 675–8; Bélanger, *Sévigny*, 258–62; *HPQ* 21: 34, 100, and 22: 86.

57 *Le Soleil*, 30 avril 1917.

58 *HPQ* 22: 191. See also *Le Soleil*, 3 décembre 1917.

59 *CAR* 1917, 679.

60 Brian Cameron, "The Bonne Entente Movement 1916–1917: From Co-operation to Conscription," *Journal of Canadian Studies* 13 (Summer 1978); W.R. Graham, *Arthur Meighen*, vol. 1, *The Door of Opportunity*, 140, 142.

61 *Le Soleil*, 24 août 1917.

62 R.C. Brown and R. Cook, *Canada 1896–1921: A Nation Transformed*, 273.

63 Cited in J.M. Beck, *Pendulum of Power*, 143–4.

64 *L'Action catholique*, 26–29 novembre 1917. Taschereau did not comment on the French-Canadian Conservative MPs who had actually voted for conscription, but Liberals generally refused them credit for any sincerity. On the campaign against Albert Sévigny in Dorchester, see Bélanger, *Sévigny*, 319–29.

65 Cited in Armstrong, *Crisis*, 220.

66 The cathartic effect of the Francoeur debate on Quebec Liberals has been far too readily assumed by English-speaking writers. Armstrong,

*Crisis*, 223-4, and Wade, *French Canadians* 2: 760.

67 A. Savard and W.E. Playfair, *Quebec and Confederation: A Record of the Debate of the Legislative Assembly of Quebec on the Motion Proposed by J.N. Francoeur*, passim.

68 *Le Soleil*, 22 janvier 1918.

69 FLAT, Discours (vol. 20).

70 Armstrong, *Crisis*, 226.

71 Jean Provencher, *Québec sous la loi des mesures de guerre*; Gérald Filteau, *Le Québec, Le Canada et la guerre 1914-1918*, chap. 14; Ward, ed., *Power*, 82-93.

72 Linteau, Durocher, and Robert, *Quebec*, chap. 18-22. See especially pp. 416-17 for statistics on urban growth.

73 *Le Soleil*, 31 janvier, 13 février 1919; *Montreal Star*, 22 January 1919.

74 The legislation of 1919 is summarized in Roger Chartier, "Les lois du salaire minimum des femmes, des grèves et contre-grèves municipales, du départment du travail et des syndicats professionnels (1919-1924)," *Relations industrielles/Industrial Relations* 17 (octobre 1962).

75 *Le Monde ouvrier*, mouthpiece of the Montreal Trades and Labour Council, congratulated Taschereau on the child labour amendment and other legislation at the 1919 session, but added the general warning that "the lack of sanctions and the application have always been the problem with [theoretically] good labour laws in Quebec." 1, 8, 15 mars 1919.

76 Dandurand, *Mémoires*, 245-61; *CAR* 1919, 539-44; Louis-Philippe Audet, "La querelle de l'instruction obligatoire 1875-1943," in Marcel Lajeunesse, ed., *L'éducation au Québec*, 120-5.

77 *HPQ* 24: 38-9.

78 *Montreal Star*, 1 February 1919.

79 On the question generally, see *HPQ* 24: 139-52. Regarding Taschereau's role, see ASQ, Université 232, no. 27, 29, Pelletier to Taschereau, 18 octobre 1918, and Pelletier to Mgr O. Cloutier, 26 octobre 1918; also Journal du Séminaire, 16 octobre 1918.

80 E.g., W.A. Riddell, *The Rise of Ecclesiastical Control in Quebec*. Defending the accuracy of official school attendance statistics, Quebec's chief Catholic schools inspector asserted that "History teaches us that compulsory education, then the compulsory school, were invented by masonic lodges and became perfidious and powerful weapons in the hands of the enemies of the Catholic traditions of France ... The same would happen here." Cited in Audet, "La querelle," 125.

81 *Le Soleil*, 13 février 1919.

82 25 February 1919.

83 Dandurand, *Mémoires*, 256-9.

84 *HPQ* 24: 48–9.

85 Ibid, 25–178.

86 *Montreal Star*, 4 March 1919; *HPQ* 24: 106, 133–4; *Toronto Star*, 18 August 1922.

87 See below, pp. 153–5.

### CHAPTER FOUR

1 *HPQ* 24: 133, 25: 20–1; questionnaires returned to Professor J.A. Lovinck by Léon-Mercier Gouin, Thomas Vien, and C.G. Power; Graham, *Opportunity*, 296–9. I am grateful to Dr Lovinck for allowing me to read the returned questionnaires.

2 Boissonnault, *Histoire politique*, 246; *Le Soleil*, 28 juillet 1920; Erland Echlin, "Speaking of Success," *Maclean's*, 15 January 1936.

3 *HPQ* 25: 12, 17.

4 Ibid., Bergeron, *Patriot's Handbook*, 171.

5 *Le Soleil*, 28 juillet 1920.

6 *CAR* 1920, 628–30.

7 *Le Soleil*, 7 septembre 1920.

8 Ibid., 28 juillet 1920.

9 Fitzpatrick Papers, R.-A. Benoît to Taschereau, 5 mars 1921 (copy).

10 Ibid., Taschereau to Fitzpatrick, 7 novembre 1921.

11 B.L. Vigod, "Ideology and Institutions in Quebec: The Public Charities Controversy 1921–1926," *Histoire sociale/Social History*, May 1978.

12 Dupont, *Relations*, passim.

13 *CAR* 1921, 654–8; 1922, 698, 700, 703.

14 Ibid., 1922, 683. The accusation is contained in PAC, Arthur Meighen Papers, Arthur G. Penny to Meighen, 11 December 1922. In reality the project had been mooted much earlier (Fitzpatrick Papers, Fitzpatrick to Taschereau and reply, 1–2 décembre 1920), and Price had his own reasons for preferring Taschereau to the provincial Conservative leader (Brig. John A. Price, interview, 12 June 1972).

15 *CAR* 1920, 630, and 1921, 660–3; *Le Soleil*, 1 août 1922.

16 C.C. Jenkins, "Quebec's Business Premier," *Maclean's* August 1921.

17 Choice quotations in Dupont, *Relations*, 42–6. For a fuller account, see Jean-Paul Lawlor, "La Commerce des alcools et la création de la Commission des liqueurs en 1921" (Thèse de D. ès s., Université de Montréal, 1970).

18 Fitzpatrick Papers, Taschereau to Fitzpatrick, 23 mars 1921.

19 Text of the act in *Statutes of Quebec*, 11 Geo. V c. 79. Regarding the haste, see Dupont, *Relations*, 76.

20 Fitzpatrick Papers, Taschereau to Fitzpatrick, 2 février 1921. This

account is drawn from my article (cited above, note 11), where additional documentation is available.

21 Henri Bourassa, *Une mauvaise loi*, 1-23; *L'Action catholique*, 17-20 janvier 1922.

22 *Le Soleil*, 17 mars 1921.

23 *Le Devoir*, 14 avril 1921.

24 FLAT, Taschereau to Mgr Roy, 20 janvier 1922.

25 Fitzpatrick Papers, Fitzpatrick to Bégin, 4 août 1921, and to Bourassa, 24 août 1921; *HPQ* 25: 117 and 26: 237.

26 FLAT, Roy to Taschereau, 12 janvier 1922 and Taschereau to Roy, 20 janvier 1922; ANQ., S.P. [Secrétariat Provincial], Taschereau to David, 18 janvier 1922.

27 FLAT, Roy to Taschereau, 22 janvier 1922.

28 B.L. Vigod, "Responses to Social and Economic Change in Quebec: The Provincial Administration of Louis-Alexandre Taschereau 1920-1929 (PHD thesis, Queen's University, 1974), 306-18.

29 *HPQ* 26: 22; FLAT, David to Taschereau, 6 octobre 1939. Educational reform throughout the decade is described in B.L. Vigod, " 'Qu'on ne craigne pas l'encombrement des compétences': Le gouvernement Taschereau et l'éducation 1920-1929," *RHAF* 28 (septembre 1974).

30 *CAR* 1920, 631; *HPQ* 25:84.

31 *CAR* 1921, 641-2.

32 Ibid.

33 FLAT, Discours (vol. 20), Speech at McGill University, 13 October 1921; "Allocution de l'honorable L.-A. Taschereau," in *Semaines sociales du Canada, 2$^{me}$ session tenue à Québec, 1921* (Montréal 1922), 389-92.

34 *Le Devoir*, 14 avril 1921.

35 FLAT, Taschereau to Mgr P.-E. Roy, 22 janvier 1922 and Taschereau to Mme Donat Brodeur, 2 février 1922.

36 Dupont, *Relations*, 175-80.

37 L.-A. Taschereau, "De l'influence de la femme sur nos destinées nationales" [1921], in Michèle Jean, ed., *Québécoises du 20$^e$ siècle*, 208-19.

38 Casgrain, *Man's World*, 51-5. Partly in response to feminists and partly out of his general interest in "modernizing" the Quebec Civil Code, Taschereau commissioned Mr. Justice C.-E. Dorion, Ferdinand Roy (then chief magistrate of the Quebec district), and two other men to examine the legal status of women in 1929. The modest recommendations were a disappointment, and the rationalization of female legal disabilities truly astonishing. See Casgrain, *Man's World*, 58-63, and Jennifer Stoddard, "The Dorion Commission, 1926-1931: Quebec's Legal Elites Look at Women's Rights," in D. Flaherty, ed., *Essays in the History of Canadian Law*, vol. 1. Taschereau strongly

opposed the admission of women to "male" professions throughout his career (*Le Soleil*, 14 décembre 1916; *Montreal Gazette*, 11 October 1930), discouraged the granting of bursaries to female students (Bibliothèque municipale de Montréal, Collection Olivar Asselin, Asselin to Joseph Rainville, 23 août 1928), and in all seriousness advised cabinet ministers to go home for lunch and otherwise monitor their wives' activities (Jean-Paul Galipeault, interview, 27 October 1976).

39 *CAR* 1922, 680–1.

40 FLAT, Discours, 27 April 1922 (vol. 20).

41 *L'habitant du Québec: La noblesse canadienne-française.*

42 Ibid.; FLAT, Mgr Eugène Lapointe to Taschereau, 1 mai 1922.

43 Gouin Papers, J.-L. Perron to Gouin, 19 avril 1922.

44 Mme Gabrielle [Taschereau] Fages, interview, 3 November 1976. The strength of the rumours was such that this author received an anonymous letter on the subject fifty-five years later.

45 *CAR* 1922, 711–15; *HPQ* 26: 158–67. Taschereau testimony in ANQ, "Royal Commission Enquiry into the Garneau Case" (ms. transcript), 20 December 1922.

46 Cited in W.R. Graham, *Arthur Meighen*, vol. 2, *And Fortune Fled*, 140.

47 Ibid., 140–3, 340–4, 487–8.

48 Ibid., 143–6.

49 *CAR* 1922, 681.

50 Ibid., 1923, 78–81; [Parti libéral], *Le gouvernement Taschereau* (1923), 161.

51 Gouin Papers, Taschereau to Gouin, 11 mai 1921, and 20 mars 1922, Gouin to Taschereau, 22 mars 1922, Edward Beck to Taschereau, 18 March 1922. Further correspondence published in *Montreal Star*, 13 March 1924.

52 King Papers, Taschereau to King, 23 April 1923. The emigration question is discussed in chap. 5.

53 ANQ, Agriculture et Colonisation, Correspondance 1922–25.

54 Taschereau's clearest public declaration on this subject was reported in the *Montreal Gazette*, 15 January 1930.

55 See chap. 7.

56 *HPQ* 25: 153–4; *CAR* 1922, 694–7.

57 *HPQ* 26: 193; Ward, ed., *Power*, 326.

58 Dossiers on the Caron-Fortin confrontation in AUL, Fonds Alfred Charpentier (32 pp.), PAC, Ernest Lapointe Papers, subject file 4a; and Archives de la Confédération des syndicats nationaux (Montreal).

59 *HPQ* 25: 93.

60 *CAR* 1920, 131, 633–5, 1922, 683; *Statues of Quebec*, 13 Geo. V c.

109, sections 26 and 31–6; *HPQ* 26: 100–3, 150–3.

61 *Le Soleil*, 11 mars, 25 septembre 1922.

62 *HPQ* 25: 100–4, 133–5, and 26: 210–12.

63 French version cited above, note 50; [Liberal party], *The Taschereau Government* (1923).

64 Gouin Papers, Taschereau to Gouin, 6 octobre 1922.

65 *Toronto Telegram*, 19 January 1923; FLAT, Discours (vol. 21).

66 FLAT, Taschereau to Jules Dorion, 9 janvier 1923; Caron to Mgr P.-E. Roy, 11 janvier 1923; *HPQ* 26: 197–200, 213–14.

67 FLAT, Taschereau to Mgr Bégin, 22 janvier 1923.

68 Ibid., Bégin to Taschereau, 24 janvier 1923.

69 Ibid., Bégin to Taschereau, 29 janvier 1923. Confident that his words could not be construed as a threat against Bégin, Taschereau allowed the correspondence to be published in *Le Soleil*, 1 février 1923.

70 *HPQ* 26: 196–234; QUA, T.A. Crerar Papers, A.K. Cameron to Crerar, 6 February 1923; Gouin Papers, Taschereau to W.S. Fielding, 6 April, and to W.L.M. King, 23 April 1923.

71 *La Patrie* and *Le Devoir*, 2 février 1923.

72 *Le Devoir, Gazette, Le Soleil*, 6 février 1923.

73 FLAT, Discours (vol. 21), Three Rivers, 3 May 1923.

## CHAPTER FIVE

1 *HPQ* 27: 71–6; *CAR* 1923, 607, 611, 628.

2 Gouin Papers, L.-A. Richard to Gouin, 12 mars 1923.

3 Ibid., Gouin to J.-E. Perrault, 3 janvier, and Taschereau to Gouin, 6 avril 1923; FLAT, Discours (vol. 21), speech to Club St Denis, 14 avril 1923.

4 King Papers, Taschereau to King, 23 April 1923; Gouin Papers, Perrault to Stewart, 27 March 1923; Taschereau to Gouin, 6 avril 1923; Perrault to Gouin, 10 avril 1923 and Caron to Gouin, 27 avril 1923.

5 King Papers, Taschereau to King, 23 April 1923; *CAR* 1923, 609.

6 See J.-E. Caron, cited in Union catholique des cultivateurs, *Rapport de la fondation et de toutes les assemblées annuelles de 1924 à 1927*, 171.

7 Vigod, "Taschereau Administration," 239–49, 255–62.

8 Gouin Papers, G.-E. Amyot to Gouin, 22 mars 1922; Gouin to Amyot, 12 avril 1922.

9 *ANQ*, Fonds C.-J. Magnan, G.-E. Amyot to Magnan, 6 avril 1923.

10 Gouin Papers, Amyot to Gouin, 3 février 1922.

11 FLAT, vol. 15, dossier b, "Remarques de M.N. Lavoie, ex-gérant-général

de la Banque Nationale," 19 février 1924; Taschereau to Beaudry Leman, 18 and 26 mars 1924; J.-A. Vaillancourt to Sir Hormisdas Laporte, 12 mars 1924; Gouin Papers, file 7, extensive Gouin-Amyot correspondence.

12 *CAR* 1924-5, 307-8; FLAT, F. Cockburn (Bank of Montreal) to Taschereau and reply, 19 and 22 January 1924; *HPQ* 27: 103-7.

13 FLAT, vol. 15, dossier b, various letters of congratulation to Taschereau, dated 18-19 January 1924.

14 *HPQ* 27: 106.

15 *Le Soleil*, 18 janvier 1924.

16 Gouin Papers, Gouin to Amyot, 25 janvier 1924.

17 Copy of order-in-council in FLAT, Taschereau to Leman, 26 March 1924; on the federal charter, ibid., Robb to Leman and reply, 24 and 26 March, Taschereau to King and reply, 26 and 31 March 1924; regarding Edmond, ibid., Taschereau to Leman and reply, 3 and 4 avril 1924; on the political risk, ibid., Taschereau to Ernest Lapointe, 31 mars 1924.

18 King Papers, Taschereau to King, 8 February 1927 and 4 May 1928. For a more sceptical view of the whole affair, see Ronald Rudin, "A Bank Merger unlike the Others: The Establishment of the Banque Canadienne Nationale," *CHR*, June 1980. But see also Leman's private summation FLAT, Leman to Taschereau, 31 juillet 1924.

19 Dupont, *Relations*, 109-15; Bourassa quotation from *Le Devoir*, 7 mars 1924.

20 *Le Soleil*, 17 septembre 1923.

21 ASQ, Université 192, no. 79, Taschereau to Mgr C.N. Gariépy, 10 mai 1924.

22 Charles Taschereau, interview, 19 November 1976. Expulsion during the final year had no practical consequences, since identical courses could be taken at Laval University.

23 ASQ, Journal du Séminaire, vol. 11, 9-18 mai 1924; Gabrielle (Taschereau) Fages, interview, 3 November 1976.

24 FLAT, Lemieux to Taschereau, 26 mai and 3 juin 1924. The running battle between *Le Soleil* and *L'Action catholique* is well described in *HPQ* 27: 150-64.

25 *Le Soleil*, 13 juin 1924.

26 *L'Action française* (juillet 1924): 58-9; FLAT, Taschereau to Mgr Gauthier, 15 and 29 août, Gauthier to Taschereau, 21 août, Mgr E.-A. Deschamps to Taschereau, 9 septembre 1924.

27 *HPQ* 17: 154-5.

28 Gouin Papers, Diary, 7 avril 1926; ASQ, Université 172, no. 63, Taschereau to Mgr Mathieu, 16 décembre 1908; Journal du Séminaire, vol. 8, 7 novembre 1911, vol. 9, 12 mai 1914, vol. 10, 1 février 1917.

29 Vigod, "Taschereau Administration," 95-7.

30 On employees and wages see *Quebec Statistical Yearbook* 1931, 364. On the growth of the industry during this period, see Vincent Bladen, *An Introduction to Political Economy* 180-96, and J.A. Guthrie, *The Newsprint Paper Industry*, 95-7, 107-10.

31 Vigod, "Taschereau Administration," 112-16.

32 Cited in Roby, *Investissements américains*, 169. This book comprehensively recounts the public debate between Taschereau and the critics of his industrial policies in the 1920s.

33 *La Presse*, 14 janvier 1925.

34 *Statutes of Quebec*, 16 Geo. v c. 20. Note the direct language of the preamble, which in addition to projecting future demand within Quebec, warns about the difficulty of stopping power exports once they have begun and proclaims the vital importance of hydro power in preventing the emigration of both workers and farmers.

35 *CAR* 1922, 681.

36 George W. Stephens, *The St. Lawrence Waterway Project*, 188-9, 209-10, 233-4.

37 Oliver, *Ferguson*, 182.

38 Public Archives of Ontario, G.H. Ferguson Papers, Taschereau to Ferguson, 18 Decembre 1925.

39 Ibid., 15 May and 7 October 1924. Not until 1926 did Taschereau publicly admit linking the issues (*Montreal Gazette*, 20 May), but he had denounced Ontario "fanaticism" in Toronto in 1923 (*Le Soleil*, 19 mars) and privately had encouraged Senator N.A. Belcourt, the leading postwar Franco-Ontarian activist. University of Ottawa Library, Archives de l'Association canadienne-française de l'Ontario, Taschereau to Belcourt, 9 juin 1924, 3 janvier 1925; Belcourt to Taschereau, 27 décembre 1924.

40 *Quebec Chronicle-Telegraph*, 21 January 1925.

41 Meighen Papers, Meighen to Ferguson (with enclosed message from Quebec Conservative Rodolphe Monty), 23 February 1924; Ferguson Papers, Meighen to Ferguson, 24 January 1925.

42 H. Blair Neatby, *William Lyon Mackenzie King*, vol. 2, *The Lonely Heights*, 225; Oliver, *Ferguson*, 185-186.

43 Ferguson Papers, Taschereau to Ferguson, 26 February and 18 December 1925.

44 Ibid., C.A. McGrath to Ferguson, 8 January 1926.

45 Ibid., Ferguson to Taschereau, 25 March 1926, and McGrath to Taschereau, 15 April 1926.

46 Ibid., McGrath to Ferguson, 14 January and 28 December 1927; see chap. 6 for further description.

47 Vigod, "Taschereau Administration," 156-8.

48 L.-A. Taschereau, *The Challenge of Canada's New Frontiers*, 4.

49 Cited in Leslie Roberts, *Noranda*, 66-7, 85. On the roads policy, see Vigod, "Taschereau Administration," 263-7.

50 1923 speech quoted in J.-E. Perrault, *La politique libérale et nos ressources naturelles*.

51 Quebec Department of Lands and Forests, *Annual Report* 1925-6, 28-30, and 1926-7, 27; *Le Soleil*, 11 janvier 1927.

52 The crisis of the 1930s is described in detail in Chap. 7.

53 Quebec, *Report on Mining Operations*, 1927, 211, 1928, 136-7, 213.

54 See especially Taschereau's speeches at Shawinigan Falls, 14 September 1922 and Three Rivers, 3 May 1923 (FLAT, Discours, vols. 20 and 21), and in the period leading up to the power export embargo (Roby, *Investissements américains*, 130-41). With brutal frankness, Perrault later argued that the government would have been irresponsible to wait for French-Canadian capital to develop Quebec's resources: "Let's admit that it was only a dream and that it was impossible." *La politique libérale*, 4, 12.

55 See above, pp. ix-x.

56 Neatby, *Lonely Heights*, 375-85; Ward, ed., *Power*, 285-6, 313, 319, 337.

57 See Stewart Bates, *Financial History of Canadian Governments*, 146 ff.

58 *HPQ* 29: 27, 186.

59 Parti libéral, *Le gouvernement Taschereau* (1927), 31.

60 Taschereau, *The Challenge*, 3.

61 Fitzpatrick Papers, Fitzpatrick to R.P. Kernan and C. Barlow to E. Beck, both 12 January 1926.

62 FLAT, Discours (vol. 20), speech at Shawinigan Falls, 14 September 1922.

63 King Papers, Taschereau to King, 18 December 1928. See also *Financial Post*, 13 and 27 January 1928, and the discussion in chap. 6. On Barclay's, FLAT, F.W. Taylor to Taschereau, 13 December 1928. Taschereau steered some government business to the bank (to L.-B. Corbeau, 10 octobre, to Omer Lapierre, 30 novembre 1929) and urged other interests to patronize it, but admitted that most big private companies were controlled by men connected with other banks (to R. Bruce, 11 February 1930).

64 *QSY* 1932, 102-5.

65 "Je vous ai payés," *L'Action catholique*, 29 avril 1926. The government contributed $1,000,000 to fund-raising campaigns at Laval and Montreal universities as well as at McGill in 1920, and in 1922 raised annual grants to classical colleges tenfold to $10,000.

66 Vigod, "Taschereau Administration," 355-69.

67 *Le Soleil*, 14 janvier 1928. The other reasons are discussed in chap. 6.

68 Vigod, "Taschereau Administration," 306–16.

69 *CAR* 1921, 654, and 1922, 680–1; *Le Soleil*, 10 juin 1919.

70 King Papers, Taschereau to King, 3 January 1923.

71 Vigod, "Taschereau Administration," 184–8, 214–17.

72 *Montreal Gazette*, 14 October 1927.

73 Quebec, *Report of the Investigation Commission on the Compensation in Labour Accidents* (1925), esp. 10, 16–17, 22–6, 40–69; *CAR* 1925–6, 378–9; CTCC, *Procès-Verbal* 1926, 69–70.

74 *Le Devoir*, 14 septembre 1927; QUA, Walter Mitchell Papers, Taschereau to Mitchell, 25 September 1927.

75 "Premier Taschereau's Outspoken Address," in *Industrial Canada*, November 1927; *CAR* 1927–8, 414–15 and 1929–30, 412–13; Parti libéral, *Le gouvernement Taschereau et la classe ouvrière*. On the social insurance question see below, pp. 152–3, 199–201.

76 *CAR* 1927–8, 421–2.

77 *ANQ*, Travaux Publiques, Félix Marois, "Notes Diverses," 1926; Vigod, "Taschereau Administration," 210–17.

78 *Le Soleil*, 19 mars 1923; *Montreal Gazette*, 14 October 1927.

79 Paul Rainville in *L'Evénement*, 17 octobre 1931; Bovey, *Canadien*, 129–39; R.T.L. [Charles Vining], "Mr. Taschereau," *Maclean's*, 1 February 1934.

80 *La Presse*, 4 décembre 1925; *Le Soleil*, 14 octobre–20 novembre 1926 (citing *Times* [London] and *Le Figaro*).

81 Gouin Papers, Taschereau to Gouin, 25 mars 1926.

82 Taschereau cited in Graham, *And Fortune Fled*, 343; Robert Borden castigated him privately for this and other statements "devised to arouse in the French Canadian people suspicion, distrust and hatred of their English-speaking brethren ... Do you believe that these actions will add lustre to your memory?" PAC, Borden Papers, Borden to Taschereau, 17 November 1925. Sauvé's condition was stated several times publicly but never too clearly (HPQ 27: 140–1, 212) and reaffirmed directly to Meighen after the 1925 federal election (Meighen Papers, Sauvé to Meighen, 26 February 1926). Meighen apologized for the lack of consultation regarding Patenaude (ibid., Meighen to Sauvé, 31 August 1925), but Sauvé still resented the loss (ibid., Sauvé to Meighen, 14 April 1926). On the Patenaude campaign's resemblance to 1911, see Graham, *And Fortune Fled*, 336–8 and 346–51.

83 Meighen Papers, Sauvé to Meighen, 12, 14, 21 April 1926.

84 *HPQ* 29: 19, 86–7.

85 Ibid. 28 and 29 passim; Roby, *Investissements américains*, 145–66.

86 L.-A. Taschereau, *Une réplique au chef de l'opposition*.

87 *CAR* 1926–7, 340–1 and 1927–8, 416–17; *HPQ* 29: 23–5.

88 Ibid., 34-7, 41.

89 Ibid., 41-5.

90 Cited in *Le gouvernement Taschereau* (1927), 25.

91 Ibid., 66-112. Taschereau did move, however, to ensure that no repetition occurred regarding a project in Temiscouata County. *HPQ* 30: 144-5.

92 *Montreal Gazette*, 14 May 1927. For a while this became a standing joke with Taschereau. Praised by Quebec manufacturers later that year for his defence of tariff protection, he couldn't resist alluding to the federal Conservative leadership convention. "Had you said that two days ago, I would probably have run at Winnipeg, and I venture to say that even Mr Meighen would have given me his support." Ibid., 14 October 1927.

93 *Une réplique au chef*, 83; *CAR* 1926-7, 355-6.

94 *CAR* 1926-7, 355-6.

95 *Le Monde ouvrier*, 7, 14 mai 1927.

96 Roby, *Investissements américains*, 167; "Outspoken Address," 48.

## CHAPTER SIX

1 *CAR* 1920, 629.

2 Cited in Quebec, *Report of the Royal Commission Inquiry on Constitutional Problems* (1956), 1: 100 (hereafter cited as *Tremblay Report*).

3 Fitzpatrick Papers, Fitzpatrick to Taschereau, 9 septembre 1922; *Le Soleil*, 19 mars 1923.

4 The one exception, Taschereau's wartime call for national bilingualism (*Le Soleil*, 23 février 1916), would not have affected Quebec, which was already bilingual. He did not hesitate, of course, to pressure Ferguson over Regulation XVII or to denounce other provinces for attacking minority rights (e.g., King Papers, Taschereau to King, 25 July 1930, regarding the Anderson government in Saskatchewan).

5 Roy, *Programmes électoraux* 1: 230.

6 King Papers, Taschereau to King, 22 March, 2 April 1926; Ferguson Papers, Taschereau to Ferguson, 28 September 1927; *CAR* 1926-7, 343.

7 Lapointe Papers, Taschereau to Lapointe, 13 janvier 1927; *CAR* 1926-7, 340. The same point arose in 1931 during final negotiations leading to the Statute of Westminster, when Prime Minister Bennett consented to a change in wording Taschereau desired. Archives of the University of New Brunswick, R.B. Bennett Papers, Minutes of 1931 Federal-Provincial Conference.

8 King Papers, Taschereau to King, 8 June 1927.

9 Ferguson Papers, Ferguson to Taschereau and reply, 2 and 4 August 1927.

10 Oliver, *Ferguson*, 292–8; Ferguson Papers, Ferguson to Taschereau and reply, 21 and 28 September 1927; Legal submission of Messrs Lafleur, Geoffrion, and Tilley, 13 September 1927. At the invitation of Charles Lanctôt this opinion was endorsed by the eminent British jurist Sir John Simon (King Papers, vol. 149).

11 Full text in FLAT, Discours (vol. 23).

12 Lapointe Papers, subject file 24, Minutes of Friday morning, 4 November 1927. The published *Précis of Discussions* is not a complete account. See also King Papers, Memoranda and Notes, file 964, and Neatby, *Lonely Heights*, 233–43.

13 *Précis of Discussions*, 25.

14 Neatby, *Lonely Heights*, 237–8; Oliver, *Ferguson*, 304–5.

15 Neatby, *Lonely Heights*, 219.

16 The federal law had already provoked division between lay and clerical leaders of the CTCC (see *Procès-Verbal*, 1926, 34–5, 60), and as late as 1933 proponents of old age pensions urged only temporary affiliation with Ottawa's scheme, pending the elaboration of a purely Quebec form. Alfred Charpentier, "La question ouvrière," in Ecole sociale populaire, *Le programme de restauration sociale expliqué et commenté*, nos. 239–40 (décembre 1933–janvier 1934). See also Suzanne Morin, "Les débats concernant la loi des pensions de vieillesse" (MA thesis, Université de Montréal, 1981).

17 Lapointe Papers, Minutes of 10 November 1927.

18 *CAR* 1928–9, 387.

19 King Papers, Diary, 9 December 1927 and 15 January 1928.

20 Oliver, *Ferguson*, 352–5; Neatby, *Lonely Heights*, 312–13; *CAR* 1928–9, 137–45; King Papers, King to Taschereau, 25 February 1929; Ferguson Papers, Taschereau to Ferguson, 25 March 1929 and Taschereau to King (copy), 19 February 1930.

21 *HPQ* 29: 158–9, 210; King Papers, Diary, 4 January 1928; *Le Devoir*, 31 janvier 1928; Gouin Papers, Diary 9 janvier 1928.

22 King Papers, Taschereau to King, 2 February 1928, King to Taschereau (confidential), 20 February 1928.

23 Ibid., Taschereau to King, 2 March 1928; Neatby, *Lonely Heights*, 329.

24 King Papers, Taschereau to King, 8 June 1927; *CAR* 1928–9, 386–7.

25 Beaulé cited in *La Vie syndicale*, février 1928; Fortin in *L'Evénement*, 18 janvier 1928.

26 *CAR* 1927–8, 328–9, 414–15; 1928–9, 545; 1929–30, 202, 412–13 (includes references to court decisions favouring the commission's authority).

Roger Chartier, "La loi des réparations des accidents du travail et la commission du salaire minimum des femmes (1925-1931)," *Relations industrielles/Industrial Relations* (janvier 1963).

27 *Le Soleil*, 6 mars 1928; *Le Devoir*, 11 janvier 1929.

28 CTCC, *Procès-Verbal*, 1929, 15-16.

29 *Le Devoir*, 15 janvier 1930.

30 Commission des assurances sociales de Québec, *Rapports* (1932-3). Other members of the commission were Canon F.G. Scott, labour spokesmen Gérard Tremblay (CTCC) and J.T. Foster (Montreal Trades and Labour Council), employer representative G.A. Savoy and the director of Public Assistance and the Provincial Health Service, Dr Alphonse Lessard. The recommendations are summarized in Serge Mongeau, *Evolution de l'assistance au Québec*, 60-2, and are discussed in chap. 7 below.

31 *HPQ* 31: 20; UCC convention resolutions and departmental correspondence, cited in Vigod, "Taschereau Administration," 239-48; Robert Migner, *Quand gronde la révolte verte*, 73, 83-100.

32 *HPQ* 29: 201, and 30: 39-41. On the danger of "politicizing" farm loans, see also Caron's speech to Caisse Populaire organizers, cited in UCC *Rapport* (1926), 171. Regarding the distinction between short and long-term credit, see Firmin Letourneau, *Histoire de l'agriculture*, 319-20.

33 Regarding Taschereau's doubts about the talents of Ouellet and Thériault, see Jean-Guy Genest, "Vie et oeuvre d'Adélard Godbout" (Thèse de D. ès L., Université Laval, 1977), 101, 122. Regarding provincial self-sufficiency as a motivating concern, see *HPQ* 31: 23-24.

34 Manifesto reprinted in Quebec, Department of Agriculture, *Annual Report* 1929, ii-viii.

35 *HPQ* 31: 18-24, 147-54; Migner, *Révolte verte*, 227-35; *Statutes of Quebec*, 20 Geo. v c. 38, 148.

36 FLAT, Caron to Taschereau, 29 novembre, 7 décembre 1929.

37 Quebec, Department of Lands and Forest, *Annual Report* 1927-8, 20. For the earlier warning, ibid. 1926-7, 27.

38 *HPQ* 30: 92-3, 145.

39 Bladen, *Political Economy*, 190-7; Guthrie, *Newsprint*, 95-6, 108-9; Ferguson Papers, Taschereau to Ferguson, 20 August 1928, 28 December 1929, 16 January 1930; *Montreal Gazette*, 12 January 1929.

40 See chap. 7.

41 *CAR* 1923, 611-12; L. Crestohl, *The Jewish School Problem in Montreal*, 1-9; Quebec, *Rapport de la Commission spéciale d'éducation* (1925), 23ff.

42 Crestohl, *School Problem*, 9-14. See also Elson I. Rexford, *The Jewish*

*Population and the Protestant Schools*, passim.

43 Harold Ross, "The Jew in the Educational System of Quebec," (MA thesis, McGill University, 1947), 28–9; Bernard Figler, *Louis Fitch, Q.C. (1889–1956)*, 3–7, 41.

44 *Commission spéciale d'éducation*, passim; *CAR* 1927–8, 427–9.

45 *CAR* 1929–30, 400–1; Gauthier, cited in Dupont, *Relations*, 259–60.

46 *CAR* 1929–30, 401–2; Dupont, *Relations*, 258–66.

47 *Montreal Gazette*, 31 October, 3 November 1930; [Parti libéral], *La question des écoles juives*, 3–5. Even Houde's denials were fraught with equivocation. See *L'Illustration*, 10 décembre 1930, 17 février, 4, 7 avril 1931.

48 Everett C. Hughes, *French Canada in Transition*, chap. 19; Lita-Rose Betcherman, *The Swastika and the Maple Leaf*, 23–5, 32–5; M. Oliver, "Nationalists," 293–4; Anatole Vanier, "Les Juifs au Canada," *L'Action nationale* 2 (septembre 1933); Jacques Brassier [Abbé Groulx] "Pour qu'on vive," *L'Action nationale* 3, 4 (janvier, novembre 1934); André Laurendeau, "Personne n'est hostile: Pourquoi nos rappeler à chaque instant qu'il est Juif?" *Le Magazine Maclean*, février 1963. The bravest and most honourable exception among nationalists was Olivar Asselin, although Henri Bourassa was also persuaded to denounce antisemitism. Honoré Mercier represented the Taschereau government at the anti-Hitler rally of 1933. Montreal was the hotbed of French-Canadian antisemitism, but the clerical press in Quebec was little better. Richard Jones, *L'idéologie de L'Action catholique 1917–1939*, chaps. 3, 11, and Louis Garon, "La Bonne Nouvelle," in Fernand Dumont, Jean Hamelin, and Jean-Paul Montminy, eds., *Idéologies au Canada français 1930–1939*, 251–2.

49 *Le Soleil*, 19 février 1932. For a further account of the debate on Bercovitch's bill, see Betcherman, *Swastika*, 14–19.

50 *Le Devoir*, 11 février 1933. On 12 April, *Le Devoir* celebrated the withdrawal of Taschereau's bill on the same page that it published Jeune Canada's denunciation of French-Canadian politicians who appeared at the anti-Hitler rally. See also Betcherman, *Swastika*, 24–7, 30.

51 *HPQ* 27: 7–8, 29: 212; I. Abella and H. Troper, "'The line must be drawn somewhere': Canada and Jewish Refugees 1933–9," *CHR* 60 (June 1979); L.-P. Audet, "La question des écoles juives 1870–1931," *Royal Society of Canada Transactions* 15 (1970): 113.

52 *Montreal Star*, 17 April 1929.

53 Ibid., 11 March, 3, 16, 17 April 1929, 30 May 1930; André Bernard, "Parliamentary Control of Finances in Quebec" (MA thesis, McGill University, 1965), esp. 232–3; Gouin Papers, Diary, 3 mai 1926; FLAT,

David to Taschereau, 20 septembre 1929; Charles Taschereau, interview 19 November 1976; Lionel Bertrand, *Mémoires* (Montréal 1972), 58; *CAR* 1933, 190.

54 Genest, "Godbout," 101–16.

55 *CAR* 1929–30, 403–4; Bernard, "Finances," 147, 163–4. Regarding McMaster's parliamentary resolution, see *CAR* 1922, 235.

56 Most literature about Houde is anecdotal and uncritically admiring, in both cases quite understandably. Houde was always colourful, his compassion for the unemployed of the 1930s memorable, and his wartime defiance of the federal authority courageous if not prudent. See Hertel LaRoque, *Camillien Houde: Le p'tit gars de Ste-Marie*, Charles Renaud, *L'imprévisible Monsieur Houde*, and Hector Grenon, *Camillien Houde raconté par Hector Grenon*. More analytical, and focused upon this phase of Houde's career, is Robert Migner, "Camillien Houde et le Houdisme 1889–1933" (MA thesis, Université de Montréal, 1971). A published version, written jointly with Robert Lévesque, is marred by simplistic ideological assertions, e.g., p. 137. *Camillien et les années vingt suivi de Camillien au goulag.*

57 *Montreal Star*, 14 and 15 November 1929 (by-elections); *L'Action catholique*, 29 novembre 1929 (Laval); FLAT, Discours (vol. 24), 7 May 1930 (Queen's).

58 Ward, ed., *Power*, 326. See also Gagnon, *Asselin* 2: 232.

59 *HPQ* 34: 131–2. In 1934 there was talk in financial circles of a Bennett-Taschereau "National Government" to lead Canada out of the depression, and when Mackenzie King won the 1935 election Robert Borden urged Taschereau to press for the appointment of a "responsible" finance minister. Partisan wrangles aside, there were few serious conflicts between the Taschereau and Bennett governments; the test case concerning radio broadcasting was initiated under King, and Bennett proved less insistent concerning jurisdiction over electric power development. "Bennett and Taschereau Can Save Canada," *Montreal Star*, 18 December 1934; Borden Papers, Borden to Taschereau, 17 October 1935; FLAT, vol. 18, dossier O ("Radio, 1931").

60 There is surprisingly little published material on Quebec's economy during the depression. For a brief survey, see Jean-Paul Montminy and Jean Hamelin, "La Crise," in Dumont, Hamelin, and Montminy, eds., *Idéologies ... 1930–1939*.

61 Canada, *Report of the Royal Commission on Dominion-Provincial Relations*, bk. 1: 166–7; Stewart Bates, *Financial History of Canadian Governments*, 149, 162–7; Robert Rumilly, *Histoire de Montréal* 4, chap. 13; Esdras Minville, *Labour Legislation and Social Services in the Province of Quebec* (App. v, *Report of the Royal Commission on Dominion-Provincial Relations*), 78–9.

62 Rumilly, *Montreal* 4: 158-9; *Le Devoir*, 10 janvier, 7 novembre 1930.
63 Cf. *L'Evénement*, 3 août, and *Le Devoir*, 4 août 1931.
64 Taschereau's tribute to Gouin in *Le Soleil*, 30 mars 1929; to Turgeon, *Le Soleil*, 14 novembre 1930.
65 E.g., *Montreal Star*, 8 July 1930.
66 Asselin Papers, Asselin to Allan Bray, 27 mai, Germain Beaulieu, 18 juin, J.-M. Savignac, 17 octobre, Antoine Giguère, 2 décembre, and Walter S. Thompson, 30 December 1930. Gagnon, *Asselin* 2: 232-49.
67 PAC, Raoul Dandurand Papers, Dandurand to Taschereau, 17 janvier 1929; Ward, ed., *Power*, 313; Neatby, *Lonely Heights*, 340.
68 FLAT, Lapointe to Taschereau, 17 avril 1931, and King to Taschereau, 1 July 1931; Ward, ed., *Power*, 275 (citing Power memo to King, 10 February 1931).
69 Ward, ed., *Power*, 315-18.
70 Ibid., 312-27.
71 *Le Devoir*, 4, 12 août 1931.
72 Bennett Papers, Alfred Mousseau to Bennett, 9 September, Dr Louis Fiset to Bennett, 30 September, and Roméo Langlais to Arthur Sauvé, 19 septembre 1931.
73 *CAR* 1931-2, 165-70; Ward, ed., *Power* 323; *Montreal Gazette*, 14 and 21 August 1931; *Le Devoir*, 14 août 1931; Bennett Papers, Victor Drury to Bennett, 20 August 1931 (still predicting a Conservative victory).
74 "Evidence and Report of the Special Committee on the Beauharnois Power Project," *Journals of the House of Commons*, 1931; Neatby *Lonely Heights*, 369-80. While there was (and is) no evidence to support Conservative accusations that the Beauharnois Corporation "bought" his support in 1928, Taschereau did issue one explicit denial (*Le Devoir*, 11 août 1931). His requests that King speed up the process of federal approval contain no hint of corruption, only genuine concern about the technical and financial problems created by further delay. King Papers, Taschereau to King, 18 December 1928, 4 June 1929. See also FLAT, Taschereau to Mercier, 6 septembre 1929, expressing impatience with provincial technical advisers. Regarding Holt, cf. King Papers, Diary, 12 September 1929 and FLAT, Sweezey to Taschereau, 20 July 1929.
75 Ward, ed., *Power*, 323-5; QUA, C.G. Power Papers, Power to Mackenzie King, 27 August 1931; *Le Devoir*, 4 août 1931. On Liberal organizational strength in Montreal, see J.A. Lovink, "The Politics of Quebec: Provincial Political Parties 1897-1936," (PHD thesis, Duke University, 1967), 180-1, and letters acknowledging Asselin's journalistic assault on Houde's credibility, e.g., Collection Asselin, Pierre

Casgrain to Asselin, 26 août 1931.

76 Bovey, *Canadien*, 131.

77 For electoral data see Cliche, "Elections provinciales," and Hamelin, Letarte, and Hamelin "Elections provinciales," 39, 42. Regarding Duplessis see Ward, ed., *Power*, 326.

## CHAPTER SEVEN

1 Ward, ed., *Power*, 329–30.

2 FLAT, Lapointe to Taschereau, 2 octobre 1934.

3 Ward, ed., *Power*, 131; FLAT, H.G. Carroll to Taschereau 18 décembre 1931.

4 Judgments dismissing early Conservative appeals in FLAT, vol. 17, dossier f. Duplessis cited in *Le Canada*, 3 octobre 1931; *L'Evénement*, 11 novembre 1931.

5 *Le Devoir*, 6 novembre 1931.

6 As claimed in Antonin Dupont, "Louis-Alexandre Taschereau, Camillien Houde et l'évolution politique du Québec de 1923 à 1936," paper delivered at the Canadian Historical Association's annual meeting, Kingston, 1973.

7 Echlin, "Success."

8 *Montreal Gazette*, 31 October 1932; *Le Soleil*, 10 mars 1933, 20 janvier 1934 (proposing a separate federal-provincial relief commission for each province); *HPQ* 33: 74, 135, 144, 177–80, 219. See also James Struthers, *No Fault of Their Own: Unemployment and the Canadian Welfare State 1914–1941*, 90–1, 104–41.

9 *Montreal Gazette*, 16 October, 23 November 1931; Robert Rumilly, *La plus riche aumône: Histoire de la Societé Saint-Vincent-de-Paul au Canada*, 159.

10 *Montreal Star*, 30 August, *L'Action catholique*, 18 septembre 1933; *HPQ* 33: 13.

11 *La Presse*, 15 septembre 1931; Bennett Papers, letter from Quebec (Conservative) caucus to Bennett, 15 September 1931.

12 *Montreal Gazette*, 18 September 1931; PAC Department of Labour, Unemployment Relief Branch, vols. 52–4 contain memoranda of agreement on bipartisan distribution (27 November 1931) and the texts of formal relief agreements (e.g., Quebec Land Settlement Agreement, 16 July 1932).

13 *HPQ* 33: 68–71, 121–3, 180–1; 34: 59–60, 80. On the evolution of relief administration, see Minville, *Labour Legislation*, 74–87.

14 *HPQ* 33: 38–41, 170, 208; Quebec, Department of Municipal Affairs, *Annual Reports* 1933–5.

15 *HPQ* 33: 69, 150–1.

16  Ibid. 33: 41–2, 51, 68, 207; Rumilly, *Montréal* 4, chaps. 14–15.

17  *HPQ* 33: 176, 207–8; 34: 22–3, 34; Minville, *Labour Legislation*, 79–80; Bennett Papers, W.H. Clark to Bennett, 9 March 1934; Rumilly, *Montréal* 4: 203, 208.

18  *HPQ* 34: 34–7, 53–4, 81–4; Rumilly, *Montréal* 4: 207–10, 213–17, 225–9, 252–3.

19  *Le Soleil*, 12 janvier 1934.

20  *HPQ* 33: 116–17.

21  FLAT, Taschereau to Vautrin, 8 mai 1933. See also *Montreal Gazette*, 31 October 1932.

22  *Le Devoir*, 6 juin 1933; *HPQ* 33: 177–8.

23  *HPQ* 33: 224–5.

24  Ibid. 34: 58.

25  *Le Soleil*, 9 août 1934.

26  Ibid., 17 octobre 1934. Opposition scepticism cited in *HPQ* 34: 96–7.

27  *Montreal Star*, 19 November 1934; Bennett Papers, Vautrin to Bennett, 20 November, Vautrin to Gordon, 5 and 20 December, Onésime Gagnon to Vautrin (copies to Bennett and Gordon) 12 décembre 1934, Bennett to Gagnon, 8 January, Gordon to Bennett, 19 January 1935.

28  *Financial Post*, 23 April 1931.

29  *Montreal Herald*, 10 April 1933; Bladen, *Political Economy*, 177.

30  Graustein testimony before U.S. Federal Trade Commission, cited in Bladen, *Political Economy*, 174–5.

31  FLAT, vol. 15, dossier d. See especially G.-C. Piché to Taschereau 24 mars, Taschereau to Alexander Smith, 1 April, J.B. White to Taschereau, 9 June, Rév. J.-V. Boucher to Taschereau, 16 octobre 1931.

32  Fitzpatrick Papers, vol. 91. See especially Taschereau's correspondence with Fitzpatrick and with the general manager, J.A. Hanrahan.

33  On the performance of Price Brothers in Bankruptcy, see FLAT, Honoré Mercier to Taschereau, 22 novembre 1934, Louis St Laurent to Mercier, 21 décembre 1934, Charles Vining to Taschereau, 28 June 1935, Taschereau to Price Brothers, 7 August 1935, Ouvriers de Riverbend to Taschereau, 10 septembre 1935, Taschereau to St Laurent, 18 novembre 1935, and John Price to Taschereau, 20 May 1936. On Taschereau's doubts about American corporations, see L. Ethan Ellis, *Print Paper Pendulum: Group Pressures and the Price of Newsprint*, 148; Fitzpatrick Papers, Taschereau to Rothermere, 4 March 1932 and D.E.. White to R.A. McInnis, 3 July 1934; FLAT, Vining to Taschereau and reply, 30–31 July 1935, and Taschereau to A. Geoffrion, 23 avril 1936. On the reorganization of Price Brothers, see *HPQ* 33: 168–70, and 34: 93–4; Guthrie, *Newsprint*, 68–9; FLAT, J.-E. Grégoire to Taschereau, 30 mai 1933, Fitzpatrick to Taschereau, 8 February and 5 August 1935, Taschereau to Fitzpatrick, 23 janvier, 6 février, and

12 août 1935, P.B. Ross to Taschereau, 25 May and 4 June 1935, Taschereau to Gordon Scott, 25 March 1936, E.C. Dean and H.J. Symington to Taschereau, both 17 April 1936.

34 Ferguson Papers, Taschereau to Ferguson, 28 December 1929, 11 and 16 January 1930; Bladen, *Political Economy*, 197–8; Eugene Forsey "The Pulp and Paper Industry," *CJEPS* 1 (August 1935).

35 FLAT, vol. 19, dossier a, Procès-Verbal, 19 décembre 1934. See also the preamble to the eventual Forest Resources Protection Act (*Statutes*, 25-6 Geo. v c. 22), H.V. Nelles, *The Politics of Development: Forest, Mines and Hydro-electric Power in Ontario 1849–1941*, 452–3, and Gustave Piché's recollections (FLAT, Piché to Taschereau, 12 avril 1940).

36 Bladen, *Political Economy*, 176; Ellis, *Pendulum*, 164–5; Fitzpatrick Papers, Taschereau to Fitzpatrick telegram, 20 November 1934.

37 FLAT, Procès-Verbal, 19 décembre 1934.

38 Hepburn cited in René Durocher, "Taschereau, Hepburn et les relations Québec-Ontario 1934–1936," *RHAF* 24 (décembre 1970): 344.

39 FLAT, Procès-Verbal, 19 décembre 1934. See also Vining's *Newsprint Prorating: An Account of Government Policy in Quebec and Ontario*. Evidently Vining tried to reassure producers that both pro-rating and legislation were temporary expedients rather than a permanent solution to the problem of excess capacity. FLAT, Vining to Taschereau, 21 February 1935, with copy of memorandum presented to manufacturers.

40 FLAT, vol. 19, memoranda (apparently from Vining), 26 January and 4 March, Vining to Taschereau 7 June, G. Piché to Taschereau 7 février, Taschereau to Hepburn 12 and 23 March, Hepburn to Taschereau 18 March and 2 April, William L. McLean Jr to Gordon Scott, 30 March 1935; Nelles, *Development*, 452–5; Durocher, "Hepburn," 346–7, 351.

41 Nelles, *Development*, 455–66; Bladen, *Political Economy*, 199–200, Carl Wiegman, *Trees to News*, 116–18, 156–60.

42 Fitzpatrick Papers, R.-A. Benoît to Fitzpatrick, 26 June 1933.

43 R.T.L. [Vining], "Mr. Taschereau."

44 Echlin, "Success."

45 Canada, *Proceedings and Evidence of the Special Committee on Price Spreads and Mass Buying* (1934).

46 J.R.H. Wilbur, ed., *The Bennett New Deal: Fraud or Portent?*, pts. 3–6.

47 Levitt, *Golden Calf*, passim; *HPQ* 24: 79–80; Roby, *Investissements américains*, passim.

48 Philippe Hamel, "Le trust de l'électricité: Source de corruption et de domination" (mimeographed ms., 1934).

49 Patricia Dirks, "Dr. Philippe Hamel and the Public Power Movement

in Quebec City, 1929–1934: The Failure of a Crusade," paper presented at the Canadian Historical Association's annual meeting, 1979; Roy, *Programmes électoraux* 2: 246. Taschereau received transcripts of Hamel's radio speeches during the last week of the campaign. FLAT, vol. 17, dossier f.

50 FLAT, Charles-Edmond to Louis-Alexandre Taschereau, 2 janvier 1932.

51 *CAR* 1932, 173–4.

52 *Le Devoir*, 29 mars 1927, 21 septembre, 2 novembre 1935; *Montreal Gazette*, 11 January 1935.

53 Regarding North American Life, for example, see FLAT, W.B. Taylor to Taschereau, 2 November 1927, Taschereau to Taylor, 31 December 1928, and Taschereau to D.E. Kilgour, 8 January 1940. On other companies, see vol. 32.

54 R.T.L., "Mr. Taschereau."

55 Bovey, *Canadien*, 130.

56 John A. Price, interview, 12 June 1972.

57 FLAT, Mercier to Taschereau, 9 octobre, 22 novembre 1934. Gérald Tremblay, the deputy minister of labour, also had to counteract businessmen's appeals for exemptions. Ibid., Tremblay to Taschereau, 13 novembre, 16 décembre 1935.

58 Ibid., vol. 20, Speech at Shawinigan Falls, 14 September 1922.

59 Ibid., Julian Smith to Taschereau, 7 August 1935; Taschereau to J.-C. Harvey, 19 mars 1932; Taschereau to J.-H.-A. Piché, 20 juin 1932.

60 Charles Taschereau, interview, 19 November 1976; FLAT, Taschereau to Smith, 15 August 1935.

61 *L'Action catholique*, 4, 7 février, 17 mars 1933.

62 Dirks, "Philippe Hamel," 16–24; *CAR* 1934, 203–11.

63 *CAR* 1933, 184.

64 *Le Programme de Restauration Sociale expliqué et commenté.*

65 *CAR* 1933, 189.

66 Patricia Dirks, "The Origins of the Union Nationale" (PHD thesis, University of Toronto, 1974), 222–4, 226, 240.

67 FLAT, Bouchard to Taschereau, 25 mars 1935 (cited at length below).

68 Ibid., Drouin to Taschereau, 15 février 1932 (with draft of Taschereau's reply on back).

69 Ibid., Taschereau to Villeneuve, 22 and 30 avril 1932.

70 *Le Devoir*, 28 juillet 1934.

71 See Taschereau's endorsement of an editorial in *Financial Counsel* in Lapointe Papers, Taschereau to Lapointe, 31 août 1934.

72 FLAT, Carroll to Taschereau, 24 juillet, 6 août 1934.

73 Hon. Hugues Lapointe, interview, 1 November, 1976.

74 FLAT, Taschereau to Lapointe, 23 août (2 letters), 29 août, 24 septembre (2 letters) 1934.

75 *Le Devoir*, 20 novembre 1934.

76 Jean Provencher, "Joseph-Ernest Grégoire: 4 années de vie politique" (MA thesis, Université Laval, 1969), 35-49.

77 ANQ, Fonds T.-D. Bouchard, Bouchard to Lapointe, 22 décembre 1934. (Dossier also contains Shawinigan Power's submission to the commission.) Bouchard's claim that he had always been fighting for a principle, and not against Taschereau personally or politically, is substantiated by letters he wrote to Hamel in the summer of 1934. Cited in Dirks, "Philippe Hamel," 26.

78 Quebec, *Rapport de la Commission de l'électricité de la Province de Québec au premier ministre de la province, 21 janvier, 1935* (1935).

79 FLAT, Bouchard to Taschereau, 28 mars 1935. See also Bouchard to Nicol, 31 janvier 1935 (unsigned copy).

80 *Statutes of Quebec*, 25-26 Geo. v c. 23, 24, 49.

81 "He'll be named a legislative councillor one day," commented Taschereau sarcastically, "though I don't know by which party." Cited in Robert Rumilly, *Maurice Duplessis et son temps* 1: 180.

82 Commission des assurances sociales de Québec, *Rapports*, 3, 5, 6 (mars, novembre, décembre 1932).

83 "Avant Propos" and L. Chagnon, "Directives sociales catholiques," in Ecole sociale populaire, *Le programme de restauration sociale*, nos. 232-3, (mai-juin 1933).

84 Conservative platform summarized in Black, *Duplessis*, 65-6; ALN platform in *Le Devoir*, 28 juillet 1934.

85 *Statutes of Quebec*, 23 Geo. v c. 2, 76.

86 *Le Devoir*, 13 janvier 1933.

87 FLAT, Taschereau to Père Henri Roy, 17 novembre, and Père Alexandre Dugré, 24 novembre 1933.

88 *L'Action catholique*, 28 avril 1933.

89 Echlin, "Success."

90 Dirks, "Union Nationale," 226-85; Black, *Duplessis*, 72-6; HPQ 24: 86-7.

91 *L'Evénement*, 16 janvier 1933; *Le Devoir*, 14 novembre 1933.

92 See Fred Monk's declaration as late as 12 juillet 1934 (*Le Soleil*).

93 Dirks, "Union Nationale," 268.

94 Ward, ed., *Power*, 332-3; Power Papers, Power to Lapointe, 17 August 1934. Power's report may well have influenced Lapointe to accept the chairmanship of the Electricity Commission - as a gesture of good faith.

95 Ward, ed., *Power*, 333; FLAT, Valentine to Lapointe (copy), 16 mars 1935.

96 FLAT, Nicol to Taschereau, 7 mai, 18 juillet 1934.

97 Ibid., Asselin to Taschereau, 15 janvier, 12 février, Taschereau to Asselin, 10 février 1934.

98 Ibid., Valentine to Taschereau, 27 novembre, to J.-H. Gaudreault, 5 décembre 1934.

99 *La Presse*, 22 septembre 1934.

100 Dirks, "Union Nationale," 290.

101 PAC, Paul Gouin Papers, Horace Philippon to Gouin, 16 mai 1935, Seraphin Vachon to Gouin, 20 juillet 1934. In January 1935, a Taschereau spy assured him that the ALN would have Lapointe's sympathy, but no public or organizational support. FLAT, vol. 35, "Notes confidentielles."

102 FLAT, Taschereau to Mercier, 30 novembre, Mercier to Taschereau, 13 décembre 1934.

103 *HPQ* 33: 149-50, 208, 212.

104 Gouin was aware that Taschereau considered his career aspirations "unworthy," but complained that the argument was not used to his face. Taschereau did express his regret at the refusal of a judgeship. Paul Gouin Papers, Gouin to Mercier, 10 septembre 1930, Taschereau to Gouin, 9 décembre 1931; *HPQ* 33: 136-7, 198.

105 FLAT, Taschereau to Claude Robillard, 20 mai 1933.

106 *Le Devoir*, 14 novembre 1933.

107 Ibid.

108 FLAT, Taschereau to Père Alexandre Dugré, 20 novembre 1933; *HPQ* 33: 213.

109 FLAT, Taschereau to Archbishop Villeneuve, 22 avril, 24 septembre 1932; Taschereau to Mgr E.-C. Laflamme, 27 janvier 1932; *HPQ* 33: 100. Hamel's personal hostility to Taschereau confirmed in Paul Gouin Papers, Hamel to Gouin, 26 mai, 27 juillet, 9 septembre 1935.

110 FLAT, Taschereau to Père Henri Roy, 17 novembre 1933.

111 Paul Gouin papers, Archambault to Gouin, 28 septembre 1933.

112 Dandurand Papers, Dandurand to Taschereau, 19 septembre 1927, 17 janvier 1929; PAC, Escott Reid Papers, interviews, C.G. Power, 157; H.B. Neatby, *William Lyon MacKenzie King*, vol. 3, *The Prism of Unity*, 90. Taschereau in fact played the same game as his federal counterparts, declining to criticize the New Deal directly, but encouraging his son to move a resolution objecting to encroachments on provincial autonomy. FLAT, Robert to L.-A. Taschereau and reply, 11, 12 février 1935.

113 FLAT, Vautrin to Taschereau, 27 décembre 1934.

114 L.-A. David, *En marge de la politique*; André and Charles Taschereau, interviews, 26 October, 19 November 1976; *CAR* 1933, 190; FLAT, David to Taschereau, 16 novembre 1933.

115 Cited in *HPQ* 33: 214.
116 Bibliothèque de l'Université de Sherbrooke, Fonds Jean-Charles Harvey, "Memoirs" (ms.), chap. 3, p. 1; Paul Gouin Papers, Harvey to Gouin, 16 juillet 1936 (recalling earlier conversation).
117 *Mémoires* 3: 106–7.
118 Neatby, *Prism of Unity*, 232–3.
119 Even in retrospect the substance of reform proposals remained obscured by distrust of the proponents. The classic example is Pierre-Elliott Trudeau. "Québec au moment de la grève," in Trudeau, ed., *La grève de l'amiante* (Montréal 1956).

## CHAPTER EIGHT

1 *Le Devoir*, 4 mars 1935.
2 Ward, ed., *Power*, 335.
3 Paul Gouin Papers, "Notes sur sa carrière 1930–1935," vol. 46, dossier 19, 17–19; Gouin to Hamel, 27 mars 1935. Bouchard apparently received an ALN delegation at his home in August 1934 (*HPQ* 34: 62), but Taschereau's ALN spy later assured him that Bouchard would not join the rebels (FLAT, vol. 35, "Notes confidentielles," 24 janvier 1935).
4 Economic data drawn from *QSY* 1936, 309, 338–43 and 1937, 276–9, 364–9, 404, 406, 423, 436, 442.
5 FLAT, Vining to Taschereau, 27 July, 13 August 1935.
6 Ibid., Mercier to Taschereau, 9 octobre, 22 novembre 1934.
7 *Labour Gazette*, January 1936, 169–70.
8 FLAT, Nicol to Taschereau, 25 juin 1935.
9 *L'Evénement*, 9 septembre 1935.
10 *Le Devoir*, 14 septembre 1935.
11 Ibid., 24 septembre, 8 octobre 1935; *Montreal Star*, 8 October 1935.
12 *Le Devoir*, 30 septembre, 7, 9, 14 octobre 1935. The text of Taschereau's radio message is in FLAT, Discours (vol. 26), 8 October 1935.
13 *Le Devoir*, 21 septembre 1935. Taschereau showed supporters his actual correspondence with federal officials regarding prosecution of coal companies under anti-combines legislation.
14 *Le Devoir* and *Montreal Star*, 15 octobre 1935.
15 *Le Devoir*, 15 octobre 1935.
16 Ibid., 18 octobre 1935; Dirks, "Union Nationale," 291–2.
17 17 October 1935.
18 *Le Devoir*, 23–29 octobre 1935.
19 Ibid., 17 octobre 1935.
20 Ibid., 19, 22 octobre, *Le Soleil*, 30 octobre 1935.
21 *Le Devoir*, *Montreal Star*, 2 novembre 1935.

22  Ibid.

23  *Montreal Star*, 5 November 1935.

24  Ibid., 6 November 1935.

25  Black, *Duplessis*, 99–100.

26  *Le Canada*, 7 novembre 1935.

27  See above, pp. 166, 170.

28  FLAT, Taschereau to Villeneuve, 14 mars 1935.

29  Paul Gouin Papers, Hamel to Gouin and reply, 26, 31 mai 1935.

30  "Le devoir électoral," 26 juillet 1935, *Mandements ... des évêques* 14: 431–9.

31  Regarding campaign activities of individual priests, see below, pp. 221–2 and notes 53, 56, and 58.

32  *Le Devoir*, 8 novembre 1935.

33  Ernest Lapointe's promise of support in FLAT, Lapointe to Taschereau, 24 octobre 1935.

34  *Le Devoir*, *Montreal Star*, 8–14 novembre 1935.

35  *Montreal Star*, 20 November, *Le Soleil*, 21 novembre 1935.

36  *L'Action catholique*, 22 novembre 1935; affidavit of witness to Lavergne speech in FLAT, Taschereau to Villeneuve, 26 décembre 1935 (dossier, pièce g); Lavergne sermon, 17 novembre 1935, in ibid., vol. 16; *Montreal Star*, 19, 23 November 1935.

37  FLAT, L.-M. Gouin to Taschereau, 6 novembre 1935.

38  *Montreal Star*, 21, 23 November; FLAT, Taschereau to Mgr Camille Roy, 21 novembre, Roy to Taschereau, 22 novembre, Nil Gosselin to Taschereau, 28 novembre 1935, Taschereau to Villeneuve, 3 janvier 1936; ASQ, Journal du Séminaire, vol. 13, 17–22 novembre 1935; Dupont, *Relations*, 321.

39  *Le Soleil*, 20 novembre 1935.

40  *Le Devoir*, 23 novembre 1935.

41  *Montreal Star*, 19 November 1935.

42  Power Papers, unpublished chapter of memoirs entitled "Church and State."

43  FLAT, Taschereau to Villeneuve, 23 janvier 1935.

44  Ibid., Villeneuve to Taschereau, 25 janvier 1935.

45  Ibid., Anon. to Taschereau, 4 décembre 1935.

46  *Montreal Star*, 26 November 1935.

47  Rumilly, *Duplessis* 1: 205.

48  *Le Devoir*, 29 novembre 1935.

49  *Montreal Star*, 26 November 1935.

50  Ibid., 2 December 1935.

51  *Le Devoir*, 29 novembre 1935, faithfully reproduced in Rumilly, *Duplessis* 1: 205. *Le Devoir*'s own appeal to antisemitism appeared 26–27 novembre 1935.

52 Rumilly, *Duplessis* 1: 207.

53 *Le Soleil*, 8 novembre 1935.

54 Dirks, "Union Nationale," 236–7, 244–5, 271–2.

55 *Le Devoir*, 3, 10, 12, 19 décembre 1935; *Montreal Star*, 19 February 1936.

56 *Montreal Star*, 26 November 1935.

57 Ibid., 3 December 1935.

58 Dominion-Provincial Conference 1935, *Record of Proceedings*, 11; *Montreal Star*, 9 and 14 December 1935.

59 *Montreal Star*, 2 January 1936.

60 Durocher, "Hepburn," 347–52; FLAT, Taschereau to H. Nixon, 21 November, J.L. Ralston to Taschereau, 16, 26 November 1935.

61 *Montreal Star*, 6 January 1936.

62 FLAT, Taschereau to Villeneuve, 23 janvier 1935.

63 *Le Devoir*, 27 novembre 1935.

64 *Le Soleil*, 6 décembre 1935.

65 FLAT, Emile Moreau to Taschereau, 9 décembre, Edgar Rochette to Taschereau, 17 décembre, Hector Perrier to Taschereau, 18 décembre 1935.

66 Rumilly, *Duplessis* 1: 210.

67 FLAT, Taschereau to Villeneuve, 9 janvier 1936.

68 Ibid., 26 décembre 1935, 3 janvier 1936. See also Taschereau to Mgr Deschamps, 24 décembre 1935, regarding clerical intervention in Montreal.

69 Ibid., Villeneuve to Taschereau, 28 décembre 1935 and 7 janvier 1936.

70 Ibid., Taschereau to Villeneuve, 9 and 15 janvier 1936.

71 "Lettre pastorale touchant certains faits publics survenus pendant la dernière période électorale," 18 janvier 1936, *Mandements ... des évêques* 15: 21–38, indicates this process had already begun.

72 FLAT, Villeneuve to Taschereau, 24 janvier 1936.

73 Ibid., Taschereau to A. Dugré, 27 janvier, 1936.

74 Ibid., copy of bishop's letter dated 11 février 1936. Original in *Mandements ... des évêques* 15: 57–65. Grégoire charged and Taschereau denied that he had leaked it. *Le Devoir*, 19 mars 1936.

75 FLAT, Perrier to Taschereau, 9 février 1936.

76 King Papers, Diary, 19 December 1935; Lapointe Papers, H.R. Renault to Lapointe, 4 décembre, Georges Parent to Lapointe, 9 décembre, Lapointe to J.B. Archambault, 10 décembre 1935.

77 King Papers, Diary, 26 November 1935; Neatby, *Prism of Unity*, 152.

78 King Papers, Diary, 9 December 1935.

79 Ward, ed., *Power*, 337–40.

80 King Papers, Diary, 12 and 19 December 1935.

81 Paul Gouin Papers, Drouin to Gouin, 18, 19 décembre, Gouin to Lacroix, 26 décembre 1935.

82 *Montreal Star*, 13, 25 January, 6, 8, 29 February 1936; *Montreal Gazette*, 5 March 1936; Joseph Couture, interview, 28 October 1976.

83 Dirks, "Union Nationale," 357-69.

84 Provencher, "Grégoire," 82-3.

85 *Montreal Star*, 18, 21, 29 January, 3-4, 18 February 1936.

86 Ibid., 19 February 1936. The alternative, for Mercier to replace Taschereau and call new elections immediately, was discussed frankly by Liberal strategists on 5 February but apparently rejected. Ibid., 6, 8 February 1935. See also Taschereau's subsequent statement to the new legislature, *La Presse*, 27 mars 1936.

87 Ibid., 20, 22, 29 February; 3 March 1936.

88 FLAT, Correspondance générale.

89 Ibid., Taschereau to Dunning and reply, 13 and 16 March 1936.

90 Genest, "Godbout," 190-1; Black, *Duplessis*, 111.

91 *Montreal Star*, 4 and 12 March 1936.

92 FLAT, vol. 17, dossier i (Institut de Montréal, 1936).

93 *Montreal Star*, 21 and 22 February 1936.

94 Judging by the tone of Taschereau's considerable correspondence with Rochette during 1935, this was the appointment he was happiest to make.

95 Rumilly, *Duplessis* 1: 215-16.

96 *La Presse*, 27 mars 1936. Black's translation, "before the session is over, to reunite all the Liberal legislators" (*Duplessis*, 113), is misleading; the passage reads: "Nous voulons, lorsque la session sera finie, à réunir tous les deputés libéraux ..."

97 Black, *Duplessis*, 113-17.

98 Provencher, "Grégoire," 95-7; Hon. Hugues Lapointe, interview, 1 November 1976.

99 Rumilly, *Duplessis* 1: 223.

100 Lapointe Papers, Taschereau to Lapointe, 2 juin 1936.

101 Black, *Duplessis*, 118-21.

102 Throughout the "Public Accounts scandal" Edmond Taschereau himself was never accused of any wrongdoing or even impropriety. Yet several witnesses who were close to the family insist that, through directors' and notarial fees, Edmond enjoyed a much higher income than any other relative or friend of the premier. Only Antoine Rivard (interview, 2 November 1976) agreed to be quoted.

103 Black, *Duplessis*, 118-27; Rumilly, *Duplessis* 1: 237-9. Typewritten transcripts of Antoine's testimony, and even an English translation, were circulated by Duplessis' followers.

104  FLAT, Richard to Taschereau, 26 février 1936.

105  Ibid., Vezina to R.F. Stockwell, 30 September 1933, and several to Taschereau, 30 mai 1932–16 décembre 1935.

106  Ibid., vol. 33 (letter composed by Alexandre which Antoine balked at signing), 2 décembre 1936; Antoine Rivard, interview, 2 November 1976.

107  Rumilly, *Duplessis* 1: 238; Joseph Couture, interview, 28 October 1976.

108  Rumilly, *Duplessis* 1: 240; Black, *Duplessis*, 127–8; both apparently misquoting Chubby Power. Ward, ed., *Power*, 341.

109  *Le Devoir*, 10 juin 1936.

110  Genest, "Godbout," 200–1; Bouchard, *Mémoires* 3: 106; Alexandre Larue, interview, 28 octobre 1976.

## CONCLUSION

1  Echlin, "Success."

2  FLAT, B. Bissonnette to Taschereau, 11 avril 1940; Taschereau to A. Godbout, 8 janvier 1940; Edouard Tellier to Taschereau, 9 décembre 1939; R.F. Smith to Taschereau, 22 April 1940; R.P. Jellett to Taschereau, 11 January 1940; Taschereau to J.A. Matheson, 20 February and 5 March 1941; vol. 35, three folders concerning Crédit Foncier; Taschereau to N.J. Dawes, 28 February 1940, and to F. Clarke, 8 November 1940. Fragmentary evidence suggests that Taschereau's income in retirement fluctuated widely, averaging about $26,000 (gross) during the war years.

3  *La Nouvelle Abeille* 5 (novembre 1948) and 7 (novembre–décembre 1950).

4  Cited in Black, *Duplessis*, 666.

5  Ibid., 151, 178, 192, 666; FLAT, Lanctôt to Taschereau, 6 octobre 1939; M. Girouard to Taschereau, 11 janvier 1940; Robert to Alexandre, 23 janvier 1940; Alexandre to Antoine, 4 novembre 1939.

6  Gabrielle Fages, Charles Taschereau, Jean-Paul Galipeault, Hugues Lapointe, interviews; PAC, L.S. St Laurent Papers, A. Galipeault to St Laurent, 18 novembre 1950; FLAT, David to Taschereau, 12 février 1940.

7  FLAT, Godbout to Taschereau, 26 juin 1936; Césaire Gervais to Taschereau, 10 juillet 1936.

8  King Papers, King to Taschereau, 17 July, and Taschereau to King, 20 July 1936.

9  Ibid., Taschereau to King, 13 January, and King to Taschereau, 5 February 1937; *Le Soleil*, 20 février and 26 octobre 1939; FLAT, vol. 14, dossier d, Ralston to Taschereau, 20 December 1939; St Laurent Papers, Antonin Galipeault to St Laurent, 18 novembre 1950; Hugues

Lapointe, interview, 1 November 1976. The federal cabinet appointment is reported in Thomson, *St. Laurent*, 8.

10 FLAT, David to Taschereau, 19 and 23 mai 1938 (with copy of David's letter to King). In case the "clinging to office" myth had been passed on as truth to St Laurent, Taschereau wrote to dispel it on 2 mars 1944.

11 Ibid., St Laurent to Taschereau, 4 mars 1944.

12 King Papers, Diary, 11 June 1936.

13 FLAT, Taschereau to King, 7 January 1939; St Laurent Papers, David, 3 mai 1949, A. Sévigny, 11 novembre 1950, and Galipeault, 18 novembre 1950, to St Laurent.

14 FLAT, Taschereau to Rumilly, 14 janvier 1948.

15 *L'Evénement*, 2, 4 avril 1949.

16 Ibid., 26 avril 1949.

17 Roby, *Investissements américains*, 188.

18 *L'Evénement*, 27 avril 1949.

19 *Le Soleil*, 5 mars 1947.

20 Union Nationale, *Le Catéchisme des Electeurs* (Montréal 1936); Black, *Duplessis*, 178, 192.

21 René Chaloult, *Mémoires politiques*, 292.

22 Jean-Charles Falardeau, "Etienne Parent," *Dictionary of Canadian Biography* 11: 584–6; Jacques Monet, *The Last Cannon Shot* (Toronto 1969), 126–8; Jean-Guy Genest, "La Lanterne 1868–1869," and Yves-F. Zoltvany, "Laurent-Olivier David et l'infériorité économique des Canadiens français," in F. Dumont et al., eds., *Idéologies au Canada français 1850–1900*, Etienne Parent, "Industry as a means of survival for the French Canadian nationality," and Errol Bouchette, "Economic development in the Province of Quebec," in Ramsay Cook, ed., *French Canadian Nationalism: An Anthology*.

23 Cf. Martin O'Connell, "The ideas of Henri Bourassa," *CJEPS* 19 (August 1953), and Levitt, *Golden Calf*, esp. vii.

24 *Statutes of Quebec*, 24 Geo. v c. 56; J.E. Keith, "The Fascist Province," *Canadian Forum* (March 1934). A fair assessment of the act in its real context is L.C. Marsh, "The Arcand Act: A New Form of Labour Legislation?" *CJEPS* 2 (August 1936).

25 This is the principal theme developed in Jean-Louis Roy, *La marche des Québécois: Le temps des ruptures, 1945–1960*.

26 The modernization model is convincingly applied in K. McRoberts and D. Posgate, *Quebec: Social Change and Political Crisis* (see esp. chap. 5).

27 Black, *Duplessis*, 688.

28 The classic cases are the ouster of Archbishop Charbonneau and pressure on Laval University authorities to control Père Georges-Henri

Lévesque. See Black, *Duplessis*, 428–34 and Roger Lemelin, "The Silent Struggle at Laval," *Maclean's*, 1 August 1952.

29  Black, *Duplessis*, 694.

30  Irving Abella and Harold Troper, *None is Too Many: Canada and the Jews of Europe* (Toronto 1982), 18, 22–3, 41–2, 50; J.L. Granatstein, "King and His Cabinet: The War Years," in John English and J.O. Stubbs, eds., *Mackenzie King: Widening the Debate* (Toronto 1978), 176.

31  Roy, *La marche des Québécois*, Conclusion; McRoberts and Posgate, *Social Change*, 77–9, 91–2.

32  The style is amusingly recalled in Pierre Laporte, *Le vrai visage de Duplessis*, chap. 7; see also Roy, *La marche des Québécois*, 182–3.

33  G. Dion and L. O'Neill, *Le chrétien et les élections* (Montréal 1960).

34  Quinn, *Union Nationale*, chap. 8.

# Bibliography

The bibliography is designed to complement the discussion of sources and of historiography in the Preface and Conclusion. It includes all primary sources consulted, except for those newspapers examined on a single occasion only. Some contemporaneous articles by and about Louis-Alexandre Taschereau are listed as secondary literature. The list of persons interviewed states their relationship to Taschereau and/or their position during his premiership. The secondary literature includes all works cited or consulted for the period of Taschereau's active political career (1900–36). The list is of necessity more select for the earlier and later phases of his life. Not included are those works bearing directly upon the subject which have appeared since the study was accepted for publication; none of these, however, would have had the effect of altering the interpretation.

## PRIMARY SOURCES

### Manuscripts

Archives de la Confédération des Syndicats Nationaux (Montreal)
Archives Nationales du Québec (Quebec)
    Fonds T.-D. Bouchard
    Fonds C.-J. Magnan
    Fonds S.-N. Parent (2 collections)
    S.P. [Secrétariat Provincial]
    Fonds Louis-Alexandre Taschereau
    T.P. [Travaux Publiques]
    "Royal Commission Enquiry into the Garneau Case,"
      Transcript of evidence
Archives du Séminaire de Québec
    *Annuaire de l'Université Laval* (1881–90)
    Bulletins du Séminaire
    Journal du Séminaire

Université [Correspondance]
Archives of the University of New Brunswick
    R.B. Bennett Papers
Archives de l'Université Laval
    Fonds Alfred Charpentier
    Fonds J.-E. Grégoire
Bibliothèque Municipale de Montréal
    Collection Olivar Asselin
Bibliothèque de l'Université de Sherbrooke
    Fonds Jean-Charles Harvey
Public Archives of Canada
    Peter Bercovitch Papers
    R.L. Borden Papers
    A.K. Cameron Papers
    Charles Fitzpatrick Papers
    Lomer Gouin Papers
    Paul Gouin Papers
    W.L.M. King Papers
    Department of Labour, Unemployment Relief Branch
    Ernest Lapointe Papers
    Wilfrid Laurier Papers
    Arthur Meighen Papers
    Escott Reid Papers
    L.S. St Laurent Papers
Public Archives of Ontario
    G.H. Ferguson Papers
    G.S. Henry Papers
Queen's University Archives
    Thomas Crerar Papers
    Walter Mitchell Papers
    C.G. Power Papers
University of Ottawa Library
    Archives de l'Association canadienne-française de l'Ontario


*Official Publications*


Government of Canada
*Dominion-Provincial Conferences*, 1927, 1935, 1941 (Proceedings reprinted
    in one volume, 1951)
*Journals of the House of Commons*, 1931
*Labour Gazette*
*Proceedings and Evidence of the Special Committee on Price Spreads and
    Mass Buying*, 1934

*Report of the Royal Commission on Dominion-Provincial Relations,* 1941 (printed in one volume, 1954).

Supreme Court of Canada *Reports,* 1876–77, 1899–1901, 1905

## Government of Quebec

*Annual reports,* Departments of Agriculture, Labour, Lands and Forests, Public Works; *Reports on Mining Operations*

*Journals of the Legislative Assembly* (Annual)

*Quebec Statistical Yearbook* (Annual)

*Statutes of Quebec* (Annual)

Commission des assurances sociales de Québec, *Rapports,* 1932–3

*Rapport de la Commission des droits civils de la femme,* 1930

*Rapport de la Commission spéciale d'éducation,* 1925

*Rapport de la Commission de l'électricité de la Province de Québec au premier ministre de la province,* 1935

*Report of the Commission on Labour Accidents,* 1907

*Report of the Investigation Commission on the Compensation in Labour Accidents,* 1925

*Report of the Royal Commission Inquiry on Constitutional Problems,* vol. 1, 1956

## Chancellerie de l'Archevêché de Québec

*Mandements, lettres pastorales et circulaires des évêques de Québec,* vols. 10, 14, 15 (1912, 1936, 1940)

## Newspapers and Periodicals

*L'Action catholique*
*L'Action nationale*
*Le Canada*
*Canadian Annual Review of Public Affairs*
*Le Devoir*
*L'Evénement*
*Le Monde ouvrier*
*Montreal Gazette*
*Montreal Star*
*Le Nationaliste*
*La Presse*
*Quebec Chronicle and Chronicle-Telegraph*
*Le Soleil*
*L'Union libérale*
*La Vie syndicale*
*La Vigie*

## Contemporary Pamphlets and Brochures

Bourassa, Henri. *Une mauvaise loi*. Montréal: Le Devoir 1921.

Confédération des travailleurs catholiques du Canada. *Procès-verbal*. Compte rendu des congrès annuels 1924-9.

Crestohl, Leon. *The Jewish School Problem in the Province of Quebec*. Montreal: n.p. 1926.

David, L.-Athanase. *En marge de la politique*. Montréal: Editions Albert Lévesque 1934.

Dorion, J., ed. *Un dossier: Le discours de M. Taschereau au Club de Réforme de Montréal, le 24 avril 1926 et les commentaires qu'il a suscités dans L'Action catholique et la presse indépendante de la province de Québec*. Québec: Action Sociale Ltée 1926.

Ecole sociale populaire. *Le programme de restauration sociale*. Montréal: Ecole sociale populaire 1933. Nos. 232-3.

- *Le programme de restauration sociale expliqué et commenté*. Montréal: Ecole sociale populaire 1933-4. Nos. 239-40.

Gouin, Lomer. *Discours-Programme prononcé par l'Hon. M. Lomer Gouin, 5 avril, 1905*. Québec: n.p. 1905.

- *Politique provinciale: Trois discours de l'Hon. Lomer Gouin*. Québec: n.p. 1908.

Hamel, Philippe. *Le trust de l'électricité: Source de corruption et de domination*. Québec 1934. Mimeographed.

Parent, Paul-E. *Au service de la province*. Montréal: n.p. 1935.

Parti libéral. *Le Gouvernement Taschereau*. Montréal: n.p. 1923.

- *The Taschereau Government*. Montreal: n.p. 1923.

- *Le gouvernement Taschereau*. Québec: n.p. 1927.

- *Les grandes lois Taschereau*. Québec: Le Soleil 1931.

- *Le gouvernement Taschereau et la classe ouvrière*. Québec: Le Soleil 1931.

- *La question des écoles juives*. Québec: Le Soleil 1931.

Perrault, J.-E. *La politique libérale et nos ressources naturelles*. Québec: Le Soleil 1931.

Rexford, Elson I. *The Jewish Population and the Protestant Schools*. Montreal: Renouf 1925.

Riddell, W.A. *The Rise of Ecclesiastical Control in Quebec*. New York: Columbia University Press 1916.

Sauvé, Arthur. *L'histoire vrai du surplus faux*. Québec: n.p. 1927.

- *La tragédie du Lac St-Jean*. Québec: n.p. 1927.

Savard, A., and W.E. Playfair, eds. *Quebec and Confederation: A Record of the Debate in the Legislative Assembly of Quebec on the Motion Proposed by J.-N. Francoeur*. Quebec: n.p. 1918.

Taschereau, L.-A. *L'habitant du Québec: La noblesse canadienne-française*. Montréal: Le Canada 1922.

- *The Challenge of Canada's New Frontiers*. New York: n.p. 1927.

- *Une réplique au chef de l'opposition.* Québec: Le Soleil, 1927.
Union catholique des cultivateurs. *Rapport de la fondation et de toutes les assemblées annuelles de 1924 à 1927.* n.d. n.p.

## Interviews

Joseph Couture (Chief Clerk, Premier's and Attorney General's Office), 28 October 1976
Mme Gabrielle Fages (daughter of Louis-Alexandre), 3 November 1976
Jean-Paul Galipeault (son of Hon. Antonin Galipeault, minister of public works and labour), 27 October 1976
Hon. Hugues Lapointe (son of Ernest Lapointe, young Liberal activist), 1 November 1976
Alexandre Larue (private secretary, Hon. Adélard Godbout), 28 October 1976
Hon. Hector Perrier (legal associate of Athanase David, young Liberal activist), 18 June 1972
Brig. John A. Price (president, Price Brothers and Company), 12 June 1972
Hon. Antoine Rivard (personal friend of Taschereau's sons, young Conservative activist), 2 November 1976
Hon. André Taschereau (nephew of Louis-Alexandre), 26 October 1976
Charles Taschereau (son of Louis-Alexandre, engineer at Shawinigan Water and Power Company), 19 November 1976

### SECONDARY SOURCES

## Books

Allaire, Violette. *Louis Guyon.* Montréal: Ecole des Bibliothécaires 1953.
Angers, F.-A., ed. *La pensée de Henri Bourassa.* Montréal: L'Action Nationale 1954.
Armstrong, Elizabeth. *The Crisis of Quebec.* Toronto: McClelland and Stewart 1974.
Bates, Stewart. *Financial History of Canadian Governments.* Ottawa: King's Printer 1939.
Beck, J. Murray. *Pendulum of Power.* Scarborough: Prentice Hall 1968.
Bélanger, André-J. *L'apolitisme des idéologies québécoises: Le grand tournant 1934–1936.* Québec: Presses de l'Université Laval 1975.
Bélanger, Réal. *L'impossible défi: Albert Sévigny et les Conservateurs fédéraux 1902–1918.* Québec: Presses de l'Université Laval 1975.
Bergeron, Léandre. *The History of Quebec: A Patriot's Handbook.* Toronto: New Canada Publications 1971.
Betcherman, Lita-Rose. *The Swastika and the Maple Leaf.* Toronto: Fitzhenry and Whiteside 1975.
Black, Conrad. *Duplessis.* Toronto: McClelland and Stewart 1974.

Bladen, Vincent W. *An Introduction to Political Economy*. Toronto: University of Toronto Press 1941.

Boissonnault, Charles-Marie. *Histoire politique de la Province de Québec*. Québec: Editions Frontenac 1936.

Bouchard, T.-D. *La domination des trusts électriques*. St Hyacinthe: Imprimerie Yamaska 1934.

– *Mémoires*. 3 vols. Montréal: Beauchemin 1960.

Bovey, Wilfrid. *Canadien*. Montreal: J.M. Dent and Sons 1933.

Brown, R.C., and R. Cook. *Canada 1896–1921: A Nation Transformed*. Toronto: McClelland and Stewart 1974.

Casgrain, Thérèse. *A Woman in a Man's World*. Toronto: McClelland and Stewart 1972.

Chaloult, René. *Mémoires politiques*. Montréal: Editions du Jour 1969.

Choquette, P.-A. *Un demi-siècle de vie politique*. Montréal: Beauchemin 1936.

Choquette, Robert. *Language and Religion: A History of French-English Conflict in Ontario*. Ottawa: University of Ottawa Press 1975.

Cook, Ramsay, ed. *French Canadian Nationalism: An Anthology*. Toronto: Macmillan of Canada 1969.

Copp, Terry. *The Anatomy of Poverty: The Condition of the Working Class of Montreal, 1897–1929*. Toronto: McClelland and Stewart 1974.

Dales, John H. *Hydroelectricity and Industrial Development in Quebec 1898–1940*. Cambridge: Harvard University Press 1957.

Dandurand, Raoul. *Mémoires du Sénateur Raoul Dandurand 1864–1942*. Québec: Presses de l'Université Laval 1975.

Désilets, Andrée. *Hector-Louis Langevin: Un père de la Confédération canadienne 1826–1906*. Québec, Presses de l'Université Laval, 1969.

Desrosiers, Richard, ed. *Le personnel politique québécois*. Montréal: Boréal Express 1972.

Dion, Gérald, ed. *Cinquante ans d'action ouvrière: Les mémoires d'Alfred Charpentier*. Québec: Presses de l'Université Laval 1971.

Dumas, Evelyn. *The Bitter Thirties in Quebec*. Montreal: Black Rose Books 1975.

Dumont, Fernand, Jean Hamelin, and Jean-Paul Montminy, eds. *Idéologies au Canada français*. 3 vols. Québec: Presses de l'Université Laval 1971–8.

Dupont, Antonin. *Les relations entre l'Eglise et l'Etat sous Louis-Alexandre Taschereau 1920–1936*. Montréal: Editions Guérin 1974.

Durocher, Réne, and Paul-André Linteau, eds. *Le 'retard' du Québec*. Montréal: Boréal Express 1971.

Ellis, L. Ethan. *Print Paper Pendulum: Group Pressures and the Price of Newsprint*. New Brunswick: Rutgers University Press 1948.

Faucher, Albert. *Histoire économique et unité canadienne*. Montréal: Editions Fides 1970.

Figler, Bernard. *Louis Fitch, Q.C. 1889–1956*. Ottawa: n.p. 1968.

Filteau, Gérald. *Le Québec, le Canada et la guerre 1914-1918*. Montréal: Editions de l'Aurore 1977.

Gagnon, Marcel-A. *La vie orageuse d'Olivar Asselin*. 2 vols. Montréal: Editions de l'Homme 1962.

Graham, W.R. *Arthur Meighen*. Vols. 1 and 2. Toronto: Clarke Irwin 1960-3.

Grenon, Hector. *Camillien Houde raconté par Hector Grenon*. Montréal: Stanké 1979.

Groulx, Lionel. *Mes Mémoires*. 4 vols. Montréal: Editions Fides 1970-4.

Guthrie, J.A. *The Newsprint Paper Industry*. Cambridge: Harvard University Press 1941.

Hamelin, Jean, and Marc Hamelin. *Les moeurs électoraux dans le Québec de 1791 à nos jours*. Montréal: Editions du Jour 1962.

Hamelin, Jean, and Yves Roby. *Histoire économique du Québec 1851-1896*. Montréal: Editions Fides 1971.

Harvey, Fernand, ed. *Aspects historiques du mouvement ouvrier au Québec*. Montréal: Boréal Express 1973.

Hughes, Everett C. *French Canada in Transition*. Chicago: University of Chicago Press 1943.

Jamieson, Stuart. *Times of Trouble: Labour Unrest and Industrial Conflict in Canada 1900-1966*. Ottawa: Privy Council Office 1968.

Jones, Richard. *L'idéologie de L'Action catholique 1917-1939*. Québec: Presses de l'Université Laval 1974.

Laporte, Pierre. *Le vrai visage de Duplessis*. Montréal: Editions de l'Homme 1960.

LaRoque, Hertel. *Camillien Houde: Le p'tit gars de Ste-Marie*. Montréal: Editions de l'Homme 1961.

La Terreur, Marc. *Les tribulations des Conservateurs au Québec de Bennett à Diefenbaker*. Québec: Presses de l'Université Laval 1973.

Lavigne, Marie, and Yolande Pinard, eds. *Les femmes dans la société québécoise*. Montréal: Boréal Express 1977.

Letourneau, Firmin. *Histoire de l'agriculture (Canada-français)*. Montréal: Imprimerie Populaire 1950.

Lévesque, Robert, and Robert Migner. *Camillien et les années vingt suivi de Camillien au Goulag*. Montréal: Editions des Brûlés 1978.

Levitt, Joseph. *Henri Bourassa and the Golden Calf: The Social Programme of the Nationalists of Quebec 1900-1914*. Ottawa: University of Ottawa Press 1969.

Linteau, Paul-André. *Maisonneuve: Comment les promoteurs fabriquent une ville*. Montréal: Boréal Express 1981.

Linteau, P.-A., René Durocher, and J.-C. Robert. *Histoire du Québec contemporain: De la Confédération à la crise 1867-1929*. Montréal: Boréal Express 1979.

McGee, J.C. *Histoire politique de Québec-Est*. Québec: Belisle 1948.

McRoberts, Kenneth, and Dale Posgate. *Quebec: Social Change and Political*

*Crisis*. Toronto: McClelland and Stewart 1980.

Migner, Robert. *Quand gronde la révolte verte*. Montréal: La Presse 1980.

Milner, Sheilagh Hodgins, and Henry Milner. *The Decolonization of Quebec*. Toronto: McClelland and Stewart 1973.

Minville, Esdras. *Labour Legislation and Social Services in the Province of Quebec*. Ottawa: King's Printer 1939.

Mongeau, Serge. *L'évolution de l'assistance au Québec*. Montréal: Editions du Jour 1967.

Neatby, H. Blair. *William Lyon Mackenzie King*. Vols. 2 and 3. Toronto: Macmillan of Canada 1963-77.

- *Laurier and a Liberal Quebec*. Toronto: McClelland and Stewart 1973.

Nelles, H.V. *The Politics of Development: Forests, Mines and Hydro Electric Power in Ontario 1849-1941*. Toronto: Macmillan of Canada 1974.

Oliver, Peter. *G. Howard Ferguson, Ontario Tory*. Toronto: University of Toronto Press 1977.

Pelletier, Michel, and Yves Vaillancourt. *Les politiques sociales et les travailleurs*. Cahiers 1 and 2. Montréal: n.p. 1974-5.

Provencher, Jean. *Québec sous la loi des mesures de guerre*. Trois-Rivières: Boréal Express 1977.

Quinn, Herbert F. *The Union Nationale: Quebec Nationalism from Duplessis to Lévesque*. Toronto: University of Toronto Press 1979.

Renaud, Charles. *L'imprévisible Monsieur Houde*. Montréal: Editions de l'Homme 1964.

Roberts, Leslie. *Le Chef*. Montréal: Editions du Jour 1963.

- *Noranda*. Toronto: Clark Irwin 1956.

- *These Be Your Gods*. Toronto: Musson 1929.

Roby, Yves. *Les Québécois et les investissements américains 1918-1927*. Québec: Presses de l'Université Laval 1976.

Rouillard, Jacques. *Les syndicats nationaux au Québec de 1900 à 1930*. Québec: Presses de l'Université Laval 1979.

Roy, Jean-Louis. *Les programmes électoraux du Québec*. 2 vols. Montréal: Editions Leméac 1970.

- *La marche des Québécois: Le temps des ruptures 1945-1960*. Montréal: Editions Leméac 1976.

Roy, P.-G. *La famille Taschereau*. Lévis: n.p. 1901.

Rumilly, Robert. *Histoire de la province de Québec*, 41 vols. Montréal: various publishers, 1940-69.

- *La plus riche aumône: Histoire de la Société de St. Vincent de Paul au Canada*. Montréal: Editions de l'Arbre 1946.

- *Henri Bourassa: La vie publique d'un grand canadien*. Montréal: Editions de l'Homme 1953.

- *Maurice Duplessis et son temps*. 2 vols. Montréal: Editions Fides 1973.

- *Histoire de Montréal*. Vol. 4. Montréal: Editions Fides 1974.

Ryan, William F. *The Clergy and Economic Growth in Quebec 1896-1914*.

Québec: Presses de l'Université Laval 1966.

Skelton, O.D. *The Life and Letters of Sir Wilfrid Laurier*. 2 vols. Toronto: McClelland and Stewart 1965.

Stephens, George W. *The St. Lawrence Waterway Project*. Montreal: Louis Carrier and Company 1929.

Struthers, James. *No Fault of Their Own: Unemployment and the Canadian Welfare State 1914–1941*. Toronto: University of Toronto Press 1983.

Trofimenkoff, Susan Mann. *Action Française: French Canadian Nationalism in the 1920s*. Toronto: University of Toronto Press 1975.

Vining, Charles. *Newsprint Prorating: An Account of Government Policy in Quebec and Ontario*. Montreal: n.p. 1940.

Wade, Mason. *The French Canadians*. 2 vols. Toronto: Macmillan of Canada 1968.

Ward, Norman, ed. *A Party Politician: The Memoirs of Chubby Power*. Toronto: Macmillan of Canada 1966.

Wilbur, J.R.H., ed. *The Bennett New Deal: Fraud or Portent?*. Toronto: Copp Clark 1968.

Wiegman, Carl. *Trees to News*. Toronto: McClelland and Stewart 1953.

## Articles and Conference Papers

Abella, Irving, and Harold Troper. "'The line must be drawn somewhere': Canada and Jewish Refugees 1933–1939." *CHR* 60 (June 1979): 178–209.

Audet, Louis-Philippe. "La question des écoles juives 1870-1931." *Transactions of the Royal Society of Canada* 15 (1970): 109–22.

– "La querelle de l'instruction obligatoire 1875–1943." In *L'éducation au Québec 19e-20e siècles*, edited by Marcel Lajeunesse. Montréal: Boréal Express 1971.

Barber, Marilyn. "The Ontario Bilingual Schools Issue: Sources of Conflict." *CHR* 47 (September 1966): 227–48.

Bonenfant, Jean-Charles. "La première table d'écoute au Québec." *Les Cahiers de Dix* 40 (1975): 87–112.

Brunet, Michel. "Trois dominantes de la pensée canadienne-française." In *La présence anglaise et les Canadiens*, by Michel Brunet. Montréal: Beauchemin 1958.

Cameron, Brian. "The Bonne Entente Movement 1916–1917: From Cooperation to Conscription." *Journal of Canadian Studies* 13 (Summer 1978): 42–55.

Chartier, Roger. "Histoire de la législation québécoise du travail." *Relations industrielles/Industrial Relations* 17–18 (janvier, avril, juillet, octobre 1962, janvier, avril 1963).

Chevrier, Bernard. "Le ministère de Félix-Gabriel Marchand." *RHAF* 22 (juin 1968): 35–46.

Cliche, Paul. "Les élections provinciales dans la province de Québec de

1927 à 1956." *Recherches sociographiques* 2 (juillet-décembre 1961): 343–66.

Craik, W.A., "The Romance of the Taschereaus." *Maclean's*, April 1914.

Dirks, Patricia. "Dr. Philippe Hamel and the Public Power Movement in Quebec City 1929–1934: The Failure of a Crusade." Paper presented at Canadian Historical Association annual meeting, June 1979.

Dupont, Antonin. "Louis-Alexandre Taschereau et la législation sociale au Québec 1920–1936." *RHAF* 26 (décembre 1972): 397–426.

- "Louis-Alexandre Taschereau, Camillien Houde et l'évolution politique de Québec 1923–1936." Paper presented at Canadian Historical Association annual meeting, June 1973.

Durocher, René. "Taschereau, Hepburn et les relations Québec-Ontario 1934–1936." *RHAF* 24 (décembre 1970): 341–55.

- "Henri Bourassa, les évêques et la guerre de 1914–1918." *Historical Papers / Communications historiques* (1971): 248–75.

Echlin, Erland. "Speaking of Success." *Maclean's*, 15 January 1936.

Faucher, Albert, and Maurice Lamontagne. "History of Industrial Development in Quebec." In *Essais sur le Québec contemporain/Essays on Contemporary Quebec*, edited by Jean-Charles Falardeau. Québec: Presses de l'Université Laval 1953.

Forsey, Eugene. "The Pulp and Paper Industry." *CJEPS* 1 (August 1935): 501–9.

Hamelin, Jean, Jacques Letarte, et Marcel Hamelin. "Les élections provinciales dans le Québec." *Cahiers de géographie de Québec* 4 (octobre 1959–mars 1960): 5–207.

Heintzman, Ralph. "Image and Consequence." *Journal of Canadian Studies* 13 (Summer 1978): 1–2, 126–8.

- "The Political Culture of Quebec." *Canadian Journal of Political Science* 16 (March 1983): 3–59.

Jenkins, Charles C. "Quebec's Business Premier." *Maclean's*, August 1921.

Laurendeau, André. "Personne n'est hostile: Pourquoi nous rappeler à chaque instant qu'il est juif?" *Le Magazine Maclean*, février 1963.

Marsh, L.C., "The Arcand Act: A New Form of Labour Legislation?" *CJEPS* 2 (August 1936): 404–19.

O'Connell, Martin. "The Ideas of Henri Bourassa." *CJEPS* 19 (August 1953): 361–76.

Rudin, Ronald. "A Bank Merger Unlike the Others: The Establishment of the Banque Canadienne Nationale." *CHR* 61 (June 1980): 191–212.

St Germain, Yves. "La société québécoise et la vie économique: Quelques échos de la décennie de la 'grande ambivalence' 1920–1929." In *Economie québécoise*, edited by Robert Comeau. Montréal: Presses de l'Université du Québec 1969.

Stoddard, Jennifer. "The Dorion Commission 1926–1931: Quebec's Legal Elites Look at Women's Rights." In *Essays in the History of Canadian*

*Law*, edited by David Flaherty. Vol. 1. Toronto: University of Toronto Press 1981.

Taschereau, L.-A. "Allocution de l'honorable L.-A. Taschereau." *Semaines sociales du Canada, 2^me session tenue à Québec, 1921*. Montréal 1922.

- "Premier Taschereau's Outspoken Address." *Industrial Canada* 28 (November 1927): 47-9.
- "Du temps que j'étais écolier." *La Nouvelle Abeille* 5 (novembre 1948).
- "Trois confrères." *La Nouvelle Abeille* 7 (novembre-décembre 1950).
- "De l'influence de la femme sur nos destinées nationales." In *Québécoises du 20^e siècle*, edited by Michèle Jean. Montréal: Editions du Jour 1974.

Trudeau, Pierre-Elliott. "La province de Québec au moment de la grève." In *La grève de l'amiante*, edited by P.-E. Trudeau. Montréal: Cité Libre 1956.

- "Some Obstacles to Democracy in Quebec." *CJEPS* 24 (August 1958): 297-311.

Vigod, B.L. " 'Qu'on ne craigne pas l'encombrement des compétences': Le gouvernement Taschereau et l'éducation 1920-1929." *RHAF* 28 (septembre 1974): 209-44.

- "Ideology and Institutions in Quebec: The Public Charities Controversy 1921-1926." *Histoire sociale/Social History* 11 (May 1978): 167-82.
- "Alexandre Taschereau and the Negro King Hypothesis." *Journal of Canadian Studies* 13 (Summer 1978): 3-15.
- "Quebec Social Legislation in the 1930's: A Study in Political Self-destruction." *Journal of Canadian Studies* 14 (Spring 1979): 59-69.

Vining, Charles [R.T.L.]. "Mr. Taschereau." *Maclean's*, 1 February 1934.

Weilbrenner, Bernard. "Les idées politiques de Lomer Gouin." *Canadian Historical Association Annual Report* (1965): 46-57.

### Theses

Angell, Harold. "Quebec Provincial Politics in the 1920's." MA thesis, McGill University, 1960.

Bernard, André. "Parliamentary Control of Finances in Quebec." MA thesis, McGill University, 1965.

Cliche, Paul. "Les élections provinciales dans le Québec de 1927 à 1956." MA thesis, Université Laval, 1960.

Dirks, Patricia. "The Origins of the Union Nationale." PHD thesis, University of Toronto, 1974.

Genest, Jean-Guy. "Vie et oeuvre d'Adélard Godbout 1892-1956." Thèse de D. ès L., Université Laval, 1977.

Lawlor, Jean-Paul. "Les commerces des alcools et la création de la Commission des liqueurs en 1921." Thèse de D. ès S., Université de Montréal, 1970.

Lovinck, J.A.A. "The Politics of Quebec: Provincial Political Parties 1897–1936." PHD thesis, Duke University, 1967.

Migner, Robert. Camillien Houde et le Houdisme 1889–1933." MA thesis, Université de Montéal, 1971.

Morin, Suzanne. "Les débats concernant la loi des pensions de vieillesse." MA thesis, Université de Montréal, 1981.

Oliver, Michael. "The Social and Political Ideas of French Canadian Nationalists 1920–1945." PHD thesis, McGill University, 1956.

Provencher, Jean. "Joseph-Ernest Grégoire: 4 années de vie politique." MA thesis, Université Laval, 1969.

Ross, Harold. "The Jew in the Educational System of Quebec." MA thesis, McGill University, 1947.

Toupin, Louise. "L'intervention du Premier Ministre Taschereau dans l'industrie de papier journal, 1927–1935." MA thesis, Université de Montréal, 1972.

Vigod, B.L. "Responses to Social and Economic Change in Quebec: The L.-A. Taschereau Administration 1920–1929." PHD thesis, Queen's University, 1975.

# Index